Personal Selling

A PROFESSIONAL APPROACH

Personal Selling
A PROFESSIONAL APPROACH

Frank Brennan

SCIENCE RESEARCH ASSOCIATES, INC.
Chicago, Palo Alto, Toronto
Henley-on-Thames, Sydney

A Subsidiary of IBM

Acquisition Editor	S. L. Fisher
Project Editor	Sara Boyd
Copy Editor	Shirley Taylor
Designer	Rick Chafian
Cover Designer	Barbara Ravizza
Illustrator	House of Graphics
Compositor	Dharma Press

Library of Congress Cataloging in Publication Data

Brennan, Frank E.
  Personal selling.

  Includes index.
  1. Selling.   I. Title.
HF5438.25.P73   1983   658.8′5   82–23118
ISBN 0–574–20685–X

10   9   8   7   6   5   4   3   2   1

Contents

About the Author

Frank Brennan is General Agent for one of America's most prestigious life insurance companies—New England Life. He is also an instructor, in Selling and Business Communication, at Avila College in Kansas City.

Like so many others who have had successful careers in selling, Frank started out in another field. After receiving a Juris Doctor of Law degree from St. Louis University, he worked briefly for a St. Louis law firm. The Korean war interrupted his career, and when he returned to civilian life it was as an agent for New England Life. During his early years as a salesperson, Frank became a life member of the Million Dollar Round Table and a Chartered Life Underwriter, and was selected as the agency's Most Valuable Associate for three years.

Not all textbook writers practice what they teach. Frank does. As he encourages all novice salespeople to do, Frank contributes his time and talents to several professional, civic, and charitable organizations. He served on Kansas City's City Council for four years, led the state's American Cancer Society Crusade Fund Drive, and is currently a member of the city's Crime Advisory Committee.

In short, Frank Brennan is a true professional.

Preface

The field of selling offers a wide variety of opportunities to those who accept its invitation to embark on a career path. It is a career that can be at the same time challenging and creative, exhilarating and exhausting, hard work and fun—but never boring.

I've been in sales for over 30 years and have enjoyed every minute of it. In this book, I share my enthusiasm for selling with you. Looking back on the many successful moments I've had in sales (and the not-so-successful ones, too), I discuss the practical techniques, psychological theories, and personal experiences that have made selling a satisfying career choice for me.

Part One of the book takes a broad look at selling as a career. Part Two, which deals with the psychology of selling, lays the foundation for Part Three's discussion of sales techniques. Part Four emphasizes the communication skills that are an integral part of the sales process. The concluding section, Part Five, deals with getting and keeping the job.

Each chapter opens with a real-life situation that sets the tone for that chapter's main topic. At the end of each chapter, two short cases based on actual sales experiences give you a chance to get a feel for the way it really is—on the road, in the office, during the presentation. You'll learn about the freedom (and responsibility) of managing a sales territory, about the necessity of paperwork, and about the importance of learning how to prospect, handle objections, get the commitment, and close that sale.

In Selling in Action, the special case study that follows Part Three, you'll accompany Beth Wilson as she goes through the entire sales cycle, listening in as she uses her people skills and product knowledge to win a new account. In the profiles that follow each Part title, you'll meet five salespeople who share the highlights of their successful careers in various industries.

In Chapter 5, you'll learn about transactional analysis and how you can make the "I'm OK, You're OK" attitude work for you on the sales call. Chapter 13 looks at body language (and why it is important to be able to interpret it), as well as written and verbal communication skills. You'll get a chance to practice creativity and showmanship in Chapter 18, where some unusual approaches to selling are covered.

Chapter 6 recognizes that it's not all fun and games out there. You'll explore ways to cope with stress and rejection by keeping both in the proper perspective. In Chapter 20, you will learn that commitment—to yourself and to your company—is the key to sales success and personal growth. In Chapter 19, you'll discover how to get and keep your first job.

Selling has been a satisfying and exciting career for me. And it has been equally rewarding to share my experiences with all of you who aspire to a sales career. Work hard—but enjoy yourselves, too. Nothing can beat the thrill of signing a new account or writing a big order—the surest signs of a job well done. Good luck and good selling!

ACKNOWLEDGMENTS

For their help in the early days of this project, I would like to thank Dr. Paulette Gladis of Avila College, who first encouraged me to write this text; Bill Eddy, Associate Dean of the School of Business and Public Administration, University of Missouri-Kansas City, who got me started; Nina Robertson, who did the preliminary typing and editing; Tom Tupper, who introduced me to SRA; and Jason Petosa, who helped me polish the first chapters I submitted to my publisher.

For contributing something of themselves to this text, I would like to thank the five salespeople who appear in the profiles: Nikki Riccelli, Bill Kron, Carol Pfander, Vergie Anderson, and Glenn Geiger. Gil Shoham's helpful suggestions for the ethics chapter improved it immeasurably; Gary Kaney generously contributed his time to photograph the body language series; Michael Bauer and Elizabeth Brennan were the cooperative models. Phil Tompkins, Associate Director of Libraries, University of Missouri-Kansas City, was kind enough to make the university's library facilities available to me.

I would also like to thank the reviewers whose comments and suggestions have made this text a stronger teaching tool: Dr. William Pace (Mississippi State Department of Education); Dr. Charolotte Mastellar (Butler County Community College), Dr. Robert Fishco (Middlesex County College); Professor Mimi Will (Foothill College); Professor Tony Alessandro (University of San Diego); Professor Frank Falcetta (Middlesex Community College); Professor Lawrence Vukelich (Portland Community College); Professor Roland Whitsell (Volunteer State Community College); Professor Roy Grundy (College of DuPage); and Dr. Rod Davis (Ball State University). I have to thank Dr. Davis for yet another contribution—preparation of the comprehensive Instructor's Guide that accompanies this text.

Thanks, too, to the people at SRA who guided a novice writer through the publishing process: Phil Gerould, Bob Yount, Susan Fisher, Sally Boyd, and Shirley Taylor.

Janey Pryor, the administrative manager of my office, put in long hours of work on the manuscript. Her talent and dedication helped beyond measure.

Finally, I want to thank my wife and best friend, Elizabeth. She encouraged me at every step of the project and filled in where needed—typing, editing, and proofreading.

Frank Brennan

Kansas City

February 1983

Selling as a Professional Career

PROFILE

Nikki Riccelli

Background Working as a sales rep for Land O'Lakes (a dairy products company) is a fulfilling career, according to Nikki Riccelli. After graduating from college, Nikki taught in an elementary school. Two years later she left teaching, seeking an alternate career that would better suit her interests and ambitions. She toured Europe with two of her friends. and upon returning to Kansas City, looked for a job in business. There were none.

Nikki then went to work as a cocktail waitress in a Kansas City restaurant frequented by a variety of business people. Some of her customers told her she ought to try sales.

Responding to this advice, Nikki sought and received help from one of her regular customers, who subsequently gave her the lead to her first sales job. Nikki was hired part-time as a salesperson with his food brokerage firm. Impressed, the president offered her a job as a full time salesperson three weeks later. Now Nikki, whose most recent raise put her over the $25,000 mark, lives in a comfortably furnished condominium in fashionable Johnson County, Kansas.

Sales Achievements Currently Nikki sells dairy products directly to distributors and also calls daily on nine food-service directors at restaurants, hotels, schools, and health-care facilities. Her sales approach includes educating the customer about the uses and benefits of the various products she sells.

Over the years Nikki has built up her territory by increasing new-product distribution and by motivating her distributors' sales forces, who sell her products directly to food-service accounts. To educate these people, she conducts sales meetings and accompanies sales people on sales calls. She also sponsors sales contests.

Her involvement with the Chef's Association and the Missouri Restaurant Association has been particularly helpful in building her territory. With these organizations, she works closely with local chefs and food and beverage directors.

In 1981 she exceeded her sales quota by 59 percent. She also was honored as South Regional Salesperson of the year for her company. Nikki has received a certificate of appreciation from the Educational Institute of the American Culinary Federation. She also has been recognized for her leadership and service by the Kansas City Chapter Board of Directors of the Missouri Restaurant Association.

Her Comments on Her Career   "My sales career allows me to be creative and to develop my own style of conducting business. I like the flexibility of movement the selling career offers. Controlling my daily routine out in the field gives me a sense of accomplishment not usually found in an office job, and because I am not guided by office discipline, I must always be self-motivated to start my day at 8 A.M.

"My advice to anyone considering a career in sales is to sell products and services that interest you. In addition, learn as much as you can about competitors' products and services. Be self-confident, positive, and assertive, as you must be able to sell yourself before you can effectively sell a product or service.

"Dressing professionally helps build confidence and gives a good impression. Salespeople should generally follow the rules of being well-groomed.

"Be able to handle a customer's objections; do not take them personally. Perceive a customer's objection as a sales opportunity instead of a personal insult, and let the objection motivate rather than deter you. Learn how to ask questions that require a statement, rather than a yes or no answer. Also, know how to be in control of your presentation at all times, which takes a lot of practice and much effort.

"After six years, I still am considered a novice. When you are new in sales (or in any business field), you are considered green. But someone once gave me very good advice: 'One should always remain green, because you are always growing and learning. When you ripen, you stop growing and deteriorate.' In essence, there should always be room to grow and learn."

1

The Role of Selling

OBJECTIVES

In this chapter you will learn:

- What personal selling is.
- Why selling is important in our society.
- How selling benefits the economy in general and consumers and business in particular.
- What advantages and challenges selling offers to those who pursue it as a career.
- What three characteristics the new professional salespeople have in common.

Bob Landau has been one of his company's top ten salespersons for five years in Little Rock, Arkansas. His products are office dictating systems. His company is a nationally known leader in the field. Bob has built a solid clientele in Little Rock and the surrounding metropolitan area. He makes in excess of $35,000 a year, and last year he received an incentive bonus of an additional $3200. He loves his work, is highly respected by his customers, and is active in the community.

Recently, an opening for a district manager in Dallas came up, and Bob was offered the position. The marketing vice-president, Abe Greene, felt Bob would be ideal for the job. After several visits with Abe, Bob turned down the job. When asked why, Bob responded:

Abe, I'm flattered you offered me the job, and I thank you for it. But, I guess I like what I'm doing too much to go into management. After all, I make good money, and Mary and I love Little Rock. But more than this I value the freedom and independence of my personal selling career. The work is interesting, and I've built up a lot of wonderful customer relationships, and I enjoy serving them. In essence, I find the career a highly satisfactory one and wouldn't change places with anyone at the moment.

This chapter discusses why there are so many Bob Landaus around. It also defines selling and points out how it benefits consumers and business as well as the country as a whole. The advantages and the challenges of a sales career are also discussed. The chapter closes with a look at the new professionals found in the sales field.

SELLING—A DEFINITION

Selling is the process of persuading prospects to buy wanted or needed products or services. In a sense, everyone is a salesperson. A waiter recommends the daily special to his customers. A dentist urges patients to brush their teeth regularly to avoid tooth decay. A daughter calls her father from college to persuade him to send her some money.

This book is about the career of selling. It is a dynamic, ever-changing, ever-growing field. Nowhere else can a person advance so rapidly in income and personal satisfaction.

SELLING AND SOCIETY

Salespeople play a vital role in our multitrillion dollar economy. Someone sells almost every product or service we consume. Take shoes for instance. A pair of leather shoes is made from the hide of a slaughtered steer. The meat packer sells the hide to a tannery. The tannery owner cures the hide and sells it to a shoe manufacturer. The shoe manufacturer makes a pair of shoes from the leather. He then sells the shoes to a retail store. There, another salesperson sells the shoes to you, the ultimate consumer.

Somewhere along the road from slaughterhouse to your neighborhood shoe store, a piece of cowhide was transformed into a pair of leather shoes. But something else was happening too. Salaries were earned, profits were made, and at every turning point of the road, the local economy was strengthened.

The selling profession's contributions to society are many.

SELLING AND THE ECONOMY

Salespeople are the catalysts of the economy—the intermediaries between producer and consumer. They keep goods and services continually moving, which in turn stimulates employment. As a result, our economy stays basically strong (in spite of the occasional ups and downs brought on by political and economic change and foreign competition).

We continually develop new products and services and rely on our salespeople to deliver them to the public. They convince the consumer to replace old items with new, improved ones. The dollars begin to move, and our economy becomes stronger.

SELLING AND THE CONSUMER

The sales process also benefits the consumer. Consumers learn of new products and services either directly from the salespeople who call on them or indirectly through the media.

The consumer also benefits greatly from the competitive atmosphere inherent in the sales process. Competition forces the development of quality goods and services at reasonable costs.

Through salespeople, consumers have at their disposal professional expertise on any given subject at any given time, and at no cost.

SELLING AND BUSINESS

Selling has a vital place in the marketing equation of any company. For companies to survive in a complex industrial society, they must keep this equation in balance. Here are the constants in the marketing equation.

1. *Developing a new product or service to be offered to the consumer.* It may be the reason for starting a new company, or the product may be the result of considerable research and development by an existing company.

2. *Establishing a price.* Companies must be careful to set prices at a reasonable and competitive level. If it costs too much to bring a product to market, the item will be dropped. For example, consider the development of plants to convert sea water to drinkable water. To date, the cost of the process is too high to compete with the cost of current water supply systems. The same can be said for the abundant oil found in shale in the Rocky Mountains. The cost of extracting it simply is too costly. It can't compete with the price of oil on the market today. When it does, it will be processed.

3. *Distributing the product or service.* The decision of how to distribute a product or service—through wholesalers, retailers, mail order—is a vital element of the marketing formula.

4. *Advertising and promoting the product or service.* Making sure the public knows the product or service is available, and is informed of its advantages and cost, is a massive effort. Millions of dollars are spent in advertising and promotion.

5. *Selling the product.* After a product is researched, designed, manufactured, priced, distributed, and promoted, it must be sold to the consumer. Without that fifth step, the other efforts would be in vain. Salespeople also keep industry informed of what the consumers want and need. They are working with the people daily, and provide continual feedback to their companies.

PERSONAL SELLING AS A CAREER

As mentioned earlier, the selling career is a dynamic, challenging career with unusual rewards for a dedicated individual.

Its Advantages

Earnings. Successful salespeople make good incomes. Furthermore, the amount they make is largely up to them. The more they sell, the more they earn. Salespeople are paid in direct proportion to the amount they produce. It is difficult to place the same dollar value on the efforts of non-salespeople. Who can measure the exact worth of someone in research and development or accounting?

Security. Contrary to popular opinion, there is great personal security in selling. Good salespeople are sought after. They realize this, and are aware that they can go to work for a competitor simply by picking up the telephone. Their companies are also keenly aware of this. Hence, they treat their successful salespeople with a measure of respect not generally found in other occupations.

Recognition. All of us like to be recognized for our efforts. Because the results of effort are easily measured in sales (through sales volume and company profits), it is easy for companies to give recognition to their top salespeople. Such recognition comes in many forms—cash awards, expense-paid trips to company meetings, plaques, recognition in company bulletins, membership in exclusive production clubs, and the like.

Membership in the Million Dollar Round Table of the National Association of Life Underwriters is the most prestigious recognition a life insurance salesperson can enjoy. Membership is open to those who achieve and maintain a high volume of life insurance sales. Because of its enormous prestige, most life insurance sales agents work hard to achieve membership in this exclusive sales organization.

Respect of customers.   Many customers rely heavily on the salespeople who sell them products or services. Wise business executives use the salespeople who call on them as sources of information about new products and services available in the marketplace. Customers rely on their salespeople to tell them how to use the products they buy in the most efficient manner possible. Salespeople who build long-term relationships with their customers enjoy a mutually profitable relationship. Out of this relationship grows mutual respect.

Independence.   Of all the benefits of selling as a career, independence, being your own boss, is one of the most attractive. Salespeople are almost separate business entities in themselves, because they have so much control over their daily activities. Of course, new salespeople are supervised by sales trainers in the early months of their careers. But once they learn sales procedures, they lead an independent life. They depend on themselves for their success. Unlike most people in business, they are not at the beck and call of their superiors.

This freedom can be dangerous if not handled properly. Good salespeople are careful not to abuse it.

Variety and interest.   Few salespeople are ever bored. The variety of products or services offered, the different personality of each prospect or customer, the ever-changing nature of the daily routine ensure a continuing interest in the entire sales process. Other aspects of selling that ensure interest are:

- Improving product knowledge through study
- Keeping up with competitors
- Opening new markets
- Finding new prospects
- Developing long-term client relationships
- Constantly practicing sales skills
- Taking part in incentive programs
- Helping newer salespeople develop

No sponsorship required.   To get ahead in any business organization today, it is always helpful to have a sponsor, or mentor. A sponsor is someone who helps lower-level personnel move up the organizational ladder. A sponsor may take on a new employee as a protégé and carefully counsel him throughout his career, running interference for him whenever necessary. The point is that few people get ahead in organizations without some personal help from someone above them.

Unfortunately, not every new employee attracts a sponsor. Personality conflicts, preconceived notions, and lack of opportunity can have a negative effect on developing useful sponsorships.

In selling, sponsorship is not a requisite for success. Salespeople are "sponsored" by their sales records. If they sell well, the system will reward them accordingly, despite whom they know or do not know in the organization. This is one of the most attractive elements of the sales career.

Opportunity for advancement.   Successful salespeople have numerous opportunities for advancement. Many chief executive officers of corporations rose from the ranks of sales. The persuasive skills developed by salespeople in the field are also valuable tools in the corporate boardroom. Hence, more and more executive talent is coming from the sales field. In the old days most senior officers of companies came from production, accounting, or law.

Salespeople have another advantage when it comes time for promotion. Management is able to measure sales performance from a dollar and cents standpoint. Thus, an outstanding sales record comes to the attention of a lot of executives in any organization. Advancement up the ladder in marketing is a natural for successful salespeople. See Figure 1-1 for a typical marketing route to the top.

Its Challenges

"Every reward in life has its price," so the saying goes. The sales career is no exception to this truism. Everyone who aspires to success in a selling career must face certain challenges.

Sales skills.   Just as a surgeon follows a set procedure for every operation, a salesperson follows certain steps in every sales presentation. To execute this process requires knowledge of the following sales skills:

Figure 1–1. A Typical Route to the Top

- Preparing during the pre-approach phase
- Presenting the product or service
- Isolating valid needs for products or services offered
- Answering prospect objections
- Closing the sale
- Delivering the product or service
- Following up the sale

It obviously takes practice to master these skills. They are discussed in depth later in this book.

Product knowledge. To sell computers successfully, a salesperson must be able to talk about them intelligently. In fact, almost all successful salespeople know a great deal about the products or services they sell. This kind of expertise takes time, effort, and a lot of study. Furthermore, products and services are constantly being improved to meet the demands of a changing marketplace. Thus, staying knowledgeable means a lifetime commitment to staying abreast of changes in one's product line. Companies help by issuing product bulletins to inform their salespeople of the latest developments. In highly technical sales fields, like computers, these changes can occur on an almost daily basis.

Behavioral skills. Salespeople must learn why people act the way they do. Salespeople can no longer rely solely on their sales skills. They have to learn how to react to what prospects or customers say to them in sales situations. Salespeople must also learn to communicate effectively both verbally and nonverbally. They must develop effective listening skills, learn to read body language, and train themselves to respond to the personality of prospects. These skill areas are covered in later chapters.

Self-discipline. Just as independence is one of the great advantages of a sales career, self-discipline is one of its great challenges. After all, nobody goes out in the field with salespeople to see that they make their calls. No one is there to criticize them if they take off in mid-day and go home to take a nap. So successful salespeople protect their independence by disciplining themselves to make up and follow a weekly activity schedule.

They begin every week with appointments usually made the previous week. They schedule appointments for the rest of the week as early as possible. Some salespeople prefer to telephone for appointments for the entire week at one sitting. Others may telephone every morning to fill up their schedules for that day. When they have open time slots on their schedule, they fill them in with calls on old customers or new prospects, or they simply make cold calls. (Cold calling will be discussed in a later chapter.) Successful salespeople work on self-discipline until it becomes a habit. They know that being your own boss is not easy.

Long hours. Very few salespeople work a typical forty-hour week. In some cases, they have to make night or weekend calls, or have breakfast with prospects.

Salespeople usually do not do their personal organization during normal working hours. This is the time they call on customers. Many salespeople find that Saturday morning is the best time to review the past week and get ready for the next. Others set aside late Friday afternoon and evening.

There is also the problem of finding time to keep up with product knowledge. Some salespeople rise early in the morning for two hours of quiet study, while others set aside one or two evenings a week for the same purpose.

THE NEW PROFESSIONALS

The back-slapping, glad-handing, high-pressure salesperson of the past has gone the way of the corner shoeshine stand. The new breed of professionals who have replaced him are more than just salespeople. They are experts in their field. They counsel their prospects and customers. They may even refuse to make a sale if they feel it is not in their customers' best interest. These new professionals have three characteristics in common:

1. The customers' welfare always comes first.
2. They possess superior product knowledge.
3. They use responsible sales techniques.

The Customers' Welfare Comes First

In their dealings with customers, professionals consider the satisfaction of the customer's needs and wants. In other words, professionals do not think solely in terms of benefiting themselves. They ask themselves what does this customer really need? They are customer- rather than self-oriented. They discuss their customers' needs and wants in an open, sincere manner. They are problem solvers, educators. Here are a few comments typical of those made in a sales interview conducted by a professional salesperson:

- I'm not here to try to sell you anything until you feel you need my products or services.
- Let's explore your needs and then determine if I can be of service to you.
- There is no sense in your buying anything from me unless you trust me.
- To build a mutually beneficial relationship, we must be completely open with each other.

They Possess Superior Product Knowledge

The phrase "superior product knowledge" refers not only to the salesperson's own product but also to the competitors'. Meet Betsy Goldstein, a manufacturer's representative in Chicago, who sells fine porcelain china to the top department stores in the Chicago area. She has been at her job for ten years, is extremely successful, and takes pride in the fact that she knows both her own line of china and her competitors' lines equally well.

Betsy gained her knowledge from years of study. There is almost no question a prospect can ask that Betsy cannot answer comfortably, adequately, and authoritatively. She rarely loses sales to her competitors.

Most professional salespeople know their competitors' products as well as Betsy knows hers. They go to school, attend seminars, read constantly about product changes, and know the weaknesses and strengths of their own products.

They often use ingenious methods to find out about competitors' products. For instance, they might be in competition with a particular product and not know what the strengths of that product are. They might make an anonymous call asking a competitor's salesperson to tell them about the product. Or they might simply call a district sales office of the company, and ask for the information. Frequently, a library, local chamber of commerce, or past or present employees of the competing company will be glad to give information on the products in question. Sometimes the customers who have been using the competitor's products can provide all the information needed.

Good salespeople usually accumulate a file on each competitor and try to keep up with every product change their competitors make. No matter what their customers' needs might be, sales people who know all about competing products or services enjoy tremendous sales leverage.

They Use Responsible Sales Techniques

Professional salespeople do not manipulate their customers. Manipulation in selling involves the use of unfair, exploitive, or fraudulent methods to achieve a sale. Behavioral psychologists tell us that victims of manipulation report that it is one of the most demeaning experiences they have ever had. It left them feeling diminished, disillusioned, and embittered.

Most people can relate personal examples of manipulative selling by retail salespeople, used car salespeople, investment counselors, life insurance agents, equipment and machinery salespeople, as well as others. But professionals avoid the use of such tactics.

The biggest factor in manipulation is the use of intimidation. This is manipulation at its worst. Most of us have had dealings with the kind of salesperson who says, "You know I am right. Why don't you sign here?" Or "Don't blame me if your copy machine goes out tomorrow when you could have my new one today."

Phrases like these can be intimidating to any customer. It takes experience, practice, compassion, and understanding for the professional salesperson to avoid falling into the manipulative sales technique syndrome.

Manipulators, then, are salespeople who:

- Exploit rather than help other people for their own gain
- Try to get customers to buy something they don't need
- Take unfair advantage of social or business relationships
- Use high-pressure selling tactics that usually involve untruths and degrading motivation
- Leave their customers diminished psychologically by the sales encounter

Influence, however, is valid and certainly has a place in selling. We live with influence every day. For example, Paul Johnson goes for his annual physical and weighs in 20 pounds heavier than he should be. His doctor tells him that for the sake of his health, he should cut down on his caloric intake. That is valid influence.

Influence, then, is professional when it helps the customer:

- Isolate a valid need for a product or service
- Realize that he must act now to meet agreed-to needs
- Say Yes to the salesperson

Most professional sales training programs address the subject of manipulation in depth. They emphasize the absolute necessity of avoiding harmful manipulation in all aspects of the sales process. Unfortunately, even professional salespeople, in the excitement of making a sale, may cross over the line between influence and manipulation. But with the true professional, it is rare.

Influence, however, is required of good salespeople. Following a good presentation and the isolation of valid customer needs, salespeople must frequently use influence to complete the sale. This type of influence is valid.

SUMMARY

This chapter began with a definition of selling as the process of persuading prospects to buy wanted or needed products and services. It then discussed the role that selling plays in our society, pointing out that salespeople act as catalysts to the economy—the intermediaries between producer and consumer. Selling also benefits consumers by keeping them informed about new products and services that are available. Selling helps business and industry introduce new products and services to the marketplace.

Personal selling as a career was discussed. Its advantages were listed: earnings, security, recognition, and independence. The challenges were also mentioned: the need to develop sales skills, product knowledge, self-discipline, and a commitment to hard work.

The chapter closed with some comments on the new breed of professional salesperson: the salesperson who is concerned for his customers' welfare, who has superior product knowledge, and who uses only responsible sales techniques.

KEY TERMS

Behavior Skills
Manipulation
Marketing Equation
Professional Salespeople
Selling

REVIEW QUESTIONS

* Define *selling*.
* Name three advantages of a sales career.
* Why is self-discipline so important in a sales career?
* What are three characteristics of professional salespeople?

DISCUSSION TOPICS

* How does selling benefit society as a whole? Individual consumers?
* Discuss the challenges of a career in personal selling.
* How do salespeople help business respond to market needs?

EXERCISES

1. Talk with a person who rose from the ranks of the sales force to management level in a company. What kind of experiences did this person have in the field that led to professional advancement?

2. Divide into groups of two and sell each other on the advantages of a sales career.

3. Give examples of manipulative selling techniques. Why do professionals refuse to use such tactics?

Case Study One

Victor Ricenzo sells computer cash registers for a large national manufacturer. His territory is Minnesota. He was born in Duluth and loves the northern winters. His sales record, while good, has not been particularly outstanding. He joined the company after graduation from a community college in Duluth. He majored in sales and marketing.

Victor has been criticized for being too pushy in some sales situations. His sales manager, Dorothy Forest, who has a record of outstanding sales behind her, is known as a professional who always places customers' needs first. After getting a customer complaint, she calls Victor in for a discussion of the matter. Dorothy tells Victor that he is very close to becoming manipulative and thus unprofessional.

- What is meant by manipulation in the sales process?
- What should Victor do to overcome his problem of being too pushy?
- Can professional salespeople justify high-pressure tactics? Explain.
- Explain the basic difference between influence and manipulation in a sales situation.

Tony Martinez works out of El Paso, Texas, for a bakery supply manufacturing company. His big sale item is the baking oven, which he has been selling for the past several years to bakeries, hotels, hospitals, and restaurants in west Texas.

Recently, a new oven that bakes French-style bread has come on the market. Restaurants find it very appealing. This oven is unique, and most customers feel it is better than the one Tony has in his product line. On checking with his company, Tony finds that they are not particularly interested in making an oven to compete with the new French baker because they believe that their ovens, if used properly, can produce the same quality of bread. In El Paso, Tony discovers that one of his largest customers, a fashionable resort hotel, is interested in buying the competitor's new oven. Tony, of course, will try to convince the hotel purchasing agent to stick with his product. To do so, however, he needs some information about his competitor's oven. He looks in the phone book and finds that the competing company has no office in El Paso.

- How should Tony go about finding the information he needs?
- Would it be professional for Tony to ask a chef who has used the competitor's product for the name of the salesperson who sold him the new oven? Are there any other local sources that could furnish this information to him?
- How about Tony's sales manager? Should Tony call him on the phone?
- Tony knows that the other company is noted for its poor service. Should this be mentioned to the chef to whom he is trying to sell his product?

2 Opportunities in Sales

OBJECTIVES

In this chapter you will learn:

- How many career opportunities there are for salespeople with varied interests and backgrounds.
- How sales careers can be categorized by where the salesperson works and what he sells.
- How salespeople are paid.

To get a good feel for the Midwest, take State Highway 2 out of Harrisonville, Missouri, and drive on through to Windsor. You'll drive through cities with typical Midwestern names—LaTour, Chilowee, Postoak, and Leeton. As you approach Windsor, you'll see the flat farmlands of the plains evolve into the foothills of the Ozark Mountain range.

And as you approach each small town on your drive, the first thing you will see is a water tower. It is often silver, with the name of the city written in black. North of Windsor, on old Highway 50, is the city of Tipton. Its water tower is in the form of a huge black billiard ball—with the figure 8 written on it. That is because Tipton is the home of one of the country's largest pool table manufacturers.

Every one of the water tanks you will see on your trip was sold by a salesperson. The city council did not just get on the phone and order one. People who sell water tanks don't make a large number of sales, but each sale brings a large commission. Selling them involves a bit of politics—getting to know who runs the city, who makes the decisions, and the like. Technical knowledge of water purification and irrigation systems also helps. It is a fascinating sales career.

Water towers are only one of a great variety of products and services that can be sold by those who want to make sales their life's work. And the variety of products waiting to be sold is more than matched by the number of opportunities open to the people who want to sell. At the time of this writing, there are more than six million people engaged in personal selling in the United States. And these people, like the products they sell, come in all shapes and sizes. There is no such thing as a typical salesperson.

We can, however, place salespeople in four general categories defined by where they work (inside or outside) and what they sell (a tangible product or an intangible service).

CATEGORIES OF SALESPEOPLE

Before we discuss specific sales careers, let's look more closely at the four categories of salespeople: inside tangible, outside tangible, inside intangible, and outside intangible.

Inside Salespeople

Inside salespeople work inside a building—a store, an office building, a specialty shop, any place where the customer comes to buy. Sometimes, inside salespeople do very little selling. They merely serve as order takers. Customers seek out the particular service or product desired, tell the salesperson they want it, and that is that. This salesperson deals with a captive clientele. In other words, the store, through ads or displays or reputation, stimulates potential customers to come in whenever they need a particular product.

Many people go into department stores simply to look around. Department store cruising is a popular lunchtime activity for surburban and urban office workers. Sometimes they buy things on impulse. You will notice, for example, that supermarket checkout counters are surrounded by displays of candy, gum, magazines, and a host of small, inexpensive items that people buy on impulse.

Inside salespeople are found in other fields, too—for instance, investment firms and travel agencies—all of which are discussed later in this chapter.

Outside Salespeople

The outside salesperson seeks out prospective customers. He does not wait for the customer to come to him. Working outside, these salespeople sell their products or services at the customer's convenience. The door-to-door encyclopedia saleswoman and the oil-drilling equipment salesman are outside salespeople. Now let's categorize salespeople by the type of product they sell—tangible or intangible.

Tangible Products

Tangible products can be seen or felt. Tangible products are easy to sell because they appeal to the senses. Automobile salespeople try to get potential customers to sit in the car because its feel and, especially its smell, can break down the sales resistance of the most reluctant buyer.

At the perfume counter, a drop or two of some fragrance gently placed on the back of a customer's hand can motivate that customer to buy. Often, sensory perception does more to sell such products than the salesperson's efforts. A well-cut suit may sell itself when the customer sees it on himself. How many times have individuals bought flowers because of their smell or sight, or a mattress because of its firmness, or cheese because of its taste?

A mini-computer placed on an executive's desk, a copying machine wheeled in for a few days' trial by the office manager, a word-processing system tested by an executive secretary—all are tangible items that may sell themselves.

Intangible Products or Services

Intangible products and services cannot be seen or felt. Rather, they offer the customer an idea, a process, or a service that represents a present or future benefit. Often people who sell intangibles must paint word pictures of their wares. They must use their imaginations to describe the offering effectively and persuasively—to emphasize the benefits it will provide. It would be very difficult to convince someone to buy a stock certificate because of its prestige value. Without the benefits of a possible increase in its value or distributed earnings, it is nothing but a piece of paper.

So, too, is an insurance policy. If you buy insurance on an automobile, it is not for the policy itself, which is merely a piece of paper. No, what you are buying is a benefit—relief from worry about repair costs or lawsuits in the event of a future accident. Life insurance salespeople explain annuity benefits in terms of freedom from economic worry at retirement.

Some of the most highly paid salespeople in the business world sell intangible products. These are the men and women who sell advertising, radio and television time, investments, computer services, public relations, self-improvement school courses, property insurance, life insurance, health insurance, and consulting services of all kinds.

The monetary reward for selling these services is often much higher than that for selling many tangible items, although sales of water towers, computers, trucks, automobiles, stereos, airplanes, and home furnishings, to name a few, can generate excellent incomes. Normally, companies pay a higher commission per dollar for the sale of intangible products and services because more creativity, more ingenuity is required to sell them.

In the next two sections, we will look at some of the career opportunities available to those who want to sell inside or outside, to those who want to sell tangible or intangible products and services.

INSIDE SALES CAREERS

Securities Sales (Intangibles)

Over the years, many people in securities sales have become millionaires. This field is strictly regulated by the federal government and the Security and Exchange Commission because of the highly volatile nature of the product sold. Stocks, bonds, mutual funds, money market funds, futures, options, straddles, and the like, are included here. These equity investments are sold by securities salespeople working for investment companies.

Securities salespeople work inside. They do business over the phone, keeping a close eye on the video display machines that show them at a glance the up-to-the-minute trading prices of stocks, bonds, and other equities.

The world of high finance is a highly complicated sales field requiring exceptional training, knowledge, and personal integrity. Contracts involving enormous sums of money are made by a "handshake over the phone." Incomes here are based on commission.

Many nationally known investment firms have exceptionally fine training programs for their securities salespeople. As mentioned earlier, the rewards can be high. A person who works hard for four to five years and builds up a substantial clientele can be assured of a substantial lifetime income. However, income in the securities field is closely tied to the state of the economy. When there is a recessionary period, the securities business will drop off a bit. As the economy improves, it bounces right back.

Commodity Brokers (Tangibles)

Commodity brokers also use the telephone to buy and sell goods—coal, steel, grain, corn, soybeans, and the like—for their customers. These brokers are basically salespeople who must understand the market in order to keep abreast of its rapid changes. Commodity sales, like securities sales, calls for exceptional training and a willingness to be involved in risky, volatile situations all the time. The income from commissions can be substantial.

Travel Agents (Intangibles)

Travel agency sales is another attractive career possibility. Who does not like to travel? To be wined and dined by the airlines, hotel chains, and top restaurants? (Travel agents are wined and dined so that they will recommend the services offered by their hosts.) Everything that travel agencies sell—airline tickets, ship tickets, train tickets, hotel rooms, package tours—brings the agency a commission. This is the only way travel agents make money, since it is not customary to charge customers a fee for making travel arrangements.

Usually airlines, steamship lines, and hotels pay commissions to the travel agency for booking their particular organization. In addition, a travel agency business provides the perfect outlet for the salesperson who loves to travel. There are other enjoyable fringe benefits, too, like discounted rates for transportation, hotels, restaurants, and tours. And building a sound clientele ensures a good living.

Transportation Equipment Sales (Tangibles)

This field includes automobiles, trucks, farm machinery and equipment, boats—anything that moves people or products from hither to yon. Despite the bad press they have received, there are many automobile salespeople who have built up a tremendous clientele who come back to them time after time to buy new or used cars. In 1976, Joe Girard made over $200,000 in commissions selling cars and trucks retail in the Detroit area.[1]

The farm machinery field is another highly paid sales career. Of course, it is subject to the swings of the agricultural economy. The sale of pleasure boats and other recreation vehicles can mean high earnings for the salesperson because of the high price tag these items carry. Most organizations in these fields have continuing arrangements with financial institutions so that customers can handily finance purchases.

Large Appliance Sales (Tangibles)

Included here are such high ticket items as television sets, stereo systems, refrigerators, freezers, stoves, furniture, and rugs. Stores that sell these items offer excellent opportunities for salespeople willing to work, to develop steady customers, and to grow with that clientele. Again, an advantage here is that customers usually come to see you. You do not have to seek them out. The mere fact that the customer walks into the store indicates that he or she is already interested in the product.

Specialty Store Sales (Tangibles)

There are a variety of such stores—book stores, shoe stores, clothing stores, bakeries, liquor stores, music stores, drug stores, camera stores, hardware stores, and so on. A few years ago, the small specialty store appeared to be an endangered species because of the growth of the large retail chains. Today, however, the small store is making a comeback. The rebirth of the specialty store offers some unique opportunities for the aggressive salesperson. Although there isn't a great deal of money to be made in these stores, they provide customer exposure experience.

Department Store Sales (Tangibles)

This is probably the best opportunity available for people who have had little experience but who are eager to try selling. Although there is little opportunity to make a fortune in retail selling, it is possible to make an excellent living. For example, there are many highly successful salespeople in some of the larger department stores who build up a sizable

---

[1] Girard, Joe, *How to Sell Anything to Anybody* (New York: Warner Books, 1979), p. 12.

clientele, keep in constant touch with their customers, and take good care of them in general. Compensation, of course, varies. Usually such salespeople are on a guaranteed hourly wage with incentives for sales commissions beyond a certain minimum amount.

OUTSIDE SALES CAREERS

Industrial Sales (Tangibles)

The industrial salesperson calls on manufacturers, wholesalers, and distributors. He or she sells raw materials, fabricating parts, or other items used in the manufacturing or assembling of all kinds of products. An industrial salesperson might, for example, sell conveyor belts to a steel foundry, or molds to a plastics manufacturer, or rivets to a fabricating plant. Because individual sales are usually substantial (in price or volume), the commission income is also substantial. This sales career requires a good technical knowledge of the product.

Manufacturers' Representatives (Tangibles)

When manufacturers feel they simply cannot afford to put a full-time salesperson in a particular area, they use a manufacturer's representative. Reps usually handle several different companies' products—called lines. And they are not employees of the companies whose products they handle. They are independent contractors.

A manufacturer's rep may have a working arrangement with several manufacturers. Their product lines are not usually in direct competition with one another, but they are generally in the same field, such as the construction field, hospital field, or paper field. The reps' agreements with the manufacturers they represent usually give them exclusive rights to sell a particular line in a particular territory. Thus, they don't have to compete with other reps selling the same product.

Good lines are hard to come by; but once acquired they can be very profitable. For example, one customer may buy from a single rep a variety of items that are made by several of the manufacturers he represents. This only happens, of course, if the rep has products that complement one another.

Computer Field (Tangibles)

The Sixties and Seventies saw the birth of the computer era. The Eighties will witness its explosion. One of the most dynamic and fastest growing fields in the world today is computer hardware and software technology. Hardware is the machine itself—the calculator, the desk terminal, or computer mainframe. Software is the programs that tell the computers what to do, for example, to write letters, send out bills, store information, or change mailing addresses. Programs are stored on chips, tapes, or disks.

The computer field has been, and will be in the years ahead, a changing field with substantial reductions in the cost of computer hardware and substantial increases in sales and usage.

Whether one is selling large computers or desk-size terminals, the field is highly remunerative. Because of the competitive nature of the business, it is particularly important for the salesperson to continually update his or her product knowledge. An engineering or math background will make this task easier.

Residential and Commercial Real Estate (Tangibles)

The dramatic shortage of single-family dwellings in this country should gaurantee opportunities in residential real estate for years to come. Studies seem to indicate that Americans still want to own their own homes. In spite of the unfavorable outlook at the time of this writing, activity in residential real estate should increase in the future. Then, as now, income from commissions should be substantial.

Commercial real estate is probably responsible for more fortunes than any other sales field. The salesperson in commercial real estate sells commercial buildings, large apartment houses, and leases for office buildings. And, although the field experiences periodic slumps, there has been a steady increase in the value of commercial real estate over the years.

Commercial real estate also furnishes unusual opportunities for personal investment in potentially profitable ventures. These opportunities simply "come with the territory."

Drug Sales (Tangibles)

Most of the larger drug companies hire people (sometimes called detail salespeople) to call on doctors and retail stores to sell their products. Although drug sales are not as financially profitable as other fields of selling, it is a sound career with excellent starting salaries.

With drug companies continually upgrading their products and devising new ones to reflect the latest research in the health area, the field will continue to be dynamic. Drug sales involve more counseling than pure selling. A knowledge of chemistry or pharmaceuticals is essential. Again, companies always provide their salespeople with updated information on their products.

Management Consultants (Intangibles)

Management consulting is a relatively new field. Smaller organizations are now entering the field, which was dominated for years by just a few large firms. Hiring a management consultant, which was once considered an admission of failure on the part of a company, now seems to be standard operating procedure. Management experts are consulting with private industry all over the country and with city, county, state, and federal governments on an unprecedented scale.

As in any new field, there is some abuse and gimmickry, but, generally selling management consulting services is highly lucrative. Beginning salespeople simply apply as they would for any other sales job. Usually some business experience is required.

Advertising Sales (Intangibles)

A media salesperson sells radio or television time (or newspaper, magazine, or billboard space) to retailers, manufacturers, or agencies that have a product to advertise. Selling space and time is a competitive field, but the income potential is high.

The account executive who works for an advertising agency is a special type of salesperson. He sells ideas (and the agency's services) to clients who want to advertise their products. Account executives are well paid and generally come up through the agency ranks—sometimes from the marketing side, sometimes from the creative side.

Insurance Sales (Intangibles)

Insurance can be divided into two broad categories—casualty and life insurance. Casualty salespeople sell insurance on automobiles, houses, property, buildings, businesses, and so on. Life insurance salespersons sell life and health insurance on an individual or group basis. Of course, there are several companies that sell both kinds of insurance. Their agents are popularly known as combination agents.

The field is so broad that there is room for all kinds of salespersons. Incomes can be exceptionally high. In fact, insurance is probably one of the more lucrative sales careers around. It is also one of the few fields that pay what is properly known as "renewal commissions." When the first premium is paid, the agent makes a commission on that; and then in future years he or she receives a small fraction of each yearly premium as commission. These renewal income residuals stimulate the agent to keep the business on the books. (In other words, to do everything possible to discourage customers from letting policies lapse.) It also allows agents to build up a source of income that will tide them over if sales are off one year.

Life insurance includes a particularly rewarding field known as advanced sales. Here the salesperson sells products like pension, profit-sharing, and deferred compensation plans to businesses and institutions.

The casualty insurance field also has its own highly profitable commercial side. Casualty agents insure all the various risks of a large company in liability, workmen's compensation, fire, personal property, business interruption, and so on. Both premium and commission income are substantial.

Office Equipment and Supply Sales (Tangibles)

This field offers a superior opportunity for alert salespeople. Business people are constantly looking for ways to cut costs in office supplies and equipment. Hence, the alert, creative office equipment and supplies salesperson can build a substantial clientele.

Word-processing machines, typewriters, dictating equipment, calculators, computers, terminals, adding machines, and duplicating machines, all come under the broad label of office equipment. Keen competition tends to improve products, and the wide variations in costs for such items affords the alert salesperson many opportunities to save his customers money and personnel costs. This is a fine way to build a clientele of repeat buyers. Because technology keeps improving these machines from year to year, there should always be a dynamic market for office products.

Printing Sales (Tangibles)

Businesses generate and receive all kinds of mail—brochures, solicitations for funds, direct-mail letters, and catalogues. And with the proliferation of forms in business and government, there is more business than ever for the people who sell printing products and services. Prompt service can lead to repeat sales.

Food and Beverage Sales (Tangibles)

Here is a broad and interesting field. The salesperson usually represents a food or beverage distributor. Chain stores, supermarkets, and small Ma and Pa establishments are typical customers. There are also food and beverage salespeople who specialize in selling to institutions such as restaurants, hospitals, hotels, distributors, or schools. They do not sell to retail outlets at all. Such salespeople are usually known as food brokers. They, like the manufacturer's representative, represent various distributors. There are thousands of salespeople involved in selling lines like soft drinks, beer, alcohol, candy, soups, nuts, canned goods, and fresh vegetables. It's an interesting field, and although the unit commissions are low, the high volume of sales makes it a profitable sales career.

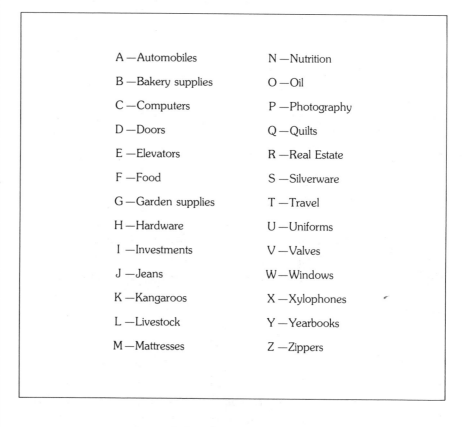

A —Automobiles	N —Nutrition
B —Bakery supplies	O —Oil
C —Computers	P —Photography
D —Doors	Q —Quilts
E —Elevators	R —Real Estate
F —Food	S —Silverware
G —Garden supplies	T —Travel
H —Hardware	U —Uniforms
I —Investments	V —Valves
J —Jeans	W —Windows
K —Kangaroos	X —Xylophones
L —Livestock	Y —Yearbooks
M —Mattresses	Z —Zippers

Figure 2–1. Sales Opportunities from A to Z

Neighborhood Door-to-Door Sales (Tangibles)

The scene is suburbia. There is a knock at the door. Mrs. Nelson answers and is greeted by a friendly sales rep of the Ajax Vacuum Company. He persuades Mrs. Nelson to take the chain off the door and let him in for one minute to talk about the greatest rug cleaner in the world, the Ajax Century.

Joe Davis, the rep, is all smiles and compliments. He shakes Mrs. Nelson's hand vigorously, and before she can say anything, dumps a pile of dirty grit on the floor, grinds it in with his feet, and says "Watch."

Horrified and upset, Mrs. Nelson puts her hand to her mouth and steps back. But Joe knows what he's doing. He plugs in the machine and presto—after a few swipes, the rug looks perfect. Mrs. Nelson buys the machine.

That's door-to-door selling; the example may be somewhat extreme, but such "presentations" do occur. Door-to-door selling entails lots of calls, many rebuffs, and numerous run-ins with neighborhood dogs. But good money can be made here because the market is so large. Most sales take two interviews, and it usually takes around 15 calls to make a sale.

A few companies have made a fortune from door-to-door selling. Items that are usually sold door-to-door are book sets, brushes, beauty items, pots and pans, vacuum cleaners, and a variety of other household items.

Other Sales Careers

To conclude this discussion of sales career opportunities, here are a few more possibilities—all with the potential for building repeat business.

- Salespeople who represent shoe manufacturers and sell their lines to shoe stores and department stores.
- Book salespeople who sell to bookstores, law offices, accounting firms, as well as schools and universities.
- Fire alarms and security alarm systems are sold to businesses, sometimes by mail or phone, sometimes from door-to-door.
- Lawn service salespeople call on everybody in the spring.
- Bankers are beginning to become outside salespeople, recognizing that in a changing financial climate, people may be reluctant to walk into a bank and ask for a commercial loan.

Fertilizer, shrubbery, cemetery, construction, industrial, paper, dental supplies, hospital supplies—you name it—if it's a product or service someone needs, you can bet that someone is selling it. It is this variety that makes the sales career generally so attractive.

Educational background is no handicap. In fact, whatever you have studied can become an asset in selling. For example, an engineer or math major can use his or her educational background to sell computers. Someone who has a degree in art can use his or her special knowledge to sell art work. The architect might go into real estate or sell building supplies. The list could go on and on.

These then are just a few of the sales opportunities available. Whether it's inside or outside, tangible or intangible, no other career offers such a large number of choices.

ENTERING THE SALES FIELD

Each sales field has its own entrance requirements. For example, to enter the real estate field, one must be 18, a high school graduate, and pass a state licensing examination. To sit for the exam, each sales hopeful must have worked for, and be sponsored by, a real estate broker. This does not pose a problem for most people. Real estate brokers can always use aggressive new salespeople.

Drug companies usually prefer to hire college graduates with a background in chemistry or biology.

Life insurance companies usually do not require a college degree. They do require an aptitude for selling. (They generally administer a battery of aptitude tests during the job interview stage.) The best way to apply is to call an agency office and ask about employment.

Retailing has no particular educational requirements. Applicants should simply go to some of the various retail outlets in their communities and apply. And there are always openings for part-time help in this field. In fact, retailers are relying more and more on part-timers.

Finding a job in sales will be discussed in more detail in Chapter 19.

HOW SALESPEOPLE ARE PAID

There are basically three methods of pay in the sales field: (1) the guaranteed salary, (2) the straight commission, and (3) a combination of the two.

Starting salaries vary. In computer selling, which requires a fair amount of technical knowledge, the starting guaranteed salary may be somewhat higher than in less technical fields. Retail selling, on the other hand, usually has a lower beginning base because no technical background is required.

No matter how much or how little they pay, most companies invest a great deal of time and money to recruit and train quality salespeople. Hence, they are usually willing to guarantee a salary for periods of up to three years before placing sales personnel on straight commission or on a salary/commission combination.

Guaranteed Salary

Most companies pay their new full-time career salespeople a guaranteed salary based on individual needs. (This takes a great deal of pressure off the new salesperson, who would otherwise have to become an overnight success to earn enough commission income to buy groceries or pay the rent.) Usually these guaranteed amounts are on a nonrecourse basis. That is, the salary or draw (against future sales commissions) has no payback requirements.

Many life insurance companies set up a three-year financing plan for their new agents. The new agent receives a guaranteed salary, which is usually based on local cost-of-living requirements. However, at various checkpoints, say every three months, the new salesperson must have earned a certain amount in commission dollars to justify continuance of the program. At the end of the three-year period, the commission dollars should equal his guaranteed salary. From that point on, agents are compensated on a straight commission basis.

Some companies, however, continue to pay guaranteed salaries to their salespeople throughout their careers. (Salaries are, of course, raised periodically to reflect increases in cost of living and individual sales achievements.) But because a guaranteed salary does not have the built-in incentive of straight commission selling, many companies have abandoned it in favor of the salary/commission combination.

Straight Commission

Salespeople on commission are paid exactly what they earn according to a predetermined commission scale. If they don't make any sales, they don't make any money. Commissions are usually based on a percentage of the actual cost of the item sold. The salesperson who sells a house for $100,000 will receive (in most parts of the country) a commission of 7 percent, or $7000. On the other hand, a computer salesperson might make a commission of 20 percent ($20,000) on the sale of a $100,000 data storage device.

In life insurance, the first-year commission might be anywhere from 30 to 55 percent of the annual premium. Casualty insurance agents usually receive 15 percent of the premium. The incentive here is performance. Only results count.

In the early years of selling, all salespeople worked on a straight commission basis. And few companies would make advances against future commissions. Salespeople had to sell to survive. That is now changed.

Today selling is a far more sophisticated profession. Salespeople need to be trained, and while they are being trained, they make few, if any, sales. That is why most companies now offer guaranteed salaries to their new employees.

Salary/Commission Combination

In the combination pay plan, a certain minimum amount is guaranteed, and anything over that amount must be earned by commissions. Most salespeople prefer this plan because it gives them both a fixed floor on their income and the incentive to sell over that floor to make more money. Usually this floor is geared to the basic income requirements of the salesperson who comes to work for the organization.

The table on the facing page illustrates median sales earnings for nine sales categories.

SALES OPPORTUNITIES OF THE FUTURE

Career opportunities for salespeople have never been better. And as more and more companies diversify through acquisition and expansion, sales career opportunities will continue to grow. The salespeople of tomorrow will be far more specialized than those of today. In the computer world, for example, some companies send out two-person sales teams. One person makes the presentation and closes the sale, and the other person delivers and services the product. This backup support system will grow, especially in the high technology fields.

Markets are going to require special attention, too. Telephone salespeople, rather than covering a specific territory will be covering specific submarkets in that territory. One salesperson may have financial institutions, banks, savings and loan companies, as a specific market. Another salesperson may concentrate on shopping centers.

Table 2–1
Median Weekly Earnings of Workers Employed Full Time
in Nine Sales Occupation

| | MEDIAN EARNINGS | | |
OCCUPATION	Both Sexes	Men	Women
Advertising agents and sales workers	$334	$418	$258
Insurance agents, brokers, and underwriters	341	402	270
Real estate agents and brokers	326	390	277
Stock and bond sales agents	535	589	—
Sales representatives, manufacturing industries	434	473	306
Sales representatives, wholesale trade	396	407	303
Sales clerks, retail trade	178	229	154
Sales workers except clerks, retail trade	288	305	—
Sales workers, services and construction	332	397	235

Source: Release 82–86, Table 3, United States Department of Labor, Bureau of Labor Statistics, Washington, D.C. 20212, March 7, 1982.

As sales functions become more specialized, the people who perform them must become better educated, more knowledgeable, and more professional. Eventually, they will also be better paid. Indeed the day will come when competent and professional salespeople will command as much respect and income as the chief executive officers of their companies. Our emerging post-industrial technological society has limitless opportunities for people willing to make a commitment to a sales career.

SUMMARY

In this chapter, we looked at the variety of opportunities available to a person who is interested in selling as a career. We saw how sales careers can be categorized by where the salesperson works (inside or outside) and what he sells (a tangible or intangible item).

Inside salespeople work inside a store or office and (usually) wait for customers to come to them. Outside salespeople work outside their offices and call on customers.

Tangible selling involves products that can be perceived by the senses—by sight, sound, smell, touch, or taste. Many tangible products sell themselves. For instance, the smell of a new car may convince a reluctant prospect to become a buyer. Intangible selling, on the other hand, requires more creativity on the part of salespeople because they are frequently selling a benefit rather than a product. For this reason, intangible selling frequently is more profitable. This is not always the case, however. A computer salesperson, for example, can make large amounts of money.

A brief overview of specific sales careers emphasized the large number of choices available to prospective salespeople. Almost any educational background will be an asset in some kind of sales career.

The chapter concluded with a discussion of how salespeople are compensated—on a pure commission basis, a guaranteed basis, or a combination of both. The combination is perhaps the most popular today.

The chapter concluded with a few comments on the future of selling, noting that tomorrow's salesperson will perform more specialized functions than the salesperson of today.

KEY TERMS

Casualty Insurance

Commodity Brokers

Guaranteed Salary

Industrial Salespeople

Inside Salespeople

Intangibles Salespeople

Manufacturers Representatives

Outside Salespeople

Salary/Commission Combination

Security Salespeople

Straight Commission Salary

Tangibles Salespeople

REVIEW QUESTIONS

- What is the basic difference between inside and outside salespeople?
- What does a tangible salesperson sell?
- What does an intangible salesperson sell?
- Name two especially lucrative types of selling careers.
- How do most companies arrive at a guaranteed starting salary for new salespeople?

DISCUSSION TOPICS

- For career salespeople, explain the advantages of building a substantial number of repeat customers.
- Why is the computer field an attractive sales career at this time?
- Why is intangible selling frequently more profitable than tangible selling?
- What does the future hold for sales as a career? Why?

EXERCISES

1. "Is selling for you?" Write a brief essay stating why (or why not) you are thinking of a selling career. Be specific about the aspects you see as advantages and disadvantages.

2. Interview a sales representative working in a field that interests you. After promising him or her anonymity, ask the following questions. Incorporate the answers in a brief essay. (Or, if your instructor prefers, make a brief oral report to your class.)
    a. Age selling career began?
    b. Products or services sold?
    c. Positives of the career?
    d. Negatives of the career?
    e. Form of compensation?
    f. Average earnings over the last three years?
    g. Thoughts on the future?

3. Obtain a job application from a local business that hires salespeople. Bring it to class and compare it with those your classmates have brought in. (There should be at least five different ones.) How do the applications differ? How are they similar? Can you arrive at any general conclusions about what qualities employers look for in the people they hire for their sales staff?

Case Study One

Mark Thompson quit his job as assistant personnel director of a large candy manufacturer in Maclean, Virginia. After considerable interviewing, he decided sales would be a good field for him. However, he does not like the thought of being an outside salesperson. He is used to working in an office and likes the atmosphere. Mark has two strong outside interests: travel and real estate investments.

You are the owner of a very successful employment agency specializing in mid-life career changes around the Washington, D.C., area where Mark wants to live and work. He is anxious to find a good inside sales opportunity with a potential for a substantial income.

- Name the inside sales careers that Mark might find attractive.
- Will his reluctance to work outside of an office limit his sales career opportunities? Explain.
- If he wanted to be a salesperson in a travel agency, could he build up a clientele without going outside the office? How?
- Can an inside salesperson succeed in the real estate field? Explain.

Sally Columbo is a vice-president in a bank trust department. Over the years, she has dealt with many of the biggest real estate investors in the Milwaukee area. She is particularly impressed with Patrick O'Malley, the owner of a well-established commercial real estate firm. O'Malley and Associates has been on the Milwaukee scene for years and has put together some of the largest real estate deals in the state of Wisconsin.

Over lunch one day, Sally mentioned to Pat that she was thinking of a career change. Her work in the trust department, while interesting, was not all that well paid. Pat responded by offering her a job on the sales staff of the commercial division of his real estate development company. He has offered her a three-year guaranteed salary with no bonus or other commissions. The salary is more than Sally makes now. (Because of her experience at the bank, passing the real estate licensing exam should be no problem.)

Sally feels very strongly that she will be a success at selling real estate. If she handles the listings herself, the commission generally runs 3 percent of the sales value of a piece of commercial property, or 5 percent of the gross value of a long-term lease—that is, the amount of the lease multiplied by the number of years of the term of the lease. O'Malley wants her to start work in approximately one month and has asked her to give him a decision on whether she wants to work on a straight commission basis or on the three-year guaranteed salary basis. Sally feels she can exceed the guarantee after the first year.

- What are the advantages to Sally, in this case, of starting on a straight commission basis?
- What are the advantages of a guaranteed salary?
- Are there any disadvantages to the three-year salary guarantee Pat has offered? Explain.
- Will her banking experience help her sell commercial real estate? How?
- What other sales careers, if any, has her banking experience prepared her for?

3

Characteristics of Successful Salespeople

OBJECTIVES

In this chapter, you will learn:

- Why employers look for prospects who are responsible and self-motivated.
- Why leadership is an important quality to be cultivated by future salespeople.
- Why employers like problem solvers.
- Why liking people is important in a sales career.
- How good communication contributes to success.
- Why employers look for independence in prospective employees.
- Why employers value personal integrity and loyalty to the organization, to the job, and to the product.
- What role self-discipline plays in a successful sales career.
- Why employers look for people who have a positive mental attitude toward life.

- What college courses best prepare students for a career in sales.

The setting is the regional sales office of a national sporting goods manufacturer. The location is the tenth floor of a Denver office building. The sales manager, Sheila Valdez, is interviewing applicants for a sales position in the Steamboat Springs area. In the winter, Steamboat is a popular ski resort; in the summer, it draws thousands of hunters, fishermen, and backpackers from all over the country. Steamboat Springs is a rapidly growing community with excellent market potential for summer and winter sports equipment.

Sheila is interviewing Skip Johnson, a native Minnesotan, who came to the University of Colorado at Boulder four years ago to earn a degree in marketing and to pursue his passion—skiing.

During school, every free moment of Skip's time was spent on the ski slopes. He knew every ski run at Vail, Aspen, Breckenridge, Winter Park, and Steamboat Springs. When the commerical runs closed down at Easter, Skip hiked into the high country with his skis on his back. Like all avid skiers, Skip became an expert in ski equipment—what kind of wax was best for various snow conditions, what type of boot offered the greatest protection, and so on. Although he was not a competitive skier himself, Skip became fast friends with several skiers on the U.S. ski team.

Skip thought he would get the sales position because of his extensive skiing experience. But he did not. During the interview it became increasingly clear to Sheila that Skip had never developed himself in other areas. His grades were average. He did not participate in any extracurricular activities in college. He held no interesting summer or part-time jobs. The only thing that appeared to interest Skip was skiing. He was an addict.

The point of this cautionary tale is that employers look for more than one dimension in the people they hire. Employers look for prospective employees who:

- Are personally responsible and self-motivated.
- Demonstrate leadership qualities.
- Can solve problems.
- Are people-oriented.
- Communicate effectively.
- Are independent.
- Have integrity and loyalty.
- Are self-disciplined.
- Have a positive mental attitude about life.

PERSONAL RESPONSIBILITY AND SELF-MOTIVATION

A sales career demands a high degree of personal responsibility. Because salespeople are not subject to the normal discipline of an office environment, they must be responsible for their own behavior.

One way to judge someone's level of personal responsibility is by the grades he or she has earned. Phil Marvin, professor of professional development and business administration at the University of Cincinnati, recently surveyed over 1200 executives who work for some of the largest corporations in the United States. A high percentage of these executives said that it's not who you know, but what you know, that counts in getting a job. The college graduate's grades are the single most important factor to the employer. Marvin mentioned that this is particularly true for students who have no job experience. Where there is no other yardstick by which to assess an applicant's potential, grades count heavily.

A history of marginal college grades usually indicates that the applicant was either too unintelligent or too unself-disciplined to do the work. In most cases, the latter is true; there may have been either too much partying or too little growing up along the way. Parents and counselors who hound students to get good grades are probably not trying to create geniuses—they simply realize the importance of academic performance in establishing successful behavior patterns for life.

There are circumstances that may reduce the impact of average grades. Working part-time to pay tuition and expenses reduces study time. Spending a great deal of time in campus activities may also cause grades to suffer. Either of these circumstances should be mentioned in an employment interview (and documented on a résumé) so that a student's grades can be placed in realistic perspective.

Good grades also imply self-motivation, another principal quality that employers seek. They want self-starters—persons who will carry out an assigned task on their own. Employers want people who do not have to be constantly prodded or pleaded with to get a job done. It is difficult to motivate people; salespeople, though, must motivate themselves. They must discipline themselves to:

- Leave the house at a specific time every day.
- Work a full day, calling on prospects or customers.
- Not waste time by visiting with friends during work hours.
- Avoid long coffee breaks or lunches when not with prospects or customers.

Salespeople have to learn to do these things by themselves to succeed. Their manager cannot accompany them on their calls, always pushing them for better performance, always pointing out the mistakes they have made. In fact, far from motivating, such authoritarian supervision can devastate salespeople. It robs novice salespeople of the chance to learn by trial and error.

Successful salespeople motivate themselves by continually:

- Making lots of sales. Success breeds success.
- Reaffirming selling as a method of reaching their life goals—job satisfaction, income, freedom, fulfillment, and personal growth.
- Accepting that field activity is the basic key to success.
- Realizing that their success is almost entirely dependent on their efforts, not someone else's.
- Appreciating that reaching a certain level of success is uniquely within their control. Unlike many other employees, salespeople do not have to wait in line to be promoted. They can work 60, 80, or even 100 hours a week if they wish. Nobody's going to stop them.
- Valuing highly the unique feeling of being their own boss most of the time.

It doesn't matter what things or money goals motivate salespeople; what matters is that they have the discipline to do the things required to realize their goals.

Employers want salespeople, then, who are motivated to achieve. And for employers, the best evidence of this trait is good grades and the activities prospective salespeople have engaged in during their college years.

Skip Johnson didn't indicate that he had the motivation to achieve anything besides the price of the next lift ticket. Employers shy away from persons who spend their college years indulging themselves. Sheila had probably seen the same pattern all too often. Although Skip was good-looking, affable, socially adept, and able to talk about skiing with the best of them, Sheila thought that there was a better than fifty-fifty chance that, on some future winter afternoon, Skip would succumb to temptation and go skiing instead of making sales calls.

LEADERSHIP QUALITIES

What did Napoleon, Hitler, Pope John XXIII, and John F. Kennedy have in common? Simple—they were all leaders. Certainly, they differed in temperament and character. And they were not all heroes. Adolph Hitler, for example, was a brutal and savagely destructive man, but he was an outstanding leader. Pope John XXIII was also a talented leader, but he brought both integrity and a sense of mission to his leadership role.

Leadership is not based on being a nice person but on the ability to inspire others to do what the leader wants them to do. Leaders have the uncommon ability to get things done through other people's efforts.

Dwight Eisenhower probably experienced the zenith of his career not as President, but as head of the Allied forces in Europe in World War II. Beneath Ike's sometimes bumbling and hesitant manner was great leadership ability. Anyone who could deal with the egos of such generals as Montgomery of Great Britain, de Gaulle of France, and Patton of the United States and get them to work as a team was truly a great leader.

Salespeople can profit from developing leadership traits because they, too, must influence others to do their bidding—that is, influence prospects to motivate themselves to buy a certain product or service. This ability to influence others is the trait that all leaders have in common. (See Figure 3–1).

One of the best indicators of students' leadership abilities is extra-curricular activity involvement. If the outside classroom activities also include holding office in one or more groups, then employers are doubly impressed. Activities such as student government, student union projects, and residence hall work usually demand organizational talent and

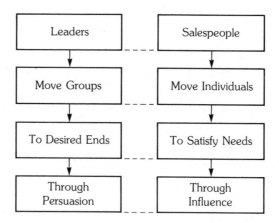

Figure 3–1. A Good Salesperson Is a Leader

are great confidence builders. Also, students who have to work their way through school are compiling solid evidence of responsibility.

Not all sales job applicants are recent graduates. Some have worked for years in others fields. In such cases, the employer looks for involvement in community activities. Thus, membership on a school board, volunteer work with a health organization, or chamber of commerce work are all indicators of leadership qualities. Again, holding an office in such organizations is further verification of leadership potential.

There are several ways that leadership talent can be developed by people of any age. Here are some practical hints:

- Find and join an organization that is active on campus or in the community.
- After attending a few meetings, ask to serve on a committee.
- Once on the committee, ask its head to give you a specific task of some importance. Then ask other committee members to help you complete the task.
- Do the task quickly and well, giving it top priority.
- Then ask for another assignment.
- Then repeat the process.

It won't be long before you are asked to head a committee. After a year or so, you will probably be offered a board membership or a chance to run for elective office. It is that simple.

PROBLEM-SOLVING ABILITY

The ability to solve problems is an attractive attribute to employers. Salespeople, especially, have to solve problems and to solve them fast. A prospect might bring up an objection about a delivery problem, or the product you sold may not be exactly what the customer ordered. The salesperson literally lives with such problems. So, learning to be a problem solver is a key ingredient to success in sales.

Evidence of problem-solving ability may be demonstrated by extracurricular or community projects. For example, a person on a school board may lead a successful lobbying effort at city council to get a tax ordinance passed for higher teacher salaries. Students may relate how they helped their student government negotiate with the school administration to provide better recreational facilities for students.

A LIKING FOR PEOPLE

People who don't like people had better not try selling. You have certainly encountered retail salespeople who were extremely rude and acted as though they were doing you a favor by waiting on you. You probably walked away wondering how such people ever got involved in sales. These are the exceptions to the rule.

Employers are looking for salespeople who like people. An introverted person who likes to work alone need not apply. Nor is there any room for the pessimist who feels that "people are no damn good." As Barbra Streisand once sang, "People who need people are the luckiest people in the world." In selling, people who like people are often the most successful salespeople in the world.

Employers have a useful yardstick for identifying people lovers. They look at the way they spend their leisure time. If they see that the potential employee spends a lot of time in group activities, then they know he or she really likes to be around people. On the other hand, if they discover that the applicant spends most of his or her leisure time collecting stamps or rocks, employers suspect that their prospect may not like people enough to sell well.

COMMUNICATION SKILLS

High on the list of desirable sales characteristics is the ability to communicate effectively. Sales managers are looking for people who can skillfully convey ideas, and who speak the English language well. Most employers shudder at the thought of one of their sales representatives saying, "It don't make no difference." Poor diction and the use of dull jargon or clichés often indicate a person who communicates in a lazy fashion.

Imagine a young man sitting opposite a prospective employer. This young man has passed his sales aptitude test with high marks. His appearance is good, his résumé indicates good leadership qualities, and he obviously likes people. The employer asks him what motivated him to investigate a sales career. He replies, "Well, I—ah—heard something about selling being a really super career. I also heard that irregardless of where you are, you will have a ton of freedom. As regards your future salaries, you kin pretty well write your own ticket, so to speak." Sounds ridiculous, doesn't it? It happens all the time, though. When employers hear someone use a nonword like "irregardless," they cringe.

Well-designed résumés, interesting application letters, intelligent interview questions all demonstrate desirable communication skills.

Thus, effective communication is high on the list of desired sales characteristics. Chapter 16 explores communication skills in depth. They are listed below to underscore their importance.

- Good oral skills—involving vocabulary, voice quality, and diction
- Assertiveness
- The art of authentic listening
- The proper use of body language
- Effective writing skills

INDEPENDENCE

Salespeople treasure their independence. In fact, it's why they like selling so much—it ensures personal freedom. Employers want to know if prospective salespeople want independence and if they will be able to handle it well. Evidence of independence usually surfaces in a job interview. The interviewer will give you high marks for independence if you:

- Pay more rent to live alone (for greater flexibility).
- Have left home to take a summer job in another part of the country.
- Blame yourself for low grades, not your teachers.
- Do not live at home with parents after graduation.
- Have worked to put yourself through school.
- Have run your own business as a part-time or summer job (tree-trimming service, house-painting, swimming school, and the like).

INTEGRITY AND LOYALTY

Salespeople work in the field, away from direct supervision. They are literally on their own. It requires ethical strength to be honest at all times in sales interviews. When a customer needs a product in two weeks, and the salesperson knows that delivery takes at least one month (and also knows that he will have moved on to a new territory by then), it requires integrity to say, "Sorry, we cannot get it here that soon."

Unprofessional salespeople may sometimes hedge, or even lie, to get an order. Not so with the professional. Honesty is always the best policy in selling. Reliability builds customer confidence. Long-term customer-salesperson relationships are built on a solid foundation of mutual integrity. As time goes by, the bond strengthens. It is often the lifeline of continuing, profitable sales relationship.

Loyalty is another key quality employers look for. Just as integrity builds customer trust, loyalty builds company trust. Companies, like people, have their ups and downs. Therefore, they need reliable salespeople who will stand by them, even in adversity.

Disloyalty disrupts the salespeople's and company's joint efforts toward getting a job done. Continual negative comments tear down the positive trust any organization needs to sell its products and services. If prospective employees cannot accept this fact, then they should not assume a sales position with a company.

The rah-rah, sing-the-company-song type of loyalty is not being called for here. Loyalty is an honest commitment to the place where you work, to its goals and ideals, to its personnel. Loyal employees do not talk down their companies to other people. They don't agree with competitors that their own company is no good.

Interviewers can identify an applicant's potential for loyalty and integrity by assessing answers to such questions as:

- If I asked you to work overtime on a Friday evening, and you had an important social engagement, what would be your reaction?
- How would you feel about postponing a planned vacation to meet a high official of the company who dropped into town unexpectedly?
- If our price is higher than a competitor's, would you sell our service record as justification for buying from us?
- What do you feel you owe the company you work for?
- What, in your opinion, are valid reasons for breaking appointments?
- What would you look for if you were hiring a person who would be handling customers' money?
- Your company offers a product similar to that produced by another company, but your product is not quite as good. Would you admit this?

These questions have no simple answers. But, their responses could reveal the loyalty potential of those being interviewed.

SELF-DISCIPLINE

Self-discipline is hard to come by. To forgo instant gratification in favor of long-range goals sometimes requires self-denial—a quality that is usually important in the short run and always in the long run. Thus a student may postpone a party in favor of studying or postpone a decision to buy something in favor of saving money for emergencies.

In selling, self-discipline is exceptionally important. After the initial training period of, say, three months, there is no direct supervision in the field. There is nobody there to see that salespeople make all their calls. It requires exceptional self-discipline for anyone to become a superior salesperson.

Employers look for this all-important quality in job applicants. An excellent way to assess self-discipline is to look at how applicants manage their money. Are they heavily in debt? If so, for what? Often employers shy away from those young, alert, dynamic, prospective salespeople who disclose during the interview that they have just bought an expensive new car or live in the latest high-rent, swinging-singles apartment complex. Such evidence of instant gratification may display a character weakness and a lack of self-discipline.

POSITIVE MENTAL ATTITUDE

Underlying all the characteristics that employers look for is a positive attitude toward life. Potential employers, like nearly everyone else, like people who are enthusiastic, positive, who have empathy for others, and who improve nearly every situation they become involved in—simply because of their attitude. They see problems as opportunities and setbacks as challenges.

Personal observation will disclose that people generally fall into one of three categories:

- Some people are realists. Accepting and honest, they deal calmly and objectively with life and its problems.

- Some people are pessimists. Generally critical and negative, they feel that life is to be endured, not enjoyed.

- Some people are optimists. Enthusiastic and positive, they view life, even its problems, as a challenge.

Good salespeople generally fall into the third category. Most salespeople become genuinely excited about the whole sales process—their products, their customers, and the dynamics of selling. Most of them will tell you that their positive outlook makes life much more enjoyable. They look forward to each new day. Their enthusiasm spills over into their social lives.

Professional salespeople use principles like these to keep a positive mental attitude:

- They can see the good side of every situation.
- They look for the best in people.
- They learn how to give genuine compliments.
- They are quick to laugh.
- They look upon their mistakes (and those of others) as an opportunity to learn.
- They refuse to drown themselves in guilt, self-pity, or self-criticism.
- They sometimes act enthusiastic when they're not, thereby ultimately becoming enthusiastic.
- They exude warmth, caring, and fun.
- They try to make people around them feel good.
- They take full responsibility for all their actions and for their attitude about life.
- They refuse to let negative people affect them.

Some of the qualities employers look for are covered in the mini aptitude tests that prospective sales trainees are frequently asked to take in advance of the interview. A typical mini test is reproduced in Figure 3–2.

COLLEGE COURSES THAT WILL HELP YOU AND IMPRESS PROSPECTIVE EMPLOYERS

Some of the most helpful courses in preparing for a selling career are in the following areas:

- Business communications. Salespeople must know how to communicate effectively, not only orally but also through letters and written reports.
- Marketing. Knowledge of the entire spectrum of marketing from product development to sales and servicing is a tremendous asset for salespeople. Marketing courses often review the pros and cons of a sales career.
- Acting. The ability to create in your audience a certain emotional response to a situation is a valuable skill indeed. The ability to present content in an exciting fashion is furthered by acting experience.

Answer Yes *or* No *to the following questions. Try to be honest even though you feel you know the answer desired.*

Circle One

1. Do you feel comfortable talking with strangers?   Yes   No

2. Do you feel uncomfortable asking for charitable contributions?   Yes   No

3. Do you usually prefer reading to talking with people?   Yes   No

4. If properly trained, would you enjoy making speeches?   Yes   No

5. Do you avoid arguing with strongly opinionated people?   Yes   No

6. Do you think sensitive people can sell?   Yes   No

7. Do you frequently start conversations with strangers?   Yes   No

8. Do friends tell you you do too much?   Yes   No

9. Do you honestly feel you are more talented than most people?   Yes   No

10. Does the thought of doing scientific research interest you?   Yes   No

11. Do you have lots of friends and acquaintances?   Yes   No

12. Generally, do you make quick decisions?   Yes   No

13. Does the thought of a job with income based on commissions from sales frighten you?   Yes   No

14. Have you regularly been involved in various campus or community activities?   Yes   No

Figure 3–2 A Mini Aptitude Test for Sales

- Debating. Many successful salespeople claim that debating is the ideal preparation for selling. Debating teaches the skill of responding extemporaneously to the opinions of others—a daily occurrence in sales.

- Speech. Not only do speech courses teach you to use the spoken word effectively, but they also emphasize proper pronunciation and usage—a tremendous help in the sales process.
- Psychology. Behavioral psychology will help you understand the sales process. The ability to interpret and react to customer behavior appropriately is often the difference between a successful and unsuccessful sale.
- Business law. Customer liability cases, manufacturing defects, delays in service, misstatements of product capabilities—all are discussed in business law courses.
- Computer science. Computers are increasingly used in sales, and computerized information sources on marketing and the selling process will become more available. Computerized proposals and terminal printouts will replace many others types of sales aids currently in use.
- Finance. Frequently, the question of how to pay for equipment or how to finance an equipment purchase surfaces in the sales process. A knowledge of finance offers a competitive advantage to professional salespeople.
- Sales. The best course of all would be one in sales. Here, all aspects of the career may be studied at a leisurely pace.

SUMMARY

Employers look closely at the personalities of potential salespeople because they believe that customers react positively or negatively to a salesperson's personality and character. Employers, therefore, look for the traits that have traditionally been associated with successful salespeople.

Employers want someone who is responsible and self-motivated, who has demonstrated leadership ability through involvement with extracurricular activities, who is intelligent and can solve problems, and who, at the same time, is people-oriented. Much emphasis is placed on good communication skills, particularly the ability to listen. Employers want someone who shows independence, good character, sensitivity, dependability, integrity, and—particularly—empathy. They also look for someone who will be loyal to the company and to the products or services he or she will sell.

Also important are self-discipline, perseverance, reliability, and a positive mental attitude about sales as a career. Employers like applicants who reveal an enthusiastic approach to life. This engaging characteristic is one of the common denominators of all successful salespeople.

This chapter also discussed some college courses that provide a good background for a selling career. These include business communications, marketing, acting, debating, speech, psychology, business law, computer science, finance, and sales.

KEY TERMS

Communication Skills

Integrity

Leadership

Personal Responsibility

REVIEW QUESTIONS

- How do grades measure personal responsibility?
- Why is problem-solving ability important to salespeople?
- What does self-starter mean?
- Can enthusiasm appear phony? Discuss.
- Name three extracurricular or community activities that would train people in leadership.

DISCUSSION TOPICS

- How would you develop or express company loyalty?
- Is it possible to disagree with some company policies and procedures and still be loyal? Explain.
- How can a positive mental attitude be developed?
- Why is self-discipline so important for salespeople to master?
- What is meant by good money management?

EXERCISES

1. List the things you have done in life that would demonstrate leadership. With your list in front of you, write a job application letter to a prospective employer who values two qualities over all others: leadership ability and humility.

2. Speak to your classmates on the subject of developing and keeping a positive mental attitude. Have them respond to your comments.

3. Enthusiasm is expressing one's thoughts in a way that can be exciting and contagious if it is not overdone. Reword and express the following phrases in an enthusiastic manner:

   - It's a nice day.
   - This product is the one for you.
   - Our company offers good service.

     Ask your classmates for their reactions.

Suzanne Martin recently graduated from a Big Ten school with a degree in marketing. Her goal is a career in sales. Although her grade-point average is only 2.3 (C), she was a starter on the women's basketball team and one of the best debaters in the school's history.

Suzanne is being interviewed by a large textbook publishing house for a sales position in the southeast. The company's traveling college recruiter is conducting the interview.

The recruiter knows nothing of Suzanne's extracurricular activities. Early in the interview, he rather abruptly states that his company feels that high grades are evidence of self-discipline and personal responsibility. She is eager to work for this company.

- How should she respond to this statement?
- Does her debating ability enhance her potential as a salesperson? Why?
- How could her athletic involvement help her in sales?

You are a manufacturer's representative in the construction business. You represent four well-known manufacturers of fastening supplies, drilling equipment, plumbing fixtures, and electrical-wiring systems. The electrical-wiring system company you represent is the fourth or fifth most successful in the industry.

You receive a telephone call from the home office of the top electrical-wiring company in the country asking you to meet with their sales director to talk about taking on their line. (You would, of course, have to drop the manufacturer you currently represent.) This position would mean an immediate jump in both sales and income.

The wiring company you currently represent has been exceptionally good to you. For example, they have insured you fully under their hospitalization plan, even though your spouse has a chronic kidney condition that predated your employment.

Even so, you must think of your own career.

- Is there a loyalty issue here?
- Should you inform your current principal company—the wiring company—of your impending negotiations?
- Should you refuse to talk to the top firm because your current company has been so good to you?

The Psychology of Selling

PART TWO

William D.Kron

Background   Bill Kron is 37 years old, married, and the father of three children. He lives in a comfortable ranch house in Saratoga, California, just one hour south of San Francisco.

He started his college career at the U.S. Naval Academy in Annapolis and completed it at the University of California, Berkeley, earning two degrees—a Bachelor of Arts in Psychology and a Bachelor of Science in Biology.

Although Bill originally intended to become a doctor, he changed his mind when aptitude tests indicated he would be happier in another field. Bill talked to several campus interviewers including Xerox, IBM, and Pan American the spring before graduation (1966). He finally signed with IBM and began his career selling office supplies in San Francisco.

Nine months later Bill was transferred to San Jose, and four years later to Palo Alto. In 1975 he moved over to IBM's small computer division. He's been there ever since.

Sales Achievements   In 1974 Bill led the entire Information Records Division of IBM in sales. He was number 1 out of 500 marketing representatives. (In 1972, he was number 3.) For six out of the past twelve years, he has been number 1 in the Palo Alto office, which has 27 representatives. Only the most successful IBM reps make the Golden Circle, a prestigious award that includes a one-week all-expense-paid trip to some exotic vacation spot. Bill has qualified for this sales achievement award six out of the twelve years he has worked in the Palo Alto office. He also has made 100 percent of his quota for twelve years, another exceptional achievement.

His Comments on His Career "I like selling because it gives me the freedom, flexibility, and high-earnings potential that few other careers offer. And I like selling a variety of products and services. I never get bored because there's always something new to learn.

"I think if I had any advice to pass on to someone just starting out in selling, I'd tell them not to get down on themselves whenever they have a bad day or week. There are slow periods in all selling jobs, but I've found that working just a little bit harder is the best way to get out of a slump.

"It's not hard for me to get out of bed in the morning. I love my job—constantly meeting new people and trying to sell them a product I have no qualms about selling, because it's first class. In fact, I don't think I'd trade places with the most highly paid corporate executive in the country."

4 Buying Behavior

OBJECTIVES

In this chapter you will learn:

- Why people buy goods or services.
- How Maslow's hierarchy of needs theory helps explain buying behavior.
- How buyers motivate themselves to buy.
- How to identify buying motives as either rational or emotional.
- How the buyer behavior of the consumer and the industrial buyer differs.
- What role advertising plays in buying behavior.
- What cognitive dissonance is (and how to deal with it).

A woman walks briskly down the street on a cool summer morning in Boston. Abruptly, she stops at a sidewalk newsstand, picks out a newspaper, hands a quarter to the aged proprietor, tucks the paper under her arm, and walks quickly on.

Why did she buy that particular paper at that particular newsstand? Was there some special news crisis brewing? Or does she always buy a daily paper there? Was she buying the paper to scan the want ads? Or did she want to read the box scores from yesterday's doubleheader at Fenway Park?

Although it is not always possible to determine why a particular person bought a particular product, we can learn something about buying behavior in general. In this chapter, we will try to discover why people buy what they do.

PEOPLE USUALLY BUY WHAT THEY NEED

People buy what they feel they need or want. A *need* is a condition that requires relief or satisfaction. In contrast, a *want* is simply a desire for something; it is not as strong as a need.

For example, if your furnace breaks down completely in mid-winter, you *need* a new furnace. You are faced with several conditions—frozen pipes, frozen feet—that require relief. On the other hand, if your furnace is simply old and inefficient, you might *want* a better furnace, but you do not need one. Effective salespeople are aware of this distinction and try to meet the valid needs, not the wants, of their customers.

Yet, many times, people do buy what they want and don't need. For example, a businesswoman buys a new blouse even though she has five very much like it hanging in her closet. Likewise, when people buy cars, their final selection is usually based not on what they need, but on what they want. Their need for a car that will enable them to get around efficiently for personal and business purposes is already established before they visit the showroom. The particular car they choose, though, is often a reflection of what they want.

GOOD SALESPEOPLE CONSTANTLY LOOK FOR NEEDS

Salespeople realize that satisfying their customers' needs is the daily challenge of selling. As mentioned earlier, good salespeople call only on buyers who may have a valid need for their products or services.

Sometimes a need goes unrecognized. Harnett-Justin, a large manufacturer of desk computers, copiers, and word-processing machines, is a case in point. The company heard that its competitors were designing a display screen for their word processors to permit users to edit keyed-in material before it is printed in final form. A display screen, which resembles a small television set, displays any portion of the keyed-in material desired. The operator can then read over the material to look for errors or poorly constructed sentences.

Harnett-Justin's research and development department, after much experimentation and in-house testing, designed a screen for the firm's own line of word processors. The screen was small and compact. Their salespeople claimed that it was in fact too small and compact to stand up well against the competition. The marketing department ignored the field force's misgivings. Marketing pointed out that research and development had discovered that a four-line screen was all anyone needed to edit written material. A larger screen would be nice to have, but not actually needed.

The marketplace proved Harnett-Justin wrong—critically wrong. The competitors' screens were much larger. Their market research had revealed that even though a four-line display was technically sufficient to detect an editing error, operators felt that they worked more effectively, more efficiently with a larger screen. Here is a classic case of misreading customers' needs despite warning from the sales force. Harnett-Justin took another year to develop and manufacture its enlarged screen—after losing a large share of its former market.

MASLOW'S HIERARCHY OF NEEDS

An eminent psychologist, Abraham Maslow, stated that people have a basic hierarchy of needs. He studied highly creative and well-adjusted living people through personal contact and the geniuses of the past through books, papers, and letters. The creative people he studied were assumed to have achieved the highest level of the need hierarchy—or self-actualization. Maslow believed that the lower needs must be satisfied before a person can fulfill his higher needs. (See Figure 4–1). An

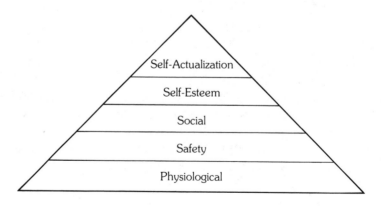

Figure 4–1. Maslow's Hierarchy of Needs

understanding of the hierarchy of needs is important for sales people, because each is fundamental to an understanding of the entire need theory of buying behavior.

Physiological Needs

Physiological needs are the most basic needs—food, air, water, clothing, sex, and shelter. Primary needs are easily fulfilled in an affluent society. In the United States, for example, most people take the fulfillment of these needs for granted. Not so in other countries. In some third-world countries with no oil, minerals, or marketable resources—like North and South Yemen—the citizens rarely move beyond this basic level of needs.

Safety Needs

Safety needs are needs for economic and physical security, including freedom from illness. The walled cities built by early man are tangible expressions of humanity's basic need for security.

Social Needs

Social needs are pursued when the physiological and safety needs have been met. Social needs include the need for love and friendship. People need acceptance and emotional support from their peers, their family, their community. When social needs are not met, the result can be devastating. Anyone who has been in the military and witnessed the "silent treatment" knows that it can break the spirit of even the most hardened soldier. Deep down, everyone likes to feel needed, wanted, and accepted. This is particularly true of salespeople.

Self-Esteem Needs

Self-esteem needs are the needs that motivate people to strive for success in their career or community. Some people need only the trappings of success—living in a certain neighborhood, driving a certain make of car, or wearing a particular brand of clothing—to satisfy their self-esteem needs.

Salespeople, like everyone else, need recognition for their achievements. If an organization fails to provide some kind of yardstick by which they can measure their own worth, they will seek satisfaction elsewhere. Therefore, most enlightened sales organizations attend to their sales staff's need for recognition. According to Maslow, if the desire for self-esteem is denied or frustrated, people become apathetic and eventually give up all attempts to obtain recognition.

Self-Actualization Needs

Self-actualization is self-fulfillment or self-realization. It comes to those who, having received the recognition they need, are now motivated to fulfill their potential as artists, scientists, businessmen and -women—or simply as human beings.

Self-actualized persons often make important contributions to their careers, their families, and their communities. Yet, Maslow implies that the whole area of self-actualization is a highly individualized thing. Fulfillment to one person may not be fulfillment to another.

Thus, to a salesperson, fulfillment may be a particular level of income and life-style; but to a teacher, it may be inspiring others to learn and to grow.

A familiarity with Maslow's theory can be helpful in the sales process. For instance, if Avery Bortwich has been told that the purchasing agent he will talk to tomorrow has poor self-esteem, Avery could take the time to try to discover some of the agent's work achievements, and then mention them during his sales presentation. Who doesn't like to hear nice things about themselves?

PEOPLE MOTIVATE THEMSELVES TO BUY

A potential buyer will not become an actual buyer unless he perceives a need and then motivates himself to fulfill it. Salespeople cannot motivate anyone, despite all the books to the contrary. Salespeople can only create an atmosphere that encourages self-motivation. They create this atmosphere by communicating an understanding of the prospect's needs, satisfactorily answering any question about the offer, and appropriately presenting products or services as fulfillments of those needs.

Creating an atmosphere that encourages self-motivation is a key element in professional selling. But it also involves an ethical responsibility. The salesperson's response to the buyer's needs must be sincere, genuine, and valid. Otherwise, there is a danger of manipulation—an insult to the prospect and to the sales profession.

There are two broad categories of buying motives—rational and emotional.

Rational Buying Motives

Rational buying motives are based on analysis, logic, and judgment. They are usually the basis for the sale of products to business and industry. Here are some typical rational buying motives:

- Flexible use
- Low purchase price
- Ease of maintenance and repair
- Availability of product or service
- Efficiency in operation
- Reduction in personnel
- Increase in profitability
- Increase in productivity
- Long product life
- Saving of time

Emotional Buying Motives

Emotional buying motives are sometimes found in industrial sales. (For example, the salesperson might know the individual who buys for the company, thereby injecting an emotional buying motive—friendship—into the sale.) Generally, however, emotional buying motives are the dominant—and sometimes only—factor in consumer sales. Here are some typical emotional buying motives:

- Amusement
- Emulation of others
- Popularity
- Pleasure
- Acceptance
- Social approval
- Better health
- Love of others
- Friendship
- Comfort
- Convenience

- Security
- Leisure
- Avoidance of pain
- Companionship
- Family security
- Status
- Monetary savings

Professional salespeople are generally well aware of rational and emotional buying motives. They sell by appealing to the needs that lie behind these motives. Thus, they project themselves to buyers as professional problem solvers. They uncover valid needs requiring relief.

Did you ever wonder why so many energetic salespeople become active in their communities? They do it to build personal prestige and thus increase their visibility when they go out to sell in their particular communities. Customers like to do business with civic leaders. Who doesn't like to spend time with well-known people? Often this willingness to buy from a community leader can make the difference in a competitive sales situation. "Both products were about equal, but one of the reasons why I bought from Joe was that he has a good reputation in the community," is a frequently heard remark. Thus, an emotional buying motive—respect for Joe as a community leader—closes a sale. The community, the buyer, and the salesperson all gain something.

THE DIFFERENCE BETWEEN THE CONSUMER AND THE INDUSTRIAL BUYER

Consumer buyers are those who go to stores to buy food, clothing, drugs, sundries, and the various other items that are consumed by a great percentage of the population on a daily basis. Industrial buyers are those who purchase items for business—office or plant equipment, supplies, tools for manufacturing, consulting services, and the like.

The difference between the two in buying traits is substantial. Consumers frequently spend discretionary income, whereas industrial buyers generally spend designated income, established by budgets in most cases, for products or services.

Consumers usually work with budgets, too, but their budgets are much more flexible. Thus, one T-bone steak might require an offsetting hamburger or two. Moreover, supermarket consumers make most of their buying decisions while in the store, as the joint study by the

Nearly two-thirds of every dollar spent results from some decision made in the store				
All Products Purchased (in percent of purchases)				
Specifically Planned Purchases 35.2%	Generally Planned + 14.8%	Substitute + 3.0%	Unplanned = 47.0%	Store-Decision Purchases 64.8%

Classification of purchases

- **Specifically planned and purchased**

  A specific brand or item purchased as planned, like OK rye bread, ABC caramels, lettuce, or steak.

- **Planned in a general way and purchased**

  A general classification like a loaf of bread, a vegetable, or some meat.

- **Purchased as a substitute**

  A change from a specifically or generally planned item.

- **Purchased without any previous plan**

  An item bought which the shopper did not have in mind upon entering the store. Unplanned purchases are often referred to as "impulse purchases.

Reprinted by permission.

Figure 4–2. Consumer Buying Decisions

Point-of-Purchase Advertising Institute and E. I. DuPont de Nemours Company points out (see Figure 4–2).

The impulse decision made in the supermarket to buy one consumer good instead of another contrasts sharply with the planned purchase approach of most industrial buyers. Hence, while professional salespeople, who usually sell to industrial buyers, are selling in a less flexible situation, they at least can count on buyer predictability most of the time.

DOES ADVERTISING MAKE PEOPLE BUY?

John Tai is sitting at home on a rainy Friday evening watching television. On the screen is one of his favorite movies, which he missed when it was in town a year ago. Just at the brink of each exciting sequence of the movie, commercials interrupt the action. Some of the commercials are neither inspiring nor convincing. But one of them is. It is a low key, honest portrayal of a large life insurance company's interest in serving its policyholders. The advertisement highlights the automatic-loan provision of its permanent policies. Under this provision, if a person does not pay his premium on time, the premium is automatically "borrowed" from the cash value of his policy, thus preventing the lapse of the policy and loss of coverage.

John is impressed with the provision since he travels a lot and is often out of town when his premium notice is mailed to him. He feels, therefore, that he needs this provision in the new life insurance he is considering. Over lunch with his regular life insurance agent a week later, John asks if this provision is in his old policies and would be in the additional coverage he is thinking of purchasing. His agent assures him it is in his old policies and the new one contemplated.

Capitalizing on this stated want, the agent explains how easily it works by explaining its benefits in depth. He enthusiastically points out that if the premium is not received on its due date, the computer automatically "borrows" the premium from the available loan amount in the policy and credits the premium as paid. Later, when the premium is actually paid, the computer reverses the process to repay the loan—all at no interest charge.

John buys the policy and is pleased with his purchase. He feels more secure than ever about his insurance. The late movie commercial helped the sales rep in the field make a sale here. But, this is not always the case. Sometimes media advertisements fall on deaf ears.

But does media advertising actually instill needs and wants to the point of prompting people to buy? What about advertisements in newspapers, magazines, or other periodicals? What about billboards? What happens at a football game when a biplane flies overhead with a long streamer reading "Eat at Barney's Pizza?" Do these advertisements really stimulate needs and wants in people?

Most advertisement agencies have copious statistics that answer a resounding yes. Advertising is properly labeled "indirect selling through the mass media." At best, advertising is a need-conditioning process beamed to a captive audience—you.

One of the purposes of magazine or television advertisements is to instill brand names in our minds, especially when there's very little real difference in competing products. Thus, when people go to supermarkets and walk down the soft-drink aisle, they may automatically pick up a particular brand because they have seen it advertised on television for so long. Sometimes television advertising has a delayed effect. For weeks, Mr. and Mrs. Consumer are bombarded with the furniture advertisements for a particular discount store. A year later, when they need a new bed or sofa, they may head directly for that furniture store. Its name has been indelibly etched in their memory by repetitive television advertisements.

Everyone would agree that advertising (and especially television advertising) can condition buyers to chose one brand name over another or one store over another. But does advertising create needs and wants? Many think so. It would be hard to believe that electronic television games, which at the time of this writing are a very wanted item, would have had the same impact on the market if they had not been advertised on television.

COGNITIVE DISSONANCE IN BUYER DECISIONS

Cognitive dissonance describes the after-purchase state of anxiety experienced by many consumers. Cognitive dissonance occurs when an individual's beliefs, opinions, or feelings are in conflict with each other. This theory was formulated by social psychologist Leon Festinger.[1]

Jim Locleer, a smoker, buys a carton of cigarettes to continue the habit. Knowing that smoking is injurious to his health, he offsets the health worry by rationalizing his behavior as follows:

- The reduction of tension is worth the risk.
- If he quit smoking, the weight gain would be more damaging to his health.
- A cure for cancer is imminent, eliminating the problem.

Thus, the dissonances here are neutralized by rationalization. Jim continues to smoke.

This same sort of dissonance often occurs in routine sales situations. The buyer doesn't feel comfortable about buying a particular product because it doesn't have all the features he wants. Thus, dissonance is inevitable at the moment of purchase. Professional salespeople anticipate this uncomfortable situation. They try to neutralize any post-purchase cognitive dissonance by:

- Discussing this possibility openly with the customer in advance of the closing.
- Pointing out to the customer the offsetting benefits of the product or service under consideration.

[1] *A Theory of Cognitive Dissonance* (Evanston, Ill.: Row Peterson, 1957).

- Getting customer agreement that very few products or services are perfect. All have their benefits and shortcomings. Yet one must be selected.
- Postpurchase contact with customers to reassure them that their decision to buy was a wise one.

Handling the problem of postpurchase anxiety well will build a favorable customer relationship, ensuring future sales. Responsible salespeople, then, always make the effort to identify this problem during the normal sales process.

SUMMARY

Generally, people have definite reasons for buying goods or services. They basically buy what they need, want, and can afford. A need is a condition requiring relief.

All people have five fundamental needs. Abraham Maslow ranks these into the following hierarchy, in descending order of importance: (1) physiological needs—food, clothing, shelter, and sex; (2) safety needs—to be free from pain and enjoy a feeling of security; (3) social needs—to be loved and accepted; (4) self-esteem needs—to have a good self-image, be favorably recognized by one's peers, and do well in one's life calling; and (5) self-actualization needs—to use one's abilities fully and to continue to strive for excellence.

Good salespeople recognize that people buy because they are self-motivated to buy—either by rational buying motives, which appeal to analysis, logic, and judgment, or by emotional buying motives, which appeal to feelings or impulses. Pleasure, comfort, convenience, approval, and status are typical emotional buying motives.

Consumer versus industrial buying was next compared. Around two-thirds of food-buying decisions are made in the store. Industrial buying is usually based on advance planning and budgeting.

The role of advertising in stimulating sales was discussed next. Finally, the role of cognitive dissonance, or postpurchase anxiety, was analyzed. Professional salespeople can do much to lessen these negative feelings by being honest about their own product's shortcomings before the sale is made and by continuing to reassure buyers after the sale is made.

KEY TERMS

Cognitive Dissonance

Discretionary Income

Emotional Buying Motives

Hierarchy of Needs

Physiological Needs

Rational Buying Motives

Safety Needs

Self-Actualization

Self-Esteem Needs

Self-Motivation to Buy

Social Needs

REVIEW QUESTIONS

- What is a *valid need*?
- What is a *buying motive*?
- How can a salesperson appeal to a combination of rational and emotional buying motives in a particular sale?

DISCUSSION TOPICS

- Illustrate the fact that customers essentially motivate themselves to buy.
- If a valid need has been established and the buyer is willing to do business with you, whose fault is it if the buyer does not buy? Explain.
- Do you feel that advertising creates valid needs? Can it be manipulative? How?
- What does cognitive dissonance mean? How do professional salespeople deal with it?

EXERCISES

1. Pick four products or services and write a short essay, stating which rational or emotional buying motive would make you buy each.
2. With a fellow student acting as the customer, role play a sales situation involving postpurchase anxiety. Ask your classmates to comment on how well you handled the situation.
3. Interview a radio, television, or newspaper person to get his viewpoint on whether ads make people buy. Report to class.

**Case
Study
One**

Mary Callahan, an executive for a local utility company, has just received an important promotion, with a substantial increase in salary. Helen Dess, a salesperson with a local real estate firm, hears about Mary's promotion at a meeting of the community organization they both belong to.

Helen's pre-approach research reveals that Mary rents a comfortable apartment in an upper-middle-class neighborhood. Helen feels that Mary's promotion should be accompanied by a move to a prestigious condominium complex. Helen's company is the sales agent for a new complex that fills the bill perfectly.

- Does Mary really really need to move?

- What, if any, appeals to emotional buying motives are involved here?

- Could there by any rational motives for moving? Explain.

- How should Helen approach Mary Callahan? (How should she open the conversation and how should she introduce the idea of moving to a larger home in a more affluent area?)

- Is Helen appealing to a want or need? Explain.

Walter Kothis, a medical supply salesperson, is talking to Lou Stern-berg, the manager of a medical clinic in Utica, New York. Lou is inter-ested in buying an ultrasound scanner for diagnostic purposes. Last week Lou talked to two of Walter's competitors, who also work for companies that manufacture scanners.

Walter, representing the Ajax Medical Supply Company, is eager to get Lou's commitment to try out his product before he decides to buy one of the two competing products. Lou, on the other hand, is in a quandary. He sees some value in all three products and finds it difficult to make up his mind. No one product is perfect. Yet, each company is reliable and well represented by a sales staff of known integrity.

In successive interviews, Walter feels that Lou is getting himself needlessly worried about making the right buying decision. Walter feels that unless he says something to reassure his prospect, Lou will make a flip-of-the-coin decision to buy and suffer postpurchase anxiety, or cognitive dissonance.

- What is cognitive dissonance?
- How could Walter handle this situation and still get the order?
- What are some after-purchase steps that Walter could take to lessen the impact of cognitive dissonance here?
- What about if Lou buys from Walter and learns that one of the competing products has more favorable features? How should Walter handle this?

5 Understanding Personality Patterns and Behavior Styles

OBJECTIVES

In this chapter you will learn:

- Why it is important to understand prospect personalities.
- How to use your adult ego state in selling.
- How to avoid crossed transactions.
- Why a knowledge of social-style profiles helps a salesperson control and predict behavior.

Henry Navarre is the buyer for a large aerospace plant on the outskirts of Los Angeles. The plant assembles instrument panels for commercial aircraft. Sheila Gustofson who represents a precision instrument company headquartered in Worcester, Massachusetts, just sold a substantial number of altimeters to Henri's company.

Sheila competed for the sale with three salespeople but she never had any doubt about getting the order. When her sales manager asked her why, her response was, "It's all very simple. I know Henry is a relationship-oriented person. He has to look at facts and figures to purchase anything, but he is more influenced by salespeople who assure him of personal service, particularly after the sale. So I catered to this when I made my presentation. Before the closing interview, I prepared a lengthy letter pointing out what our company would do to see that the altimeters were delivered and serviced as promised. Then I put in a few sentences about how I personally would be available if any problems came up. I assured him I would not delegate any postsale service. He liked that very much."

Sheila made the sale because she knew Henry's social style profile and catered to it throughout the presentation. The other salespeople did not.

In this chapter, we will discover why salespeople like Sheila, who understand their prospects' personality patterns and behavior styles, are more effective than those who do not.

KNOW THYSELF / KNOW THY PROSPECT

Successful salespeople make sales because they are able to look at the presentation from the prospect's viewpoint. After determining whether the prospect needs the product he has to sell, the professional salesperson askes himself: What will cause this prospect to react favorably to my presentation?

Every good salesperson is a student of human nature. And the study of human nature, like charity, begins at home. In other words, salespeople must know what motivates them before they can understand what motivates others. They must learn, if they do not already know, what kind of behavior is likely to elicit a particular response. We will see how behavior affects human transactions in the following section.

BERNE'S THREE EGO STATES

Salespeople must establish and maintain an adult relationship with prospective buyers. This stands at the heart of professionalism in selling. Professionals must understand the Parent-Adult-Child ego states popularized by Eric Berne in his book *Games People Play*. Essentially, Berne said, people have three distinct ego states—the parent, adult, and child—co-existing in their person at all times. It is important for everyone—and especially important for people in sales—to be aware of these states in any transaction, or social interaction. Berne puts it this way:

> The unit of social intercourse is called a transaction. If two or more people encounter each other . . . sooner or later one of them will speak,

or give some other indication of acknowledging the presence of others. This is called transactional stimulus. Another person will then say or do something which is in some way related to the stimulus, and that is called the transactional response.[1]

Let's look briefly at the characteristics of the Parent, Adult, and Child.

The Parent can be:

- *Nurturing.* That is, supportive, understanding, loving and caring. "Don't worry, I'll handle this service problem."
- *Critical.* The critical parent dictates orders, is domineering, is always right. "If you don't buy today, you won't be able to get it."
- *Both nurturing and critical.* Obviously, there are times when salespeople must cross over from nurturing to critical and vice versa.

Good salespeople are basically nurturing. High-pressure salespeople are usually critical parents. That is why they eventually fail.

The Adult can be:

- Objective
- Calculating
- Analyzing
- Creative
- Thoughtful
- Evaluating
- Realistic

The adult aspect of our personality is a storehouse of information and is as objective as a computer. It is this particular aspect of the adult ego state that successful salespeople must continually project. Successful salespeople maintain superior product knowledge. They study their competitors. They stay abreast of product changes. They view the inevitable setbacks of a sales career dispassionately, and they do not become discouraged simply because things don't go their way. They don't rant and rave when their company does not change a product immediately, just to be competitive. They are tolerant.

---

[1] Eric Berne, *Games People Play* (New York: Grove Press, 1964), p. 29.

The Child can be:

- *The natural child.*   This is the fun-loving self that looks at life with a sense of wonder, loves people encounters, is eternally optimistic, expresses emotions freely and often. Salespeople can let this state express itself after closing a substantial sale, winning a contest, or receiving some kind of special recognition.
- *The adaptive child.*   The adaptive child does not question authority, is always seeking approval, is easily manipulated, and does not want to upset the apple cart. Salespeople in this state cannot last long for obvious reasons.
- *The spoiled child.*   This child is petty, stubborn, inflated with a sense of his own importance, selfish, headstrong, and usually has been socialized to believe that he is better than others. Sometimes salespeople display this state when they have lost a sale or experienced a slump. Therefore, they may lash out at people around them.

All three of these personality aspects—parent, adult, child—have a special place in selling. Each ego state is called into play precisely when needed. Perceptive salespeople become aware of these various ego states in themselves and with practice learn to keep them in balance. For example, good salespeople never lose their temper or insult their prospects, even though such behavior may be completely justified. Early in their careers, people in sales realize that such outbursts destroy forever the possibility of establishing a trust. So, they very rarely lose their cool in front of prospects. They feel the trade-off, a potential sale, is worth the swallowed pride.

Professional salespeople, then, try to avoid the kind of conflict that arises from a crossed transaction.[2] (See Figure 5-1.) For example, instead of answering the customer's objections with an adult response like "I certainly understand your feelings," a salesperson might lose the whole sale by saying, "There is absolutely no reason for you to feel that way."

Thus, the Adult in us should always try to avoid crossed transactions. The Adult should strive to maintain a positive, mature attitude in all customer relationships.

[2] A crossed transaction is a transaction between, say, one person's Child and another person's Adult. Crossed transactions are rarely productive in sales presentations or in any other aspect of life.

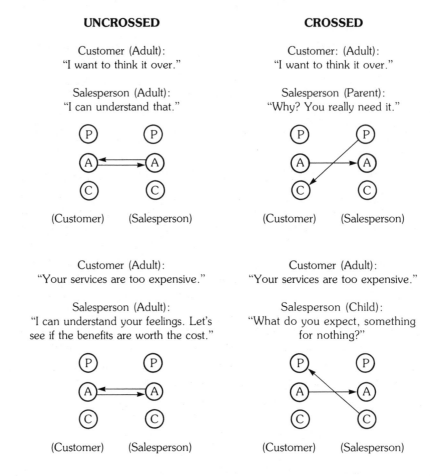

Figure 5–1. Sales Transactions

I'M O.K./YOU'RE O.K.

The concept of a positive mental attitude is defined and discussed by another member of the school of Transactional Analysis, Dr. Thomas A. Harris, in his enlightening book *I'm OK—You're OK*.[3] Dr. Harris tells how to develop a positive mental attitude in interpersonal relationships by eliminating negative feelings as a judgment base. These feelings come from experiences early in life.

- I'm not OK/You're OK. Usually what a child feels in the early months of life. The helpless child craves the reassurance that comes from contact with others.

[3] Thomas A. Harris, M.D., *I'm OK—You're OK* (New York: Harper and Row, 1967).

- I'm not OK/You're not OK. If the parent is cold and nonstroking, the child feels abandoned and isolated.
- I'm OK/You're not OK. The child is abused by the parents. If the abuse continues, the child may withdraw from all contact with adults in order to survive. Nobody is OK. Everyone is against the child.

These three conditioning processes, if not alleviated, produce maladjusted adults who have a tough time in life. The fourth position—I'm OK/You're OK—is the ideal. Almost anyone can reach the fourth frame of mind by practice, according to Dr. Harris. In selling, a positive mental attitude is the best way to create and maintain a healthy, open, and constructive relationship with customers.

Conflict Resolution—When Everything Is Not OK

Conflict between buyers and salespeople arises when the buyer behaves in a way that threatens the well-being or self-image of the salesperson. A customer might say, "How do I know your products and services are as good as you say?" To the seasoned professional, this is not threatening, but an honest concern. There are generally three ways to resolve such a conflict:

1. Deny the criticism. ("That's not true.")
2. Attack the prospect. ("Why do you say that?")
3. Neutralize the conflict by trying to find out what the prospect really means. ("Obviously I haven't described my products or services very well, may I try again?")

The last statement should resolve the conflict and allow the interview to proceed in a favorable manner. Thus, the adult reestablishes the I'm OK/You're OK relationship on an adult basis and continues the process.

PERSONALITY TYPES

Professional salespeople study the personality traits of individuals so that they may present their products or services in the most favorable customer climate. Is this unfair? Is this manipulation? Of course not. This process simply removes communication barriers between salespeople and the customers who may need their products. Professional salespeople understand the importance of good communication in the sales process and develop competence in responding to individual personality characteristics in order to facilitate it.

The First Theory of Personality

The Greek physician Hippocrates, who lived 400 years before the birth of Christ, is called the father of modern medicine. He postulated that personalities are determined primarily by the dominance of one of four body fluids. This theory lay dormant until Galen, who practiced medicine about 100 years after the death of Christ, revived and refined it. Also Greek, Galen was an exceptional scholar. His perceptive studies of humans and animals make him the father of modern physiology.

Expanding on Hippocrates' body fluids theory, Galen concluded that a person's general disposition, or humor, was indeed based on the dominance of one of the four body fluids. (See Figure 5-2.) Until the Middle Ages, these fluids were thought to control a person's disposition. This kind of scientific thought may seem strange to us now, but it does give us some idea of how long scientists have been trying to explain and categorize different personality types.

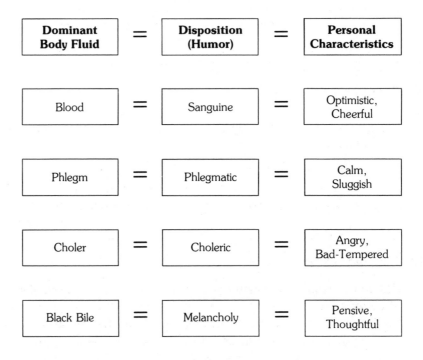

Dominant Body Fluid	=	Disposition (Humor)	=	Personal Characteristics
Blood	=	Sanguine	=	Optimistic, Cheerful
Phlegm	=	Phlegmatic	=	Calm, Sluggish
Choler	=	Choleric	=	Angry, Bad-Tempered
Black Bile	=	Melancholy	=	Pensive, Thoughtful

Figure 5–2. The Four Humors

Carl Jung

Carl Jung, the Swiss psychiatrist, added a new dimension to the study of personality when he classified people into two behavior types—extrovert and introvert. The extrovert looks outward; the introvert looks inward. Thus, extroverts have been generally categorized as outgoing, fun-loving, highly social individuals. Introverts, on the other hand, are usually thought to be retiring individuals who engage in careers like engineering, accounting, and research. Jung felt that people are born with the potential for both types of behavior, but that one eventually dominates.

The Social-Style Profile

One of the most perceptive modern theories of behavior —and also one of the most useful for salespeople—is the four social styles described by David W. Merrill and Roger H. Reid. Merrill and Reid extensively researched various behavioral characteristics and evolved workable social-style profiles of individuals. Their Social-Style Profile and the Style Awareness Training developed by Personnel Predictions and Research, Inc., has helped more than 100,000 people improve their understanding of their own and other people's social styles. When salespeople learn how to control and predict behavior, their ability to interact with others is dramatically improved. As Merrill and Reid put it:

> Thus, we take a practical view: Other people must deal with your actions every day, whether or not they understand why you behave the way you do. Because of this, your personal actions have an effect on your success. The way you act when you are with others—your social style—sends a message that influences the way that they, in turn, act with you. And thus, the better you understand these interactions, the greater are your chances of having positive relationships with people.[4]

Merrill and Reid feel that social style does not really describe an individual's full personality because it does not include such things as individual beliefs, ethics, and abilities. But it does describe what they call the three basic dimensions of human behavior—assertiveness, responsiveness, and versatility.

[4] From page 5 of *Personal Styles and Effective Performance* by David Merrill, Ph.D., and Roger Reid, M.A. Copyright 1981 by the Tracom Corporation. All extracts and figures from Merrill and Reid are reprinted with the permission of the publisher, Chilton Book Co., Radnor, Pa.

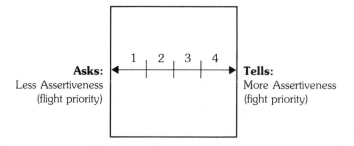

Figure 5–3. Assertiveness Dimension Diagram

Assertiveness.   Assertive people "state their opinions with assurance, confidence, or force."[5] They can be demanding, forceful, and aggressive. There are four classes of assertive behavior, ranging all the way from the highly aggressive, who tend to fight, to the cooperative, who tend to prefer flight to fight. Figure 5-3 shows this in diagram form.

Responsiveness.   "The more responsively people behave, the more they appear to react to influences, appeals, or stimulation."[6] Here again, there is a wide variety of responsive behavior, ranging from the highly impulsive to the controlled. Less responsive persons are cautious, intellectual, and serious. They rely on reason and logic, are stiff and formal, and tend to avoid getting involved with others. They are more achievement-oriented than accepting.

More responsive people are just the opposite. They are people-oriented, informal and fun-seeking in social relationships, and dramatic, open, and impulsive. More responsive people, then, show their feelings, while less responsive people control theirs. (See Fgure 5-4.)

The authors conclude:

> These two dimensions of behavior—assertiveness and responsiveness—can be observed in everyone, and, whether consciously or unconsciously, we often decide how to deal with our acquaintances and co-workers on the basis of our perceptions of their assertiveness and responsiveness. But remember, when we do this, we are reacting only to other people's behavior—not to their intentions. The person who ap-

[5] Merrill and Reid, p. 44.
[6] Merrill and Reid, p. 48.

Controls Emotions

Less Responsiveness (achievement priority)

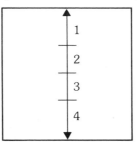

More responsiveness (acceptance priority)

Emotes

Figure 5–4. Responsiveness Dimension Diagram

pears warm and friendly may not, in fact, like us any more than the one who appears serious and detached. Similarly, the dynamic, forceful-appearing individual may not have a better idea—or even believe in it as strongly—as the quiet, less assuming one. These labels do not define what a person is thinking or feeling; they only describe aspects of observable behavior.

As we begin improving our ability to observe these two basic dimensions of human behavior, it will seem that assertiveness is easier to identify. In fact, in our interpersonal relationships, we can almost immediately pinpoint a person's assertiveness. For example, we can all tell the difference between "shy" and "outspoken" people. Thus with the clues which we have described, plus your previous understanding of assertiveness, you'll probably be able to recognize the extremes of this behavior dimension fairly easily, in others and in yourself. The responsiveness dimension, however, usually is more difficult to identify, even though our research shows that people respond to the emotional content in a relationship almost as frequently as to the assertiveness dimension.[7]

If we overlay Figures 5-3 and 5-4, we come up with four individual social style quadrants, with no racial or sexual predominance in any one group. (See Figure 5-5.)

[7] Merrill and Reid, p. 51.

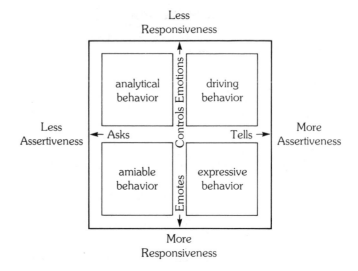

Figure 5–5. Four Social Styles

As the authors describe it:

> In the model's upper right-hand quadrant, we can place individuals whose behavior is usually characterized by "telling," but who "control" their feelings. They are primarily assertive, serious people. These individuals make an effort to tell people what they think and require, and they appear severe because they don't display feelings or emotions readily. We call this social style *Driving*.
>
> In the lower right-hand corner of the profile, we find the person who tends to "tell" and to "emote." This style is also assertive, like the Driving style, but these individuals are generally much more willing to make their feelings public. Rather than trying to control emotions, the person with this style will show both positive and negative feelings. This style is called *Expressive*.
>
> As we move to the lower left-hand corner of the profile, we find a social style that "asks" and "emotes." Like the person with an Expressive style, this individual usually displays feelings openly, but is less assertive and more interested in being agreeable and cooperative. This is called the *Amiable* style.
>
> Finally, as we look at the upper left-corner of the profile, we find a style that "asks" and "controls." This style is low in assertiveness, but high in control of emotions. Rather than being decisive or forceful, like

Analytical   **Driving**

Slow reaction	Swift reaction
Maximum effort to organize	Maximum effort to control
Minimum concern for relationships	Minimum concern for caution in relationships
Historical time frame	Present time frame
Cautious action	Direct action
Tends to reject involvement	Tends to reject inaction
Unhurried reaction	Rapid reaction
Maximum effort to relate	Maximum effort to involve
Minimum concern for effecting change	Minimum concern for routine
Present time frame	Future time frame
Supportive action	Impulsive action
Tends to reject conflict	Tends to reject isolation

Amiable   **Expressive**

Figure 5–6. Behavior Typical of the Four Styles

the person with the Driving or the Expressive style, the individual displaying these behaviors will tend to ask questions, gather facts, and study data seriously. This style is called *Analytical.* [8]

For salespeople, being able to ascertain early whether their prospects or customers are Drivers (action-oriented), Expressives (intuition-oriented), Amiables (relationship-oriented), or Analyticals (thinking-oriented) has telling implications. They will be able to relate to potential customers far more effectively, resulting in increased sales for the seller and increased benefits for the buyer.

In Figure 5-6, we see behavior typical of the four styles. In Figure 5-7, we see the positive and negative adjectives that Merrill and Reid have ascribed to each.

[8] Merrill and Reid, pp. 52-53.

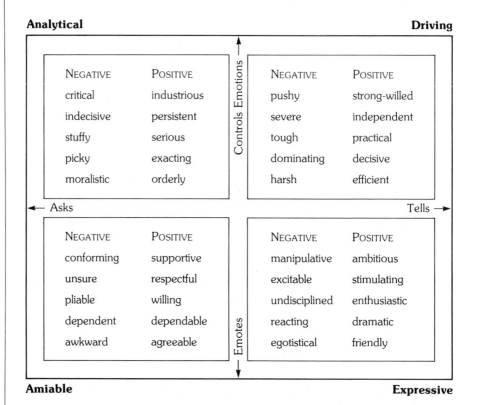

Analytical   **Driving**

Controls Emotions ↑

NEGATIVE	POSITIVE
critical	industrious
indecisive	persistent
stuffy	serious
picky	exacting
moralistic	orderly

NEGATIVE	POSITIVE
pushy	strong-willed
severe	independent
tough	practical
dominating	decisive
harsh	efficient

← Asks   Tells →

NEGATIVE	POSITIVE
conforming	supportive
unsure	respectful
pliable	willing
dependent	dependable
awkward	agreeable

NEGATIVE	POSITIVE
manipulative	ambitious
excitable	stimulating
undisciplined	enthusiastic
reacting	dramatic
egotistical	friendly

Emotes ↓

Amiable   **Expressive**

**Figure 5–7. Positive and Negative Adjectives Used to
Describe the Four Styles**

Selling particular styles

- *Drivers* are geared toward results rather than people. They don't respond to socializing. They want to get on with the business at hand. They like to know the options available and the probability of success of each option.

  Sales Hints: Present several alternate summarized solutions to the client's problem. Never tell him what to do. (Drivers' behavior is unpredictable.)

- *Expressives* are warm and outgoing. They are dreamers and highly opinionated. They like to explore ideas and solutions with salespeople. They don't like to argue and can be very emotional. They act impulsively, but opinions of others are important.

  Sales Hints: Keep proposals short. Use visuals. Spend time dreaming with these customers. Use testimonial letters supporting ideas and concepts being presented. The more prominent the person or organization giving testimony, the better. Expressives like social recognition; hence they like to be asked to lunch or to be otherwise entertained. They like extra incentives for their willingness to act promptly.

- *Amiables* are even more people-oriented than Expressives. They thrive on close relationships. They are warm, friendly, cooperative, and sentimental. They like to feel secure and avoid taking needless chances. They are pliable and patient.

  Sales Hints: Salespeople must not hurry Amiables. They must allow plenty of time for each interview. A warm, open, genuine relationship is a prerequisite to influencing amiables. Testimonial letters praising salespeople, not their products or services, impress Amiables. Hence, two or three letters from long-standing satisfied customers are ideal. These, coupled with simple concepts and conversational suggestions for solving problems, will go far in creating a sound customer relationship. After each sales interview, the salesperson should outline, in writing, what the Amiable may expect from him.

- *Analyticals* like lengthy proposals. The more facts, figures, graphs, and service contracts, the better. They are preoccupied with making the right decision. They are in no hurry. The one-interview sale is completely foreign to them. They are logical and live by fixed principles. They are thinkers.

  Sales Hints: Let the facts speak for themselves. And the more facts, the better. Thus, a written proposal of what your product or company intends to do for them is quite acceptable. All facts and figures should be accurate, leaving no room for surprises during the interview. Surprise is an upsetting experience for Analyticals.

Versatility.   The third dimension of human behavior, versatility, is really the extra dimension, according to Merrill and Reid. This dimension permits people to deal successfully with each social style.

> Versatility is not simply the ability to get along with others. Rather, it is dealing with others in such a way that they come away from encounters with us feeling better about themselves, thanks to what we said and did. In other words, a truly versatile relationship increases the effectiveness and productivity of both parties.[9]

[9] Merrill and Reid, p. 89.

The authors point out that we can learn versatility by learning how to listen attentively, to live with confrontation, and to resolve conflict. It takes practice. Good use of feedback—that is, seeing whether your message is understood and how the receiver feels about it—will help develop versatility.

The authors also urge individuals to ascertain their own social style through insightful study and through feedback from friends. They suggest preparing four 3×5 cards listing the characteristics of each style on each card and asking friends to rank them according to each style. Hints for observing styles are also outlined by Merrill and Reid:

1. Avoid trying to define a style too quickly. Since we all tend to jump to conclusions, we should try to observe a person in as many situations as possible.

2. Get out of the way. Our personal feelings toward the people we are observing can only hinder the accuracy of our objective observations.

3. Learn to observe more accurately and describe what a person does without making early "good," "bad," or "why" judgments.

4. Separate style clues from assigned authority or roles. We often jump to conclusions based upon assigned roles; for example, we might say, "He's a football player, a competitor, so he must be assertive."

5. Moderate stress clarifies style. As already mentioned, we often fall back on those patterns of action that have worked well for us in the past, our styles, in social situations that cause us moderate tension.

6. Set the stage for the person being observed. If someone is busy reacting to you and your social style, you will find it very difficult to observe that person's style. Thus, you must give the other person a chance to show his or her style by effectively "setting the stage." To do this, approach the individual in an open, nonthreatening way; demonstrate an interest in the person. After the normal greetings, begin the conversation with nondramatic questions, rather than with statements.[10]

Most people do have secondary style tendencies. Frequently, these may interchange. But, most people seem to be dominated by one style.

---

[10] Merrill and Reid, pp. 80-81.

Here are a few other points to keep in mind when dealing with someone you have never met before—in either a business or social setting:

- *When a person's basic style is frustrated* by another's behavior, he may fall back on a secondary style. Thus, Drivers become autocratic, Expressives overwrought; Amiables acquiescent, and Analyticals withdraw. This is an important point for salespeople to remember. If their behavior triggers a backup response in a prospect, there may be little meaningful communication and feedback.

- *It takes practice* to become adept at recognizing the various styles. Yet, anyone can learn.

- *Salespeople subordinate their styles* to those of others. Merrill and Reid discuss the way salespeople, knowing their own styles, sometimes have to control their natural tendencies to be effective.

- *The Platinum Rule* is the author's version of the Golden Rule: "Do unto others as they'd like to have done unto them."

- *All styles can be successful.* Dr. Merrill compiled overwhelming statistical evidence to prove this point. His study of a major midwestern insurance firm revealed the following about its 3000-person sales force: 38 percent were Expressives, 27 percent were Drivers, 24 percent were Amiables, and 11 percent were Analyticals.

Thus, a knowledge of social styles will help salespeople recognize the dominant personality tendencies of their customers. A knowledge of transactional analysis will help them deal intelligently and maturely with their customers' concerns and objections. Knowledge of these two techniques will also help salespeople to resolve conflicts with customers successfully.

BECOMING A WHOLE PERSON

Being a whole person means not being limited in interest to the narrow confines of the company or the products it sells. Professional salespeople do not allow themselves to become narrow in focus nor restricted in their opinions about life and work. Professional salespeople want to grow. So they keep themselves well informed about what is going on, not only in their industry but in the world at large. They develop an interest in their communities because they know that communities thrive only when citizens at all levels take an interest in them.

Becoming a whole person is not an easy process. It is a matter of arranging priorities. A typical program of personal development involves competency at various levels. In this order, salespeople should:

- Integrate family, business, and community life so that no one area suffers at the expense of another.
- Learn their company's products and services from A to Z, and keep current on changes.
- Learn competitors' products and services from A to Z.
- Get involved in the industry through trade associations and clubs.
- Get involved in community or church work.
- Assume leadership roles in industry organizations, community, or church groups.
- Expand life to include cultural and other interests.
- Begin to read for private enjoyment as well as for knowledge.
- Keep abreast of current events at the community, state, national, and international level by reading newspapers and periodicals.

This whole person concept is one of the main reasons why so many salespeople teach, serve on school boards and participate in community fund drives. Such involvement obviously benefits the community, but it also brings rewards to the salesperson who participates. The salespeople benefit because they:

- Find more prospects for their products and services.
- Get to know decision makers, who may buy from them.
- Become known as more responsible than the salespeople not involved. (Customers like to deal with responsible salespeople.)

Communities are well served because the salespeople who become involved are:

- Superior communicators, badly needed in most community projects.
- Comfortable asking for funds in charitable drives.
- Competent in resolving conflicts among varying interest groups.

SUMMARY

This chapter urges salespeople to place themselves in their customers' shoes. In this way, they can better understand, and cater to, their prospects' personality patterns and behavior styles. The ideal seller-customer relationship is conducted in an I'm OK/You're OK atmosphere by two Adults.

One way for salespeople to discover the dominant personality tendency of their prospective customers is to examine the three dimensions of human behavior studied by Merrill and Reid: assertiveness, responsiveness, and versatility. Combining the quadrants of assertiveness and responsiveness, Miller and Reid define four distinct social styles of behavior: the Driver who acts, the Expressive who dreams, the Amiable who relates, and the Analytical who thinks.

The chapter closed with a discussion of how important it is for a salesperson to become a whole person by undertaking a program of personal development that involves allocating the right amount of time to personal, business, and community affairs.

KEY TERMS

Amiables	Extrovert
Analyticals	Introvert
Assertiveness	Parent/Adult/Child
Conflict Resolution	Responsiveness
Drivers	Social-Style Profile
Expressives	Versatility

REVIEW QUESTIONS

- Name the three ego states.
- What is a crossed transaction?
- What are the three basic dimensions of human behavior defined by Merrill and Reid?
- Name the four social styles of human behavior.

DISCUSSION TOPICS

- Discuss the role of versatility in the sales process.
- How do you determine the social-style profile of a prospect?
- What place does conflict resolution have in the sales process?
- How do successful salespeople avoid crossed transactions?

EXERCISES

1. Form two small groups, one of which answers customers' objections in an uncrossed manner; the other in a crossed manner. Demonstrate your techniques to the rest of the class.

2. Write a short essay on whether you are primarily an introvert or an extrovert. Give specific examples.

3. Prepare three 3 × 5 cards asking three of your friends to define your social-style profile: Amiable, Analytical, Driver, Expressive. Then summarize them for discussion in class.

Case Study One

Jamie Walsh is a successful salesman for Pritchard's Patio Furniture, a Charlotte, North Carolina, manufacturer. Chicago is in his territory. He has just been told that an exclusive furniture store on fashionable Michigan Avenue is interested in adding a line of patio furniture to its inventory.

Jamie is an outgoing, impulsive type of salesperson who likes to sell clients over lunch. He does not like complicated detailed proposals. He always sells from his well illustrated catalogues.

He has been told to call Roland Agnew, the third-generation owner for an interview. By talking to other furniture contacts in the area, he finds that Mr. Agnew is a no-nonsense workaholic. Mr. Agnew works long hours and runs a very tight ship. He gets things done and does not like to waste time. His store is quite successful.

- What is Mr. Agnew's social-style profile?
- Should Jamie take Mr. Agnew to a nice restaurant for lunch? Explain.
- How should Jamie present his furniture line to Mr. Agnew?
- What role does versatility play in this situation?

Joyce Vanderschmit has been selling steel castings in the Pittsburgh area for three years. After graduating from her community college in Harrisburg, she accepted a sales position in Pittsburgh. She is single. Joyce loves to sell and is a hard worker. She puts in a long work week and devotes most evenings to reviewing her day's activities and reading up on company product changes.

A friend, John Strong, whom she dates occasionally, claims Joyce is working too hard. Joyce denies this, claiming it's vital for a new saleswoman to work very hard in the early years of her career. John counters with the argument that it's important to keep everything in perspective, that there's more to life than being a successful saleswoman. John argues that Joyce is not working at becoming a whole person.

- What is a whole person?
- How does being one, or not being one, affect a sales career?
- Explain why community or industry involvement helps an individual become a whole person.

Case Study Two

6

Dealing with Fear, Stress, and Rejection

OBJECTIVES

In this chapter you will learn:

- What the drawbacks are in selling.
- How to put the drawbacks in perspective.
- How to understand and conquer fear.
- How to keep stress at a minimum.
- Why rejection does not have to be personally demeaning.
- What the ego trap can do to salespeople.

Ed Paschek sat before Charles Condon holding back his emotions. He had been in the agency for two years and was just now starting to become a really successful salesperson. At the age of 31, after working for a bank and a real estate agency, Ed thought the life insurance sales field the ideal career for him. He was intelligent, energetic, and highly motivated.

More and more, however, he was feeling that he could not take the rejection that all salespeople experience. This past week, in which he had been turned down five times, had been particularly bad for him. So he had decided to talk to his sales manager about it. "I just can't stand having the majority of people I see every week say no. I'm tired of being regarded by potential customers as bothersome—discussing death and retirement and things they don't want to think about. Mostly, I just don't like being in a situation where people are always being negative. I'm beginning to have a real fear of making calls. I feel nervous every time I walk in to keep an appointment. It has gotten so bad that I'm afraid I'm going to have to leave the insurance business."

What Ed was telling his boss is not unusual, especially for salespeople at the outset of their careers. Charles Condon understood perfectly and tried to reassure Ed that he should not take rejection personally.

"I understand your point," Ed said, "and I know that the rejection is not of me but of what I am trying to sell. When I get myself in that frame of mind, I'm OK. As a matter of fact, I thought I had the whole problem licked until this week."

Again Charles understood. "You probably never will get it completely licked, Ed. But stay with it, and eventually it will become tolerable. You won't feel it's such a personal thing. I don't know any successful salesperson who has not experienced the same thing in the early months of selling. It's one of the minor drawbacks to the career. Come to see me whenever you're bothered by it and we'll continue to analyze it. Frankly, you have a lot of sales talent and will go far, once you put the negatives of selling in their proper perspective."

THE DRAWBACKS IN SELLING

Every career has some drawbacks. Investment salespeople have to be near the telephone all the time. Doctors are always on call. Most lawyers and accountants are confined to their offices because they bill on an hourly basis. Business executives must endure the steady pressure of deadlines and a hectic pace. But these careers are rewarding.

Selling is no different. It has drawbacks and rewards, and one who embarks on a career of selling must learn to recognize the drawbacks, and learn how to react to them.

The most common drawbacks in selling are fear, stress, and rejection—as with Ed Paschek in the example. There can also be loneliness and boredom, a feeling of lack of prestige, with sales slumps. For some there is the ego trap, the danger of becoming a workaholic. Other associated problems can be more indirect—delivery problems, a poor sales manager, or, sometimes, unethical or illegal company practices. Let us look at these drawbacks from a salesperson's perspective and see if we can learn to understand them and deal with them.

FEAR

Most of the psychological and psychiatric studies on the subject of fear are concerned with extraordinary or psychotic behavior. Very little is known about the kinds of fears we experience in everyday life, usually related to an anticipation of physical or psychological pain. In an article on fear in the *Monthly Letter* of the Royal Bank of Canada the kind of fear that sales people commonly encounter was described this way:

> Among the most pervasive of the elusive fears that insinuate themselves into people's minds in western society today is fear of failure. It makes its bid for control of a person early in life, perhaps in a grade one classroom or on a Little League baseball field. As it progresses it appears in a variety of subsidiary forms: fear of making mistakes, fear of breaking with convention, fear of one's occupational superiors, fear of dismissal from a job, and finally fear of trying. In the latter form it can destroy the spirit of an individual—and without spirit, what is life?[1]

Salespersons are haunted by fears of failure, of being rejected, of being looked down upon, of looking bad. To overcome these fears, a salesperson first has to recognize how fear can influence behavior and then try to understand the reactions to fear. Too often in life we try to counter fear by denying that it exists, by subordinating what are perfectly normal apprehensions—either of physical pain, or as in selling, psychological pain. By not making appointments, a salesperson can postpone dealing with fear—but only temporarily. To get over the hurdle, a reluctant salesperson should recognize that the worst that can happen in making a call is a verbal rejection. Few prospects are going to risk being sued for assault and battery! And the salesperson should also bear in mind that if he fails to make a sale, it is not he but his product or service that is being rejected.

Having arrived at an acceptance that it is normal to be afraid as a salesperson, then we *release* ourselves to follow alternative courses of action where fear would have originally defeated us.

Many experienced salespersons work out their own formulas for coping with fear and apprehension and bolstering confidence. Practicing the formula eventually makes the response so automatic that it can be relied upon to help even when fears intrude in a sales interview. The formula usually goes this way:

---

[1]"The Meaning of Fear." From the *Monthly Letter*, published by the Royal Bank of Canada, December 1978.

- Rejection is not personal.
- I know much more about my products and services than my customer does.
- No one is perfect, including myself.
- I have done a lot of good for a lot of customers in the past. I am not a bad salesperson.
- No salesperson can sell everyone he sees—otherwise we all could have retired years ago.
- It's all part of the career.
- My customer doesn't have to like me personally in order to buy from me.

STRESS

Stress, in the sense of anxiety and worry, is one of the most common modern afflictions. It is blamed for much of what seems to ail our contemporary life, especially in the United States and other highly developed societies. It afflicts salespeople quite as much as other people who deal with the public in competitive situations. To some degree, stress, even in its usual sense of pressure or anxiety, can add zest to life, but continual stress can be destructive.

In salespeople, negative stress and anxiety is a disquieting state brought on by a mentally or physiologically disruptive or upsetting experience. It can occur when one begins to find a prospect's comments confusing or when the discussion seems to be going beyond one's depth of knowledge about some product or service. In certain situations, such as making a presentation to an executive committee or to the chief executive officer of a company, stress can be merely acute stagefright.

The physical symptoms may be queasiness, a rise in blood pressure, sweating, a dry mouth—a general feeling of impending doom—and inarticulateness or rapid, defensive speech. Every salesperson has probably experienced these unpleasant symptoms in some degree or another, but what overwhelms one salesperson may be a stimulant for the next. Some degree of stress is normal. It is only when stress becomes extreme and prolonged that it becomes seriously detrimental to performance.

To keep this condition in perspective, salespeople should understand that it occurs in other occupations too. Several years ago, a study was made of 100 top executives of certain American corporations, excluding any who had got their jobs by virtue of birth. Half of those studied suffered such symptoms of stress as headaches, stomach trouble, nervous disorders, and other job-related pressures; the other half declared themselves to be happy and stable in their work. The study showed that those who were able to manage the stress in their lives had five things in common:

1. They were not in spiritual turmoil about religion or the existence of a Supreme Being, but religion was a separate part of their lives. They neither blamed nor praised God for their success.

2. They were completely at peace with their personal lives, whether married, divorced, remarried, or single.

3. They were willing to risk making mistakes. As their careers blossomed, they realized that they would have to take risks to grow, and if they made mistakes they took them in stride and learned from them.

4. They had gained a lot of experience as they climbed to the top. They spent adequate time at each level. Recent studies are showing that some of the MBA business school whiz kids are proving to be disappointments in high-level executive jobs because they simply have not had enough experience at the lower levels. They lack the wisdom that only time can bring. Salespeople often try to move ahead too fast. They are impatient and do not realize that big sales cannot be made overnight.

5. Every one of the happy 50 had five friends with whom he or she could discuss the intimate details of business as well as personal affairs. This was one of the most significant findings in the survey.

The kind of stress that merely quickens the heartbeat and arouses healthy anticipation—exercise, sex, athletic competition—can be emulated by a salesperson in his work. Like an actor or a good speaker who knows his business and can get the adrenalin flowing to ensure a good performance, a salesperson can work out a little routine for arousing his selling verve. But since personalities differ, someone else may find it better to cope with stress by meditating, or listening to music, or exercising. For stress in the usual negative sense, as the survey mentioned above showed, the support of other persons—friends, family, colleagues, professional counselors—can be the most helpful of all. As the saying goes, "A problem shared is a problem halved." Sharing an experience or doubt—not indulging in mere self-revelation but respecting the other's position—can diminish the impact and may lead one to a solution.

Above all, you should have faith in your capacity to handle stress, to leave bad experiences behind and save your energy for new situations. There is nothing wrong with a happy optimist, who can look forward to a life full of the healthy stress that is necessary, enriching, and enjoyable. Particulary for salespeople, healthy stress can be a great source of continual self-confidence.

Dr. Hans Selye, a Houston psychologist, suggests in his book *Stress Without Distress* that to achieve peace of mind and fulfillment, most persons need to work for some cause they respect.[2] Highly motivated artists, musicians, painters, writers, scientists, or businesspeople can, he says, suffer great stress if prevented from doing their work, and one of the most difficult things for any active person to bear is enforced inactivity, such as sickness, retirement, or prolonged absence from work. Dr. Selye concludes that a way of life based on the understanding of a person's responses to stress and to constant change is the only way to cope with the constant polarities of contemporary life. Here are a few of his stress management techniques:

- Accept stress as part of life.
- So far as possible, avoid persons or situations that cause negative stress.
- Develop a solid belief in yourself, your values, your goals, and stick to it.
- Take up some physical activity—walking, swimming, jogging—in which winning is not the goal.
- Use simple imagery techniques—lying on a beach, sleeping in the shade of a tree, or floating in water.
- Learn to laugh more.
- Don't waste energy worrying about things you cannot change.
- Accept your mistakes as growing, learning experiences.
- Eliminate guilt feelings—even if you were wrong. What's done is done.

Obviously, some of these techniques are less useful than others for a salesperson: the career itself is full of negative stress, and winning is a goal. But they are useful pointers, and developing one's own techniques along some of the lines suggested can help a salesperson to offset the tensions and stress of his daily work.

[2] *Stress Without Distress* (Philadelphia: Lippincott, 1974).

A successful salesperson may become cocky, and customers may show their disapproval by not buying. A good salesperson realizes why he is being rejected, and since he doesn't like losing customers he will try to improve his image. He wants to avoid the pain of being disliked (though he may also tell himself that it is the product that is being rejected, not himself) and will correct his ways. ("I feel I am not really a bad person. I feel good about myself. I have a good self-image. Why risk having it impaired by being rejected here?")

Most salespeople do not want to risk impairing their hard-won self-esteem. They do not want anything to become an unwanted projection of their personalities. This fear stands at the very heart of why most salespeople fail. They dread having to close a sale because they fear being rejected personally. There is no denying the reality of this fear, but it can be overcome. It *has* to be overcome if a person wants to succeed in selling. It *can* be overcome if the salesperson works at it.

Again, salespeople must learn that when a customer says no, it is not a personal rejection but nearly always a rejection of the product, concept, or services offered. Unfortunately, learning this underlying fact requires a basic change in rational beliefs about situations involving the closing of sales.

You Can Cope with Rejection

Some psychologists think our personalities and our reactions to life situations are largely formulated by irrational beliefs. Salespeople should take heed here. Here are some very commonly held irrational beliefs listed by Dr. Albert Ellis, a New York psychologist:[3]

- Bad effects of my childhood have to control my life.
- People must love or approve of me.
- Making mistakes is terrible.
- People should be condemned for their wrongdoings.
- My emotions cannot be controlled.
- Threatening situations must keep me terribly worried.
- I cannot stand the way people act.

All these find their way into the daily routine of most salespeople. The second one particularly applies to the closing situation in sales. Granted, it is preferable to be liked rather than disliked, even nicer to be loved, but

[3]Cited by Jean Baer, *How to Be an Assertive (Not Aggressive) Woman in Life, in Love, and On the Job* (New York: New American Library, 1976).

the notion of individual approval has no place in selling. As long as what you are selling is useful and sound, why waste energy worrying about what the customer thinks of you personally? Why try to be all things to all people all the time?

Instead of worrying about being rejected, you should try to be aware of your own personality and goals, and build up, first, self-esteem and then self-confidence. If your goal is to become rich and powerful, well and good, but you should carefully analyze your ideas about getting there, lest you impair your self-esteem or self-confidence.

You do not have to deny your fears; you only have to accept them and use them as a way of learning more about yourself. You can learn to understand that when people say no to you, they are rejecting not you but your idea. Even when someone seems to ignore you by looking out the window or staring at the clock, remember that it is not a personal rejection but only a way of saying, "I'm not interested."

Using Rejection to Advantage

Successful salespeople are honest about themselves. They are able to take stock of their own feelings and are aware of their own value systems. For instance, they try to qualify for a sales convention because they know they want to learn something at the convention, and they know that qualifying will in itself enhance their self-image. They purposely build their self-image, because it is one way of becoming inured to rejection.

They use proper methods in selling contests, too. They are not willing to compromise their self-esteem by using nonprofessional sales techniques. ("I'd like to win the trip, and I'll give it a go. If I don't make it, it's not the end of the world; but I'd really like to go.")

Thus professional salespeople build their self-confidence by establishing realistic goals and pursuing them wholeheartedly. They are motivated by their willingness to be responsible for themselves. Toward this end, they will, step by step, week by week, year by year, restate to themselves—through performance—their confidence in their ability to achieve. As self-confidence grows and self-esteem is heightened, they are inspired to continue, because they like feeling good about themselves. Rejection is no longer a problem.

LONELINESS

It is a soft morning in early May. Spring flowers are in blossom everywhere, perfuming the air. Bill Ainsworth has three closing interview appointments that should result in three sure sales. All three prospects need the product, can afford the cost, and have all but said yes. It's great to be in sales, Ainsworth thinks.

Then the roof caves in. The first call at nine o'clock results in the customer hurriedly putting him off, after a few minutes of the interview. "Something has come up, Bill. Please call me next week." His next appointment, right across the street, is cancelled by Mr. Norton's receptionist, who says he was suddenly called out of town. Then the third interview, too, is cancelled, because of an unexpected visit from a home office official. Three unexpected cancellations instead of three sure sales are enough to upset any salesman.

But Ainsworth recovers quickly and over a cup of coffee reviews his other customer cards in the area. He always brings such file cards for just such a contingency.

After a few more sips, he plunges into some cold calling at nearby businesses. One person indicates some interest in one of his products, and grants a future appointment. Ainsworth is pleased: he could have sat over his coffee longer and really felt sorry for himself. He is glad that he has the habit of always carrying back-up cards.

Like other professional salespeople, Ainsworth knows that there will be cancellations and delays, long hours, sometimes, to spend alone, and he anticipates them. If you are prepared for the unexpected cancellation, you can use the extra time to advantage. Cold calls, calls on customers in the same area, paperwork such as filling out prospect cards with notes from earlier calls, or reading can all be profitable. Selling is a career for people who can succeed on their own, and resourceful salespeople learn to come to terms with this early in their careers.

Though joint selling with a trainer can be helpful to the beginning salesperson, too much of it gives a false sense of security. The first taste of loneliness can be a devastating experience. Here are some hints about handling loneliness:

- Loneliness is part of the career; accept this.
- From experience, learn to expect a certain number of cancellations every week.
- Carry reading or work material to fill in extra time.
- Cold calling is always possible and may be surprisingly successful.
- Never seek to indulge your loneliness by running to the nearest bar, particularly during normal office hours. Bars are the seductive downfall of many salespeople.

- Listen to audio casettes of helpful sales ideas or motivation while driving in your car.

EGO TRAP

If you have a sustained "hot streak" with high commission earnings and are climbing high in the office sales standings and your fellow salespersons are showing their admiration for the outstanding job you are doing and you are beginning to believe you are pretty super, watch out! You are in danger of being snared by the ego trap. Carried away with your own importance, you will lose your humility and perspective, and your whole life may lose its balance.

Salespeople need recognition just as others do in business. But too much ego building can distort and destroy. To some extent companies themselves are responsible: if they go overboard in encouraging competition among their salespeople, the successful sellers naturally respond to the rewards. To avoid the pitfalls, the salesperson should look out for the following:

- View contests, awards, and high sales results as motivators rather than as ends in themselves.
- Watch over commitment of your life to business success.
- Keep your life in balance. Many persons will continue to love you for what you are and not for what you do.
- It is all right to bask in the spotlight, but keep it in perspective.
- Be grateful for your achievements and express your new-found leadership by helping others to succeed.

SALES SLUMPS

If three weeks have elapsed since you sold anything, you are probably in a sales slump. Slumps—even one or two severe ones every year—are part of selling, and they can be the making of a successful salesperson in that they force one to reevaluate one's techniques. Slumps are warning signals which tell salespeople that something is out of step in their operations. The fault may of course be of a personal nature, such as boredom, lack of enthusiasm—or, on the other side, too much enthusiasm which borders on arrogance. The most usual explanation, however, is that one has become rusty in sales fundamentals or has lapsed into shoddy habits of prospecting, closing, and / or personal organization.

Slumps can be anticipated. Frequently, when salespeople are writing a tremendous amount of business, turning in orders at a rapid rate, their enthusiasm is so keen that they begin to feel infallible. Suddenly, the streak can end, and a prolonged slump may set in. In this case, the super salesperson has probably allowed his successes to overtake his methodical application of sales fundamentals. He has relaxed when he should have been concentrating.

To break out of a slump, you must analyze your sales objectively to determine what went wrong. You should ask yourself these questions:

- Did I make my sales presentation properly?
- Was I as effective as possible in every closing interview?
- Are my work habits falling off?
- Am I calling on nonbuyers?
- Am I calling back on people too many times hoping for a sale when actually I know there is not a chance?
- Have I been failing to get referrals on calls that ought to have produced them?

After you have found out what your problem seems to be, decide what you ought to do about it and take action. If you think that your main problem is poor prospecting, don't sit back and admit that you are very poor in prospecting but go out into the field. If the problem is closing, ask your trainer for more instruction. If you are not getting a need commitment, make a special point of trying to. Breaking slumps requires one to take corrective action. Here are some corrective action steps that have worked for salespeople in slumps:

- Look upon this slump as natural and approach your profession with renewed vigor.
- File away all the supposedly good prospects you've seen, except for two or three who you think are actually going to buy. For the present, at least, assume the rest to be nonbuyers.
- Devote at least two days a week to prospecting with absolutely no plans for selling interviews at all.
- Spend two days making goodwill calls on present customers or centers of influence.

- Do a lot of cold calling; it allows you to try new sales techniques without risk.

- Consult your sales manager for constructive criticism regarding your selling habits. Go over your techniques very specifically. Arrange for some clinics on basic sales skills.

- Seek out some of your fellow salespersons and have them listen while you go over sales presentations or closing techniques.

- Make a joint call or two with someone whose ability you respect; listen carefully.

- For the next two weeks, keep in close touch with your sales manager and try to analyze your performance.

WORKAHOLICS

Super salespeople, driven by ambition, can easily become workaholics. So can those who, less successful, are compelled to put in long, usually inefficient, hours to get ahead. Varieties of workaholics fall in between, but all have in common a meager social life, few intimate relationships with others (often including their own families), and an unbalanced existence.

Unchecked, such a pattern can lead to a warped approach to life and mental and emotional fatigue. Quantity of work, rather than quality of work, becomes a way of life.

Burn-out, or mental fatigue, occurs when salespeople push too hard for too long. They discover that they have lost their energy, become sullen, and just plain bored. Recent studies on workaholics show that such excessive work achieves little. Workaholics do not succeed any faster or reach higher levels of success than their less fanatical peers.

Successful salespeople usually reach the top by working more skillfully, not harder. To avoid becoming a workaholic, bear these points in mind:

- Heed the first warning signals.

- Immediately take some time off to think about the problem.

- Acquire some new interests.

- Force yourself to start and quit your workday at fixed hours.

- Take a half-day off each week for one year. Do anything you want except business.

- Start laughing more.

BOREDOM

Boredom and loneliness can go hand in hand, but even a very busy and successful salesperson can become bored saying the same thing again and again, answering the same sorts of objections, hearing the same old responses. Boredom exists in all kinds of work, at all levels, from highly professional careers on down. You must accept the inevitability of certain mundane and repetitious aspects of selling, but there are some things you can do in the field to lift yourself from what seem to be the doldrums.

- Try a completely new and creative approach.
- Try talking about products you don't usually sell.
- Do some cold calling.
- Ask your manager to make some joint cold calls with you.

Obviously, what you do after working hours can make all the difference. The suggestions for the workaholic may apply equally well to the bored salesperson.

PRESTIGE IN SELLING

In selling, prestige is achieved by performance, not by job title. Many salespeople in a variety of fields enjoy a high level of prestige with their customers. Frequently their prestige exceeds that of doctors, lawyers, bankers, and so on—professions which the public has customarily regarded as most influential.

Sales prestige is earned by salespeople by building solid customer relationships over the years. This is achieved by a consistent pattern of excellence:

- Being reliable.
- Being honest.
- Going out of your way to give customers good service.
- Building a fine community reptutation.
- Putting customers' needs first.
- Admitting product problems.
- Being available for service.
- Eliciting company action on a customer's behalf.

Indeed, the integrity of a salesperson helps more in building a good relationship of trust and confidence than all the product knowledge in the world.

INDIRECT DRAWBACKS

Despite all the skill and care and enthusiasm he can muster, a salesperson may sometimes find himself losing out through no fault of his own. After all, he is only representing a company—sometimes a huge one—and there may be problems over which he has no control. They may be only minor inconveniences, or they may prove insurmountable.

Product and Delivery Delays

When dealing with a factory, delays in delivery are bound to occur—as a result of a backlog of orders, or a strike, or whatever. When this happens, a good salesperson has to be patient, and honest with his customers, hoping that if they know the reasons for the delay they will be patient too. If during the sales process you are aware of a probable delay, be frank. If your product or service is needed and wanted, a little delay can be accepted.

Salespeople who have earned the respect of their companies as well as of their customers through their professional approach and proved company loyalty often find their companies will try a little harder to make their deliveries on time.

Poor Sales Managers

Not all sales managers are good at their work. Even those who seem best suited to train others can fail to inspire, and super salesmen can sometimes prove to be the worst of managers. The problem is certainly not unique to the field of selling, and salespersons can complain just as much as others do when they have a supervisor they do not admire.

On the whole, successful salespeople have in the past looked upon the sales manager as a facilitator, a provider of services, and a necessary representative of the head organization to keep the office going and to provide help in making sales. Today, the trend is more and more toward independent, self-reliant salespeople, who prefer not to depend on a sales manager to tell them what to do. They want services and availability from the sales manager, but they want to be free to go at their own, usually rapid, pace. More and more, the really top members of a quality sales organization are making higher incomes than their managers.

Capitalizing on the freedom that originally attracted them to the field of selling, many of these great successes strike a workable balance between their families, their clients, and whatever else interests them. They look upon their companies as resource centers to help them serve their clients in a professional manner.

Most of these top salespeople have a certain detachment from their district office operation. But though they prize their independence and abhor sales contests, they are often happy to share their success by helping other salespeople to succeed. Thus, although they are cooperative and friendly with their manager, they are inclined to ignore any direction that seems too rigid or dictatorial. But all salespeople, however independent, should keep certain things in mind about sales managers:

- Most sales managers are competent.
- They are also human.
- They have different styles of leadership.
- They are paid to make their salespeople effective.
- They have their ups and downs just as their sales trainers do.
- You, not the manager, are responsible for your own sales success.
- If your sales manager seems a hindrance, recognize that this situation is temporary and will pass in time.

Unethical or Illegal Company Practices

Finally, one of the most difficult—though fortunately infrequent—problems for a salesperson is that of unethical or illegal practices by his or her own company. Suppose your company wants you to sell off what is left of an old model, although you know that the new model, already in production, is much better. What do you do if your sales manager suggests that you lie about a product feature or delivery date in order to make a sale?

It is grossly unethical for a company to urge its sales staff to sell off the inventory of a product that it knows to be defective. Yet it does happen, and persistent behavior of this sort can only be answered by resigning. Even before the consumer movement began bringing problems of this sort out into the open, most reliable companies were already handling these problems wisely, and it is to be hoped that the trend will continue. (More about this will be said in Chapter 22, "Law, Ethics, and the Consumer.")

SUMMARY

All walks of life have negative aspects which must be viewed in realistic perspective. In this chapter we have discussed the various drawbacks to the sales career. Fear—especially of failure—stress and anxiety, and rejection are all closely interlinked, and the remedies are similar. The important thing to remember is that some fear and stress are natural and inevitable, and if you keep in mind that it is not you as a salesperson who is being rejected but only your product or service, the fear of failure is lessened and anxiety stays in its proper place.

Loneliness, not necessarily unwelcome to everyone, also has its remedies, and a good salesperson learns how to use time profitably. The ego trap, which may lead to sales slumps—and to the life of a workaholic—and boredom, too, may set in. These are drawbacks that can enter into most careers. The best answer for all such ills is self-awareness, evaluation, and a balanced, well-rounded life. If you as a salesperson have these things, you will not need to worry about the matter of prestige, for you will know that you are doing a good job in work that you enjoy.

Finally, product delivery problems, having a poor sales manager, or unethical or illegal company practices are not routine to the career. They must be handled as they occur. Professional salespeople will not risk their hard-won reputations by doing anything that would consciously hurt their customers.

Salespeople must remember that all these drawbacks can be handled as long as they understand them. They are for the most part impersonal and should not in any way damage their own self-images. Above all, useful energy should not be wasted worrying about what, after all, are only a minor, if inevitable, part of an interesting and satisfying career.

KEY TERMS

Ego Trap
Sales Slumps
Workaholics

REVIEW QUESTIONS

- Do you agree that salespeople can cope with fear? Explain.
- Is it possible for a salesperson to come to terms permanently with the fear of rejection? How?
- What are some ways of transforming loneliness into a useful aspect of the sales career?
- Should one be determined to be the top salesperson in an organization? Why or why not?
- What is the difference between quantitative work and qualitative work in a sales career?

DISCUSSION TOPICS

- How can slumps be a positive experience for a salesperson?
- How can salespeople cope creatively with boredom?
- Can stress really be the spice of life? Explain.
- If you have a continual product delivery problem from the factory, how would you deal with this in your day-to-day selling activities?
- How would you deal with a poor sales manager?
- What would you do if your company asked you to do something that is illegal or unethical?

EXERCISES

1. Walk up to another student on campus and introduce yourself. Put down in writing your feelings before, during, and after the introduction. Discuss your fears in class and relate this to salespeople calling on prospects for the first time.
2. Interview a salesperson about sales slumps. Find out if he or she experiences them, how often, and what remedy to overcome them is used.
3. Discuss types of stress salespeople experience, and how one deals with negative stress.

As a successful industrial salesperson for several years, you have been asked by your local chamber of commerce to address a workshop it is sponsoring on mid-life career changes.

You got into selling at the age of 38 after spending years in a dead-end job in a large manufacturing concern in your city. After an arduous start, you have become quite successful. You like your work. It has given you a new perspective on life and a new sense of purpose, besides producing a greater income than you had before.

You are enthusiastic about the selling career and what it has done for you, and the invitation to address the group is flattering and exciting.

As part of the presentation you have been asked to answer five questions chosen from the group at random. How would you respond to the following questions?

- Is it normal to experience fear in selling? Explain.
- How do you cope with being alone in the field every day?
- Do you ever get bored? If so, how do you handle it?
- In the beginning years, don't you almost have to become a workaholic? Explain.
- What does positive stress in selling mean?

Sidney Pendleton has been highly successful in selling to attorneys and bankers. Suddenly he falls into a slump. None of his customers seems to be buying. The economic situation is good; there is no recession in the business world for his two markets. He cannot figure out what is wrong.

- Do slumps happen to all salespeople? Explain.
- What are some positive aspects of sales slumps?
- If he cannot figure out the problem, whom can he turn to?
- Suggest three things that might help Pendleton get out of his slump.

The Sales Process

PART THREE

PROFILE

Vergie Anderson

Background   Vergie Anderson was born in Tennessee and reared in Glencoe, Illinois, a suburb of Chicago. She attended New Trier East, one of the nation's finest high schools, and Loyola University, where she received a degree in political science. While in college, Vergie worked for her family's real estate firm. She liked the real estate business so much she decided to forgo further studies in political science in favor of a full-time job as a real estate agent. She still harbors some political aspirations, however, and feels that the real estate business would be a wonderful platform from which to run for political office someday.

Vergie enjoys her career immensely and has been extremely successful, earning a substantial income over the past several years. She is also active in various political and community organizations. She enjoys her single life, living in a fashionable condo on Lake Michigan just off Lakeshore Drive on Chicago's near north side. Vergie is listed in *Who's Who of American Women*, *Who's Who in the Midwest*, and *Outstanding Young Women of America*.

Sales Achievements   The family real estate firm is the largest minority brokerage firm on Chicago's North Shore. For seven of the last nine years Vergie has been the leading salesperson in the firm. She has done committee work with the North Shore Board of Realtors and has served as co-chairman of the Legislative Committee of the North Shore Board of Realtors. She has also done a substantial amount of committee work with the Illinois Association of Realtors.

Her Comments on Her Career   "I like the sales field because it gives me a chance to meet a lot of people under different circumstances. Real estate offers the unique satisfaction of helping people realize the 'American Dream' of home ownership. In selling I pay attention to the psychology of relationships between people. I use counselor selling techniques without any high pressure tactics. I think the key to being a successful real estate salesperson is to keep a positive mental attitude, despite temporary setbacks. In the real estate sales career, setbacks include high interest rates and inflationary prices. I have found that they can always be overcome by working a little harder, using creative sales ideas, counseling people in the whole area of sound budgeting, and using creative financing approaches.

"The satisfaction of helping people realize the 'American Dream' is unique to the real estate sales field. My advice to those starting out in real estate is to get to know people, what motivates them, and to approach the entire field of real estate sales with the idea of helping people own their own home. If you put others' needs first and your commission dollars second, you will be highly successful."

7 Prospecting

OBJECTIVES

In this chapter you will learn:

- What prospecting is and why it is an essential part of the sales process.
- Why qualifying prospects is important.
- What methods of prospecting work.
- How salespeople develop new markets for prospects.
- What target marketing is.
- How to establish a prospect-support group.

It's 4:00 P.M., Friday, on a spring day in Chicago. Jim Rosenkowsky, who sells tax services to major law and accounting firms, is completing his personal organization work.

Looking out the window of his twenty-fourth floor office on La Salle Street, Jim can gaze down on Chicago's Gold Coast to the north and Lake Michigan to the east. Today, however, he has more important things to do. He smiles broadly to himself as he begins to write down the names of new prospects on his prospect sheets. (Jim's prospect sheet is shown in Figure 7-1.) It's been a wonderful week. He picked up 26 potential customers. Here's where they came from:

- Twelve were referrals from three of his long-time customers. When Jim asked them, they freely mentioned possible prospects. They also told him what they knew about each one.

- Six came from a federal district judge Jim has known for several years. The judge's work brings him into contact with a great number of law firms. A valuable center of influence, the judge gave Jim these leads over lunch at the Drake Hotel, a favorite luncheon spot of lawyers.

- Three came from the managing partner of one of the Big 8 accounting firms that Jim had targeted as a specific market worth developing six months ago.

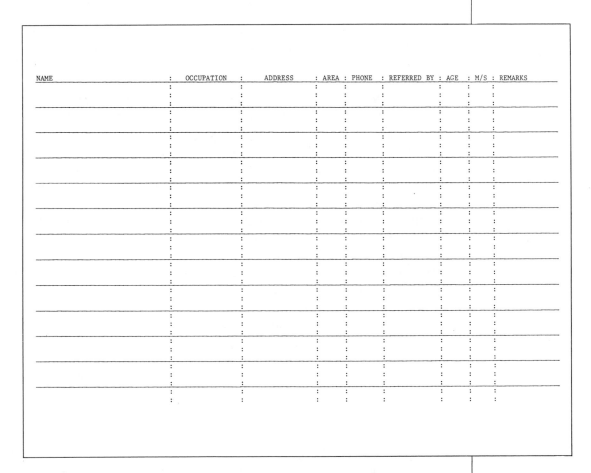

Figure 7–1. A Prospect Sheet

- Five came from two friends with whom he is involved as a volunteer fund raiser for the American Cancer Society. These friends are also salespeople, and the three of them share leads at the monthly Cancer Crusade report meetings.

Jim knows that a great deal of his success depends on his skill at prospecting. Jim knows that even though there is a strong market for his services, he must see new people constantly, or business will fall off. Old customers get transferred, move away, or change their tax service company as a matter of policy. Hence, Jim—and all successful salespeople—must continually develop new pools of prospective customers.

Prospecting is the sine qua non (without which not) of successful selling. Successful salespeople accept its necessity. They don't fight it. They realize it is—and always will be—essential to their careers.

Prospecting is not a catch-as-catch-can procedure. It is a systematic process that, once mastered, will ensure a steady stream of new customers.

In most industries, customers normally do not initiate sales contacts. Most salespeople have very few customers who call them for appointments. Granted, with certain products, such as office supplies, people do call to order or reorder. Generally, however, salespeople have to initiate and build customer relationships. The professionals pursue prospecting relentlessly—day in and day out. It is not easy, but it need not be difficult either. It simply is a process that must be mastered and then applied on a daily basis.

Some salespeople have built-in prospects. They are selling in a market that ensures a steady flow of new names. For example, a law book salesperson may call regularly on certain law firms in a particular territory. These firms may furnish more leads to that salesperson than he can ever use. Other salespeople are assigned exclusive territories for much-in-demand products or services. They always have plenty of people to see. These are the exceptions, however.

Most professional salespeople work hard at prospecting. Let's take a look at some of the techniques they use.

- Referred leads (also known as the endless chain method)
- Centers of influence
- Nests
- Personal observation
- Cold calling

- Lists
- Direct mail
- Pre-approach letters
- Newspaper and business journals
- Yellow pages
- Target marketing
- Prospect support groups

QUALIFYING PROSPECTS—THE FIRST STEP

A name procured through any of the above sources does not mean a guaranteed sale. Obviously, some of the potential customers simply don't need the product or service proposed. To avoid wasting both the prospects' and the salesperson's time, professionals "qualify" the names on their prospect lists to see if they have enough potential to warrant an interview. This generally involves getting as much information as possible from the source who recommended the prospect in the first place.

Appropriate questions might be:

- Do you feel Mr. Darby might need my products or services?
- Do you know anything about the financial status of his company?
- Do you feel there would be an objection to doing business with me?
- Is there any information you can comfortably share with me that will help me assess the potential here?
- With whom do they now do business?

These, and other questions, should help salespeople determine whether the leads procured are worth developing or not. Let's discuss the sources of such leads.

THE REFERRED LEAD, OR ENDLESS CHAIN METHOD

Satisfied customers are often happy to give their salespeople the names of potential customers, often for no other reason than to reassure themselves that their decision to buy from a particular salesperson was judicious.

Here is an example of the endless chain in operation. After he has delivered his product to a satisfied customer, Perry Horton says: "Marv, there is something else I'd like to discuss with you. Now, I'm not going to ask you to buy anything more today. But, there is something you can help me with, and I'd like to visit with you about it. Is that okay?"

Usually the customer will be quite interested and open to the next comment.

"Marv, my inventory and stock in trade is people—people who potentially have a need for my products or services—with whom I can talk on a favorable basis. I am sure there are many persons you know that I don't, who would be good people for me to meet. Now I'm not going to embarrass you by calling these people and telling them that you told me to sell them a new copying machine. That would be unfair to both you and them. But, I would like to approach them on this basis. When I do call them for an appointment, I will tell them that I know several people in their particular field, and I would like to mention your name among them. If that person says, 'Oh, I know Marv Smith'—you wouldn't mind if I told her that she could call you for a reference on me? Does that sound okay to you?"

Usually the customer will say that it's all right to use his name if it will not be used to pressure a friend or colleague to buy something.

Perry continues, "Well, with these thoughts in mind, who are some of the people that you know who would be good people for me to meet? For example, what about some of your competitors? Or what about successful people you know in the community who might need my product? Or what about people in your church or social clubs, or in your neighborhood?" And so on.

Perry doesn't expect Marv to mention many names right away because people usually draw a blank when first asked for referrals. But if the salesperson continues to make suggestions, the satisfied customer will usually think of several prospects. Listed below are a number of useful tips that should help you keep your endless chain well oiled.

TIPS

- It takes a while to jog the memory of customers. So follow up your request for referrals by asking questions about various occupations, neighbors, or competitors that will remind the customer of names of prospects.
- Always call back and inform the customer of the results of your appointments with the referrals.

- Build solid relationships with your customers. This might involve seeing them periodically—perhaps once every two or three months or so. These visits frequently produce names of new prospects.

- Always send them a thank-you note after referrals are given.

THE CENTER-OF-INFLUENCE SYSTEM

Any person who has considerable clout in a particular city, area, industry, or profession is a potential center of influence. In effect, such a person sponsors the salesperson. A center of influence becomes a mentor, anxious and willing to help the salespeople he or she believes in.

Where do you find centers of influence? They might be satisfied customers, ones that the salesperson has done something special for, or they may be acquaintances in civic or church organizations. For younger salespeople, centers of influence are usually their customers. As salespeople mature and begin to expand their involvement in community affairs, they will meet more potential centers. Acquaintances at first, these centers can become close friends and even mentors.

Centers can be found in the salesperson's own backyard—a neighbor, a successful sister-in-law. They are everywhere. The more active salespeople are, the more they become exposed to potential centers. Salespeople who don't expand their horizons—who come home every night and sit down in front of the television set—are less likely to meet them.

Centers of influence are marvelous sources of prospects. Salespeople who develop such centers are fortunate indeed. Ten or twelve centers should be enough to provide a rich source of referrals. Each week, the salesperson should contact one center of influence for possible referrals.

When a salesperson feels that a particular center is a likely prospect, he should call and make a breakfast or luncheon appointment. The purpose of this meeting is to give the salesperson an opportunity to formally solicit the center's help in furthering his career.

If the center agrees to help, the salesperson then tells him that he will send him a help sheet (see Figure 7–2). The purpose of this sheet is to jog the center's memory in the hope that he will come up with some actual referrals. The salesperson then calls the center in two or three weeks to make another breakfast or lunch appointment. Normally, at this second meeting, the prospective center says that he hasn't quite gotten the hang of it and has no names to suggest. The salesperson again asks the center to review the outline of various occupations on the suggestion list. Two

TO: Jonathan Smith

FROM: Fred Brown

SUBJECT: Referrals for Fred

Thank you for agreeing to help me by suggesting acquaintances who might be potential customers. Below is a suggestion list that might stimulate your thinking. I will call soon to pick it up. I can't thank you enough for your thoughtfulness. In helping me succeed, you may also be helping an acquaintance who will benefit from my products.

Source	Name	Occupation	Address	Phone
Competitor				
Friend				
Neighbor				
Business Associate				
Doctor/Dentist				
Lawyer				
Accountant				
Civic Leader				
Church Friend				
Club Friend				
Other				

Figure 7–2. A Help Sheet

weeks later, at the third lunch, the floodgates seem to open, and the names of many prospects come tumbling out. The center of influence relationship is now secure.

Although this procedure may seem slightly awkward to the beginner, it does work. For one thing, people tend to feel they should reciprocate in some way when someone buys them lunch. Three lunches can only intensify the sense of indebtedness. Unfortunately, some of the younger people in the business feel that it is a waste of money to spend money entertaining someone who will never be a customer. Certainly, it does take time, and some money, to develop centers of influence, but it is worth the effort.

TIPS

- Although buying someone lunch can be expensive, the buyer has a tremendous psychological advantage. Salespeople are not trying to buy anything here, but are striving to develop a mutually satisfactory relationship.

- Remember that most centers of influence, if properly developed, really want the salespeople they help to succeed.

- Centers of influence like to be thanked—and thanked often.

- After calling on referrals, centers should be informed of what happened.

- At least 13 active centers of influence should be developed. Call on each one four times a year.

THE DEVELOPMENT OF NESTS

A nest is a cluster of potential customers. Nests are found everywhere—in a certain profession, geographic location, or business. In a hospital, for example, nests are organized by profession—nurses, pharmacists, anesthetists, social workers, and so on.

Nests are surprisingly easy to find and develop. Life insurance agents find nests, for example, in dental schools, where they sell insurance to dental students before graduation and keep them as clients for life. A law book salesperson develops a nest of customers in one large firm. An investment counselor might develop a large nest of accounts in the same firm.

When a nest is developed in one firm, the imaginative salesperson tries to sell from the top down—to the firm as a whole, first, then individually to the top executives and the rest of the organization. This technique can generate from the one sale at the top a continual flow of good sales at the bottom.

Mary Arnold makes a lot of commissions selling office supplies to a nest of government offices in one large metropolitan area. Even though her products are bought pretty much on a bid basis, she was able to develop nests of people who think favorably of her and who make decisions on buying office supplies. She has done well.

TIPS

- Always work from the top down where feasible.
- Be very careful not to call on too many people in the nest at the same time. It might look like you are taking too much advantage of your opportunity.
- Be careful not to reveal confidential information to other members of the nest.
- Be especially careful about company or nest gossip that might be detrimental to development of potential customers.
- Be informed about competitors' products or services, since people in the nest may have bought from them in the past.

PERSONAL OBSERVATION

Successful salespeople keep their eyes and ears open—looking and listening for the distant sound of opportunity knocking. An alert salesperson attending some social or civic event can pick up many leads. Somebody who is just about ready to make a buying decision may complain about the product's drawbacks or mention that he wishes the service or product was a little better. The listening salesperson picks this up. There are literally millions of dollars of commissions earned by personal observation at such gatherings.

In Denver recently, an alert office equipment salesperson, Tim Means, observed that a new building was going up in the city. Investigation revealed that it was being built by an out-of-town company.

Tim also noticed in front of the office building the usual sign, stating the name of the architect, the engineering firm, and the owner. He hiked himself right over to the architectural firm and got in on the ground floor in selling wall partitions and other basic equipment for the offices—all because of personal observation. It is wise to walk around different neighborhoods or to drive a different route to work every day, just to observe the names of new companies, stores, and office buildings.

TIPS

- Observe new construction projects in town.

- Survey newly occupied office buildings.
- Listen for prospect probabilities at social or civic events.

COLD CALLING

Cold calling has a valid place in the sales process. Cold calls are a wonderful way to fill the time gap created by canceled appointments or shortened interviews. And certainly there is nothing to lose. The salesperson on a cold call selects an office and walks in. She says something like, "Hi, I'm Sally Jones from the Ajax Word Processing Company. My company is making a market penetration survey of our products in this area, and I wonder if I may have a few minutes of your time now, or perhaps set up an appointment in the future." That's all there is to it. Often the prospect's reaction is positive, and sometimes there is an opportunity to make a sale.

Another approach to cold calling. Go to an office building that houses several small businesses—advertising agencies, law firms, manufacturers' representatives, or accounting firms. These small businesses are often good prospects because many salespeople pass them by, considering them an unfruitful market. They are good potential customers, and the people you meet there may turn into marvelous centers of influence because many have time to spare and look forward to informal drop-in visits.

Assuming that you are able to talk to a prospective customer, you could say something like, "Hi, my name is Barbara Stewart. I am with the Ajax Printing Company. I was making a call down the street, and saw your office. Would it be possible for me to visit with you for a few moments now about what we do? Or would it be more convenient if we talk sometime in the future?"

TIPS

- Use cold calling to test new sales ideas. (You can do it without hurting yourself.)
- While visiting an area away from your usual territory, spend an hour or two making cold calls. You may discover a new territory worth developing.
- Use cold calling to counteract a slump. It stimulates activity and often produces sales.

LISTS

There are four types of lists available in most metropolitan areas that are fruitful sources of prospects.

- Dun and Bradstreet business listings
- Standard and Poor business listings
- Contacts Influential, a listing of preferred people by income or profession.
- Newcomers, a listing of new arrivals in communities.

Such lists provide name, address, occupation, and other pertinent qualifying information. (See Figure 7-3.) Then, there are chamber of commerce directories, service club rosters, and country club rosters. There are those from the professions. There are also alumni associations. One could go on and on. Lists are excellent silent prospectors.

Where do you find these lists? Some organizations subscribe to the business listings published by Dun and Bradstreet and Standard and Poor to help their sales staff. Each service furnishes valuable information

Figure 7–3. Club Rosters

on the companies they list, information that may furnish good sales leads.

The Contacts Influential and Newcomer lists are less detailed. They concentrate primarily on individuals, not businesses. These lists provide leads for sales to individuals—insurance, investments, real estate.

All four of these services are listed in telephone directories if the metropolitan area is large enough to support the sale of such services.

Chamber of commerce directories are usually available, for a modest charge, at chamber headquarters. They are an excellent source of potential prospects for individual or business sales. Service and country club membership rosters are more difficult to get. The best way to obtain such lists is simply through acquaintances who might know an individual member who is willing to lend one to the salesperson.

The same applies to professional rosters, although they are usually easier to come by. A doctor, for example, might be persuaded to help out a patient in sales by furnishing such a list.

TIPS

- Be sure to get up-to-date lists.
- Ask the people you do business with for rosters of their clubs and organizations.

DIRECT MAIL

Direct-mail prospecting usually works this way. Sales letters and brochures are mailed directly from company headquarters to a list of prospects. (The list is generally compiled by the company's sales staff in the field.) Their purpose is to create interest in the company's services. If the recipient of the letter shows some interest by, say, sending in for more information on the product, a salesperson from the local sales office calls for an appointment. (Sometimes the salesperson calls in any case.)

Over the years, prospecting by direct mail has had its critics as well as its proponents. But it does work. People are continually flooded with direct mail of all kinds, offering everything from magazine subscriptions to business opportunities. If salespeople are selective about their lists, each mailing will generate a fairly predictable response. A 5 or 6 percent response is considered standard for 100 pieces of mail. That would be five leads a week for a 100-piece weekly mailing. Most good salespeople try to keep a continual direct-mail program in operation.

The lists mentioned previously are an ideal source of direct-mail names. For example, a salesperson might direct mail a complete chamber of commerce roster over a period of several weeks. Thus a 500-person list might be mailed out at 50 per week for 100 weeks. Then a week after letters are sent, the salesperson calls for an appointment to talk about the "idea my company recently wrote you about" or something similar.

The letters themselves are usually designed by marketing departments familiar with the particular business, profession, or occupation being solicited.

TIPS

- Make sure the mailing addresses are current ones.
- Use letters the company has found most effective over the years.
- A second mailing after a period of time may be productive.
- Be sure to call on prospects as soon as possible after they reply.
- Calling the nonrepliers on the list for appointments may also yield results.

PRE-APPROACH LETTERS

An outgrowth of the direct-mail method, pre-approach letters are considerably more selective than direct mail. First, the salesperson develops a list of prospects—perhaps gleaned from one of the lists mentioned earlier. Each week, he or she sends a certain number of pre-approach letters to selected people on the list. Sometimes the letters are sent over the signature of the sales manager, or even the president of a firm.

Figure 7-4 illustrates a typical pre-approach letter. It was sent by a restaurant food supply company to a restaurant manager.

These letters are effective. Who doesn't pay attention to a personal letter from the president of a corporation? Such a letter must, in effect, offer a valuable service. Who wouldn't like to cut down on restaurant food costs? And, who wouldn't like to have somebody help them with the quality control of their inventory? These letters, if well written, usually result in appointments. Many successful salespeople, rather than using a stereotyped direct-mail letter, rely on the pre-approach letter, sending out five or ten a week.

The Ajax Food Company

6560 Columbia Avenue, Milwaukee, Wisconsin 53202

Dear Mr. Johns:

We are uniquely qualified to help you do two things that will make your operation more successful--buy quality food at affordable costs, and institute more efficient quality control methods.

As you may know, the Ajax Food Company has been serving fine restaurants in the Milwaukee area for the past 22 years.

In these days of rising food prices, it is important for you to work with someone who is aware of these problems, someone who will help you keep your food costs within reasonable bounds.

I have asked Michael Ansarie, our representative in the Milwaukee area, to call you for an appointment next week to see if he may discuss this matter of mutual interest. Thank you for your cooperation,

Sincerely,

Henry Jordan, President
THE AJAX FOOD COMPANY

Figure 7–4. A Typical Pre-Approach Letter

TIPS

- Be selective in compiling lists for pre-approach letters.
- Make sure the letter is concise, inoffensive, and to the point.
- Always call the prospect within 10 days after sending the letter.

NEWSPAPERS AND BUSINESS JOURNALS

If an experienced salesperson were to go to a strange city and start from scratch, he would probably use local newspapers and the local business journals as a prospect source. In newspapers, articles announcing promotions, new businesses, and newly arriving businesses are a continual source of prospects. So are the classified advertisement sections. Simply subscribing to local newspapers or local business magazines, which can now be found in every major metropolitan area, guarantees a steady stream of people to call on.

TIPS

- Eliminate the names of all who don't look like prospects for your products or services.
- Assemble several names and phone numbers before calling.
- Try to call the prospects promptly. Other salespeople may also call.
- If there are lots of names, tear out the section and put it in a special prospecting file for later.

THE YELLOW PAGES

The Yellow Pages of telephone directories, if used properly, can be an instant source of new names. Not only does this source isolate a market by type of business, but, used from year to year, the Yellow Pages reveal other useful facts. For example, a comparison of last year's entries with this year's will produce a list of new business addresses. A new address usually means that either a new business has been started or that an older one has moved to larger facilities. Either event should prompt a telephone call from alert salespeople who know that business changes require reviews of most product or service needs. (Older Yellow Pages directories are often filed in public libraries.)

The Yellow Pages will also give you an effective overview of the size of particular markets. If you look at the listings under architects, lawyers, cleaning establishments, manufacturing concerns, automobile dealerships, or any kind of business, you will get an instant picture of the relative size of the market. You may even find a big market you were not aware of.

Bell Telephone recently introduced white business pages, which list businesses alphabetically. Used in combination with the Yellow Pages, this source can generate all kinds of potential sources for sales.

TIPS

- Make sure the directory is up-to-date to avoid wasted calls.
- Keep personal copies from year to year to check new listings each year.

TARGET MARKETING

A particular market (or market segment) is researched to see if it has enough prospects to warrant development. For example, if an investment counselor wants to reach the doctors' market, he may target a particular medical specialty as the object of his energies. The counselor then investigates the market to see if there are enough people to justify it as a field worthy of extensive development.

Sometimes a potential market is created because it is a buying target for a specific product. If a salesperson is selling, say, word processing systems to law firms, she might look at the number of firms that are likely to use these systems. If there are enough prospects here, say 200 or so, then they may comprise a valid target market for her company's word processors.

The concept behind target marketing is that the commonality of the occupation or business makes the approach worth the effort. For example, a telephone equipment sales company may target markets in certain industries, say, the financial industry. This market would include banks, savings and loan companies, investment houses and insurance companies. Particular salespeople are assigned to this market exclusively. Then they are trained in the specific needs of that market. By becoming so specialized, they are better able to answer their prospects' questions and design more efficient phone systems.

This is in marked contrast to the general approach of assigning salespeople to particular territories and expecting them to sell to all kinds of prospects in their areas.

As technical equipment for use in business becomes more complicated, the people who sell it will be more effective if they concentrate on particular markets. Their in-depth knowledge will put them ahead of their competitors who try to be all things to all customers. Target marketing is similar to the nest concept. Such markets must be researched to determine the best approach.

How is a target market researched? One of the best ways is to seek out some people who work in that market—perhaps a contact from a friend, some referred lead, or simply by calling up and asking for information about some of the products used in the market. Then make an appointment with such a person.

Sal Cordero represents a company distributing specialty gourmet food items in White Plains, New York. He is in Buffalo today for the first time, trying to get a profile of Schwabs Fine Food Stores, which carry a lot of specialty food items for their selective clientele.

His only contact is a friend-of-a-friend who works in Buffalo as an accountant in a bank. His name is Patrick Finnegan. Here is Sal calling Patrick for an appointment to fill out a market analysis on Schwabs.

"Mr. Finnegan, Patrick Finnegan?"

"Yes."

"My name is Cordero, Sal Cordero. We have a mutual friend—Sara Goodenoff in White Plains."

"O yes, how is Sara?"

"She's fine—she just got a huge promotion at the bank. She is now a full vice-president."

"That's wonderful. Be sure to congratulate her for me, will you?"

"Well, that's not the only reason I called you. Patrick, I'm a salesperson with Gourmet Foods, and I'm in town today to do a market profile on Schwabs Fine Foods here in Buffalo."

"I see."

"Well, since I don't know anyone else here, I'm wondering if I could take a few minutes of your time today and make a few notes on Schwabs."

"Well, that's OK, I'm afraid I don't know too much about Schwabs. I shop there, but that's about all."

"I understand. But could we still get together, say, late this morning, or would afternoon be better for you?"

"OK. I'll see you at 4:00 P.M. if you can drop by my office."

During the interview, Sal will make notes on a predesigned form. (See Figure 7–5.) Many successful salespeople design a form for this purpose. It helps them assess the market potential. Interviewing three or five people working in such a market should produce a valid picture of its potential as a market.

Suppose that a salesperson for a printer is investigating a new market. The printer she works for wants to expand his business to include forms for data processing. The salesperson will try to find out how many computer companies are in the area, what kind of (and how many) forms they use, and how well they have done financially. If the market looks promising, the salesperson can then approach prospects on an individual basis.

MARKET ANALYSIS FORM

Company:_____ Name of Contact:_____

Position Held:_____ Phone:_____

1. Type of Organization (check one):

   ( ) Sole Proprietorship   ( ) Partnership   ( ) Professional Corporation

   ( ) Subchapter S Corporation ( ) Other_____

2. Type of Business (check one):

   ( ) Sales ( ) Service ( ) Industrial ( ) Manufacturing ( ) Professional

   ( ) Other_____

3. Number of Employees: Union_____ Nonunion_____

4. Member of any Association (if so, please name)_____

   _____

5. Principal Thrust of Business:_____

   _____

   _____

6. Is It Successful?:_____

7. Any Idea of Annual Volume:_____

8. Any Idea of Annual Worth:_____

9. Miscellaneous Information:_____

   _____

   _____

10. Could you introduce me to anyone who might know something more about the business

    so I can have an even better profile?_____

    _____

    _____

    _____

Thank you for your help.

Figure 7–5. A Market Analysis Form

Many successful travel agents have developed large companies as clients by this target-market approach. They isolate five or six large companies whose personnel do a lot of travelling. They then interview selected employees to assess their traveling requirements or habits and tailor their services to meet those needs. It takes time to target any market, but once secured, it can be a permanent and profitable source of new sales.

TIPS

- Make sure the group is large enough to merit special targeting.
- Wherever possible, interview an employee or someone with particular knowledge of the company.
- Procure at least three interviews in each potential market.
- Analyze results realistically to see if the approach is justified.

PROSPECT SUPPORT GROUPS

Prospect support groups are creative vehicles for generating prospect names. Here, groups of salespeople from different fields get together specifically to exchange leads.

Prospect support groups are usually started by enterprising salespeople. Generally, there is a particular salesperson who sees the value of such a venture. That person then looks around for sharp salespeople in other, noncompetitive fields.

An approach is made. The matter is discussed at length, and through networking, a group of, say, 10 or 12 people is isolated. They all get together, perhaps over breakfast, and form a group, setting up future meeting dates and places.

Each person in the group constantly looks for leads that will benefit others in the group. Thus, industrial equipment salespeople calling on plants might pass along the names of their contacts to those who sell food services to plants. Office equipment salespeople might exchange leads with office supply people and so on.

Support groups help salespeople help each other. This help can be expanded to other aspects of the sales career. Thus, the group could set up workshops to share sales techniques or hire outside speakers to talk on subjects of mutual interest.

To keep such a group going, meetings should be scheduled regularly and all members be required to bring a minimum number of new prospects to every meeting.

Besides leads and talks by outsiders, the mutual help in all aspects of selling is valuable.

TIPS

- Early breakfast meetings, say, every other week, are best.
- All members must be noncompetitive with each other.
- Strict membership criteria should be established.
- Membership should be limited to 15 or 20 people.
- Assess dues to pay for outside speakers, social gatherings, and the like.
- Each sale based on an acquired lead requires a small payment to club treasury for future use.
- Occasionally, a meeting may be devoted to one or two people who have not been given enough leads recently.
- Ambitious salespeople make the best members.
- Remember—patience is the key to survival.

Such support groups are becoming a popular, useful tool for dedicated professionals. They can create valuable contacts and lasting relationships.

SUMMARY

Prospecting is the sine qua non of any sales career. Sales cannot be made without buyers. Successful salespeople are aware of the importance of prospecting and continue to accumulate names even when they appear to have more than enough. In this way, as they hit slumps or dry spells, they will have plenty of people to call on. Professional salespeople qualify prospects to determine whether they are worth contacting.

The first prospecting method discussed was referred leads, the endless chain method. Satisfied customers usually furnish qualified leads—that is, they usually tell the salesperson something helpful about each lead given.

Centers of influence were discussed next. Nurtured properly through frequent contact, centers of influence can provide a rich source of prospects. They should be called on three or four times a year.

A cluster of prospects or customers in a particular organization or profession is known as a nest. Nests are easy to find and develop, if one is willing to make the effort.

Personal observation is another source of prospects. If salespeople stay alert at civic and social gatherings, they will come up with many prospects that might not be obtainable in any other way.

Cold calling, calling on prospects picked at random, allows salespeople to practice sales skills and find new sources of business.

Other methods discussed were lists, direct-mail prospecting, and pre-approach letters. The newspapers, business journals, and Yellow Pages were also discussed as fruitful sources of names from many occupations and businesses.

Target marketing, where the salesperson targets particular markets, companies, or professions, and then investigates them through interviews can produce markets worth developing.

Finally, the value of prospect support groups was considered. Hints on effectively organizing such clubs were presented.

KEY TERMS

Centers of Influence

Cold Calling

Direct Mail

Help Sheet

Market Analysis

Nests

Pre-Approach Letters

Prospect Sheet

Qualifying Prospects

Referred Leads

Target Marketing

REVIEW QUESTIONS

- Why is prospecting the sine qua non of selling?
- Why are referred leads the best source of prospects?
- Who is the best person to act as a center of influence for you?
- Is cold calling a waste of time? Explain.
- When is the best time to ask customers for referrals?

DISCUSSION SUBJECTS

- What is meant by the statement that prospecting must become a permanent part of salespeople's lives?
- How would salespeople start building prospecting files in a strange city?
- Explain why most salespeople do not generate several centers of influence.
- Explain the value of target marketing.

- Why is it important for salespeople to keep their eyes and ears open at every gathering they attend?

EXERCISES

1. With another student, role play asking a satisfied customer for a referral.

2. From the Yellow Pages, select three markets in which you might sell printing services. In a short essay, explain why you have chosen each market.

3. Assume you are a life insurance salesperson. For a period of one week, accumulate a list of prospect names from personal observation. (Collect the names of both individuals and businesses.) Report the number of names accumulated in class.

Case Study One

Francine Paliterre is married to an executive in an electronics company. When Francine's last child went off to college three years ago, she took a job selling office supplies. Now she must give up the job she enjoys so much because her husband is being transferred to a distant city.

Francine plans to continue selling office supplies for her old company in the new location. Her company has never done business in this state, so Francine will have no built-in accounts to service. And she has agreed not to use any of her husband's contacts or sell any office supplies to his business, because it might prove embarrassing to him.

- How could Francine break into the office supplies sales market in this strange city?
- Describe three methods she might use, assuming she knows no one in the city, to begin to build a prospect list for immediate calling.
- How could the local chamber of commerce help her?

Case Study Two

Jake Pretorious recognizes that the large nationally known agricultural service company headquartered in Kansas City would be a wonderful source of prospects to whom he could sell his travel services. He has just entered the field and discovers that his present travel service agency does not list this company as one of its accounts.

- How would Jake go about developing the company as a nest of prospects?
- Would a pre-approach letter be wise in this case?
- How would he go about target marketing this organization?
- Where could he obtain a list of the executives of the company?

The Pre-Approach

OBJECTIVES

In this chapter you will learn:

- How to prepare for a sales interview by following a three-step pre-approach process.
- Why a well-written pre-approach letter brings results.
- How to improve your telephone technique.
- What items should be on every salesperson's interview checklist.

It is spring in Los Angeles. The March winds have cleared the air of smog. The city sparkles.

Frank Chain is a manufacturer's representative in his early thirties. His product lines include office furniture and furnishings—ashtrays, pen holders, desk file trays, and the like. His most profitable line, however, is shelving.

Frank, a liberal Democrat, was very active in the Students for a Democratic Society at UCLA. Since his graduation ten years ago, he has built up a substantial clientele in southern California. He has lost some clients, though, because he frequently expresses his opinion on controversial issues.

Today he is calling on Michael Frost, the owner of a large national paper products distribution company. The company's five-story office building on West Santa Monica Boulevard contains thousands of feet of shelves (to store the inventory) and sixty desks (for the order processors).

Frank, with the assistance of his sales manager, Margaret Halpin, has researched the company at great length in preparing for this all-important interview. First, he asked a friend on the staff of the Los Angeles Chamber of Commerce for a brief history of Mr. Frost's company. Frank's contact was able to give him valuable information about both the company and its owner. Frank learned that Mr. Frost was a conservative businessman who had a passion for fishing.

Armed with this information, Frank called Mr. Frost's company and asked the receptionist the name of Mr. Frost's secretary. He waited a day, and then called the secretary, greeted her by name, and asked if a fellow fisherman could possibly see Mr. Frost for a few moments at his convenience about a matter of mutual interest. The secretary asked Frank to hold and came back with an affirmative response. Mr. Frost would see Frank the following Tuesday at 8:30, his usual arrival time.

As Frank enters the office, Mr. Frost gets to his feet, shakes hands, and motions Frank to a chair. Mr. Frost then glances at the headline in the *Times* and comments to Frank, "It looks like Senator Muragishi [California's Republican senator] is not running for reelection."

Frank (who should have bitten his tongue) blurts out, "That makes my day. Maybe we can elect a young, wide-awake Democrat to fill his seat."

Mr. Frost looks icily at Frank. "I certainly hope not," says Mr. Frost. "As a matter of fact, I think Senator Muragishi has done an excellent job. I'm proud of the fact that I was one of the largest contributors to his campaign."

The interview is over. Frank Chain has lost his opportunity to sell this man—today and in the future.

Professional salespeople should not make controversial remarks in any sales situation unless they know they are on safe ground. If there is any doubt at all, silence or a noncommital comment is the only intelligent response.

If Frank had done his homework more thoroughly, he might have avoided his indiscretion—and ultimately developed a substantial account.

In this chapter, you will learn how to prepare for a sales interview so that you, unlike Frank, will never find yourself in the wrong office, talking to the wrong person about the wrong subject.

THE PHASES OF THE PRE-APPROACH PROCESS

A lawyer does not go to court without having adequately prepared her case. A contractor does not bid on a big construction project without taking into account every board and nail he will use. And a salesperson does not walk into a prospect's office without having done his homework. The amount of research, of course, is determined by the magnitude of the sale. Obviously, if the item to be sold is inexpensive, preparation may not be extensive. But every potential sale, no matter how small, merits preparation.

All preparation has three specific phases, which are discussed in the following sections.

1. Gathering the Information

Prospecting, as you learned in the last chapter, means accumulating as much personal and business information as feasible before contacting prospects personally. Such information may be listed on a prospect card or any other place where it is accessible for review just before the interview. Company information should include:

- The background of the company
- The growth potential of the company
- The authority of the prospect (Is he or she empowered to buy?)
- The financial condition of the company
- The markets it serves
- The products and services it provides
- The morale of company employees

Personal information about the prospect should include:

- Name, occupation, age, family status, resident address, and education
- Hobbies, interests, and personal activities
- Personal characteristics and preferences
- Community involvement

Some sources for the above information are:

- Employees of the company. Be cautious, however. Some employees, out of loyalty, resent outsiders who are too curious.

- Other salespeople who deal with the company. Professional salespeople do not share privileged information (they believe it unethical), but they might give you a general opinion of the company.
- Customers of the company. If not bound by confidentiality, most customers will talk freely and frankly about the companies they buy from. Even here, though, prejudice can color an evaluation. An otherwise satisfied customer who has had a recent problem with the company might make negative comments just to let off steam.
- Annual reports or company newsletters.
- Centers of influence. A banker, a chamber of commerce board member, a well-known civic leader, all can produce a wealth of facts and opinions about businesses in their communities.
- The local chamber of commerce is a clearing house of helpful information on local businesses.
- The library. Ask at the desk for annual reports, local business magazine or newspapers, or any of the other sources available. In large metropolitan areas, many libraries have data banks that may be accessed by computer.
- Observation. Pay attention to gossip, newspapers, community acquaintances of the prospect, people with whom the prospect does business.

A great deal of information can be gleaned from the above sources. Supposing your contact at the company is Mario Fellice, the vice-president of operations. Information about his personal preferences can be obtained by asking such questions as:

- "Oh, by the way, do you know what Mr. Fellice's hobbies are?"
- "Didn't I hear he was quite active in his church?"
- "Does he jog or play tennis?"
- "Do you know where he goes on his vacations?"
- "Is there anything unusual or interesting about him?"

The way people spend their leisure time may reveal a great deal about them. If nothing else, you will have something to talk about when you walk into the office.

Pre-approach information allows salespeople to become more "political" in their approaches to prospects. "Political" in this sense means creating a more productive interview climate. This is not manipulative. It is common sense for salespeople to try to impress their prospects favorably.

Having qualified the prospect, we move on to the second phase of the pre-approach.

2. Assessing the Information

After all the information has been gathered it must be analyzed to see if the prospect is indeed a potential buyer. Perhaps he isn't—for various reasons. Perhaps the prospect simply has no need of the products or services offered. Or he may have a friend or relative he prefers to do business with.

The financial condition of the company must also be considered. If it is known to be in financial trouble, why call on the company?

If the outlook is positive, and the prospect valid, then the information gathered can be put to good use in the small talk portion of the interview. For example, many potentially difficult interview sessions have turned into a warm exchange of ideas when the salesperson and prospect reveal themselves as avid Doonesbury fans.

Once the information has been assembled and assessed, it is time to turn to the final phase of the pre-approach.

3. Preparing the Approach

A well-organized, effective visual presentation not only helps demonstrate the product or service but also tells the prospect that the salesperson is both competent and professional. Salespeople represent their firms. If they are unprepared or uninformed, prospects will view their firms in the same manner. If salespeople cannot make professional presentations, prospects will question their ability to give adequate service after the sale.

The selling process is similar to other professional endeavors—performing an operation, trying a lawsuit, acting on stage, to name a few. Preparation is necessary for success.

What does the salesperson prepare? A pre-approach letter (in many cases) and the visuals he or she intends to use—catalogues, pictures, computerized proposals, charts, graphs, slides, written statistics. These should be arranged in the sequence they will be used in the interview itself. Professional salespeople constantly refine this process, artfully shifting from oral comments to visual, then back to oral comments.

If visuals are not in order, the approach to the sales interview must still be organized and committed to memory. If salespeople have to concentrate on what to say rather than how to say it, a great deal of the impact of the presentation is lost.

PRE-APPROACH LETTERS

Pre-approach letters are sent to the prospects in the hope of getting an appointment. There are many pros and cons about such letters. Some salespeople don't use them because they think such letters are ignored. They prefer to use the telephone. However, many salespeople use pre-approach letters with superior results. They contend that a creative, well-written pre-approach letter conditions the prospect to view them and their product favorably.

```
Ms. Patricia Nelson
Vice-President, Consumer Training
The Soya Company
501 Main Street
Harrisburg, Pennsylvania

Dear Ms. Nelson:

     Increased people productivity in your organization will
save you dollars.  If I could show you how to do this, would
you be interested?
     I was pleased to read in the newspaper about your recent
promotion.  I will be calling you for an appointment.  I am
eager to meet you.

               Sincerely,


Ms. Patricia Nelson
Vice-President, Consumer Training
The Soya Company
501 Main Street
Harrisburg, Pennsylvania

Dear Ms. Nelson:

     I hear you're heavily involved in the Women's Movement.
So am I.  I have some ideas that could save your company
money and will be calling you for an appointment.

               Sincerely,


Dear Ms. Nelson:

     In these inflationary times, the only antidote to falling
profits is to increase the productivity of people or machines.
     I have some ideas that have been of extreme value to
other organizations like yours in increasing people produc-
tivity at little cost.
     There is no obligation to you, of course.  May I call you
for an appointment?

               Sincerely,
```

Figure 8–1. Three Pre-Approach Letters

There are no hard and fast rules for the use of these letters. However, if they are used, they should be effective. They should not be presumtuous or too personal. Discretion is the keynote here. If there is any doubt about using a certain piece of information, don't. For example, if you read in the paper that a prospect's son has received an award for scholastic achievement in high school, don't mention it. This kind of information is too personal. On the other hand, if you know that your prospect is on the board of the local symphony, it might not be offensive to mention this fact in a letter. Again, it's a matter of discretion. Most salespeople shy away from mentioning anything having to do with the prospect's personal life. They concentrate instead on the prospect's business or business conditions in general. Three pre-approach letters are shown on the facing page. The first is weak because it uses too many "I's" and sounds a bit phony. The second is too personal and abrupt. The third is a positive, confident letter that would probably result in an appointment.

One week after such a letter is sent, a telephone appointment is made. The telephone is an extraordinary tool.

EFFECTIVE TELEPHONE TECHNIQUES

The telephone is to salespeople what the elevator is to the modern skyscraper. Think how difficult it must have been for salespeople in the pre-Alexander-Graham-Bell days to make contact with prospects. Think of the thousands of fruitless calls that must have been made.

The telephone is the most valuable time-saving tool a salesperson has. Properly used, it can be a substitute for a person-to-person encounter on a post-sales service call. It is a wonderful resource for the person who can use it with skill. Nevertheless, some salespeople shy away from using it. Yet, a good telephone technique is not difficult to learn if certain rules are followed. These rules should be written down, and practiced, until they become almost second nature.

- Be cheerful and sincere on the phone.
- Speak directly into the instrument.
- Speak firmly and clearly without shouting.
- Concentrate on good diction.
- Identify yourself and your purpose for calling. (Generally, it's to get an interview.)

- Be brief and to the point without being rude or curt.

- Always sound confident and in control.

- Be frank and honest. Most successful phone users say that frankness is the heart of a good telephone technique. In other words, you should not try to obtain an interview under false pretenses.

- Remember that the overall objective of the telephone call is to get an appointment, not to make a sale.

- Once you have begun telephoning, continue to make calls one after the other. Successful salespeople say this is the best way to ward off fatigue and boredom.

- Keep at it. Be persistent. Telephone technique improves dramatically with practice.

Like other skills, telephone techniques can only be mastered by practice, practice, practice—until they eventually become a habit. Role playing is ideally suited for such practice. One salesperson plays the caller and another the prospect. This can be done face to face, or over telephones in different offices of the same company.

Salespeople who are comfortable using the telephone can plan a whole week in advance. Several studies indicate the following preferred times to call:

- Middle managers after 9:30 A.M.

- Executives and business heads after 10:30 A.M.

- Purchasing agents between 9:00 A.M. and 4:00 P.M.

- Contractors and builders before 9:00 A.M.

- Doctors, dentists, and osteopaths after 11:00 A.M.

- Lawyers between 11:00 A.M. and 2:00 P.M.

- Merchants, store owners, and department heads after 10:30 A.M.

- Accountants anytime during the day.

- Government employees anytime during the day.

- Bankers before 10:00 A.M.

- Stockbrokers before the market opens and after it closes.

In the following section, we will see how one salesperson uses the telephone effectively.

Using the Telephone to Make Appointments

Before you pick up the phone, have a list of names and telephone numbers in front of you. It generally takes five to six calls to get one appointment. Hence, 20 weekly appointments require a list of 100 to 120 names.

THE BASIC SCRIPT

Mr. Alden, please. [Mr. Alden comes to the phone] Mr. Alden? [Yes] Mr. John Alden? [Yes] My name is Harry Smith of the Ajax Office Supply Company. Have you just a moment, please? [Yes] I have some office supply ideas that have been extremely valuable to many successful people like yourself. They could also be of great value to you. I'd like to drop by and explain them to you. Would Thursday at three or Friday afternoon at four be better? [Friday at four] Thank you. I'll be there. Good-bye.

WITH A REFERRED LEAD

Same script as above except after "Have you just a moment, please?" say the following:

I was speaking with Mr. Nominator from ABC Company the other day, and he mentioned that you might be interested in meeting me to talk about your office supply situation. I'd like to drop in and talk to you for a few moments. Would Tuesday at two or Thursday at four be better? [Thursday at 4] Thank you. I'll be there. Good-bye.

WITH A PRE-APPROACH LETTER

Same script as the first, except after "Have you just a moment, please?" say the following:

I sent you a letter the other day. Do you remember reading it? [Yes or No] Well, in that letter I mentioned how I could increase your bottom line by saving you a substantial amount in office supply costs. So, I'd like to drop in and talk to you for a few moments. Would Tuesday at ten or Thursday at three be better? [Wednesday at 10] Thank you. I'll be there. Good-bye.

WITH A SCREENED CALL

I would like to speak to Mr. Alden, please. [Who is calling and what is it about?] It is about an important business matter, and I need to speak to Mr. Alden directly. [He's busy right now. May I give him a message?] No, thank you. Because it does involve his business, I will have to call another time. [*Secretary will probably put you through. She may not want to be responsible for blocking a call involving her employer's business. But the secretary may respond with: "I probably haven't made myself clear. Mr. Alden is a very busy man and has asked me to screen his calls carefully. He has requested me to find out what any call is about before I put it through to him." In this case, you probably will not get through. But there is no point in giving up. Another attempt just might work*]. I understand Mr. Alden's position. But I have some information that may be of extreme value to him. If you can put me through, I'll take just a few moments of his time to explain it.

Answering Objections on the Telephone

OBJECTION: WHAT DO YOU WANT?

The reason I'm calling, Mr. Alden, is to arrange a time when I can show you a new service offered by my company. Would Tuesday at two or Thursday at four be better? Thank you. I'll be there.

OBJECTION: I'M AWFULLY BUSY

I can understand that, Mr. Alden, and that is why I called in advance. What I have in mind will not take long to explain—about five or ten minutes. Would Monday at three or Wednesday at two be better? Thank you. I'll be there.

OBJECTION: I'M NOT INTERESTED

I can understand that, Mr. Alden. I can see why you might not be interested in something I haven't really explained. To properly explain my work, we need to get together. Would Tuesday at four or Thursday at two be better? Thank you. I'll be there.

OBJECTION: I DON'T NEED ANY OFFICE SUPPLIES

Of course, Mr. Alden. I wouldn't expect that you need them at this exact moment. Maybe someday you will, and at that time I hope to be of help to you. Meanwhile, I would like to visit with you about the kind of work I do. When can we get together? Would Tuesday at three or Wednesday at four be better? Thank you. I'll be there.

OBJECTION: TELL ME NOW WHAT YOU WANT

Mr. Alden, at best it would be confusing to give you all the information over the telephone. I need to discuss it face to face with you. This will take only a few minutes. Would Tuesday at two or Thursday at four be better? Thank you. I'll be there.

OBJECTION: NO! NO! NO!

Okay. I understand, Mr. Alden. I surely do not want to offend you. Let's leave it this way, Mr. Alden. The next time I'm in your area, I would like to call again to set up a meeting with you. There's no obligation on your part. That's fair enough, isn't it?

Having mastered the telephone and obtained an appointment, you are now ready to prepare for the interview.

PREPARING FOR THE INTERVIEW

As mentioned earlier, the amount of preparation for an interview is usually determined by the magnitude of the potential sale. Extensive interview preparation for a small sale may not seem worth the effort. Nevertheless, most salespeople who are trying to grow horizontally (that is, sell more units to current customers), prepare properly for any interview for which an appointment has been secured.

Basically, preparing for an interview involves three fundamental steps, which are discussed in the following sections.

1. Knowing the Product

Successful salespeople anticipate what products or services are likely to be needed by a particular customer and then prepare accordingly. A reasonable knowledge of the competitors' product is also helpful.

Too much preparation is better than too little. Overpreparing builds the salesperson's confidence. This shines through to the prospect, helping to build trust between the prospect and the salesperson. A relationship of trust is essential to successful closings.

To summarize, salespeople should:

- Be knowledgeable about pending product or service improvements
- Learn where they can find answers to product questions asked by prospects
- Learn the strengths and weaknesses of the competitors' products
- Be prepared to turn around product or service shortcomings with acceptable counter-answers

When a salesperson knows the product, he or she is ready to prepare the actual presentation.

2. Assembling Material for the Presentation

In the old days, good salespeople prided themselves on their skill at "back of the envelope" selling. They did not need glossy brochures to show the customer what their product looked like. That has changed. Although some still use notes on a scratch pad to make a point, today most successful salespeople use printed proposal material in their presentations. They might use pictures or other visuals or the products themselves. Not only do these materials form a natural track to run on, but as the old saying goes, "A picture is worth a thousand words." Other types of presentation materials are:

- *Samples.* When tangibles are involved, samples are usually powerful motivators by themselves. A sample may stimulate a prospect's interest by appealing to his senses of sight, hearing, touch, and (sometimes) taste, and smell. Hence, one who is selling hand calculators can evoke strong interest merely by placing the item on the prospect's desk. A calculator salesperson can talk all day long about the fine quality of the Japanese chips that make up the memory, but his words will not have the impact that letting the prospect handle the item will.

- *Catalogues.* Many industrial sales organizations display their wares effectively in catalogues. Industrial catalogues often contain specifications as well as pictures.

- *Testimonials.* Often professional salespeople will ask their satisfied customers to write letters of endorsement for use in other sales situations. Usually customers are willing to write about a product they are particularly happy with. If nothing else, they like to attest to their

THE ASLOW COMPANY

1448 QUIMBY LANE • KELLY, LOUISIANA 71441 • (318) 716-9200

Ms. Marie Beauchamps
The Hornsby Company
1352 Mills Avenue
Baton Rouge, Louisiana

Dear Marie,

It's been six months since our firm purchased the annotated Louisiana Tax Service from your organization.

It has been extremely helpful to us--particularly to our
field auditors. I wonder how we ever got along without it.

I'm looking forward to our next visit, Marie.

Thanks again,

**Figure 8–2. A Testimonial Letter Emphasizing Customer
Product or Service Satisfaction**

own wisdom in making such an intelligent purchase. Such testimonials should be appropriate to the situation and related to the needs of
the prospect. Professional salespeople have an inventory of such
letters to use as the situation demands. (See Figures 8-2 and 8-3.)

910 State Street • Lexington, KY 40502 • (606) 524-3344

Mr. Anthony Soares
Stigmare Manufacturing Company
964 Front Street
Louisville, Kentucky

Dear Tony,

Your continuing superior service of the conveyor system
we bought from you two years ago is appreciated.

You are a credit to your company and your profession.
Please feel free to use me as a reference any time. I enjoy
our relationship.

Regards,

**Figure 8–3. A Testimonial Letter Emphasizing
Salesperson Satisfaction**

- *Demonstration aids.* These tools enable salespeople to demonstrate their products, verifying their claims by proving them on the spot. Professionally done, demonstration aids have great impact. Visuals help salespeople:

1. Dramatize the product.
2. Make points more vividly, leaving prospects with lasting impressions.
3. Stimulate prospects by appealing to two senses—sight and hearing.
4. Hold the prospect's attention. It can be difficult for a salesperson to hold the interest of prospects for an extended period of time without some outside focus.
5. Simplify the description of a product or service. For example, computers or complicated manufacturing equipment can best be demonstrated through visuals. A simple lecture on the merits of the latest computer mainframe usually goes in one ear and out the other.
6. Enhance retention. Psychologists tell us that people retain about four times as much through sight than through all the other senses combined. Furthermore, international research on sales and marketing executives, published around four years ago, found that a combination of hearing and sight guarantees 65 percent retention.

Visuals should be presented in orderly fashion. Many salespeople carry optional visual material, like a testimonial letter, to use at their discretion. Chapter 14 describes the specific types of audio-visual aids for use in the interview.

3. Reviewing a Pre-Interview Checklist

Successful salespeople keep a checklist with them at all times, and as they are waiting to see a prospect, they glance at the list to remind themselves to follow the correct procedures in the interview. Airline pilots who have been at their jobs for 25 to 30 years insist on going through a checklist every time they prepare to take off or land. They simply will not trust the procedures to memory. Here is a typical pre-interview checklist:

- Review all the personal information about the prospect to try to determine his or her personality type. Which profile trait is dominant here—amiable, analytical, driver, or expressive? How will you take advantage of this knowledge in your interview?

- Consider the subject of introductory small talk. Should it be about the prospect's business or some personal aspect of his life (for example, a hobby)?

Review personal and business information?
Decide on small talk?
Review presentation - everything in order?
What are the product or service needs here?
Know competition?
Rehearsed objections and answers?
Smile and Listen! Smile and Listen!

Figure 8–4. A Pre-Interview Checklist

- Go over the steps you plan to follow in your presentation. Keep the sequence in mind. Remember not to spend too much time on one part at the expense of the others.

- Rehearse your visual presentation. Experienced salespeople will always go through their visuals immediately before an interview just to make sure they will not omit anything.

- Rehearse in advance any objections the prospect might have to your product or service, trying to anticipate the answers.

A pre-interview field checklist generally covering the above points should be written on a 3 × 5 card (see Figure 8-4) and carried at all times. It will serve to remind salespeople of key things about the impending call. Being thus prepared, the salesperson is now ready to conduct the interview.

SUMMARY

Successful pre-approach preparation will ensure a favorable climate for conducting the sales interview. If the potential sale is substantial, it is almost impossible to overprepare for an interview. If the sale is small, professional salespeople still prepare thoroughly. They use such interviews to practice their skills for the bigger sales.

The three phases of the pre-approach were discussed: gathering the information, assessing the information, and preparing the approach. The pre-approach letter, if used, should be creative but never personal.

Persistence is the key to developing effective telephone techniques. These techniques must be practiced until they become habit. Role playing helps most people develop better telephone techniques.

The chapter closed with a discussion of preparing for a sales interview by (1) studying the product or service (and the competitors'), (2) preparing appropriate presentation materials, and (3) reviewing a pre-interview checklist.

KEY TERMS

Demonstration Aids	Pre-Approach Process
Interview Checklists	Samples
Pre-Approach Letter	Testimonials

REVIEW QUESTIONS

- What is meant by qualifying a prospect?
- How does the pre-approach research help the sales process?
- Why are visuals better than oral presentations?
- What is a testimonial?
- What is a pre-interview checklist?

DISCUSSION TOPICS

- Name three sources where you can obtain information about a large company in your community.
- Discuss the role the telephone plays in the sales process.
- Is it important to use an identical telephone technique each time? Explain.
- What is the purpose of a pre-approach letter?
- Why should the pre-interview checklist be referred to every time before each interview?

EXERCISES

1. At a recent social event, you met the owner of a small manufacturing concern. She mentioned that she is thinking about acquiring an in-house computer. As a salesperson for a computer company whose primary market is small businesses, you are anxious to make an appointment to see her. Write a pre-approach letter.

2. Choose another student to help you practice telephone techniques. You play the role of the salesperson, the other student the prospect. Make the situation as real as possible. The prospect should not grant appointments too easily. Ask the class to criticize your performance.

3. A friend of yours is a loan officer of a large bank in your area. Over lunch he mentions a possible lead to you. The lead has been a regular bank customer for years and a well-known community leader. She heads her own trucking firm. You are a printing salesperson and see an opportunity here for a potential sale. To qualify this prospect, what questions would you ask your friend?

Case Study One

Janice Barton is a sales rep for a large cosmetics company. She works out of Lincoln, Nebraska. The headwaiter at the Riverside Plaza has told Janice that the hotel's fashionable gift shop has dropped the cosmetic line it has carried for years. He has given her the name of the hotel's assistant manager, who is the person who will decide on a replacement for the old line.

In her pre-approach research, Janice discovers some interesting facts. Through a mutual friend, she learns that the hotel gift shop did not drop the line. Instead, the distributor decided to place its line with another retail outlet because of a "slow pay" problem with the hotel. There were some cash-flow problems in the hotel, and the management took advantage of its prestigious position in the community by delaying payment on most bills beyond the usual late period. The hotel took as much as 120 days before paying some of its bills.

In spite of this information, Janice wants the account. It is, after all, a very prestigious account that would help her reputation locally and impress the people at the home office. Even if she made no money at all on this account, it would be useful as a third-party influence to use in other calls throughout the Lincoln area.

- How could Janice find out if her friend is right about the hotel not paying its bills on time?
- Should Janice discuss the hotel's cash-flow problems with the assistant manager in making her presentation?
- If so, what should she say?
- Since Janice is interested in getting this account, would it be wise to ignore the "slow pay" situation?
- Should she discuss the point with her own sales manager? Why?
- How would you advise Janice to approach this account?

Tony Gameiro works for a large office supply house in the Hartford, Connecticut, area. He has heard that one of Hartford's large insurance companies is about to change office suppliers.

Tony has been trying to get an "in" with this insurance company for years. He has heard that the person who will be making the decision is the vice-president in charge of company operations, Margaret Sampson. Ms. Sampson is a weekend golfer and part-time painter.

Tony does not know much about the insurance company and only heard of this opportunity at a social gathering.

- Name four sources where Tony can get information about the company.
- Discuss ways Tony can find information about Margaret Sampson's interests in golf and painting.
- How else would he go about qualifying his prospect?
- Would a pre-approach letter help here? What should be said in such a letter?

Presenting Products or Services

OBJECTIVES

In this chapter you will learn:

- How to stay on the sales track with the Formula-Need theory of selling.
- Why sales presentations are more successful if accompanied by visual aids.
- What visual aids are available (with examples of each).
- Why it is important for salespeople to present themselves as professionals.
- Why customer satisfaction should always be foremost in every salesperson's mind.

Ted Arscott is the assistant superintendent of the St. Paul, Minnesota, school system. He is in charge of purchasing supplies for the entire school district—35 grade schools and 9 high schools. Annual purchases run into hundreds of thousands of dollars.

Last week Ted called the Minnesota Instruments Company, a large manufacturer of calculators and mini-computers, whose national headquarters are also in St. Paul, to ask for a quote on 200 hand calculators.

The sales manager told Ted that he would have his best salesperson call him for an appointment. Carl Johannsen is his best salesperson. Carl has led the Minnesota division in sales for the past five years.

Carl's pre-approach research revealed three interesting things about Ted Arscott. One, he likes to do business with St. Paul companies. He feels very strongly that the citizens' tax dollars which are used to support the school system should be spent, if possible, in the local community. Second, Ted loves the local baseball team, the Minnesota Twins. (So does Carl.) Third, Carl discovered that Ted's social-style profile is Expressive—he loves to talk. Carl makes a 10 o'clock appointment on Thursday to see Ted Arscott in his office at the school board headquarters.

"Hello, Mr. Arscott," Carl says as he enters the room. "My name is Carl Johannsen, from Minnesota Instruments Company."

"Nice meeting you, Carl. Please be seated."

"Thank you."

Next Carl engages in some appropriate small talk. "I like your office, particularly your desk. Did it come with the office?"

Ted replies, "No, it's my own. I brought it from my last assignment several years ago when I was principal at Center High School."

Carl now has Ted's attention and decides that this is the moment to bring up the Twins. "So," Carl says, "How about our Twins? Wasn't that something—winning three in a row from the Yankees, in Yankee Stadium no less?"

Ted, beaming, turns his chair around to face Carl squarely, leans forward with obvious interest in his eyes, and says, "They were really terrific! I think the Twins are going to go all the way this year." He then starts talking at length about the team, going through the roster position by position.

Carl is equally entranced by the conversation because he has been a devoted fan for years, and he's always delighted to meet someone who shares his enthusiasm and interest. The two fans devote the next 45 minutes to a discussion of the Twin's chances to win the pennant.

Almost abruptly, Ted looks at his watch and says, "Good Heavens, it's almost eleven, and I'm due in the superintendent's office for a school board meeting in five minutes. Carl, I'm very sorry, but you'll have to drop by some other time. I really enjoyed talking about the Twins. Maybe we can see a game together sometime."

Carl smiles, but he leaves the office with a sinking feeling. He knows he let the interview get out of control. He knows he should have cut off the conversation about the Twins early and gotten down to business. Now he wonders if he has perhaps jeopardized his chance to make the sale. Perhaps the next salesperson Ted Arscott talks to will not be a Twin's fan.

Carl did something that all salespeople, even good ones, occasionally do. He got off the sales track—the selling path most successful salespeople follow. It starts the moment the salesperson walks into a prospect's office and ends (ideally) with the purchase of a product or service.

The Formula theory of sales, which was popular in the early 1900s, was one of the first sales "theories." Later, the Formula theory was combined with the Need Satisfaction theory to form the Formula-Need theory, the theory we will be looking at in this chapter.

The five stages of the Formula-Need sales track are *attention, interest, desire, conviction,* and *action* (or *aid*). Many salespeople remember it by the name AIDCA. Each stage of the sales track must be successfully negotiated in the proper sequence. For example, the interest stage cannot begin until the attention stage has been completed. Needs (conviction) cannot be ascertained until desire has been stimulated. (See Figure 9-1.)

THE FORMULA-NEED THEORY

When the Formula-Need theory was developed early in this century, it was generally used in conjunction with a canned sales presentation. A "canned" presentation is a memorized, word-for-word presentation de-

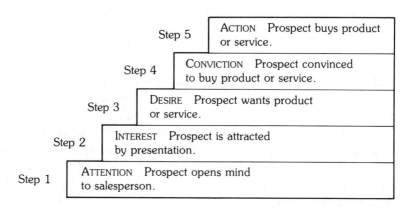

AIDCA is a five-step process; each step must be taken in sequence.

Figure 9–1. The Formula-Need Theory

signed by the company for their salespeople to use in every interview. Although sometimes helpful for new salespeople, the canned presentation is generally too stilted and mechanical for proven professionals.

For example, suppose a salesperson is interrupted by the following question, "Excuse me for interrupting, but didn't I read somewhere that your company is announcing a brand new line of sportswear in the fall?" Thrown off the track by such an unexpected turn of events, the salesperson must interrupt his memorized presentation. Perhaps he will never get back on the right track.

The Formula-Need theory, then, should be looked upon as a guide, a track to run on. Although all salespeople should keep the five stages in mind, and follow them in sequence, they should be flexible enough to deal with interruptions.

ATTENTION—THE FIRST STEP

The purpose of the attention stage is to get the prospect's mind off other matters and open to the sales presentation. An enthusiastic greeting followed by the salesperson's identification of himself, his company, and his product should open this stage. A little small talk, initiated by the salesperson, is the next step.

The small talk should be centered around an object in the prospect's office, his hobbies, or his involvement in community activities. (Remember Carl Johannsen's comments about Ted Ascott's desk.) Small talk should break the prospect's chain of concentration, removing all other thoughts from his mind. Thus, the first few interview moments are critical. Sales can be lost in the opening moments of a presentation, as Carl Johannsen discovered. This is also, of course, the time when the prospect will be evaluating the salesperson. Appearance, posture, voice quality and tone, all of these count heavily at this point.

Experienced salespeople become expert at uncovering subjects for small talk. As soon as they walk in the door, they look for unusual office decorations or personal items like family pictures, plaques, awards, sports trophies, and paintings. All reveal areas of interest appropriate for small talk. If the salesperson knows something about the prospect's interests outside the office, he or she might take advantage of this knowledge to introduce a suitable subject.

Here are some points to remember about the attention phase:

- Prospects must become attentive before they can become interested.

- All small talk should be about the prospect's interests, not the salesperson's.

- This phase should not last too long. Most prospects want to get down to business.

- The salesperson should appear to be interested and enthusiastic, even if his client is talking about his grandchild's new tooth.

The attention phase, then, is the time to build rapport with customers. If handled well, this period of small talk can create a very positive first impression of the salesperson. Such discussion also fosters understanding of the customer's approach to life, the wave length he is on, and the kinds of things that motivate him. It allows the salesperson to adjust his thinking to the prospect's method of thinking, thus increasing the probability that the presentation will end in success.

INTEREST—THE SECOND STEP

Having secured the prospect's undivided attention, the salesperson then moves on to the interest stage. This is the point where he tries to stimulate interest in his products or services.

A word of caution. Since the purpose of sales interviews is to sell products and services, the salesperson must arouse the customer's curiosity about the products or services he has to sell—not about the Minnesota Twins, the customer's business, or the salesperson's company's overall goals. Professional salespeople always remember this. They view the interest stage as the opportunity to introduce their products or services.

The interest phase begins with an opening statement that is broad enough in scope to cover all probable needs for the product offered. Here is a typical approach, one that Carl Johannsen could have used with Ted Arscott if he had cut short his discussion of the Minnesota Twins.

The Opening Approach

"In these days of constant changes in the marketplace it is important to do business with someone who tries to stay abreast of the times. Now my company, the Minnesota Instruments Company, is an excellent company. We make outstanding hand calculators. But so do other companies. So, I make it my business to keep up with our competitors' products and services—to know how their products compare to ours and what we can offer that they can't. Of course, I represent my company, but

I also feel I can represent you and your needs—without any sense of conflict or disloyalty. So, if you can tell me what you need, I can tell you whether or not I can help you."

What this approach does is put the prospect at ease by identifying some of the general business condition problems that everyone in business experiences. Carl's admission that other companies make good calculators also puts Ted at ease. Ted now feels that he will not be pressured to buy. He also feels that Carl is a professional salesperson representing the school district's interest as well as those of his company.

In this case, Carl knows that Ted is interested in buying hand calculators. Often, however, a salesperson has no idea what particular product or service the prospect might need. In such cases, the salesperson might say, at the end of his approach, something like, "With these thoughts in mind, what is your situation with reference to office equipment [or insurance, investments, office supplies]?"

An approach like the one Carl should have used is successful because it is intelligent, inoffensive, honest, and professional.

Such an approach is also responsible. It does not make any false promises. It focuses on the prospect's welfare.

The Transition Between Interest and Desire

After the opening approach has been made, the prospect should be encouraged to supply some basic facts about his needs. This information enables the salesperson to gather his thoughts in preparation for the next stage—creating desire.

Let's assume, for the moment, that Carl did not know in advance that Ted Arscott was interested in hand calculators, but was merely calling on him as a routine prospective customer. Carl has made his approach, concluding with, "What is your situation with reference to mini-calculators in the school system?"

Ted's response might be, "Well, we do use quite a few calculators in our school system. And we do need to look into buying replacements for those that no longer work. And we certainly don't want to do business again with the company that sold us those defective calculators."

Immediately, Carl would log this as a potential sales situation, but he does not know whether buying calculators is Ted's number-one priority. So he would proceed with some remark such as, "I understand. So you're interested in buying some hand calculators. Are there any other mini-computer products or services that you have been thinking about?"

"Not really," says Ted. "We do have a minor problem with the desk terminals used for our courses in computer programming, but we're not interested in getting into that right now."

"Are there any other areas that might be of interest to you?" Carl continues.

"No, I don't think so."

Thus, with a minimal amount of probing, Carl discovers that the school board's immediate interest is in acquiring some hand calculators.

How about an unwilling prospect—one who is reluctant to part with the information necessary for the sales process to continue. Salespeople try to overcome the problem by statements like these:

- "In order for you to determine if we should proceed further, I need to have some idea of your situation."

- "Is there something I've said or done to upset you?"

- "Perhaps this is not a good time for you. May I make another appointment?"

Phrases of this kind will usually break the ice and cause customers to state frankly why they are reluctant to offer needed information. Occasionally, personality conflict will bring the interview to a premature close. Even successful salespeople cannot be all things to all people. The wise salesperson recognizes the situation and bows out gracefully before ugly words are exchanged and feelings hurt.

DESIRE—THE THIRD STEP

Having attracted his prospect's attention and aroused his interest, Carl is now ready to start stimulating Ted's desire to consider his product. The actual presentation of the product now begins. Carl opens by saying something like, "Mr. Arscott, my company has been making quality hand calculators for years. I feel strongly that our CZ-280 model might be the ideal one for you. Let me show it to you." Carl now reaches into his briefcase, pulls out a calculator, and places it on Ted's desk. Ted immediately picks up the calculator. His eyes examine it carefully. His fingers press the function keys.

There is nothing spontaneous about a good sales presentation. It is a well-thought-out procedure designed to produce sales. All effective presentations have certain characteristics in common. They should:

- Immediately attract the attention of the prospect.

- Maintain the interest of the prospect.

- Be clear, concise, and have impact.
- Stimulate desire.
- Help solidify a confidence relationship between the salesperson and the prospect.
- Be delivered with honest enthusiasm.
- Involve the prospect through questions and discussion.
- Be controlled by the salesperson (but not so rigidly that momentum is lost if there is an unexpected interruption).
- Uncover valid needs.
- Motivate the prospect to buy from the salesperson.
- Lead naturally to a close.

Sales presentations are more effective if accompanied by visual aids. These generally fall into one of the five categories listed below.

1. *The product itself.* Here the salesperson displays the item. The prospect can see it, feel it, touch it, hear it, and, in some cases, smell it. Placing an attractive hand calculator in Ted's hands, for example had an immediate impact. Unfortunately, many products or services do not lend themselves to display. They are either too large to be portable or too intangible to be displayed.

2. *Graphics.* In the days before catalogues were commonplace, sales-people had to sketch a figure on the back of an envelope or a diagram on a piece of scratch paper to illustrate their products. The days of do-it-yourself product art are fortunately gone forever. To-day, there are many attractive graphic visuals designed specifically as sales aids (See Figure 9-2).

3. *The proposal (case study).* The proposal, sometimes called a case study, is a written description of the way a product or service can be designed to satisfy a customer's need. Proposals are written for specific products or services to be used by specific clients in a specific environment.

    Obviously a salesperson cannot write up a proposal for a pros-pective client on the spot. But he or she can show the client a sample proposal. For example: "Mr. Johnson, here's the proposal for a telephone system we installed for the Candid Distributing Company. Let me show it to you."

    Then the salesperson simply goes through the proposal page by page explaining what his company did for another customer. The presentation could end with: "What I'd like to do is prepare a similar

House of Graphics
A GRAPHIC ART STUDIO

You'll like our faces:*

Aachen Medium
Aachen Bold
American Classic
American Classic Italic
American Classic Bold
American Classic Exbld.
Antique Olive
Antique Olive Medium
Antique Olive Bold
Antique Olive Compact
Aquarius No. 8
Avant Garde Gothic Book
Avant Garde Gothic Medium
Avant Garde Gothic Bold
Bauhaus Bold
Bookman
Bookman Italic
BUSORAMA MEDIUM
Century Textbook
Century Textbook Italic
Century Textbook Bold
Century Textbook Bold Italic
Clarendon Book
Clarendon
Clarendon Condensed
Cooper Black
Cooper Black Italic
Egyptian Bold Condensed
Floridian Script
Friz Quadrata
Friz Quadrata Bold
Futura Light
Futura Light Italic
Futura Book
Futura Book Italic
Futura Demi
Futura Demi Italic
Futura Bold
Futura Bold Italic
Futura Light Condensed
Futura Medium Condensed
Futura Bold Condensed
Futura Extrabold

Goudy Oldstyle
Goudy Oldstyle Italic
Goudy Oldstyle Bold
GOUDY OLDSTYLE-SMALL CAPS
Helvetica Light
Helvetica Light Italic
Helvetica
Helvetica Italic
Helvetica Bold
Helvetica Bold Italic
Helvetica Extrabold
Helvetica Condensed
Helvetica Condensed Italic
Helvetica Bold Condensed
Helvetica Bold Condensed Italic
Helvetica Extrabold Condensed
Helvetica Extended
Helvetica Bold Extended
Helvetica Exbld. Ext.
Korinna Regular
Korinna Kursiv
Korinna Bold
Korinna Kursiv Bold
Korinna Extrabold
Korinna Kursiv Extrabold
Korinna Heavy
Korinna Kursiv Heavy
Korinna Outline
McCollough
Melior
Melior Italic
Melior Bold
Melior Bold Italic
Microstyle Extended
Microstyle Bold Extended
News No. 2
News Bold No. 2
Old English
Optima
Optima Italic
Optima Bold
Optima Bold Condensed
Palatino
Palatino Italic
Palatino Semibold
PALATINO-SMALL CAPS

Park Avenue
PENYOE Bold
Revue
Serif Gothic Light
Serif Gothic Regular
Serif Gothic Bold
Serif Gothic Black
Serif Gothic Outline
Souvenir Light
Souvenir Light Italic
Souvenir Medium
Souvenir Medium Italic
Souvenir Demi
Souvenir Demi Italic
Souvenir Bold
Souvenir Bold Italic
Stymie Light
Stymie Light Italic
Stymie Medium
Stymie Medium Italic
Stymie Bold
Stymie Bold Italic
Stymie Extrabold
Stymie Extrabold Condensed
Tiffany Light
Tiffany Medium
Tiffany Demi
Tiffany Heavy
Times Roman
Times Roman Italic
Times Roman Bold
Times Roman Bold Italic
Univers 45
Univers 55
Univers 65
Univers Medium Italic
Univers Ultrabld. Exp.
University Roman
University Bold
Windsor Bold

Латинский Шрифт
Современный Шрифт

*Each line is shown in 18 point for size comparison.

OUR SERVICES INCLUDE Art Direction and Design; Technical Illustration; Book Design and Illustration; Photo Retouching and Complete Production of: data sheets and catalogs, direct mail pieces and periodicals, brochures and books, instruction manuals and annual reports, visual aids including slide and viewgraph presentations; Typography and Darkroom Services.

930 Commercial Street
Palo Alto, California 94303

(415) 493-1213

Figure 9–2. A Graphic Aid Produced by a Company That Sells Design and Typesetting Services

proposal for you based on your needs and the amount of money you have budgeted for a telephone system." This is an impressive sales aid. Few prospects can resist having their problems solved for them. (A sample proposal is shown in Figure 9-3.)

```
                        PROPOSAL

    We propose to install and service the following solid state
    telephone system, based upon your specifications.

    EQUIPMENT
    1  J.T.S. 4C electronic JPBX switching system with the
          following features:
          call forward--follow me
          complete class of service
          group hunting
          consultation hold
          call transfer--individual
          add-on conference
          attendant conference
          paging access
          call pick-up
          power failure transfer capability

    1  JTS-4D console with busy lamp field
    8  central office trunk lines
    30 station lines
    34 4X-200 telephones

    SUPPLIES
    All hardware, cable, extension lines, and necessary miscel-
    laneous equipment

    SPARE PARTS
    1 common service card
    1 processor card PR-1
    1 processor card PR-2
    1 attendant line card
    1 attendant register card
    1 station line card
    1 central office trunk card

    LABOR
    No cost for basic installation.  One year free maintenance
    service guaranteed.

    COST
    For purchase, installation of above equipment     $33,294.58
        Sales tax @ 3%                                     998.84
                                TOTAL                  $34,293.42

    NOTES:
    a.  Depreciation on a double declining balance method and
        investment tax credit will further reduce cost.  Your
        accountant will be able to furnish this information.

    b.  Financing is available on a 5-, 8-, or 10-year basis at
        favorable interest rates.
```

**Figure 9–3.   A Proposal Created by the Jarboe Telephone
Company for a Prospective Client**

4. *Computerized printouts.* Computer printout visuals are obviously a relatively new sales visual. Let's see how they work.

The salesperson says something like, "Let me get the facts and information from you and send it to our computer center. We'll see what the computer recommends." The intention here, of course, is to introduce an objective element—computer analysis—into the sales process.

Computer printout visuals are particularly appropriate when costs are a major selling point or when a service like financial planning is being offered. A sample printout might be shown to a prospect with a comment like "Here's an estate analysis we ran for some clients of mine." (An excerpt from an estate analysis printout is shown in Figure 9-4).

```
III. ESTATE TRANSFER COSTS:  Type of Distribution -  Husband (Two-Part Trust/Minimum Total Taxes)
     --------------------                             Wife (Two-Part Trust/Minimum Total Taxes)

                                                    Order of Death(1)

                                   Husband 1st       Wife 2nd        Wife 1st      Husband 2nd

       Gross Estate(2)           $  1,246,000  $      577,010  $      211,000  $    1,256,000
       Less: (Expenses and Debts)      76,490          41,630          20,010          81,530
             (Marital Deduction)      516,010               0         160,000               0
             (Charitable Deduction)         0               0               0               0
       Taxable Estate                 653,500         535,380          30,990       1,174,470
       Plus: Adjusted Taxable Gifts         0               0               0               0
       Tentative Tax Base             653,500         535,380          30,990       1,174,470
       Tentative Federal Tax         212,595         168,891           6,218         417,333
       Less: (Unified Credit)         62,800         192,800          62,800         192,800
             (Credit for State Death Taxes)  16,140    11,415               0          43,566
             (Credit for Gift Taxes Paid)        0         0               0               0

       Net Federal Estate Tax        133,655               0               0         180,967

       State Death Taxes(3)           16,140          11,415               0          43,566
                                   ------------    ------------    ------------    ------------
           Total Transfer Costs    $  226,285  $     53,045  $       20,010  $      306,063

       Net Distribution to Spouse  $  516,010  $          0  $      160,000  $            0


   IV. LIQUIDITY ANALYSIS:
       ------------------

       Total Transfer Costs        $  226,285  $     53,045  $       20,010  $      306,063

       Available Liquid Assets         41,000           1,000          41,000          21,990

       Cash Surplus / (Deficit)    $ (185,285) $    (52,045) $       20,990  $     (284,073)

           If Husband Dies First: Total Shrinkage Both Deaths $   279,330 (21.4%)

           If Wife Dies First: Total Shrinkage Both Deaths $   326,073 (24.9%)

   (1) Assumes spouse survives 10 years with no change in asset values.
   (2) Includes gift taxes paid, and certain gifts made within 3 years of death. (IRC 2035)
   (3) State death taxes are based on state of residence and are in approximation. Consult your tax advisor.
```

Figure 9–4. A Printout Created by a Life Insurance Salesperson for a Prospective Client

The salesperson takes the prospect step-by-step through the sample printout and offers to order a similar program for the prospect, stating, "I'll need some basic information to feed to the computer and let's see what it comes up with."

Computer analyses are the wave of the future. Their accuracy, immediate availability, flexibility, and moderate cost make them an attractive presentation tool. They are available for virtually any kind of sale, but, as mentioned earlier, seem best when costs or services are involved.

5. *Testimonial letters.* Letters are often used to support the sale of a service—for example, a training program. Such presentations do not necessarily lend themselves to computer visuals, proposals, or graphics. Certainly, there's no product to show. Testimonial letters are ideal presentation vehicles in such cases. There is no better endorsement than a satisfied customer. (See Figure 9-5.)

Here are some sales fields in which testimonials are particularly effective:

Consulting services

Travel agencies

Bookkeeping services

Investment counseling

Office cleaning services

Repair services of all kinds

Banking and financial services

Testimonials can also be used effectively by those who sell for small businesses, including their own. These salespeople simply do not have access to the kind of selling aids that salespeople for large organizations do. Hence, a few letters praising their work are invaluable.

Presenting Yourself as a Professional

The last opportunity for a salesperson to intensify the desire stage occurs after the presentation has been made. Presenting oneself as a professional can intensify the desire of the customer to continue the relationship. At this point, Carl says to Ted, "Before we proceed, Mr. Arscott, I would like to explain how I operate. I try to operate as a counselor to my clients. By this I mean that I try to keep up with all of the changes in our industry because if I didn't I couldn't help my clients choose the products that will best serve their needs.

GLOBAL CITY BANK

480 N. LASALLE STREET • CHICAGO, ILLINOIS 60606 • 312/662-2100

Sandra Weiner
Communications Consultants
1040 Dinsmore Road
Winnetka, Illinois

Dear Ms. Weiner:

The communications training program you recently ran for our employees is having its desired effect.

Morale has been greatly improved, personality conflicts neutralized, and an overall positive attitude exists around here for the first time in years.

Feel free to use me as a reference any time. Let's stay in touch.

                            Regards,

                            Roger Allison
                            Vice-President
                            Global City Bank

Figure 9–5. An Endorsement from a Satisfied Customer

"Second, as a professional, I have had a lot of experience helping my clients set priorities. So, I can help you find out what you really need, and them help you set priorities on satisfying those needs."

If properly articulated, such expressions will go far to establish a productive working relationship with the prospect. By this time, the prospect should be well at ease, interested, and open to discussing basic needs. Isolating needs and getting a commitment to buy is the subject of the next chapter.

CONVICTION—THE FOURTH STEP

Conviction, which usually occurs at the closing interview, is discussed in Chapter 10. In this stage, the prospects are convinced that:

- They need the salesperson's products or services.
- They do not need the competitor's products or services.
- They want to do business with that particular salesperson.
- They are ready to buy now.

ACTION—THE FIFTH STEP

Prospects take action to buy. This occurs when the prospect:

- Signs an order blank or some other instrument acknowledging his purchase.
- Issues a check in partial or full payment, or
- Indicates verbally that a purchase has been made by such phrases as: "I know I'll like your product or service," "I feel better knowing I've bought this," "When will you deliver this?," "How do you want me to pay for this?"
- Calls in a subordinate to take over the installation of the product or service.

Following the Formula-Need theory, then, in sales presentations is crucial. Professional salespeople make this process the foundation of *every* presentation. They know each stage well, and learn to *sense* when each stage has been successfully completed. Professionals follow the Formula-Need theory for the five basic reasons listed below:

1. It is professional.
2. It is objective.
3. It builds trust and confidence.
4. It puts the salesperson, not the prospect, in control.
5. It results in sales.

CUSTOMER SATISFACTION

Ideally, the Formula-Need theory should culminate in customer satisfaction. Even if each step is followed in sequence, and a sale is made, the sales process cannot be considered successful if the customer is not satisfied.

Obviously the important thing here is follow-up. After getting the signed order, the process must be carefully followed through to see that:

- The product or service is available as promised.
- It is delivered on time and in working order.
- It is explained or installed properly.
- Any minor problems are promptly solved.
- In-house training for proper usage (if necessary) is given.
- An open line of communication is established between salesperson and customer.
- Any other promise made incidental to the sale is kept.
- Where indicated, reassurance is given that the customer made the right decision in buying.

Unless all these matters are promptly attended to, the customer may have second thoughts or long for a newer product wilth better features. By continually following up as outlined above, postpurchase anxiety will be properly neutralized.

SUMMARY

This chapter emphasized the importance of following the five-part sales track of the Formula-Need theory of selling—attention, interest, desire, conviction, and action. Each stage of this process must be reached in proper sequence, or the sale could be lost.

The first three stages were discussed in detail. The importance of the first few minutes of the interview was stressed. The salesperson must be careful not to permit prospects to talk too long about hobbies and interests. The salesperson must control the pace of the interview and keep it on track.

The opening approach in the interest stage was discussed at length. A good approach conditions prospects to accept the salesperson as a professional and assures them that they will not be pressured to buy.

In the next stage, desire, the salesperson makes his presentation. Several methods of presentation were discussed—the product itself (when possible), graphics, proposals, computer printouts, and testimonial letters.

The chapter closed with a discussion of customer satisfaction as the only desirable outcome of presenting products and services.

KEY TERMS

Action	Formula-Need Theory (AIDCA)
Attention	Interest
Conviction	Presentation
Desire	Proposal

REVIEW QUESTIONS

- What are the five steps of the Formula-Need theory?
- Why are the opening minutes of the first interview so important?
- Should the content of the sales track be memorized? Why?
- What does the attention phase do?
- How do salespeople sell themselves as professionals?

DISCUSSION TOPICS

- Wasn't the opening approach illustrated in the text somewhat contrived and therefore manipulative? Explain.
- Why not get all the facts instead of just preliminary information after the approach?
- How can salespeople control interviews and keep themselves on the sales track?
- Discuss the pros and cons of the five basic presentation aids.
- Why is customer satisfaction more important than making a sale?

EXERCISES

1. Using the AIDCA formula, try to sell a business or professional person on making a scholarship contribution to your school.
2. Break up into groups of three to role play the first and second steps in AIDCA. One acts as the customer, one as the salesperson,

and the other as a critic. Reverse roles until all three have played each part.

3. A customer, 60 days after buying a product, telephones the salesperson complaining about poor post-sales service. In a short essay, discuss ways of reestablishing a good relationship.

Case Study One

Bob Hernandez represents a glassware manufacturer who sells primarily to restaurants and hotels. Bob is in Tucson, Arizona, calling on Joe Guitterez, the owner of a successful chain of Mexican restaurants. Joe came up the hard way (his father was a migrant farm worker in the Rio Grande Valley) and still keeps track of every dime he spends or earns. Joe is also tough, efficient, and somewhat impatient. He believes that all Chicanos can reach the top if they are willing to work as hard as he did. Joe is also exceptionally open to women in his organization. Half of his 32 restaurants are managed by women.

Bob Hernandez finds out most of this information in his pre-approach research. Bob, himself, is not too sympathetic to the cause of women in business. He feels that it is hard enough for a male Chicano to get a decent job and that Joe, by giving so many managerial jobs to women, is taking jobs away from men.

- Should Bob bring up his views on women in the work force in the opening interview? Why?
- What appropriate opening comments could Bob make during the all-important early moments of the first interview?
- In view of Joe's impatience, are there any things for which Bob should be particularly prepared in the first interview?
- What visual materials would be appropriate for Bob to use?
- What things do the two men have in common that Bob could bring to play in the interview?

A small desk-size digital adding machine, with optional tape for a hard-copy record of totals, is the product leader of the Add-On Corporation of Portland, Oregon. Marlene Jacobsen, a salesperson with Add-On, likes the product. Her sales record is outstanding.

Three years ago, Marlene worked in the personnel department of Add-On. She asked for a transfer to the field because she knew that sales experience is a must for any meaningful promotion up the executive ladder. After two and a half years in the field, and a hefty earnings increase, Marlene is not so sure she ever wants to leave sales. She likes to sell creatively. She begins every interview with the usual personal introduction and small talk. She then likes to say to her prospect, "Mr. Peabody, do you mind if I show you something?"

Somewhat intrigued, the customer usually says, "No, not at all." Whereupon she carefully unveils her company's latest digital adding machine and places it on the prospect's desk. She steps back, staring at it lovingly. She says nothing.

After a somewhat awkward pause, the customer usually says something like, "It looks nice; how does it work?"

She then goes into an effective oral presentation and demonstration.

The Portland Power Company has called her company to arrange for a sales demonstration. They are planning to purchase 53 digital adding machines for their office staff. Since the company is in her exclusive territory, the sales manager informs Marlene of the request.

She is ecstatic at the prospect of such a substantial sale. In discussing the case, her sales manager urges her to use a more sophisticated presentation than the one she has been using to sell one machine at a time.

She balks. Marlene feels that if she changes her proven presentation, she might lose the whole sale.

- What are the pros and cons of using her proven techniques in the larger sale?
- How else could she present the Attention, Interest, and Desire stages of the Formula Need theory here?
- Is Marlene's kind of showmanship unprofessional? Explain.

Getting the Commitment

OBJECTIVES

In this chapter you will learn:

- Why it is important to help prospects isolate and establish priorities for their needs.
- How to use counselor probing to help clients bring their needs to the surface.
- What a commitment to buy is (and how to obtain it through tactful probing).
- What three qualifications a prospect must have before a salesperson can obtain a valid commitment from him.

Hartford, the capital of Connecticut, is the home office for several national life insurance companies. That's why Paulette Gladdon lives there. Paulette is a successful life insurance sales agent with one of the large national companies.

When Paulette got out of college, she taught for a while, decided teaching wasn't for her, and drifted into the life insurance business when she was twenty-eight.

One of the first things she did, at the suggestion of her manager, was to get involved in a voluntary health organization in her spare time. The organization Paulette joined was run by a particularly bright young man, John Daley. John, who is in his mid-thirties, has made a career of working with voluntary health organizations. He knows only too well how the nature of the relationships between volunteers and professional staff affects the efficiency of health organizations.

When Paulette called to introduce herself, she discovered during the course of the interview that John was concerned because volunteer/staff relationships had deteriorated almost to the point where the two groups were not speaking to each other. John told Paulette that he had been looking for a confident and capable volunteer who could forge a consensus between volunteers and staff, help with volunteer training, and see both sides of the picture. Paulette told John she would try to rectify the situation.

The rest is history, as they say. Paulette not only did an outstanding job, but received an award from the national office of the health organization for almost single-handedly revitalizing the spirit of cooperation between volunteers and staff. Paulette was asked to give an acceptance speech at the annual national meeting in New York.

In her speech, Paulette stressed the importance of having competent volunteers and staff working in harmony. She pointed out that if the voluntary staff is too strong, the good professional staff members leave. And, conversely, if the professionals ignore or limit the contributions of the volunteers, only the weak volunteers remain. The strong ones seek an outlet for their talents elsewhere.

Two years after this meeting, the national health organization authorized each state to purchase its own group life insurance program. Hearing of this, Paulette asked John Daley if he felt it would be all right with the board if she made a bid for the Connecticut organization's business. John talked to some of the voluntary board members who said, Of course—as long as Paulette's bid was competitive, why shouldn't they do business with her? Several bids were submitted, and after lengthy deliberations, Paulette was named the agent of record. She wrote the group life policy and has serviced it well for the past several years.

As might be predicted, several of the organization's volunteers are local agents. These agents are constantly calling John Daley with the suggestion that the organization change its carrier from Paulette's company to their own. But, according to John Daley, there is no way that the organization is going to switch its carrier as long as Paulette Gladdon is around. John is always careful to point out that if there was a tremendous difference in price, he would be happy to change, but he knows that this is unlikely in light of the competitive spirit of Paulette's company. John Daley feels that because of Paulette, he will do almost anything to keep that policy with her company.

John's loyalty is not a payback or rebate for services rendered, but an appreciation of what Paulette has done for his organization. There is a lesson here, however, and all salespeople should learn it well. Before you can make a sale, you must secure the customer's commitment to buy from you. You may have the lowest price, the best service reputation, the most ideal product, but unless you secure the decision-maker's support, there will be no sale.

This chapter explores two vital phases in the sales cycle, isolating needs and getting the commitment. To obtain a true commitment from a prospect, that prospect (1) must have the financial capability to buy, (2) must have the authority to make the buying decision, and (3) agree to buy from the salesperson making the presentation.

ISOLATING NEEDS

When Paulette Gladdon first talked to John Daley about group life insurance, he indicated that there were needs for all kinds of employee benefit plans. The organization needed a disability plan, a retirement plan, and an accident insurance plan. (They already had a health insurance plan.) John was convinced, however, that the primary need of the organization was a group life insurance plan. And, although Paulette felt that some of the other plans were equally important, it soon became obvious that John had given top priority to a group life insurance program. So Paulette pursued this avenue and deferred discussion of other needs to a later time.

In a sales interview, several needs, or so-called hot buttons, may emerge. The skilled salesperson uses counselor probing and discussion to explore these needs with the prospect. The purpose, of course, is to find out the priority need—the one the customer wants to satisfy right now. Frequently, salespeople will misinterpret the first need expressed as the priority need, and may not attempt to uncover other more pressing needs. Hence, the sale is lost. Professional salespeople therefore expend a great amount of energy and skill uncovering all needs at the beginning of the interview. They do this by engaging in a "fishing expedition" type of probe with the prospect.

The Fishing Expedition

Serious fishing is not a simple activity. It is more like an expedition. Those who fish go adequately prepared, not only with the right kind of physical equipment but with proper mental attitude. People who like to fish do it leisurely. They know success in this unpredictable enterprise requires plenty of probing and patience. But the end result is worth the reward.

Once the lake is selected, and the boat is in the water, the probing begins. The fishermen look first at the weather. If the sun is bright, fish usually seek shady coves or deep water. If the day is cloudy and relatively cool, the fish may gather closer to the surface anywhere in the lake.

After settling on a particular place to fish, the bait is chosen. Should worms or plugs be used? It probably depends on past successes in similar circumstances. Then the question of line strength comes up. This depends on the anticipated size and type of the fish to be caught.

Despite all these preparations, there is still no guarantee that the fish will be biting. If they have no luck, the fishermen move to another location. The probing process is repeated. And if even no fish are landed at the next spot, the fishermen will row home with a cheerful "wait till next time." It isn't that they don't like to catch fish. That's the reason they go fishing. The point is that they are willing to probe interminably and are not discouraged when their probes are temporarily fruitless.

The fishing expedition analogy is particularly apt for this phase of the sales process. Professional salespeople spend much energy probing for needs of their products or services through discussion with prospects.

The Counselor Probing Process

The dictionary defines *to probe* as "to examine or investigate penetratingly; delve into." Adding counseling to probing makes it professional because it places the customers' needs first. (Some professionals call this process *counselor selling*. Both terms describe a process in which the salesperson, by asking a series of general, indirect questions, helps the prospect isolate and identify valid needs). It takes time to master the skill of productive thinking, not inhibit it. Here are some guidelines for successful probing:

- Begin by asking general questions.
- Continue the questioning process to delve into prospect's thinking about the products or services you are offering.
- Keep the converstion focused on prospect's specific needs, not general ones.

- Talk in untechnical terms.
- Allow plenty of time for prospect's answers.
- Listen attentively, feeding back to prospects their expressed ideas by paraphrasing their statements. Use such comments as "I see," "I understand," and "I see what you mean."
- As needs begin to emerge, explore each one in depth with your prospect.
- After disclosure of all needs, help client set priorities for satisfying them.
- Be a counselor-seller, not a selfish seller. See Figure 10-1.
- If no agreed specific needs surface after a reasonable time, terminate the interview.

This is the time to build rapport with your prospect. It is at this stage in the sales situation that a prospect must be convinced of your sincerity. This is when you start building a trust relationship.

Here is a portion of a typical counselor interview. Berta Mehlick represents the meat division of a large food brokerage house in Cedar Rapids, Iowa. She is in the office of Marty Glassman, the manager of a large independent supermarket located in a downtown shopping mall. The store has used one line of top quality meat products for years.

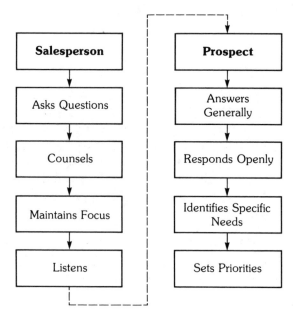

Figure 10–1. The Counselor Probing Process

Berta's company sells top quality meats. She is eager to sell Marty on using her products.

Berta has made her overall approach and showed Marty some visuals of her company products. She is now ready to isolate needs. As usual, she starts this segment of the interview with an open-ended question.

QUESTION   So you can see, Mr. Glassman, my company does have a quality meat line that would complement the other quality lines in your store. What is your meat counter situation, if I may ask?

ANSWER   Well, we have dealt with several meat distributors for years for our middle quality lines. And Cornell has been our top line for several years. We are really quite satisfied with all our supplies.

QUESTION   Yes, I can see that, and I agree that Cornell makes top products. But if you could increase your meat department profits by 10 per cent by adding another top line, you would probably do it, wouldn't you?

ANSWER   Of course. Profit is the name of the game.

QUESTION   Top meats are purchased by top spenders. I am sure you want to do everything you can to keep them happy. I notice you carry an exceptionally wide assortment of meats for the average customer. Isn't it possible that most of your top dollar customers would like a bigger assortment of top of the line meats, too?

ANSWER   Sure, that's always a possibility.

QUESTION   Mr. Glassman, I've noticed that Cornell's frozen cornish hens don't seem quite as plump as ours. I think ours weigh substantially more. Do you have much of a call for cornish hens?

ANSWER   No, as a matter of fact, we don't. I guess I never gave it much thought. (Berta mentally logs the specific need here and moves on to others.)

QUESTION   Well, more on that later. I also noticed that you don't carry top-of-the-line smoked briskets. Doesn't Cornell carry smoked briskets?

ANSWER   No. But we do sell a lot of our middle line briskets. The customers don't seem to complain much here.

QUESTION   I see. Well, I guess if you've never had a top brisket line, your customers wouldn't know the difference. So maybe my company's line here would make you some extra sales, don't you think?

ANSWER   Well, perhaps it would.

At this stage, Berta has isolated two specific needs—for frozen cornish game hens and beef brisket. She will continue probing until possibly three or four product needs surface. Then she will help Marty set a priority of needs to be fulfilled. She will then obtain a commitment to buy before she makes her proposal and asks for the order.

Good and Bad Probing

Good probing attracts prospect interest; bad probing discourages it. Often the manner of asking a question, the actual words used, makes the difference between good and bad probing. Here are some examples:

GOOD   If our new copying machine can cut your paper costs by 40 percent you'd be interested, wouldn't you?

BAD   People would be dumb not to buy our machine if it could save them 40 percent, wouldn't they?

GOOD   Let me see if I understand what you're saying. You're saying you don't feel a need for this tax service at this time. Is that correct?

BAD   You're telling me you don't need my tax service, right?

GOOD   May I explain something?

BAD   Let me tell you something.

GOOD   Yes, I understand your feelings. However, there are other approaches to the problem. Are you open to exploring them?

BAD   Despite your feelings, you ought to look at my alternative.

GOOD   If I were in your position, I'd be upset with my company's service, too. Is there any way we can reestablish our credibility with you? I'm eager to serve you.

BAD   Well, no company's perfect. But I guess you feel differently. Can't I do business with you?

GETTING THE COMMITMENT

Of all the mistakes beginning salespeople make, none is more costly than the failure to get a fixed commitment to buy before attempting to close the sale. They might move through the other phases of the sales cycle with the flair of a professional, but unless they get a buying commitment from their prospect, they are wasting their talent and their time.

Once a saleserson gets a commitment, the rest of the sales process is simple. It is a matter of filling out the order blank. There are three basic elements to obtaining a valid commitment:

1. Agreement on prospect's financial ability to buy
2. Affirmation of prospect's authority to make the buying decision
3. Agreement to buy from the salesperson making the presentation

Here is how Berta Mehlick obtained a commitment to buy from Marty Glassman.

QUESTION Are there any other products of ours, like frank-furters, link sausages, hams, or smoked cold cuts, that you feel might be worth a try here, Mr. Glassman?

ANSWER We always sell a lot of link sausages. I don't know why. And I've always been proud of our quality hams. Maybe those two deserve a try.

QUESTION Well, we could certainly try all four products. Of course, it all depends on your budget situation. We could place a trial order of all four products. A two-month commitment would be ideal. After all, it's going to take your customers that long to become aware of our products, let alone buy them in great quantities. For a representative display, we're prob-ably talking about a two-month commitment of, say, one thousand dollars to do the job. Do you see any problem with that?

ANSWER Well, things are a little tight right now. I don't think our budget could expand that much at this time.

QUESTION Fine. I understand. So maybe we're looking at, say, just one or two products—perhaps brisket and cor-nish hens. That makes sense, doesn't it? Or do you prefer to try one or two of the other products I've mentioned?

ANSWER   Frankly, I like your idea of the brisket. What about hams instead of the hens? What would a two-month trial of those cost?

QUESTION   Oh, I suppose about half that or around five hundred dollars. Do you think you could handle that comfortably?

ANSWER   Well, that's more like it. Yes, I could rearrange some budget items and come up with five hundred but no more.

QUESTION   Let me make a note of that. (Berta writes the figure $500 on the order blank.) In other words, you could allocate five hundred dollars out of your current budget for the trial of our briskets and hams, is that what you're saying?

ANSWER   Yes. I'm not saying I'm buying it today, but yes, I do have the funds available.

Berta now has a firm financial commitment. The prospect has the ability to buy. If, after probing, Berta had been unable to get a financial commitment, she would end the interview and make a date to return whenever Marty's budget situation improved enough to afford her trial run costs.

Now Berta moves to the second aspect of obtaining a commitment—affirmation of the prospect's authority to make the buying decision.

QUESTION   I understand that you're not saying you're buying right now. But if you were, $500 would be no problem, right? (Berta is reaffirming the dollar commitment.)

ANSWER   Right.

QUESTION   Speaking of making the actual purchase, are you authorized to make these decisions yourself or do you have to clear things with someone else?

ANSWER   No, I'm allowed to select products at will and for whatever cost I desire, so long as it's in the budget. After all, that's what I'm paid for—to manage this operation.

Now Berta has confirmed that Marty can make the buying decision. All that remains now for her to do is to get his agreement to buy from her, the third and last aspect of obtaining a valid commitment. Then she'll be ready to close the sale.

Sometimes, it is impossible to get that commitment for reasons beyond the salesperson's control. Perhaps the prospect has a long-standing commitment to another salesperson or company. Berta continues her probing to see if this is the case with Marty Glassman.

QUESTION   All right. Let me note that you make the decisions around here. (Berta again makes a note on her order blank. This physical action on her part conveys to Marty that she is eager to do business with him.) Now, finally, there's just one other area I'd like to clarify. Is there any reason you can't buy from me or my company, Mr. Glassman? I mean, do you have any personal commitment that would preclude you from buying from me or my company?

ANSWER   No, not that I can think of. Several years ago the owner tried to tell me who I should buy from. But I told him I wouldn't work under such restrictions, and he backed off. So, no, there's no reason I can't buy from you or your company.

Berta is relieved. She feels she can now move to the close. She has obtained a valid commitment to buy. She sums up the commitment in this way.

QUESTION   Then as I understand it, Mr. Glassman, you can afford five hundred dollars right now, you alone make the buying decision, and there is no reason you can't buy from me or my company. If this where we are?

ANSWER   Yes, it is.

Ability to Pay

The buyer's ability to pay for a needed product is a key element in any sale. Hence, it stands at the top of the list of the pre-closing commitments.

As the salesperson helps the prospect isolate needs, he should always keep costs in mind. For example, if the prospect is entitled to a discount if he purchases a certain quantity, the salesperson should point this out. (Note: If the competitors' prices are lower, the salesperson should stress the quality aspects of his product. If the competitors' prices are higher, then of course he should play up price.)

When a prospect does not have the dollars for a purchase, sales-people frequently help them find the money. Sometimes, what seems at first glance to be an inability to pay for a certain product is simply a reluctance to reallocate available monies. Let's see, for example, what Peter Barnes did when he encountered this situation.

Peter Barnes, a word-processing salesperson, has convinced the managing partner of a large law firm that his word-processing machine is more efficient and less expensive than the one the firm presently uses. Nevertheless, the partner tells Peter that the firm cannot afford a new word processor now. Peter does not know that at a recent meeting of the partners, it was determined that no money would be spent for word-processing equipment because the machine that had been bought two years earlier was adequate. By continued probing, however, Peter uncovers the problem and suggests a solution.

"Mrs. Jostad, I can undersand your reasoning, you just don't have funds allocated to purchase this word processor, right?"

"That's correct."

"I see. Well, you know this word processor can save the cost of up to two full-time typists once it's up and operating, isn't that correct?"

"Yes, you covered that point very convincingly."

"Well, you know that the savings in salaries could easily pay for this machine. In fact, the machine costs about the same as the annual salary of one of those typists. If there was a way to install it now, would you be willing to?"

"Oh yes, it's just that I have my instructions, so to speak."

"Yes, I realize that. I'm just sitting here wondering. Do you suppose the priority of some of those budget items could be rearranged so we could install this processor now?"

"Well, I hadn't thought of that . But yes, that's a possibility."

"Well, perhaps you could discuss it with the other partners. I'm sure a temporary postponement of another item in the budget would be more than offset in the future by saving the salary of one full-time typist, don't you agree?"

"Yes, I do."

In all probability, then, Mrs. Jostad will go back to the other partners and tell them she would like to rearrange the present budget to find the money to pay for Peter Barnes's new word processor.

As we've just seen, determining whether a prospect can afford a product is largely a matter of tactful probing. (But remember, the strong-est need in the world will go unfulfilled if the company simply cannot afford it.) Here are several ways a prospect can finance the purchase of a new product or service:

- Budget rearrangement
- Postponing other, less needed purchases
- Temporary bank loans
- Lease-purchase plans in which items are leased on a monthly-payment basis with an option to buy at the end of the lease term. Sellers of large equipment items like telephone systems, office computers, copiers, furniture, and plant equipment usually arrange such financing plans as part of their customer service.
- Balance sheets. After study, a balance sheet may reveal sources of money for purchases. Sometimes "reserve-for-contingencies" items might provide the dollars. Or a postponement of dividend distribution on company stock might suffice.

After the money has been found, a commitment to buy must be obtained. You don't want your prospect saying later on, when the sale is being closed, "I can't afford it." It's too late then to try and find the needed dollars.

Authority to Buy

Ideally, a salesperson should deal directly with the person who is empowered to buy what he has to sell. However, as the cost of products and services increases, purchases over a certain amount must be authorized by someone in top management. Frequently, these top-level decision-makers delegate initial contacts with the salesperson to subordinates. The subordinate then reports all the pertinent data to the decision-maker, who in turn makes the buying decision. Professional salespeople, of course, want to have the decision-maker in on the sales process early. They frequently achieve this by convincing screeners that they can discuss their product adequately only with the decision-maker.

Here is a list of counseling techniques that might be used with the lower-echelon person to ensure the decision-maker's presence:

- "Rather than my burdening you with the technical aspects of my products, why don't we discuss it jointly with Mr. Johnson?"
- "It would save you time if we discussed this matter directly with Mr. Johnson."

- "I'm sure Mr. Johnson would have some questions that only I can help you answer adequately."
- "Why can't both of us appear before your board? You make the presentation; I'll be your technical expert."

Usually, if a good rapport has been established with the screener, comments like these will lead to a meeting with the decision-maker. Professionals often refuse to make complicated presentations without the presence of such a person.

Willingness to Buy from You

Even though firm needs have been established, fixed dollar commitments have been determined, and the decision-maker's presence ensured, it still must be ascertained whether prospects will actually buy from the salesperson making the presentation. As noted earlier in the case of Paulette Gladdon, the chances of John Daley's buying from anyone else, even at a more competitive price, were quite remote. Because of her strong relationship with John, Paulette had the inside track.

Nevertheless, there are several reasons why prospects may not buy from a particular salesperson. These should be uncovered in the sales process. A logical place is in the final phase of getting the commitment by asking a question such as "In view of all these matters, is there any reason why you would be unable to do business with me or my organization?" Again, professional salespeople insist on getting this matter settled before proceeding. Here are some reasons prospects may not buy from salespeople even when they need and can pay for their product:

- The prospect may have a strong loyalty—to another salesperson or company.
- The prospect may have had a bad experience with the salesperson's company in the past.
- The prospect may simply not like a salesperson's personality, or the way he conducts himself.
- Somewhere in the sales process, prospects may have been intimidated, insulted, or otherwise turned off by the presenters.
- There may be undisclosed personal reasons ("I always buy from my brother-in-law") involved.

To summarize, before a salesperson can obtain the all-important commitment to buy he must establish that the prospect has the money to pay for the product, the authority to make the buying decision, and no objection to doing business with the salesperson involved.

Some sales organizations use rating systems to help their salespeople assess closing possibilities after the initial interview. Salespeople must submit rating sheets on the prospects they have interviewed in the past week. This procedure reminds salespeople to procure commitments.

Larry L. Howard, a unit manager with IBM on the West Coast, designed a particularly effective prospect rating chart. Larry has received several awards from IBM for his sales achievements. He is also a very successful recruiter and trainer of salespeople for the IBM computer line. His rating form rates prospects in four categories, with 4 the highest and 1 the lowest. (See Figure 10-2.) Each of the four categories can be rated from 1 to 4. Thus, a score of 16 means that the prospect is ready to be closed, with the chances of success very high. Lower total scores, of course, indicate a smaller probability of closing.

Citing all elements as important, Larry feels strongly that decision-maker contact is the key element to any sale. If the executives who are the decision-makers will not come to IBM seminars to see demonstrations of computer capabilities, or if they will not allow salespeople to visit them personally, then Larry feels the chances of making the sale are very limited.

SUMMARY

This chapter discussed the key elements in isolating needs and obtaining the commitment in the sales process. Usually several needs will surface; these are called "hot buttons." Salespeople must then counsel with prospects to help them establish a priority of needs.

Needs are isolated and commitments obtained by means of a process similar to a fishing expedition. Counselor probing (for which guidelines were listed), listening, and other good communication techniques are enlisted in this exploratory process to isolate areas of need.

The chapter continued with a discussion of the three qualifications necessary for a valid commitment. Namely, the prospect must have the financial capability to buy, the authority to make the purchase, and no objections to buying from the salesperson making the presentations.

PROSPECT CODES

Top Executive Coverage

4—IBM has contacted the decision-maker directly and has a plan to see him on a regular basis.

3—IBM has contacted the decision-maker, but has no specific plans to see him again.

2—IBM has not contacted the decision-maker, but plans to do so, and has access to him.

1—IBM has not contacted the decision-maker, and has no plans to contact him.

Resources (Financial and Personnel Resources Necessary to Afford a Computer.)

4—The prospect has more than enough personnel and financial resources to afford the system they are considering.

3—The prospect appears to have enough personnel and financial resources to afford the system they are considering.

2—The prospect may not have enough personnel and financial resources to afford the system they are considering, but they definitely could afford a smaller system.

1—The prospect's resources would be stretched if they installed any in-house system.

Desire

4—The prospect is totally convinced that his organization can benefit from installing a data-processing system. We will most likely have an order within thirty days.

3—The prospect can see the potential value in having a data-processing system. He and I have agreed specifically on what must be shown before securing final commitment.

2—The prospect is somewhat dubious about the value of an IBM system to his organization. He and I have agreed generally on what would have to be shown before proceeding further.

1—The prospect is not interested in a data-processing system at this time and has told me specifically why not. I agree with his reasons.

Account Knowledge

4—I understand all elements of this organization. I can communicate with top management as an equal. I know specifically the benefits a data-processing system would produce.

3—I understand the objectives of this organization and can generally describe the advantages a computer system would provide. My survey shows some areas that need further study.

2—I understand the general objectives of this organization, but have not as yet been able to translate these into saleable computer advantages—a survey is in process.

1—I do not understand how this company could use a computer. I have no plans to do a survey at this time.

Reprinted with permission.

Figure 10–2. A Prospect Rating Chart

KEY TERMS

Commitment

Counselor Probing

Decision-Maker

Isolating Needs

Hot Buttons

REVIEW QUESTIONS

- Why is a fishing expedition like a sales interview?
- Name three methods to finance purchases.
- Why is it important to deal personally with the decision-maker?

DISCUSSION TOPICS

- Why is it important to isolate and establish a priority of needs?
- What is counselor probing?
- Discuss several reasons why a customer who needs a product, and can pay for it, might still not buy from a particular salesperson.
- Can salespeople overcome deep-seated prejudices against companies they represent? How?

EXERCISES

1. You play the role of a purchasing agent for a large manufacturing concern. You need three products offered by a salesperson (played by another student). They are a new conveyor belt system, a new molding machine, and a new delivery truck. The budget permits the purchase of only one. You are the only one who knows which need is the most vital. The student playing the salesperson will, through counselor probing, try to find your "hot button" item. Your fellow students are your audience. Ask them, at the end of the role, if they can guess what your hot button is.

2. Write a two-page essay on the basic difference between counselor selling and self-interest selling.

3. Divide into small groups and practice various methods of getting the financial commitment to buy. The goal here is to make sure the salesperson secures a firm dollar commitment and not a decision to buy the product or service offered. (Those students not involved in role playing can act as critics.)

Case Study One

As the administrative manager of the Computer Services Corporation in Springfield, Missouri, Mary Pryor reports directly to the president of the company. CSC is a computer time-sharing company that serves savings and loan associations throughout a five-state region.

Although Mary reports directly to the president, she is the person who actually runs the company on a day-to-day basis. The president, John Pierce, spends a good deal of his time on the road looking for new clients. He has a background in marketing and has done a remarkable job in selling CSC's services to various savings and loan associations.

For the past six months, the company has been considering the purchase of an up-to-date dictating system. It will be an expensive installation because it will be used by both the salespeople on the road and the people in the home office. Mary usually handles all preliminary interviews on major purchases and then consults with John, who makes the final decision. Mr. Pierce seldom meets the salesperson involved. He feels that Mary is competent to make preliminary decisions; he is only interested in her final recommendations.

Tony LaCotta is his company's most successful dictating equipment salesman. His company is the leader in the entire industry, but because of its quality, Tony's product is more expensive than the dictating system that his closest competitor is offering to CSC.

Tony has made many presentations to Mary, and she has informed him that while his company is certainly in the running, the chances of buying his product are quite low because of budgetary considerations. Tony feels that the only way he can overcome this objection is to meet with John and Mary together. Mary, of course, says that such a meeting is not necessary and probably would do no good. As an experienced salesperson, Tony knows his only chance of making this sale is to have an interview in the presence of John Pierce.

- How should Tony go about setting up such an interview?
- Is there any way he can placate Mary Pryor and still have that interview?
- Should Tony utilize his own sales manager here? If so, how?
- How could Tony capitalize on his reputation as a professional salesperson to procure such an interview?
- If Tony fails to arrange the joint interview, what other courses of action, if any, are available to him?

Case Study Two

Max Berenbaum and Associates is a marketing consulting firm in Minneapolis. Max, who majored in psychology in college and then worked five years as a sales rep for a large office equipment company in Cleveland, set up his own company ten years ago. His clients are medium-sized companies that have anywhere from two to twenty sales-people selling their products or services. Max himself designs a complete marketing plan for such companies and then sees that it's executed properly. He does this by working with the client company's marketing directors or sales managers on a continuing-fee basis.

To get new business, Max runs seminars in the greater Minneapolis area. He is not interested in making money from the seminars (his fees are modest); he conducts them to drum up business for his consulting firm.

The next scheduled seminar is on "Effective Sales Training." Max himself has been heavily involved in the preparations; he has put together an attractive workbook and supplements to hand out to attendees. Max hopes that this seminar will bring in a great deal of new business.

Max particularly hopes that Bob Doyle, the president of a very progressive local advertising firm, will attend. However, Bob was turned off by the aggressive tactics of Max Berenbaum's salesperson Marian Cartwright, when she tried to sell him on the idea of attending the last seminar six months ago. Although Marian is generally professional and usually successful in her attempts to sell Max's seminars, Bob Doyle was not amused by her efforts. He told Marian she was not welcome in his office.

Max does not hold anything against Marian for her aggressiveness. Nevertheless, he is still interested in procuring Bob Doyle's firm as an account and wants his organization represented at this upcoming seminar.

- What can Max do to placate Mr. Doyle?
- Should Marian Cartwright be kept out of any future contacts with Bob Doyle? Why or why not?
- How could Marian herself go about establishing a good relationship with Mr. Doyle?
- Are all salespeople who offend prospects unprofessional? Defend your answer.

11 Answering Objections

OBJECTIVES

In this chapter you will learn:

- Why objections are a routine (and welcome) part of the sales process.
- How to tell the difference between an objection and an excuse, a valid and an invalid objection.
- How to recognize the three kinds of valid objections.
- How to answer objections effectively.
- What part attitude plays in this phase of the sales process.

Mary Martinez works for an advertising agency in Chicago. She is the account executive for a large travel agency account. An excellent worker, she is a valuable asset to the agency.

Mary travels a great deal, partly for pleasure and partly to get a feel for the market her account is trying to reach.

On this particular day, Mary has taken an extra long lunch hour to go shopping. She is looking for a navy blue blazer to go with several skirts that are already in her wardrobe. Mary feels the combination will be perfect for fall traveling.

She walks into an exclusive women's store on Michigan Avenue and is immediately captivated by two blue blazers hanging on a rack. Her budget, however, will not stretch to accommodate the more expensive one, even though she likes it better. The less expensive one is made of worsted wool, which is both serviceable and comfortable. However, her eye keeps returning to the cashmere blazer, which is soft and luxurious. Cashmere doesn't wrinkle as much as worsted. It is ideal for travel. The only drawback is the price. She finally motions to Miss Johnson, the nearest salesperson, and asks her several questions about the two blazers. As every question is answered, she comes to the conclusion that she really must have the cashmere blazer for her wardrobe.

Miss Johnson does not press the issue. It seems that Mary is going to have to make this decision on her own. Suddenly, Mary gets that funny feeling in her stomach, the same feeling she always gets when she feels pressured.

So what does Mary do? She says to Miss Johnson, "Thank you very much for your time. I want to think this over. I'll drop by next week."

Smiling, Miss Johnson says, "Do you mind if I ask you a question before you go?"

"No, go ahead," says Mary.

"Well, in the first place you agree you really need a blue blazer, isn't that right?"

"Yes, I do."

"Second, I think we both agree that the cashmere is the one you should buy, isn't that correct?"

"Definitely."

"But apparently the cost is all that stands between you and possession of that fine jacket. Am I correct?"

"Yes. I just cannot afford it right now."

After asking leading questions to help Mary get in a yes mood, Miss Johnson decides to use a mirror response in an attempt to influence Mary to buy the more expensive one now. So she says, "Mary, if I read you correctly, you are saying that you can't afford the higher price right now for the cashmere blazer."

"That's right."

Now Miss Johnson turns the objection around to her advantage, stresses the benefits, and closes the sale. She concludes, "Well, the very reason you should purchase this blazer is that it will save you dollars in the long run. Because it sheds wrinkles so quickly, you will not have to send it out to be pressed every time you unpack it. The soft texture not only feels more comfortable but projects an image of prosperity and good taste. Besides, there is something about wearing the best that improves your self-confidence."

Mary nods agreement. Miss Johnson continues. "Look, we can put this on your revolving charge account. That way you can walk out of the store with it."

Mary smiles but says nothing.

"Let's have alterations take a look at it," says Miss Johnson. "I think the sleeves may be a tad too long." As they walk together toward the back of the store, Mary feels good; she's excited about her new purchase; she can't wait to wear it. She pulls out her charge plate and hands it to Miss Johnson.

What can we learn from this story? We saw that when it got right down to decision-making time, Mary became very nervous about buying the more expensive blazer, mainly because she thought it was beyond her budget. But the salesperson knew full well that most budgets can be adjusted to accommodate special purchases. So the salesperson stressed the product's benefits and influenced Mary to buy it.

But why didn't Mary feel comfortable about making the decision to buy? Psychological studies offer some insight. Many purchases, even insignificant ones, change a person's life. With Mary, the purchase will mean a temporary adjustment to her budget. The change might make her uncomfortable, might interrupt her sense of security. Thus, she attempted to head off this threat to her well-being by saying, "I want to think this over."

The salesperson helped Mary make a buying decision by answering her objections, thus neutralizing her uncomfortable feelings.

The major point of the tale of Mary and the blazer is that objections are a natural part of the sales process. Experienced salespeople look for objections and neutralize them where feasible. They are worried to death when their sales talk evokes no response. No response at all, no interest at all, no objections at all usually mean that the prospect is not only not sold but not even interested in buying.

OBJECTIONS ARE A NORMAL PART OF THE SALES PROCESS

Because prospects are normally reluctant to make decisions, they generally bring up objections during the sales process. Very few professional salespeople expect to go into any sales situation without meeting some initial resistance. In fact, sales objections are a normal—and welcome—part of the sales process. Most objections indicate one of two things: the prospect needs more information about the product or the prospect is reluctant to make a buying decision because of some special circumstance.

So, salespeople should have a very positive attitude about answering objections in the sales process. They should realize that objections are the essential ingredient to making a sale of any kind because they reveal how a prospect is thinking and feeling.

THE DIFFERENCE BETWEEN AN OBJECTION AND AN EXCUSE

Objections arise from confusion, interest, need for further information, or reluctance to buy. (Persistent objections might be due to the salesperson's failure to follow the Need-Formula theory outlined in Chapter 9. If so, the salesperson must go back to the point of failure and start over. This point is usually the desire stage.) Excuses are generally attempts on the part of the prospect to avoid being involved in the sales presentation at all.

For example, if a prospect says, "I simply cannot see you today or next week—maybe sometime after the first of the year," she is making an excuse. For reasons peculiar to herself, the prospect simply does not want to become involved in a sales presentation at that time. The only way to counter an excuse is with a statement such as, "Mrs. Jones, I know you are busy, and you probably have seen too many salespeople in the last month. However, because you are a busy person, I am sure that you would like to know about my product. I can show it to you in a very short time. It could relieve some of the pressures on you and save you time in the long run. You can then turn your attention to other things in your business." If that doesn't work, you should either drop the customer or call back at a more convenient time.

RULES FOR ANSWERING OBJECTIONS

There are certain rules for answering objections. The most important of them are listed below:

- Listen sincerely as the objection is made by the prospect.
- Maintain eye contact.
- Let the prospect express the objection over and over again until he feels that he has really communicated it to you.

- Indicate by nodding and by paraphrasing to assure the prospect that you understand the objection.

- Think before giving your answer to the objection, making sure it is a reasonable and proper answer.

- Answer the objection fully and completely.

- Try to personalize your answers.

- Immediately return the focus to the order blank by asking for a decision on a minor point.

Suppose, for example, that a salesperson is trying to sell an industrial conveyor belt to a large steel fabricator. This is the third interview, and the close is at hand. Many of the prospect's previous objections have been dealt with satisfactorily, and the salesperson is ready to begin writing the order when suddenly the prospect says, "This is a big decision we are making. I think I'd like to discuss it a little more with my staff before we place the order."

The salesperson looks the customer in the eye and nods while the prospect continues to hedge. The salesperson then paraphrases the objection by saying, "Now, as I understand it, you want to think about it a little bit, is that correct?"

With that, the customer says, "Yes, I want to think about it. There are just a few things here that I feel merit some further discussion with the staff before making the final decision."

Meanwhile, the salesperson maintains eye contact, nodding to indicate understanding of the point. The prospect feels that the salesperson really understands his need to talk to his staff.

A customer who does not feel that a salesperson is sympathetic to his objections generally sets up a communication barrier that makes it pointless to continue the sales process. An experienced salesperson does not let that happen. He remains sympathetic as he tries to discover any hidden objections.

"Well, Joe, is there something you don't understand about the conveyor? I think you know how it works. We have discussed the fact that it's practically maintenance free. We have discussed the fact that the rollers with the ball-bearing assemblies should last for at least 20 years with very little maintenance. You understand all of that, don't you?"

"Yes," says Joe. "I understand all of that. It's just that I feel I really am not quite ready to make the decision today."

Now it's obvious that there's a hidden reason for the delay. The salesperson continues: "Well, Joe, it's difficult for me to figure out exactly why it is that you don't want to go ahead. You seem to understand all about the belt. You like it. You can afford it. And, you know that you need it. For some reason, and probably a very valid one, you have a feeling that you cannot go ahead today. Is there something you feel you can tell me so that I can at least try to respond to your objection?" The salesperson's tone of voice is gentle, not harsh.

At this stage, Joe might look at the salesperson and say, "Well, as a matter of fact, I was just talking to Mr. Smith today, and he said, 'Before you make any final decision on this belt, I sure want to see it. I know I told you in the past you could go ahead, but now I want to talk to you about it in view of some budget cuts we have to deal with.'"

By answering the objection properly and by thinking it through fully, the salesperson has finally gotten at the real hidden reason for not going ahead—because there have been some budgetary reconsiderations. Now, the salesperson can address himself to a valid objection.

THERE ARE ONLY THREE VALID OBJECTIONS

There are only three valid objections for anybody not purchasing a particular product or service after the proper groundwork, approach, and presentation have been made. An objection is called valid when it is impossible to overcome—in other words, when it arises from one of the three circumstances that preclude the possibility of a sale.

- **"I don't need it."**   A perfectly valid objection, and one that professional salespeople understand and respect. But sometimes prospects do not always know what they need. Competent salespeople recognize this. Every day they help prospects uncover hidden needs. For example, a word-processing department may have a machine that is not working as well as it should. The supervisor realizes the machine is inadequate, but she thinks it would be too much trouble to lobby for a replacement. Then, lo and behold, a salesperson comes along and shows her that there is a product that will not only overcome the shortcomings of the deficient word processor, but is more efficient than all the other word processors in the department. The superviser now decides that she needs a new word processor. You now have a sales situation. It happens every day.

- **"I can't afford it."**   If a person cannot actually afford the product involved, salespeople are squandering their time visiting with them. The best thing to do in such cases is to try to ascertain when money will be available and set up a date for a return call at that time.

Industrial salespeople know that the end of the fiscal year is a poor time to make sales. Budgeted funds have run out, and there is no way that a company can buy even needed equipment. Hence, professional salespeople set up a lot of their sales interviews immediately after the beginning of a new fiscal year, when the "cannot afford" objection is less likely to be heard.

- **"I won't buy from you."** The final valid objection to buying is that, for some reason, the customer won't buy from a particular salesperson or manufacturer. In many situations, the personality of the salesperson clashes with that of the customer, and they have a difficult time getting together. Clues that might help reveal this circumstance:

The prospect has no apparent interest in the presentation. He looks away, leans back with arms folded.

The prospect continually interrupts the presentation.

The prospect challenges every statement made by the salesperson.

Some talented salespeople relish the experience of selling to customers who are "tough nuts to crack." To get through that wall, that defense, that defiance, and isolate a need—and eventually close the sale—is like winning an Academy Award.

There are many "I won't buy from you" situations that have nothing to do with personality conflicts. For example, top management may have made a commitment to buy office supplies from a particular company. Or perhaps the decision-maker has a special rapport with a particular salesperson and buys only from his or her company.

In some cases, it is a credit to the salesperson who locks up a particular customer so that the customer will not buy from anybody else, no matter what price or service is offered by a competitor. But there is a time bomb ticking away here, too. Salespeople enjoying such relationships must not take them for granted. Many such arrangements turn sour because the salesperson involved fails to keep customers informed of product and service changes or price changes, all of which are constantly occurring.

Thus, there are only three valid objections to buying (See Figure 11-1). The prospect (1) does not need the product, (2) cannot afford it, or (3) does not want to buy from a particular salesperson or manufacturer. Good salespeople are quick to recognize valid objections and to move on to greener pastures when they encounter them.

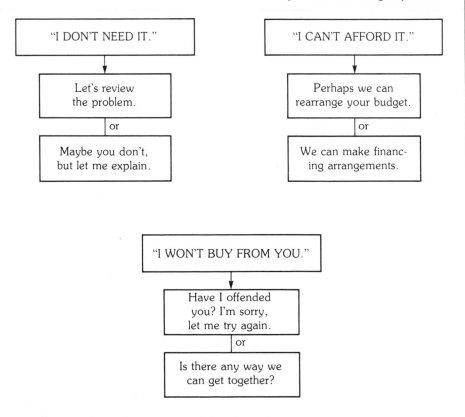

Figure 11–1. The Three Valid Objections and Strategies to Overcome Them (when possible)

INVALID OBJECTIONS

All objections other than the three mentioned above are invalid objections. (Invalid objections are those that can be overcome.) If the salesperson has made a professional and proper presentation, invalid objections should not stand in the way of closing the sale. In fact, as mentioned earlier, they can actually help the sale. At best, invalid objections are usually strong buying signals. At worst, they are only expressions of reluctance to buy. The prospect is simply saying to the salesperson, "I'm not quite ready to buy yet. If you can answer my objection, I will go ahead."

Here are typical invalid objections found in the normal sales process:

- "I want to think about it."
- "How do I know yours is the best company?"
- "How do I know your product is the best one?"
- "Will you call me in a couple of months?"
- "Do you mind if I check with some other companies?"
- "I'm not ready to buy today."
- "I want to talk it over with management."
- "I don't like to rush decisions like this."
- "I don't really understand the service you're offering."
- "Will your service be adequate?"

These objections are buying signals. They are telling the salesperson that the prospect is definitely interested, but that a particular objection must be dealt with first. Of course, it is here that professional salespeople demonstrate their developed techniques to overcome objections.

ANSWERING OBJECTIONS EFFECTIVELY

One of the earmarks of professional salespeople is their inventory of effective methods of answering routine objections. But even these methods will not work unless salespeople are able to convey to the prospect that they understand the objection. This is the key to becoming a good closer—listening carefully to the prospect's objection and responding to it with courtesy and interest.

The ability to listen attentively can be developed by sharpening your listening skills. You learn to convey to the prospect that you are listening by body language and eye contact. Salespeople must also discipline themselves to listen carefully to the objection. Merely giving the appearance of listening is not enough. Many sales have been lost because of a failure either to listen to the prospect's objections or to convey to the prospect that his objections were being listened to. Chapter 13 explores listening skills in depth.

Only when listening skills have been mastered are salespeople ready to answer the objections. Here are several proven techniques in answering objections. They are not listed in any special order of importance.

The Mirror Response

The salesperson does not repeat verbatim what the prospect has just said. He or she captures the substance or the form of the prospect's statement in paraphrase. "As I understand you, Mr. Prospect, you are saying that . . ." or "Correct me if I'm wrong, but did you say that you don't understand the service requirements of this machine? If I read you correctly, you are saying you are concerned about the maintenance costs. Is that correct?" (An answer to the latter point about maintenance costs might be, "The maintenance costs may be high, but that's because we use highly skilled service people in this work. In the long run, they will save you money because when they repair something it stays repaired for a long time.")

The "Yes, But" Method

The salesperson introduces a point that challenges the prospect's objection—but only after affirming a point of agreement. Salespeople do not like to contradict anything a customer says. There is no point in winning the battle and losing the war. Therefore, although the salesperson actually challenges the prospect's statement, he first neutralizes the contradiction. For example, "Yes, I can understand why you feel that this paper is too expensive for your copying machine. But research indicates that a lighter paper will not last in permanent records, and the picture will actually begin to fade in later years." Or, "Yes, I know this policy is more expensive than that of Ajax Company, but having our claim service located in your area will ensure more rapid claim service."

The Boomerang Method

The salesperson cites the very reason for the objection as the reason for buying the product. Thus the objection boomerangs back on the customer. For example, a customer might say, "Business is really slow now, and we are trying to tighten up on budget matters. And even though I told you we could afford to buy this machine, I feel that in view of our current business situation, we should not go ahead with this fabricating unit right now."

The boomerang answer to that would be, "Well, I can understand why you're concerned, Mr. Prospect. But have you thought that a slowdown might be the very reason you should buy the fabricating machine now. With the features we have shown you, you will be able to fabricate the same kind of steel products; only they will be of higher quality. And this, of course, should help you recover from your off year."

The Question Method

The salesperson counters the objection of the customer by asking questions. The questions should never be intimidating or designed to confuse the prospect. Let's assume that a prospect is objecting to buying a pair of shoes because they cost a lot more than the prospect thinks they should. She objects with, "I really think these are just too expensive for me to buy today." Here is how the salesperson might respond:

SALESPERSON	Mrs. Prospect, what you're saying is that you would like to buy a cheaper product. Is that right?
PROSPECT	Yes.
SALESPERSON	And, I think you would be the first to agree that you usually get what you pay for. Don't you agree?
PROSPECT	Yes, I do.
SALESPERSON	I feel that we would also both agree that our feet are very important to our health, our attitude, and our performance, and so should be well taken care of. Isn't that right?
PROSPECT	Yes, you're correct.
SALESPERSON	So, in the long run, paying a little more today will save you money because these shoes will far outlast a cheaper pair. Don't you agree?
PROSPECT	I guess you're right.

The Counterpoint Method

This is a good way to counter a customer's statement that a competitor's product has more favorable features. The salesperson admits to the truth of the statement and then counters the effect.

For example, a customer might object to buying your copying machine because she has heard that a competitor is coming out with a better one. Your answer could be something along this line: "Mrs. Jones, I understand your feelings, and I know that the Ajax Company's machine will duplicate material on both sides, and that it's much faster than ours. I also understand the price will be a bit higher. But, the features you mentioned are not useful in your business at the present time. As we discussed before, you rarely need to have both sides of the paper copied.

And second, the fact that it will guarantee a rapid, high-volume production of copies really doesn't apply in your organization. You've told me yourself you do not need to have numerous copies of the items you reproduce.

The "Can't Be Perfect" Method

"How do I know your company is the best company?" The salesperson responds that his company may truly not be the best company at all times, in all ways. But then, what company is? Often this is an effective way of answering the objection because most people have an innate suspicion of anyone who claims to be the best at everything.

Here's how a salesperson might respond to a typical customer objection: "Well, Mr. Prospect, I don't claim that our company is the best. If our company were the absolute best at everyting, we wouldn't have any competitors. In fact, competition is the best friend you have—it leads to better and better products. No, my company is not perfect, but we can certainly try to offer you the best service available and as good a product as you can find anywhere else on the market."

The Third-Party Method

Sometimes, when a prospect voices a particularly strong objection, the salesperson does not try to counter it directly. Instead he tries to neutralize it by mentioning other people who have used his product or service. In a typical case, the customer says, "Look, we are only a medium-size law firm, and we don't need your particular tax service for the type of business we have."

The salesperson might answer: "Well, I can understand the thinking behind that, but Miller and Smith across the street are about the same size law firm, and they believe this tax service is one of the most valuable services they have ever purchased. Because they are small, they do not have the staff to do the research we can provide."

All these methods for handling objections, then, are things that salespeople use every day. It keeps them current and competent. Keeping a file of answers to objections is one of the most productive things salespeople can do. They continually accumulate answers to objections, and review them periodically—particularly as they prepare to close sales.

You can find sample answers to objections in most sales training manuals. Conventions, seminars, and workshops on proven sales skills are another fruitful source.

USING ANECDOTES
TO OVERCOME OBJECTIONS

A picture is frequently worth a thousand words in a sales situation. So, too, is the anecdote, a picture created by words. In fact, anecdotes, when used with tact and restraint, can be highly effective in overcoming objections.

We are not talking about the "rolling up the hearse" method that is a great favorite with unscrupulous life insurance salespeople. These salespeople try to intimidate people into buying insurance by painting graphic pictures of the breadwinner dying and his widow and orphans losing their savings, their home, and ultimately their respectability.

A properly told anecdote helps the customer visualize the benefits of a product. A good anecdote can have a positive influence on a customer's decision to buy.

Evelyn Guidon is having her third interview with Becky Sorenson, the administrative manager of a large medical clinic in suburban Fort Worth. Evelyn, the clinic's interior decorator, is trying to sell the clinic seven framed prints for the patients' waiting room.

It is time to close the sale. The need has been established, the price is right, and Ms. Sorenson has no objection to doing business with Evelyn. As Evelyn starts to write the order, Ms. Sorenson says, "Evelyn, why don't you come back next Monday after five and I'll write you a check then." After listening intently to the objection, Evelyn decides an anecdote might lead to a sale.

So she says something like, "You know, Becky, I can understand why you're a bit reluctant to sign the order today. After all, this is a substantial purchase, and these pictures will be here for a long time. But visualize what these pictures will mean to your patients. Their bright colors will lighten their spirits. Their pleasant scenes will calm their anxieties. Their beauty will take their minds off their ailments, and isn't that what we are trying to achieve here—a feeling of welcome and comfort that will take their minds off their troubles?"

ATTITUDE IS IMPORTANT

It doesn't matter how skillfully a salesperson answers objections, if he doesn't have the proper attitude, he will not make the sale. Good salespeople know if there is anything that will alienate a customer, it is a superior attitude. Thus, the salesperson's attitude as he answers objections should be geared toward gaining the prospect's respect by a display of confidence, helpfulness, and empathy.

The importance of a good attitude is perhaps best exemplified by the following anecdote. A successful life insurance salesman was the subject of an article written several years ago. The author of the article interviewed the people this agent had sold policies to in one particular plant. Top executives, middle-managers, supervisors, and nonmanagerial employees were on the list. Each made the same response to the question, "Do you feel you are more intelligent than this agent?" All of them answered yes. This particular salesperson was obviously doing his job.

SUMMARY

This chapter discussed one of the most important aspects of the sales process—answering objections. Objections are not only a normal but a desirable part of the sales process. In fact, a person who is quiet and does not make any objections is less likely to be a potential buyer.

There is a difference between an objection and an excuse. An excuse is usually an attempt to put off the sales presentation altogether, whereas an objection frequently indicates interest and is often a signal that the prospect is ready to buy.

After presenting guidelines for answering objections, the text discussed the three valid objections to buying: (1) the product is not needed; (2) the prospect can't afford it; (3) the customer, for one reason or another, will not buy from a particular salesperson. All other objections are invalid, that is, they present no true obstacle to closing the sale. Next, there was a review of techniques for answering objections. It was stressed that these techniques are effective only if the salesperson is a good listener.

Anecdotes may also be used to answer objections. Used skillfully, they can have a positive influence on a decision to buy.

Finally, the chapter closed with a discussion of the importance of attitude in the answering-objections phase of the sales process. Salespeople should treat their prospects with respect.

The whole area of answering objections is a vital part of the sales process. Superior sales results are usually in direct proportion to the skill with which objections are answered.

KEY TERMS

Boomerang Method

Can't Be Perfect Method

Counterpoint Method

Invalid Objections

Mirror Response

Question Method

Third-Party Method

Valid Objections

"Yes, But" Method

REVIEW QUESTIONS

- Explain the difference between an objection and an excuse.
- What is an *invalid objection*?
- Why do salespeople welcome objections?
- What objections are not buying signals?

DISCUSSION TOPICS

- List the rules for answering objections.
- Why is it important for a good salesperson to accumulate an objections file?
- How can anecdotes help in the sales process?
- What is meant by being humble in the answering of objections in the sales interview?
- There is a fine line between humility and insincerity. Explain.
- Do you agree that there are only three valid objections to buying? Can you think of any other possibilities?

EXERCISES

1. With another student, role play the answering-objections phase of the sales process. You are the salesperson. Ask your fellow students to comment on your performance and to vote on whether or not they think you will close the sale.

2. Write out three motivating anecdotes that could be used in response to a prospect's sales objection. (You are selling hot tubs.)

3. Demonstrate the question method of answering objections in front of your classmates. Ask them for criticism.

You are a salesperson for an American manufacturer of quartz digital watches. You are attending the regular morning sales meeting presided over by your sales manager. You have had a fairly good week, but you lost a big potential sale at a department store in your territory.

In reviewing your sales report, the sales manager mentions that you should have used some kind of third-party influence by relating an anecdote about another customer who bought your product and was satisfied with it. One such anecdote you could have used, your manager says, is the one about the Japanese customer who found that your watch not only kept better time than the Japanese import product he was wearing, but was cheaper and more attractive.

The sales manager then asks you why you didn't use a third-party story to help you close the sale. He feels that if the buyer had had some evidence that other people had been satisfied with your line of watches, the department store probably would have bought your product. Your response is that you don't really need to rely on such stories to make sales.

Richard Price, one of the top salespeople in the organization, disagrees. He feels that anecdotes have a positive influence on customer buying desions. They are similar to the effect drama and showmanship have in the sales process.

- Do you agree with Price? Why or why not?
- Do you feel it violates privacy or confidential relationships if you do use true anecdotes, including names and incidents, without permission?
- If you were the sales manager, what advice would you give your sales staff about using anecdotes?
- Is it possible to be a successful salesperson without using anecdotes? Explain.

Case Study Two

You represent the wire division of a large steel manufacturing company. Last year, your company was cited for giving kickbacks to government officials in order to get defense contracts. The publicity was bad, but your company entered a consent decree in federal court, paid a substantial fine, and agreed never again to engage in such practices. You have been with the company ten years, and your division has never received (or asked for) a contract from the United States Government.

In spite of strong competition from foreign manufacturers, you have always been able to keep your customers by appealing to their sense of patriotism. You have also stressed that although foreign steel is cheaper, your company is able to provide superior service and follow-up.

You are in the process of closing a sale to a large midwestern steel fabricating plant. The company is a strong customer.

The person responsible for purchasing wire obviously has had pressure from his superiors to look into buying lower-priced materials. You feel, too, that the kickback scandal has made it easier for the company to consider dealing with one of your foreign competitors—in this case, a Swedish wire manufacturer.

The purchasing agent is anxious to find an excuse to do business with your competitor. He says to you, "Look, for the past three years I have purchased your product, even though your Swedish counterparts have quoted cheaper prices. Now, with your company's recent involvement in a completely unethical situation of giving kickbacks to the government, I feel obligated to recommend to my superiors that we switch our account from your company to the Swedish company."

Answer his objection using:

- The "Yes, But" method
- The Counterpoint method
- The Third-Party method
- An anecdote

Closing the Sale 12

OBJECTIVES

In this chapter you will learn:

- Why closing starts with the first customer contact.
- How good closers build customer trust and confidence.
- Why it is important to react to the personality of the prospect.
- Why successful closers (1) assume the customer will buy from them, (2) control the sales interview, (3) concentrate on the business at hand, and (4) close as soon as they receive a buying signal.
- How to close by using the alternative-question method.
- How to use four effective closing techniques in any sales situation.

Norman Sanders is the top salesperson for a large national manufacturer of electronic office calculators. He is completing his third interview with Nina Ross, the office manager of a large Big 8 accounting firm in Houston. Norman's involvement in this particular sales situation began when Nina called his company headquarters to ask for a demonstration of its line of calculators. The initial interview and demonstration led to a second in-depth fact-finding interview. In the second interview, Nina told Norman she would like to purchase 12 machines. Nina also told Norman that she would have to discuss the proposed purchase with the managing partner, but that the firm probably would buy. She asked Norman to come back for the third time.

Now, in the third interview, Norman is following his regular closing procedure. The merits of the product have been discussed. He has answered the few objections Nina raised in a satisfactory manner. He now is ready to close the sale.

Over the years, Norman has developed an alternative-question closing procedure that works most of the time. Throughout the interview he keeps an order blank in front of him, and after he successfully answers an objection, he pauses, writes something on the order blank, and then asks the prospect for a decision on a minor point.

We are now at the stage where Norman has answered Nina's last objection, obviously to Nina's satisfaction. Note how Norman actually closes the sale:

". . . For these reasons, I'm sure you can see why these machines will not only meet your needs but will also bring a much higher trade-in price than any other company's machines. Now, as I mentioned earlier, we have only six of these on hand. I know you want twelve. Shall I go ahead and send the six that we have in the warehouse to you now, or do you want me to wait until all twelve come in?"

"I think I'd like to get started as soon as we can, so why don't you go ahead and send me the six?"

"Okay, Nina, I'll do that. Now all you do is sign right here, and give me a check for the down payment. The check should be made out to my company in the amount of $569. The rest of the payment will be due upon delivery of the other machines."

As he says this, Norman leans over and starts to go through some of his papers. He does not want to watch too intently as Nina signs the order, fearing it might in some way interfere with that process. Nina signs the order, leaves the room for a moment, and comes back with a check.

Norman thanks her for the business and assures her she has made a wise decision. He promises delivery within the week. He leaves promptly. Usually, good salespeople leave as soon as the close is made because they know their client is busy with other things. Also, they do not want to open the door to any further discussion that might eventually nullify the sale.

Norman is simply following a procedure that has worked for him in the past. He answers all objections and then closes by getting an affirmative response on some minor matter.

Selling is closing. The ability to get the order—to ask for it, to write it up, to get the customer to sign on the dotted line—is the payoff in selling.

And yet, there are sharp, intelligent salespeople who cannot seem to close at all.

They fail because they are not willing to ask for the order. They are afraid of rejection. But, to be successful, one must risk it. A salesperson who understands the nature of rejection, as pointed out in Chapter 6, and puts it in perspective, will not be afraid to ask for the order. In most sales-training seminars, closing is discussed as if it were a separate part of the interview. It isn't. Professionals start closing the first moment they talk to the customer, whether by telephone or in person. Surveys indicate that good closers are successful for two reasons. They rely on proven techniques (acquired by training and experience and polished to perfection) and they have certain behavioral traits in common:

- They radiate excitement throughout the sales process.
- They are sincere, sensitive, and open.
- They are eager to help customers solve problems.
- They develop I/you, rather than I/it relationships with their clients. They treat each client as a unique human being, not just as another customer.
- They seem to project an intense personal interest in the client's problems from the beginning of the sales process.
- They abhor any kind of manipulation.
- Most of all, they enjoy what they are doing.

In addition to the behavioral traits listed above, good closers have other characteristics in common.

- They feel good closers are made, not born.
- They build relationships of trust and confidence with their customers.
- They are good at analyzing and reacting to the personalities of their customers.
- They always assume the customer will buy from them.
- They control the sales interview.
- They concentrate on the business at hand.
- They know why they are effective.
- They close as soon as possible, watching for early buying signals.
- They use (and constantly practice) effective closing techniques.

We will discuss each of the above characteristics in the sections that follow.

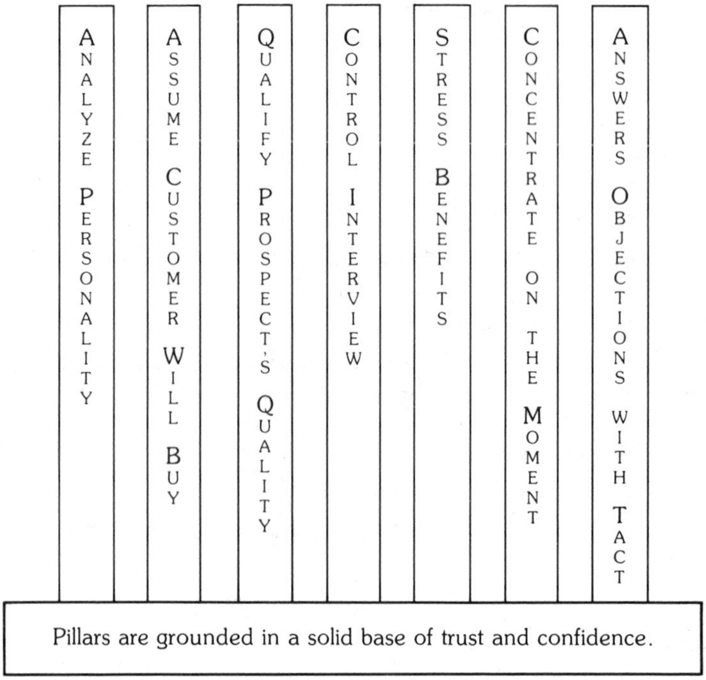

ANALYZE PERSONALITY | ASSUME CUSTOMER WILL BUY | QUALIFY PROSPECT'S QUALITY | CONTROL INTERVIEW | STRESS BENEFITS | CONCENTRATE ON THE MOMENT | ANSWERS OBJECTIONS WITH TACT

Pillars are grounded in a solid base of trust and confidence.

Figure 12–1. Closers Build Solid Foundations

GOOD CLOSERS ARE MADE, NOT BORN

One popular misconception about selling is that salespeople are born, not made. A corollary of this misconception is the stereotype sales- man —the dynamic and personable drummer; the Music Man, selling a dream to a whole town. (No saleswoman stereotype has evolved yet, but her time will no doubt come.) Salespeople are not born any more than engineers, actors, or electricians are born. Success at selling, like success in any career, is the result of training, apprenticeship, and experience.

THEY BUILD TRUST AND CONFIDENCE

Dishonesty heads the list of all the criticisms about salespeople. And sometimes the criticism is justified. Most of us have heard at least one nonprofessional salesperson say something like, "Buy this today, it won't be available tomorrow." This kind of manipulation, which, by the way, is seldom successful, gives selling a bad name. Professional salespeople won't use it. Instead, they build trust with customers by being objective, open, and honest. Eric Fromm, the psychologist, states in his writings that disciplined objectivity is the key to building good or loving relationships between people.[1] Objectivity is also the key to building trust in a sales relationship.

Trust, then, is the foundation for rapport between salespeople and customers—trust in the salesperson, trust in his products, trust in his company's services.

THEY ANALYZE AND REACT
TO THE CUSTOMER'S PERSONALITY

If a salesperson calls on a prospect who has no interest in classical music and proceeds to give him a detailed description of last night's concert on television, that person will probably never build a sales relationship with his prospect.

Good closers study the interests and personality types of their prospects, and put this knowledge to work in the opening moments of the first encounter. They note the prospect's dominant personality tendency. Is he an extrovert or introvert? Is she an Expressive or Amiable?

An intelligent salesperson also tries to discover whether his prospect is a basically positive or negative person. Negative persons may be difficult to sell, but they need products and services as much as positive people. Some enterprising salespeople make successful careers out of selling to negative personalities. They develop the ability to deal with negative people, to understand their problems, to sympathize with their "problems," and to cater to their negatively expressed needs for love and understanding. As a result, such salespeople are able to establish a rapport in a market that few others care to enter.

Effective salespeople learn early in their careers to react to the personality traits of prospects. It takes extreme patience, for example, to deal with someone who is tense. A tense person can be brusque, impatient, unreasonable, and exceptionally negative. The salesperson has to be a good listener, keep the presentation low key, and constantly reassure the prospect, but such behavior can bring wonderful sales results.

Clark Alexander, of Jacksonville, Florida, was a successful coal broker. A tough-talking, no-nonsense businessman, he was able to operate on a thin profit margin because he had a huge volume of business.

[1] Eric Fromm, *The Art of Loving* (New York: Harper and Row, 1956) p. 101.

Alexander was hard to contact, let alone see. Bob Warren, who knew how to work with such people, finally secured an appointment, and after waiting in an outer office for 30 minutes, was ushered in to Alexander's office. Bob introduced himself, sat down, and was just about to begin the sales approach when Alexander said, "Mr. Warren, I don't have much time, so I don't want you to give me your usual pitch. I want you to get on with what you have to say. Besides that, I think all salespeople are sons of . . . ."

Bob, smiling broadly, cut off Alexander by saying very politely, "Mr. Alexander, I resent people insulting my mother." Whereupon Mr. Alexander laughed and said, rather meekly, "I didn't really mean that. It is just that I have a very busy schedule. Okay, what do you want to talk about?"

He became one of Bob Warren's best clients. Bob broke through the veneer that had kept other salespeople away for years. And even though Mr. Alexander is still abrasive, Bob Warren is able to live with it very profitably.

Then there are those who love to put salespeople on trial. They are always trying to interrupt the sales process or to put the salesperson on the defensive. These clients seem to enjoy the discomfort they cause by not responding to sales presentations. Even the best salespeople wonder if it is worthwhile to even talk to such people.

Nevertheless, a salesperson who demonstrates superior knowledge of his product or service, who uses tact and patience, and who makes his approach in a solid and convincing manner can convert some of these prospects. At times, motivational analysis will break this strain of hostile indifference:

"Mr. Prospect, it seems to me that you are continually questioning my motives, as though I am trying to put something over on you. I am not." Or, "You've mentioned several times that your store layout is hurting your sales. You asked me to come up with a reasonably priced design to improve your sales, not mine. Shall we try again?"

How can one object to approaches such as these?

Then there is the silent type. These people seem hardly to react at all. They may simply be preoccupied. Until the salesperson breaks this shield of silence by asking questions or being courteous (for example, encouraging the prospect to talk about himself at length), a working relationship will never be established.

How about sensitive, timid, and quiet persons, who are afraid to make a decision of any kind on their own? They convey the feeling that they have never made decisions of this kind and now is not the time to start. By being gentle, sympathetic, and genuinely helpful, a salesperson can sell these people. Lowering the voice, using more subdued body language, these things tend to open up shy people.

Finally, there are the commonsense customers—the ideal persons to sell. They are usually intelligent, thoughtful, considerate, open to what the salesperson is talking about. The best way to close these customers is to give them exactly what they expect and deserve—good professional selling.

Most productive closers, then, become amateur psychologists. Over the years, they learn through reading, clinics, training, and study, that a failure to understand their client's personality traits may result in a failure to close sales.

A note of caution: Be careful about classifying people too rigidly. Do not rely totally on first impressions. First impressions are not always that reliable, despite the old saw that "a first impression is a lasting one." It is dangerous to categorize anyone. Generally speaking, people are basically alike in their goals and aspirations in life. Good salespeople keep all of these things in mind as they turn that doorknob and enter the prospect's office.

THEY ASSUME THE CUSTOMER WILL BUY FROM THEM

If a successful salesperson has a product that will fill a prospect's need, then he feels certain that the prospect will do business with him. This assumption usually conveys itself to customers, and begins to build the trust and confidence needed to secure a sale and a future client. Thus, in the initial contact with the prospect, by telephone or otherwise, the good closer assumes the customer will buy. This positive attitude is infectious, and often rubs off on the customer. Who wants to do business with someone who is not confident, who is not trustworthy, who is not enthusiastic and excited, who does not know what he is doing? Proven closers, then, just assume the customer will buy from them. To do otherwise would be to court defeat before the session even starts. Furthermore, most good closers are so confident that they are genuinely surprised when people refuse to buy from them.

THEY CONTROL THE SALES INTERVIEW

By Requalifying Prospects

Effective closers do not like to waste time. They know that although it is fun to visit about last night's concert or yesterday's speech by the

President, the basic purpose of the sales interview is to get a sale. Hence, good closers requalify their customers as quickly as possible. As we learned in Chapter 7, qualifying means finding out if a prospect needs, and can afford, the seller's product or service. Closers also want to determine early in the interview whether the customer has any objection to doing business with them personally. If any one of these three valid objections exist, the experienced salesperson cuts the interview short and moves on to the next prospect.

Generally, before leaving, the salesperson will ask for referrals or probe to see if the prospect might be able or willing to buy at some future date. Often the prospect is glad to get off the hook and is more than willing to name some referrals.

By Controlling Digressions

Inexperienced salespeople have a tendency to let the prospect lead them off the sales track by extraneous small talk. Professionals stick to the sales track. The sales track (discussed at length in Chapter 9) offers a permanent way of controlling the interview. Each step must be complete before the next begins. For example, the prospect says, "By the way, that was an interesting comment on the news last evening about the Secretary of State, wasn't it?" The good salesperson will respond with something like, "Yes, it was. I thought it was provocative, and I would like to discuss that with you at a more convenient time. Meanwhile, about this service we were discussing . . ." and swings right back onto the sales track.

The customer here is not necessarily trying to sabotage the interview or the salesperson. It is normal for customers to want to exchange pleasantries. Prospects may want to visit, but good salespeople know that general conversation does not lead to sales. Good closers, then, persist in controlling their interviews from initial contact to product or service delivery.

By Stressing Benefits

At every opportune moment, good closers stress product or service benefits. That is why they are there in the first place, to convince the prospect that their product's benefits will satisfy his expressed needs. For example:

"You say your staff spends too much time typing right now? That is why our word processor would be ideal for you. It would allow your staff to do other things. And, perhaps, a position can even be eliminated."

"Of course, this service costs a lot of money, but your investment counselors will be able to spend less time doing research and more time selling customers, increasing your bottom line."

"This new solar heating system may be costly at first, but over the years, as energy costs rise, you will see your utility bills drop."

"I guess we have been talking about dollars and cents too much here. What this savings plan will really give you is peace of mind and security. Rainy days may come and go, but, with this plan, you will always be prepared."

THEY CONCENTRATE ON THE BUSINESS AT HAND

Competent salespeople develop solid communication skills. One of these is an ability to focus all their concentration on the business at hand. They are able to convey to the customer the feeling that the present interview is the most important interview of their career. They are able to purge their minds of outside thoughts and concentrate entirely on the moment at hand. This concentration pays off handsomely.

Conversely, there is nothing a prospect finds more annoying (and insulting) than a half-hearted sales presentation. The conveyed preoccupation, the communicated desire to get on to the next sale, or a listless going through the motions, are all fatal sales errors that customers perceive very quickly. Yet, so-called salespeople continue to diffuse their concentration and make half-hearted presentations. No wonder they fail.

THEY KNOW WHY THEY ARE EFFECTIVE

Knowing why they are effective, and what closing techniques actually work best for them, is another earmark of productive salespeople. They know their strengths and avoid their weaknesses. They know when and why they are at their best. They know, for example, that if they are particularly skillful at closing over lunch, they should schedule closing luncheon interviews every day.

They evaluate their closing techniques constantly, always looking for more effective ways to write their orders. They keep learning and growing. They know which market is best for them and what type of person buys from them most frequently.

If a salesperson learns from experience that a particular technique works in a given situation, he will use that technique every time. For example, most salespeople make sure that the customer sees them handling the order blank in the closing interview. It signals to the customer that they expect to close the sale momentarily. Most salespeople use good body language and eye contact. They learn when to smile, when to be still. They know themselves well.

Professional golfer Tom Watson practices endlessly because he wants to develop the perfect golf swing. This is a goal he knows cannot be reached; but in the process, he will win many tournaments.

Attend any sales convention; you will not be surprised to find that when salespeople get together, they spend most of their time exchanging ideas on how to improve their techniques. Even experienced professionals never stop learning. As they get older, they continually try to improve as a matter of personal pride, of personal dedication to their profession.

THEY UNDERSTAND HUMAN MOTIVATION

No one can honestly motivate anyone else to buy anything. This is one of the great myths of selling, and it is just that—a myth. People must motivate themselves to buy. Successful salespeople recognize this.

A customer who is pressured to sign an order blank before he is ready will probably not buy. This is manipulation. It is unethical (and ultimately unprofitable) to try to bully people into buying.

Professional closers have a whole library of techniques and motivating anecdotes to call on when they feel the customer needs help in motivating himself. In the last chapter, you saw how Evelyn Guidon used a motivating anecdote to sell her framed prints to a buyer who was having second thoughts at closing.

THEY CLOSE AS SOON AS POSSIBLE

Salespeople learn early in their careers that as soon as a customer seems ready to buy, they should try to close the sale. A buying signal should be followed immediately by a trial close. Successful salespeople develop a sixth sense that helps them recognize buying signals. So they stop the presentation process and attempt a trial close by saying something like, "Ms. Prospect, are you willing to sign the order if I can get you a favorable trade-in on your present copier?" If the response is positive, then the sale has been made. If it is not, then the salesperson returns to the presentation. No harm has been done.

Surprisingly there are customers ready to buy when the salesperson walks in the door. They may have already made up their minds to buy and will respond positively to a trial close.

Trial closes are routine for good salespeople. Most orders are written on the fourth or fifth try. Hence, professionals realize they are probably going to have to attempt three or four closes before they write that order. It is standard operating procedure. Unfortunately, new salespeople have a tendency to try only one close. When that fails, rather than risk rejection, they give up and leave. Experience usually overcomes this problem.

Years ago, people believed a sale could only be closed at the "psychological moment," the precise instant that everything came together and meshed perfectly. The salesperson who missed the psychological moment did not make a sale.

Today, salespeople know there is no single moment, psychological or otherwise, to close a sale. Rather, there are several times during the sales interview when it could be closed. Apt salespeople recognize these moments and act quickly. (See Figure 12-2.)

Rosalie Conrad is calling on a local travel agent in Chicago to solicit an advertisement for the *Chicago Business Executive* magazine. She is ushered into Peter Gillingham's office, and he motions her to sit down as he completes a telephone call. Peter owns the agency.

Rosalie has called on Mr. Gillingham before, and he has always refused to buy an ad on the grounds that it would not do much good for his agency. Peter feels that he has built a word-of-mouth reputation as a top-notch travel agency for executives. He has plenty of business, has moved to bigger quarters, hired a larger staff, and, as a matter of fact, is eager to cut expenses.

Rosalie knows this, because when she called Peter for an appointment, he went over this very specifically, repeating his contention that "I am not in the market for any advertising, Rosalie, but come on over anyway. I'll be glad to see you." Rosalie comes because she feels he is worth developing for future business.

As soon as Rosalie sits down, Peter hangs up the telephone. Rosalie tries to sell him an advertisement one more time. After all, she reasons, what harm can it do? And someday he will buy.

She starts the attention (small talk) phase with, "I'm impressed with your new quarters." They exchange pleasantries about his office.

As she begins to move toward the interest phase by talking about her magazine's new Series III ad promotion, he interrupts her with, "Rosalie, what would a one-quarter page ad in your January issue cost me?"

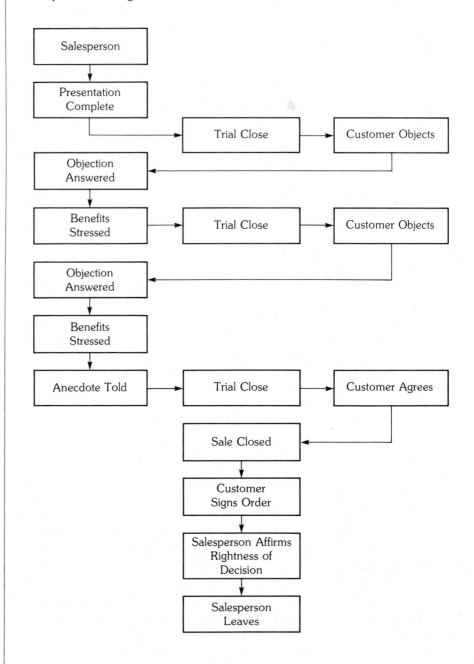

Figure 12–2. Closing the Sale

Bang! Right out of nowhere, a strong buying signal jumps out at Rosalie. She quickly responds, "If you ran it once, $325; twice, $300; and three times, $275 each."

"I want it once," he says.

"That will be $325," she counters.

Rosalie confidently pulls out an advertisement contract from her briefcase, since his "I want it once" comment means to her he is buying right now. "Do I work with you or your administrative assistant on the copy?" she says, presenting Peter with a decision on a minor point that she hopes will close the sale.

"Oh, I guess we'll both sort of work on it."

"Okay," says Rosalie. "If you'll just sign here, I can get right on it. We don't have too much time before our January deadline."

Peter signs the order and the sale is made.

What happened here? Why did Peter Gillingham, who had been so negative about advertising in the past, agree to buy an ad in Rosalie's magazine? What happened was that between Rosalee's telephone call and her appointment, Peter attended a travel agency seminar. There, the president of one of the most successful executive travel agencies in the country said it was a must for a growing travel agency to advertise regularly in the most prestigious business magazine in the area, citing several statistics to make his point.

Not every buying signal will be as strong as the one Peter gave to Rosalie, but she displayed adroitness by immediately moving to the close. Peter had made his mind up; he wanted that advertisement and wanted to sign the order immediately.

New salespeople often fail to recognize buying signals. Experience often spells the difference. It takes time to learn to recognize them. Sometimes they are blatant, out in the open, in the form of a question like, "When can I get this?" Sometimes they are more subtle. Often they are misinterpreted. What salespeople might think are buying signals may not be signals at all. For example, the customer who shifts his body and leans forward may be doing so simply to become more comfortable.

Buying signals fall into two broad categories—verbal and physical. Some examples of verbal buying signals are

- Maybe I want another color.
- I think that's what I have in mind.
- It would work well around here.
- We really need this machine.

- When could you deliver one to me?
- May I pay for this by the month?
- What does your service warranty say?

Physical buying signals also tell the salesperson that the customer is ready to buy. Some examples are

- Making notes on what the salesperson is saying
- Leaning forward in the chair excitedly
- Smiling
- Picking up a pen
- Agreeing with your comments by nodding the head in "Yes" fashion
- Touching the salesperson

These are just a few of the signals that prospects may telegraph at any time during the interview. Resourceful salespeople watch closely for signals, stop everything, and immediately try to close. Many sales have been lost by a failure to react instinctively to a buying signal.

As mentioned in Chapter 11, "Answering Objections," objections are sometimes buying signals, too. "Why can't I get this item this month instead of next month?" or "Why don't you let me think it over, and then we will see." These kinds of objections also can be interpreted as buying signals, but objections must be answered before the sale can be closed.

THEY USE EFFECTIVE CLOSING TECHNIQUES

Since most sales are made on the fourth or fifth try, salespeople try to close at least five times before giving up. To help them, they rely on certain physical props. For example:

- An order blank requiring a signature or date
- A contract requiring a signature or date
- A receipt with the amount of dollars to be filled in
- A warranty contract requiring the initials of the customer
- A certificate of title to be initialed or dated
- Other appropriate documents—such as a proposal—to be initialed or signed as authority to write the order

These props are kept in broad view throughout the entire closing interview. In Rosalie's case, she was caught by surprise and had to reach into her briefcase for a contract. But most salespeople keep them close at hand and use them to record the responses to the alternative questions they ask their prospects in an attempt to close. Here are some examples of alternate questions asking for a decision on a minor point:

- Shall I order one or two dozen?
- Shall we make the effective date today or on delivery?
- Do you want to pay me now or later?
- Do you want to give me cash or a check?
- Shall we put this in your name or your company's?

The answer is always written down and the document handed to the prospect for initialing, signing, dating, or whatever.

There is a wrong way to do this, too. For example, if a salesperson is trying to sell a new cold medicine to a clinic, and the purchasing manager emits a buying signal such as "How soon can you get me this product?", the salesperson might answer with, "Well, although it's a very popular item, I can ensure delivery in three weeks. Would that be OK?" This leaves the customer open to say yes or no, which most salespeople feel is asking for trouble. The customer is being asked to make a decision to buy without the salesperson's help. Perhaps, the best action to take in such situations is to respond to the buying signal by asking some minor alternative question, such as:

CUSTOMER   How soon can you get me this product?

SALESPERSON I think we can get it for you in two weeks. (Pause) Now, do you want me to go ahead and deliver it to you in person, or may I just drop it off with the ffice manager? (or) Do you want to go ahead and order three gross of these, or shall we just start out with half that number?

A question that does not give the customer an opportunity to state whether he will buy or not, but merely asks him to state a preference on some minor detail, is important here. Proficient salespeople use this technique constantly because they know that prospective buyers rarely say, "Yes, I'll buy it." Prospects don't want to concede defeat, to admit that they have been sold. Some prospects look upon a sales interview as psychological warfare. The wise salesperson permits them to save face. So, the more salespeople can avoid this kind of confrontation, the better. And they do so by using an order blank, an application, or similar prop as a vehicle for recording the customer's decision on a minor matter. But this decision is often the thing that cinches the sale. (The case study that follows this chapter examines this procedure in detail.)

Proven Closing Techniques

The assumptive close. The salesperson assumes that the prospect will buy from him. His attitude conveys confidence in a successful outcome throughout the entire sales process. At the appropriate moment, the salesperson might say, "Do you want this delivered this month or next?" or "Whom do I see to get a check?"

The summary-of benefits close. After completing the presentation the salesperson summarizes the benefits, then asks for the order. "So, as I said, Mr. Prospect, this life insurance policy will create an estate value of $50,000 in case of your death. If you live, it will provide over five hundred dollars a month income, if you choose, at age 65. In the meantime, through your accumulated policy values, you have cash available for emergencies. Now, would you care to have the examination for this made here or at the doctor's office?"

The impending-event close. "Mrs. Prospect, on July 31, the price on this machine will increase. It is now June 15. If you sign the order today, we can process the sale before July 31, saving you over $150. It makes sense to act now, doesn't it? Fine, now do you want to pay for it fully today or make a down payment?"

The offer-of-premium close. "We are having a special on our tax service for the month of February. If your law firm buys it during this month, we will give you this free *Estate Planning Guide* as a special incentive. Now, do you want me to set aside one of these for you today?"

Much more important than the actual closing technique used is the way it is used. Remember, always ask for a decision on a minor point. If you look again at the above closings, you will note that in each instance, the customer was asked, not whether or not he wanted the product, but to make a decision on an alternative matter.

SUMMARY

This chapter began with the statement that good closers start to close the minute they come into contact with their prospects. Contrary to popular opinion, closers are made, not born. They have integrity (and therefore earn the trust and confidence of their customers), are students of human nature, and are confident that people will buy from them.

They control the sales interview, by requalifying prospects, controlling digressions, and stressing product benefits. They have a capacity for focusing their attention on the business at hand and for understanding human motivation. A professional salesperson learns to recognize buying signals and close as soon as possible.

Professionals develop and use proven closing techniques. For example, they usually carry an order blank or some other kind of prop to use in the closing interview situation. They accept the fact that four or five attempts to close is routine. They have learned to close by asking the prospect for a minor decision on an alternative matter.

It is in the closing encounter that salespeople can put to use the behavioral techniques they have learned, practiced, and perfected.

The chapter closed with a discussion of four closing techniques.

KEY TERMS

Alternative-Question Closing

Assumptive Close

Closing Props

Impending-Event Close

Offering-of-Premium Close

Requalifying Prospects

Summary-of-Benefits Close

REVIEW QUESTIONS

- Why is it important for a salesperson to analyze the personality of the customer?
- How can a salesperson build a trust relationship with a customer?
- Why must salespeople control digressions?
- Why is it important for salespeople to know why they are good in their work?

DISCUSSION SUBJECTS

- Most people fail as salespeople simply because they cannot close a sale. Do you agree?
- Explain why good closers are made and not born.
- Do successful closers use identical closing procedures or techniques in every sale? Why or why not?
- Why is it important to understand human motivation in the sales process?

- Why do good closers condition themselves to ask at least five times for the order in every closing situation?

EXERCISES

1. Interview someone who sells cars, and find out the most effective closing technique that person uses. Report it to the class.
2. Choose a partner to act as the prospect, and demonstrate to your classmates the closing process by asking alternative closing questions.
3. Discuss the pros and cons of using closing props at the closing interview.

Case Study One

Bob Follett, a black, is a highly successful computer terminal sales-person in Atlanta, Georgia. Most of his sales have been to minority-owned businesses, but he has a number of white clients who are exceptionally loyal to him. Impressed with his performance, Bob's company has recently expanded his territory to include several businesses owned and operated by whites.

Today, Bob is sitting across the room from the vice-president in charge of operations for a large manufacturing concern. The two men are discussing the feasibility of installing a terminal system in the company. Such a sale would result in one of the largest orders of Bob's career.

During the small talk, Bob senses that the vice-president might harbor a prejudice against blacks. Bob has nothing specific to go on, but the vice-president seems preoccupied, as if he wants to get the interview over. The questions he asks are short and to the point. Bob senses a lack of warmth; he sees a communication wall rising between them. Bob knows the feeling. He has dealt with prejudice before. Bob grows increasingly uneasy and more and more convinced that no sale will be made unless the issue is brought out into the open.

- How should Bob state his suspicions and still keep communication lines open?
- Should Bob smile, leave the interview, and then talk to his sales manager about how to handle the situation?
- Can Bob still win the trust and confidence of the vice-president?

Fred Dillon works for a very successful small communications company that specializes in selling, installing, and servicing new telephone systems. Because of the company's size, it is able to offer both product and maintenance service at a much lower price than the huge national concerns. Fred has obtained an appointment with the president of a major real estate sales organization, who is eager to look at his product.

In analyzing Fred's presentation, the president is impressed. But, he balks at Fred's continually mentioning low price as the main reason for buying. "What are some of your other benefits besides price," the president asks.

- What should Fred say?
- What errors, if any, did Fred make in emphasizing price over other benefits?
- What other benefits can Fred mention about his system?
- Name some comments from the president that would be buying signals for Fred.

Selling in Action: A Case Study

OBJECTIVES

In this case study you will learn:

- The steps in the formula-need theory and the sales cycle.
- How to use them in the sales process.
- How to control the sales interview.
- How to identify closing signals.
- How to respond to buyer objections in a closing interview.

In the following account of an actual interview, we will examine the sales process from the initial contact through writing the order.

Chicago is a lively, bustling Midwestern metropolis, a good business city. Many national companies have regional offices there, and some large companies have their headquarters there.

Chicago Creative Visuals, better known as CCV, is a Midwest distributor of audio-visual equipment for several manufacturers, including Japanese and German firms. Though it is not a large firm, it has for several years been competing directly with two giant companies. One of these is Unicom, a conglomerate giant that spans the globe in its operations. The other is an old and well-known German manufacturer called Stuttgart Optics. Both these competing firms, like CCV, offer equipment such as cassette tapes and recorders, microphones, earphones, video cameras and playback systems, overhead and slide projectors, and other allied products and service.

Beth Wilson is the top salesperson in CCV's Chicago sales office. She entered sales to get line experience, a key to advancement to executive levels in many large corporations. She chose the communications field because it is one of the fastest growing fields in today's business world.

Even though the prices on some of CCV's equipment are somewhat higher than those of Unicom and Stuttgart, Beth has been successful in direct competition with these firms because of her selling ability. After a few frustrating months getting started, after five years, she now has an established clientele. She makes an excellent salary and bonus, and has a car and a generous expense account. And she likes selling so much that she recently turned down a job with the marketing division of a competitor. Beth is beginning to feel that she would like to stay where she is, despite her earlier idea of moving into management.

Carl Brown is the president of Carl Brown and Associates, a highly successful business consulting firm that specializes in the presentation of motivational seminars and workshops. From a modest start with seminars in the Chicago area, Carl has gradually expanded, until his firm now covers the continental United States.

Carl has worked out a simple and effective marketing and promotional system to sell the seminars in most major cities. Each year his research and development department settles on 30 different subjects to be presented the following year—some new, some repeats of particularly successful current seminars. By using mass mailings and local telephone follow-ups by professional callers, Carl has been able to turn out an average of 75–100 people for each of his seminars. His speaking staff is small, mostly people who live in local areas and have other occupations like teaching or counseling. They are retained for the seminars on an individual-fee basis.

Now, after two years of study and research, Carl has decided to make a major change in his operation. He has a plan by which, over a period of three years, the number of seminars per year should increase from 300 to about 900. His plan divides the country into six regions and calls for hiring four persons full time in each region to conduct the seminars. He is in the process of hiring several of these people and believes that, although the expansion may be expensive at first, it will in the long run be enormously profitable.

For some time, the seminar material has been standardized in outline form so that those who conduct the sessions can present more or less the same thing, but audio-visual material has varied greatly. Some people have used slides, some motion pictures, some chalkboards, and some flip charts. Only a few have used overhead projectors.

After discussing this matter at length with Phil Jerrell, the national marketing manager of the firm, Carl has decided that an overhead projector is the best visual equipment for his presenters to use. He has decided to buy 30 projectors, which will allow one for each presenter with one back-up machine located in each region in case of equipment failure.

Beth Wilson has been calling on Phil Jerrell for years and has sold him a moderate amount of audio-visual equipment. Phil has kept her abreast of Carl's interest in overhead projectors and from time to time has asked her for information on projection equipment to pass on to Carl. Beth herself has so far not met Carl, but she has been very helpful to Phil and welcomes the opportunity to make a presentation to Carl.

In addition, Beth has had the chance to learn something about Carl as a desirable prospect for the purchase of CCV's overhead projector. As a result of several conversations with Phil, Beth has concluded that Carl's social-style profile is basically expressive. He likes people and is rather impulsive, and when he conducted seminars himself always had a good rapport with his audiences. Beth is sure that Carl will respond to a stimulating approach. He will expect immediate answers to his objections, and in the interview she will dream with him about the future expansion of Carl Brown and Associates.

But Beth has also inferred that along with his impulsiveness Carl has an analytical side: though he may be impulsive, he is trying to look at this expansion with complete objectivity and will want all the facts. Beth therefore knows that she must have firmly in mind for the interview all the pertinent technical information about her own company's projectors, as well as those of Unicom and Stuttgart, her main competitors. (Phil has suggested that Carl seems predisposed to those companies because of their nationwide service outlets.) As part of her preparation, Beth carefully reviews CCV's projector versus those of her competitors. For the first interview, discussion will be enough. She will save the sample projector for the closing interview.

Beth has arranged an appointment with Carl through Phil, and at her suggestion Phil has written an introductory note praising her and her company. For half an hour before she leaves her office, Beth goes over her file notes about Carl Brown and Associates and carefully reviews her pre-interview checklist (Chapter 8, Figure 8-4). As a reminder, she takes the checklist along and scans it again quickly just before going into the reception area. She is ready.

THE SALES PROCESS IN ACTION

Every successful salesperson follows a set process in making sales. There is no exception. The outpouring of ideas and phrases may sound natural and spontaneous, but usually every phrase and word has been time-tested and permanently incorporated into the sales process by the salesperson.

Behind the sales process is also a philosophical base. This base has evolved into the Formula-Need theory discussed at length in Chapter 9. The interview process should follow those five phases in order. They are: attention, interest, desire, conviction, and action.

The practical application of these five principles is found in the sales cycle (Figure 1) which encompasses the entire sales procedure. The sales

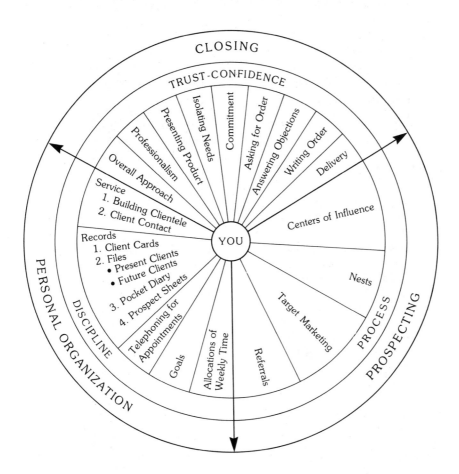

Figure 1. The Sales Cycle

cycle breaks down selling into three basic skill areas: prospecting, personal organization, and closing, the subject of this chapter. The interviews between Beth Wilson and Carl Brown show how a skillful salesperson can make use of the five phases of the Formula-Need theory in an actual sales situation. In the interviews that follow, the left-hand column gives the conversation, and the right-hand column explains which stage of the formula-need theory and the sales cycle Beth is using.

The interview begins as Beth enters Carl Brown's office.

The Sales Process
FIRST INTERVIEW

Formula-Need (FN) Stage

Sales Cycle (SC) Stage

"Mr. Brown? I'm Beth Wilson with Chicago Creative Visuals." They smile and shake hands. She has not brought a projector with her.

FN Stage—Attention.

SC Stage—Greeting, leading to overall approach. Carl gives Beth his full attention by answering her question about the projector screen. Beth avoids upsetting the rhythm of the interview by too much small talk. She does not bring her projector on this first interview because she feels that it will be much more effective at the closing interview.

"Nice meeting you, Ms. Wilson. Won't you sit down?" She does.

"I like your office. It looks very efficient."

"Yes, it is."

"I see that you have a retractable projector screen in here. May I ask why?"

"Well, we design and review a lot of our seminar transparencies right here."

"Oh, I understand—and I suppose it's just as useful here in your office as it would be somewhere else?" Carl nods. "Well, Mr. Brown, I'm not here to sell projector screens, but I do have some ideas on overhead projectors that might be of extreme value to you. Before I get to them, however, I should like to bring up two preliminary considerations.

FN Stage—Interest.

SC Stage—Overall approach. Here Beth begins to arouse Carl's interest, and she is projecting confidence by speaking with authority. She leans forward slightly and looks straight at Carl. She will maintain this posture throughout the interview, glancing away occasionally for mutual relief. She looks pleasant and relaxed. Note how Beth personalizes her approach by pointing out problems peculiar to Carl's field. It indicates that she has done her homework. Then she begins to stimulate interest in herself—not her products

"First, in these days of inflation, high costs of travel, and dramatic product changes in the whole audio-visual area, it is important that you work with someone who tries to keep abreast of all these

changes—someone whom you can trust and have confidence in.

"Second, it is important that such a person be flexible. Let me explain. My company distributes some of the finest audio-visual equipment on the market today. But we can't be all things to all customers constantly. Our overhead projector is not so easily portable as some others, nor quite so compact. But it is portable—small enough to go under any airplane seat—and not much heavier than the lightest ones. And I must admit it doesn't look as sleek as the German model.

"And if you need a feature that my company doesn't have in an overhead projector, then I think I know as well as anyone which competitor might have that feature. In other words, Mr. Brown, I am here to represent you as well as Chicago Creative Visuals and to help you choose wisely. Now, with these thoughts in mind, what is your overhead projector situation at this time?"

"Well, Ms. Wilson, I'm interested in buying 30 portable overhead projectors for our district presenters to use. We're making a major shift in operating procedures and have decided to standardize our presentations with overhead projectors. This will allow us to make uniform presentations and give us more quality control over our seminars."

"I see. What features do you feel are important?"

"Well, obviously, since our presenters travel a lot, convenient portability is a must. Secondly, we want a product that's easy to set

yet—by admitting that her company is not perfect and praising one aspect of her competitors' products, though without mentioning any names. This is professional selling. Carl likes this. His mind begins to open up to Beth. Trust is beginning to build.

Beth knows she can overcome the more attractive look and portability of Unicom's product in the closing interview. If she didn't feel she could, she would have ignored these features. She considers this a closing point, and is saving it for the closing interview. This is one reason she's been successful. She mentions competitors' product features all the time, but only if she can counter them with her own product's features or service.

FN Stage—Interest.

SC Stage—Professionalism, presenting products, isolating needs. Beth begins to project professionalism, present her products, and isolate a valid need for her projector. This part of the interview is crucial. She controls it by asking questions designed to draw affirmative responses that will lead to getting Carl's commitment later on.

Beth is now forming in her own mind how her product will satisfy Carl's needs.

up. Sometimes our people fly to, say, Denver and arrive at the airport just an hour before the seminar begins."

"I see," says Beth. "And, of course quality transparencies mean a lot, too, don't they?"

"Definitely," Carl replies. "We need transparencies that can be used over and over again. They get a lot of handling. Reliability is also important. The Stuttgart representative—they're a German company . . ."

"Yes, I know," Beth nods.

". . . was here last week and they have a bulb that's guaranteed for 75 hours, which is what we need. In other words, we need a quality product all the way. After all, we expect to conduct about 500 seminars a year with our new marketing plan."

"I agree, Mr. Brown. You need a quality product, which is what CCV offers. I think that our product will serve all these needs as well as any other product on the market today. And from the information you've given me today, I would like to return with our version of the ideal overhead projector for your needs. Would that be agreeable to you?"

"Sure."

"Good. May I clarify one or two points before setting a time?"

"Of course."

"First, you obviously need 30 quality overhead projectors, am I correct?"

"Yes. We've already decided that other audio-visual products simply won't do."

Every question Beth asks is carefully phrased. She is helping to pin down valid needs here. She also knows her competitors' features well and the reasons for doing business with her company.

In this interview, Beth will not counter with features of her own company's product. Those comments are closing points and are to be saved for that interview.

FN Stage—Desire.

SC Stage—Commitment.

Beth feels that she has made a reasonable beginning, established her professionalism, and isolated a valid need for 30 high-quality overhead projectors. She now describes her product briefly as one to satisfy the need. She is ready to conclude the first interview by getting a commitment from Carl that he needs a product similar to hers, that he can afford her product, and that he has no objection to doing business with her or her company.

"And, second, I assume that you have budgeted funds for such a purpose?"

"Oh, yes. By the way, what do yours cost?"

"Well, our X-20 model, which is ideal for you, runs $350 with our unusual 5–10–15 quantity discount. You get 5 percent off list for each one if you buy 10 or more, and 15 percent off for 30 or more."

"I see. Your price seems a bit high to me. I mean, Unicom's product is around $340, and Stuttgart's is around $330, as I recall."

"That's correct. But of course those huge companies can cut prices by their large production. We try to make up the difference in quality. I take it that our price would be no problem?"

"No, not really."

"In other words, if you really like our product despite the slightly higher cost, you would be willing to pay our price?"

"Oh, yes. Now I'm not saying I'm buying your product, but the price would be no problem if your product is the one we finally decide on."

"Fine." Perhaps I can mention one more thing . . ."

"What's that?"

"Please don't misunderstand me, but do you have any reason for not buying from me or my company?"

"No, but why would you bring that up?"

"Well, you might have some obligation, a friend, or some other reason for buying from someone else. And if so, I'd like to know about it now. After all, I want to build a lasting relationship with

Beth firmly removes these potential objections in advance of the second interview which will go far toward assuring a sale here.

you and if there is any reason this cannot be done, I feel it's only fair to discuss it."

"No, I don't think so at all. We don't have any commitments. We want to buy the best product we can."

"Splendid. Now, when can I show you our X-20? How about next Tuesday at three or Thursday at four? I have both times free."

"Thursday at three-thirty would be best for me," Carl says, glancing down at his desk appointment calendar.

"Excellent. Next Thursday at 3:30 P.M., right here," Beth says, rising. "I'm sure you'll like our projector, Mr. Brown, and I hope CCV can join with your company in this project of yours. The thought of bringing your distinguished motivational programs to thousands of people every year is exciting, and we look forward to helping you bring those dreams to life. Thank you for your time. I'll see you next week." Smiling broadly, she shakes hands with Carl and exits quickly.

Here Beth strongly appeals to Carl's expressive social style by appealing to his dreams of the future.

Beth has conducted a classic first interview. She controlled it entirely, using effective communications skills. She built customer confidence by following the sales cycle in order. She started with customer-oriented small talk, then moved to her personalized approach, followed by the general product presentation, even though she didn't bring her projector with her. She isolated valid customer needs and ended the interview with a fixed financial and personal commitment by Carl. The second interview should result in a sale.

Beth is confident as she leaves Carl's office. She has 40 minutes before her next appointment in the same area and uses the time, back in her car, to get out her notebook and jot down the important details of the interview just completed. Among other things, she now knows that her competitors are, as she had expected, Unicom and Stuttgart. Though she is already very familiar with their lines, she makes a note to herself to review her up-to-date "competition files" to refresh her memory.

Before going on to her next appointment, she finds a pay telephone, calls her office, and requests the word processing staff to prepare a form letter thanking Carl for his time and reaffirming their appointment for "next Thursday in your office at 3:30 P.M." She also adds her own P. S. to the form letter: "All progress begins with dreams."

That Saturday morning, Beth is in her office preparing for the second interview. She customarily uses Saturday morning from around nine-thirty to twelve-thirty for organizing and planning. It is a good time to record notes and complete files on her past week's activities, to fill out her weekly activity report, and write birthday cards to good customers. Sometimes she just daydreams a bit, reviewing her progress. She is disciplined about spending this particular time in her office and always concludes these sessions by preparing for the coming week. Then, when twelve-thirty comes, she gets up, leaving her sales job behind until Monday morning. Saturday afternoon and Sunday, away from her job, refresh her.

She spends most of this particular Saturday morning on the coming interview with Carl. She analyzes the first interview and mentally outlines the second. She rehearses her part for the second, going over and over possible objections and reasons Carl should buy her product. She knows that CCV's fine service shop will be one of the keys here. Neither Unicom nor Stuttgart has local service facilities. They farm the work out to commercial repair shops—not nearly so satisfactory as CCV's on-the-spot service. She also reviews some specific product differences, anticipating that Carl's secondary analytical personality trait will demand straightforward answers on some product differences.

At twelve-thirty, Beth stands up, stretches, and leaves her office for a tennis date to be followed by a late lunch. She's ready for next week.

On Thursday, driving to Carl's office, Beth rehearses her presentation one final time, going over in her mind all the possible objections that Carl may raise. Experience has taught her that this last rehearsal always helps her in the closing interview. Despite the preparation, Beth still feels slightly tense and nervous. This used to bother her and make her wonder whether selling was worth the worry, but a wise sales manager assured her that it was all part of the job, not unlike what other professionals experience in other fields—surgeons, actors, athletes, musicians. And for Beth, the after-sales elation is definitely worth it.

THE SECOND INTERVIEW

Promptly at 3:30 P.M., Beth, carrying a portable projector, is ushered into Carl's office. Carl rises and they shake hands warmly. Carl gestures Beth to a chair, and as she sits down she places the projector on the floor beside her. Beth starts the interview casually: "How has your day been going?"

"So, so," says Carl. "And yours?"

"Oh, fine. I've had a very productive day." Then Beth reaches down, picks up the projector, and places it, unopened, on Carl's desk. "Now, before we begin, I assume that you are still prepared to buy 30 overhead projectors."

"Yes, I am."

"Well, let me show you our model—the remarkable X-20." Beth says this with enthusiasm and vigor. She opens up the projector and snaps the optical lens arm into place and then quickly feeds out the extension wire and plugs it into the nearby wall socket whose location she took note of in her first visit. As Carl watches, Beth switches on the machine and focuses it to a bare portion of the wall opposite Carl's desk.

"There we are," she says, smiling. Then she flips the switch to Off, feeling she is prepared to make her presentation. Looking at Carl straight on, and speaking pleasantly and clearly, Beth says, "Now let me tell you about one of the finest overhead projectors on the market today."

As Carl looks on with interest, she enthusiastically points out the various features and explains them,

FN Stage—Conviction.

SC Stage—Asking for the order, answering objections.

Trust and confidence have already been established. Lengthy small talk is no longer necessary to stimulate attention or interest. Beth knows that Carl is busy and wants to make a decision. She has only to reaffirm the need and commitment.

Beth must make an interesting presentation. A boring, detailed presentation could turn Carl off here. Everyone likes to be entertained, even in a buying setting.

Fortunately Beth exudes enthusiasm, warmth, and confidence throughout. She stands during her entire product presentation. Partly this is to give her a greater sense of control, but also it makes the demonstration easier.

always remembering to look directly at Carl as she does so. She smiles confidently as she enumerates one product feature after the other. From time to time she asks Carl, "Do you understand what I'm saying here?" Brown nods affirmatively.

After this preliminary explanation, Beth puts a plain pale-blue plastic-bound transparency on the machine and switches the starter button. With a yellow pencil, she writes on the transparency "Carl Brown and Associates.

"Isn't that effective? You can either prepare these in advance or write on them as you're speaking. And they are very durable." She shows Carl how tough the plastic frame is. "Here, try to tear the frame apart," she urges. He takes it and twists it. It won't crack. He's impressed.

After discussing in detail the variety of other transparency uses, she assures Carl that she will be available to show his staff how to design and prepare effective visuals for his presenters with his current office copier. She also offers her time to show his presenters how to use these transparencies for maximum effect. While explaining this, she is careful to answer any questions along the way. She does not dwell too long on the answer or explanation of a particular feature. Beth wants to make sure she gets through her entire presentation in a reasonable time—30 minutes in all. After finishing her formal presentation, she pulls out of her packet a purchase order with the name of Carl's company already typed in and a big penned X at the place of the signature. Carl notices

Beth continually asks for reassurance. Thus, Carl is continually approving her presentation.

Here is showmanship at its best. Asking Carl to try and tear the transparency apart is highly effective.

Beth feels she can make a quick trial close here, because Carl seems so interested. Even his body language transmits buying interest. He is leaning forward now, moving a little closer to Beth. He is this. As she places the purchase order in his full view, she says, "What do you think about our projector?"

"I like it," says Carl.

"I'm sure you agree it will be ideal for your presenters, isn't that right?"

"Yes," nodding his head.

smiling broadly, not the formal smile of resignation, but one of genuine interest, and he keeps looking either at Beth or the projector. However, Beth also expects him to make some objections, which she accepts as valid buying signals. After all, she has never had someone like Carl say, "I'll take it"—no matter how effective her presentation. She knows she must always expect objections; it's part of any sales process.

Beth stimulates the nodding approval again.

"Wonderful. I knew it would be the ideal projector for you. Now, do you want all 30 delivered here or sent around to your various offices as required?"

"Well, I'd rather have them all sent here so we can conduct a two-day training seminar with all our reps. But wait a minute. I'm not ready to buy just yet."

Here Beth moves her pen toward the order blank by asking an alternative question on a minor point. It is her first attempt to write the order.

"I understand, Mr. Brown." Beth puts down her pen, leans back a little, and, looking directly at Carl, says, "If I understand you clearly, what you're saying is that you're not ready to buy just yet. Is that it?"

"Yes, that's right," says Carl, slightly relieved.

As Beth responds to Carl, she first makes sure that he feels she understands his objection. She does this by relaxing her closing posture and paraphrasing or repeating Carl's objection. Beth listens intently for his reaffirmation. She knows that if Carl doesn't feel she has really understood his objection, it will be a mistake to continue. She will begin to lose control of the interview and eventually the sale. She therefore listens intently to Carl's objections. Genuine listening is honest, sincere, open listening which conveys itself to customers through body language and eye contact. It is a powerful communication skill.

Even though Carl needs these projectors and has budgeted

"Mr. Brown, I understand what you're saying. You're just not ready to buy yet. May I point out a few things?"

"Sure."

"First, you need 30 projectors."

"Yes."

"Second, I'm sure our X-20 can do the job."

"I think so."

$10,000 for the order, he is beginning to feel that reluctance which most buyers feel when they're about to make a purchase. Beth recognizes his feeling immediately and understands that she must now subtly ease the situation and lead Carl into a positive buying mood. She cannot supply him with the motivation, but she can help him realize that he has the motivation.

"Well, a point to consider is your 30 presenters in the field. Delaying the purchase of projectors and asking them to continue making inferior presentations by using whatever visual aids they've been using unsatisfactorily seems to me counterproductive and almost unfair to them. Now," Beth says, *after a slight pause and letting her pen drift back to the order form, "would you like to pay for these by check today or upon delivery next week?"*

"Look, Ms. Wilson," says Carl, I *like your product, and I like you personally. But frankly, I don't know whether Unicom's or Stuttgart's products aren't more to our liking. For example, Unicom's projector fits ideally into a handsome executive briefcase. It looks good, it's narrower than yours, and it's easier to carry. Yours does look a bit clumsy, if I may say so."*

Beth is relieved to hear this objection, because she has known all along that Carl really likes this feature in Unicom's product. She does too, and wishes her company's product were better looking, but that is beside the point, she feels. At least she has done her

By referring to the actual plans for using the projectors she is on the point of selling, Beth is bringing Carl back to thoughts of the real need he has for them.

Here, Beth again assumes that Carl is going to buy from her. She maintains control and always listens intently to his objections and comments. She again asks her alternative question on a minor point. A positive answer to either closes the sale.

Now Carl is really opening up. He is mentioning specific product differences. He is getting close to buying.

research and can counter with a valid response to this objection.

I see your point, Mr. Brown. That executive carrying case of Unicom's is beautiful. But that doesn't make it a better overhead projector. It's a cosmetic feature. I'm sure your reps would much rather have a machine like ours, which is equally portable, has tough plastic-bordered transparencies, and has the unique automatic snap-out lamp changer. Unicom's may look a lot better, but for actual performance, I'd certainly rather have ours, and so would your reps."

Carl sits there, obviously convinced of Beth's points.

"Now," Beth says again. "On service calls, I find a lot of time is saved if you assign one person in your organization to be my contact. Would such a person be Phil Jerrell, or someone else?"

"No, Phil would be the man to see."

Beth writes Phil's name down on the order blank. She feels a close is near and is just about to ask again for a 10 percent down payment when Carl says: "Look, I like your machine, and I like you. You've made a fine presentation, but I'm just wondering if the Stuttgart machine isn't the one we ought to buy. After all, it's slightly cheaper than yours. It has lamps that last 75 hours—you know how the Germans engineer things."

"Mr. Brown, I understand your views here. The Germans are en-

Beth praises the looks of the competitor's product and counters by reiterating the good points of her own product, which override those of the competitor's.

Beth realizes she must not allow a pause here. Once again she turns to her order blank, as she suggests another telling point in the form of a question to which Carl must reply. She gets him to make an alternative decision on a minor point before going on. She never expects customers to say, "I'll take it," even if she has answered their objections convincingly. Nor does she want them to feel that it is she who has won the day. Therefore she always relies on her alternative questions to close the sale.

FN Stage—Action.

SC Stage—Writing the order.

At this stage Beth feels that she has almost reached her goal. She maintains her enthusiasm, concentrates on listening to Carl's objections, and keeps smiling. Her eyes constantly seek his.

Again, Beth listens intently. With Unicom eliminated, she feels the sale is near. All she has to do is get over this last hurdle and the sale will be hers.

gineering geniuses. And Stuttgart certainly has a wonderful reputation. As I said before, we make up for our price difference by quality and service. Let me tell you about our service. In the early years, we did what Unicom and Stuttgart did—we contracted our service out to commercial audio-visual repair shops. But this never worked well for us. Repair completion dates were always delayed and we were unable to find responsible contacts. So we started our own shop.

"If one of your reps in California has a problem with his projector, right after the coffee break, a phone call to us will send a spare one on its way to him by Air Express within the hour, if the rush-hour traffic at O'Hare isn't impossible. And if you have any problems with our shop, have Phil call me and I'll see to it that you get help. We may be small, but we work like Trojans to satisfy our customers. You're number one with us. Now, should I see Phil Jerrell about setting up those staff training sessions, or will you have him call me?"

Carl is sold. Sounding somewhat relieved, he says, "No, I'll have Phil call you. But we're anxious to get started on this soon. I hope your schedule is flexible the rest of the month."

"I'll make it flexible for you, Mr. Brown. I think you have made a wise decision, and I'm sure that in the years ahead you'll see why Chicago Creative Visuals has such a fine service reputation."

Carl has Beth see Phil Jerrell to get a down-payment check and to arrange for delivery, staff training, and so on.

Beth has, of course, kept in mind her company's local service as a strong reason for buying from her and has saved this point to use in the closing interview. By asking about service calls, she has got Carl away from his thoughts of appearance and into practical matters. Good salespeople always save such points for the close.

She again moves her pen toward the order blank to make this note.

Beth reassures Carl of his wisdom in buying from her. Customers always like reassurance for buying, even from the salesperson who sells them.

At approximately 4:45 P.M., Beth leaves Carl Brown and Associates. She is exhilarated. This has been one of her biggest sales. She hurries back to the office and turns in the order blank and check. She writes Brown a thank you letter with another P.S.: "Thanks for allowing CCV to be part of your dream." Her sales manager is elated too and tells her the president of CCV said he would buy her lunch tomorrow if she got the sale. She glows at the recognition. Beth leaves for another tennis date at 6:00 P.M.. She knows she'll win—after today, she can beat anyone!

SUMMARY

This case study is an example of the sales process in action, including a step-by-step description of a closing. Also reviewed were the five stages of the Formula-Need theory: attention, interest, desire, conviction,and action. This is the philosophical base upon which the sales process operates. The sales process itself involves the application of the philosophy of the Formula-Need theory on a practical basis.

The case study described the sale of an overhead projector to a client who had made known his need for 30 such projectors. A typical two-interview sales process was presented, culminating in a successful writing of the order for the projectors.

From first contact through the final sales, the salesperson, Beth Wilson, followed the sales cycle. After getting an appointment, she conducted the first interview in professional fashion. She started off with small talk, then continued with the overall approach. She then proceeded to establish her professionalism, present her products, isolate valid needs, and obtain a commitment that Brown could afford the product and was prepared to buy. She did not bring the projector with her on the first interview, feeling that it would be much more effective as a tool in the second, closing, interview.

The second interview also followed the sales cycle process. Beth restated the results of the first interview and reaffirmed Carl's wish to acquire 30 projectors. In making her presentation, Beth controlled the interview. She concentrated fully on her client and his reactions to her demonstration. She acknowledged his objections before answering them, taking her time to assure him that she understood his point.

As typical objections arose during the sales process, Beth met them successfully. Meeting objections depends upon listening intently, showing the customer that you understand the objection, countering the objection with other telling points, and asking the customer to make an alternative decision on a minor point. The order blank was shown to be an effective closing tool.

The use of an alternative decision on a minor point with the order blank eased the tension for both Beth and Carl. Effective salespeople never act as if they had "won" when they make a sale. Customers don't like to feel they have lost a psychological battle to a salesperson.

Finally, Beth's elation at having made a substantial sale is part of the psychological rewards of selling. Salespeople frequently experience this sense of achievement. Beth acquitted herself well. Her superior professional knowledge of her own and her competitors' products paid off. She never talked down the competition. She always thought in terms of her client's interest. She used responsible sales techniques.

KEY TERMS

Answering Objections

Asking for the Order

Buyer Interest

Buyer Reluctance

Buying Signals

Formula-Need Theory

Overall Approach

Sales Cycle

Valid Needs

REVIEW QUESTIONS

- Why didn't Beth bring her projector on the first interview?
- Would a picture of it have helped?
- Why is it important to build trust and confidence in the sales process?
- Does selling with drama violate professionalism?

DISCUSSION TOPICS

- Explain what is meant by using a purchase order blank as a closing tool.
- Why is it important for prospects to feel that salespeople have heard their objections?
- How do salespeople control the interview?

EXERCISES

1. In a short paper, comment on the Formula-Need theory as applied by Beth Wilson. Did she use it well? Did she successfully complete one step before going on to the next?

2. Demonstrate in class other ways (than asking him to try to tear a transparency) Beth could have used showmanship in her presentation to Carl Brown.

3. Ask a salesperson how he or she deals with a competitor's known superior product feature in a closing interview. Report your findings in class.

Case Study One

Sidney Greenburg sells drilling rigs to large oil companies. Since most companies have stepped up drilling activities, particularly in the continental United States, the competition is high. Several companies that have been dormant in the field for several years have revitalized their oil equipment divisions.

Recently, after months of negotiations, Sidney lost a large sale to a major oil company embarking on a drilling effort in Wyoming. Dismayed at his loss, Sidney had a talk with his sales manager and gave him, so far as possible, a word-by-word repetition of the actual closing interview. The sales manager came to the conclusion that one of the reasons Sidney did not make the sale was that he was too impatient and did not listen closely enough to the objections of the prospect. Sidney thought he had and got into a rather heated discussion with the sales manager about it. The sales manager's main point was that customers must feel that the salespeople understand their objections.

- Why is it important for customers to feel that salespeople understand their objections?

- What is meant by genuine listening to customers' objections?

- What is the value of repeating the objection of the customer in different words?

- Is body demeanor or language helpful in answering objections and is it useful in a closing sale?

- Are all objections buying signals? Explain.

Marian Shannon is a very successful real estate saleswoman in Dallas, Texas. Although the city has grown enormously in the past several years and numerous new subdivisions have been built, there is still a shortage of good housing in the area and real estate prices are high.

While speaking recently at a sales seminar in San Francisco, Marian was asked how she actually closed a sale. Her answer was, "When I get a buying signal."

In reply to the question, "What is a typical buying signal?" she said, "When the person who is thinking about buying a house says, 'I wonder if my furniture will fit in here,' I know that I am getting a strong buying signal. At that stage I usually remain silent and, after a pause, return to the subject by asking how large their furniture is. Then they start imagining a sofa here and a desk there, or a breakfront here or a plant there, and even start hanging their pictures on the wall.

"When this happens, I always pull out a letter-of-intent form for them to sign, which is an offer to buy the house, based upon their financial condition and the availability of money and interest rates, and so on."

One of the persons in the audience asks Marian why she uses the letter of intent as a closing vehicle. Why doesn't she simply say to the customer, "Are you ready to buy the house?" or, "Shall we write up the papers?" or some such direct question.

- What is the reason for not asking the customer whether he will actually buy the product?
- What does getting a decision on a minor alternative mean?
- In the closing interview, why is it important to have the customer sign something or write a check?
- What is the risk in ignoring buying signals? Explain.
- Is it normal for customers to raise objections during closing interviews? Explain.

Sales Techniques

PART FOUR

PROFILE

Glenn G. Geiger

Background   Glenn Geiger, a native of North Dakota, is the father of four sons and two daughters. Glenn, Jr., is an attorney in New Hampshire; Grant is in the life insurance business; Scott is in space sales; and Daniel is a forestry major. Nancy is finishing her master's degree in counseling, and Lori is a senior at Middlebury College in Vermont. Glenn's attractive wife, Mary, a graduate of Yale Nursing School, is very active in adoption work, the Kidney Foundation, and the local hospital auxiliary. She is president of the local Republican Club.

Glenn is the president and owner of Executive Benefit Consultants, a firm that specializes in packaging executive compensation arrangements for top corporate executives and professionals. Glenn entered this field 34 years ago when he took a temporary job (while he studied for the New York Bar examination) with Lambert Huppeler. (Thirty-four years ago Mr. Huppeler was on his way to building the largest life insurance agency in the United States.) The temporary job with Mr. Huppeler led to a full-time job in sales and sales management, and Glenn finally ended up with his own agency in New York City.

Sales Achievements   Glenn has led the New England Mutual Life Insurance Company for the past five years. He is a life member of the Million Dollar Round Table and its exclusive Top of the Table. He is past president of his local Chartered Life Underwriter chapter, and is active in the National Association of Life Underwriters. He also is a director of the University of North Dakota, and a president of the Leaders' Association of the New England Life.

In the sales field, he ranks in the top one percent of all salespeople in the United States, with an income in the middle six figures.

Glenn sells executive compensation plans to large corporations. Professional to the core, Glenn exemplifies all that is admirable in the sales career. His customers' needs always come first. His product knowledge, including that of his competitors, is exceptional, and he uses responsible selling techniques.

His Comments on His Career   "I do not like detail work, or the unscrupulous competitors that I occasionally face in the market place. I believe that integrity of purpose and person is extremely important in establishing the trust so important to customer–salesperson relationships.

"My advice to anyone entering the field of selling basically is three things:

1. Learn to manage time.
2. There is no substitute for being in front of prospective customers.
3. Learn to live with rejection; it is not personal.

"Although I take nearly three months' vacation and devote up to two months to charitable and industry activities every year, my income continues to grow as I confront new challenges. I keep my interest. I have no plans to retire and will remain active well past 65 if my health permits."

13 Communication Skills

Ingrid Hoevin sits at her computer terminal, ready to transmit her customer's request for more aluminum fasteners from her company's manufacturing plant in far-off Pennsylvania. The procedure is to ask the main plant what other company plants around the United States might have a temporary surplus of the aluminum fasteners, then transmit a request to that plant so that within hours they will be on their way by air freight to Ingrid's customer in Colorado.

Her customer is Philip DeNaegler, who owns a substantial manufacturing plant in the greater Denver area. He manufactures such things as aluminum doors and window frames for the home building industry. He gets the fasteners for binding the window frames together from Ingrid's company.

Ingrid got this particular order because Philip's company has had a large, unexpected order for several thousand window frames from Colorado's largest home builder. All Ingrid has to do is find where the fasteners are and place an order.

It sounds simple enough, and it would be simple if computers always worked as they are supposed to, but in this case the computer is not helpful. Ingrid goes through the usual procedure, checking her message and symbol usage, and types the message to the home office with the request encoded according to the manual. She waits for confirmation and the coded terminal address of the plant with the extra fasteners. Nothing happens. After a long pause, the computer asks her to recheck the accuracy of her message symbols. She does. The terminal then asks for a repeat of the message. She repeats it, but no answer comes.

As she waits impatiently, the phone rings. It is Philip, wondering when he can expect the fasteners: his assembly line is shut down and he wants them soon. Ingrid has to explain that she is having trouble with the computer.

"Look, Ingrid," Philip says "we can't wait on the computer. I've got orders to fill, people to keep working. Get on the phone to the home office right now. OK?"

"All right," she says, and hangs up. But what can she do now? Old Fred Johnson, who used to handle these requests at the home office, was long ago phased out by the computer. She decides she will have to call the other plants herself, and for the next several hours she sits at the telephone trying to track down the new fasteners. At last she gets through to the operations manager of the South Carolina division, who promises to ship the order immediately. The crisis is over and Philip is relieved.

This sort of thing is all too familiar in our computer age. Computers are marvelous communication vehicles when they work, but when they don't work, it is very hard to find a person around who can answer your questions. Because of computers, much of the human communication between the field and home offices—even between departments—is disappearing. It may seem, too, that the art of communicating person to person is no longer very important. But not in selling. Computers cannot sell. People sell. And they sell by communicating effectively.

THE ART OF COMMUNICATING EFFECTIVELY

There is no magic involved in learning the skill of communicating effectively, but to be a consistently effective communicator, one must practice. This chapter reviews the basic verbal and nonverbal communication skills and discusses how to practice and improve your use of them. Remember, the primary object of all communication is the receiver, not the sender, and a good communicator seeks to get messages to recipients, not to build up his own ego. The focus is always on the receiver. Successful salespeople work on an I/You rather than an I/It relationship. The person to whom they direct their messages is all important. No one else matters at that moment. By focusing their eyes on the receiver's eyes and by positive body language (discussed later in this chapter) salespeople assure themselves of a receptive audience.

Everyone knows a few incessant talkers who go on and on, dominating a conversation to the exclusion of all others, seemingly unaware of how boring, and rude, they are being. Woe to the salesperson who allows his sales talk to get the better of him and uses verbal bombast instead of verbal skills.

Basic Communication Model

Meaningful communication has four distinct elements: the sender, the message, the means of communication, and the receiver. One of the important communications models was conceived by C. E. Shannon, and it applies, in general to all means of communication. It was originally published in the Bell System technical journal and was later included in the *Mathematical Theory of Communication*, written jointly with Warren Weaver.[1] Figure 13-1 shows the current model, known as the Shannon Weaver Model, which includes feedback not found in the original. The theory of the model is that communicated messages are subject to outside noises during their transmittal and also result in feedback from the receiver back to the sender.

In selling, good communication skills are essential. Especially important to salespeople are encoding, noise, and feedback. The sales message must be stated properly to ensure full understanding. It must be stated clearly without outside noise interference, and it must prompt feedback. If there is no response, then the sales process ceases.

[1] Claude Shannon and Warren Weaver, *The Mathematical Theory of Communication* (Urbana: University of Illinois Press, 1949) p. 7.

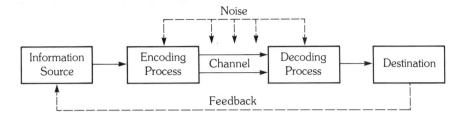

Figure 13-1. The Shannon-Weaver Communication Model

VERBAL SKILLS

Listening

Since most of what we hear from prospects is spoken, the art of listening correctly falls under verbal communication skills. It is one of the most important skills for a salesperson to master and it can be a powerful way of getting a message across.

Laura Anders goes to a cocktail party with her friend Anthony. They engage in separate conversations in different rooms. As they leave the party for dinner, Anthony says, "Did you have a good time?"

"I did indeed," replies Laura. "I met a fascinating man who was a stimulating conversationalist. I really enjoyed talking to him."

"What did you talk about?"

Laura pauses to think. Then, grinning broadly, she says almost apologetically, "Why, we talked about me! He kept asking me questions about what I did, where I went to college, where I work, what my interests in life are, and so on. After each question, he sat back and listened. I did all the talking. He made me feel that I was the most important person in the room. He didn't once take his eyes off me. He seemed so *interested* in me!" Obviously, this man was communicating by being a genuine listener. He talked hardly at all, but he made a strong impression.

Good listening is one of the most effective tools salespeople can employ, for listening can literally make sales. Attentive salespeople listen for the customer's reactions, for their hidden objectives, for their reasons for not buying. It is a key element in every sales situation. Most salespeople think they are good listeners, but numerous studies prove that people absorb only about one-third of what they hear.

Here are some concepts about good and bad listeners:

GOOD LISTENERS	BAD LISTENERS
• They open their minds and train themselves to be receptive to what is actually being said.	• They do not have open minds.
• They listen with their eyes. They "look" interested. They constantly look at the eyes of the speaker.	• They have a wooden look which indicates lack of interest.
• By looking at the tip of prospects' noses, they can outstare anyone—a powerful psychological advantage in sales.	• Their eyes wander all over the room.
• They concentrate on what is being said.	• They try to fake attention to the other person.
• They ask questions on the subject being discussed.	• They listen mainly for facts rather than for ideas.
• They show interest by body language and facial expressions; they smile frequently.	• They use poor body language; they slump back in their chairs or fold their arms and look unreceptive.
• They let the speaker talk freely, nodding agreement or interest. They take mental notes of what is being said and in their minds (not aloud) try to anticipate what the speaker will say next. This sharpens their attentiveness and keeps them focused	• They frequently finish someone else's sentence.
• They pay attention to the speaker's ideas, rather than listening only to the style.	• They listen for errors in speech, diction, and the like.
• They hear out the other person.	• They interrupt before the other person is finished.

Figure 13–2 shows the guidelines to follow to become a genuine, active listener.

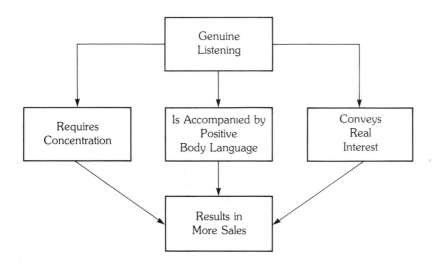

Figure 13–2. Guidelines for Good Listening

Diction and Grammar

Diction is the choice of words, especially "with regard to correctness, clearness, or effectiveness" (Webster's). Diction also relates to enunciation, and would-be public speakers often take special training to rid their speech of unpleasant mannerisms, such as ah's and uh's and other inarticulate sounds.

Good diction, in both senses, is important to the salesperson, who regularly uses speech as a means of communication. It goes hand in hand with good grammar, for it means little if one has impeccable grammar and yet cannot speak clearly or correctly. No salesperson should mumble. No salesperson should limit his vocabulary to sales lingo or slang or other trite expressions. Circumlocutions, roundabout high-flown expressions, euphemisms, or pompous-sounding terminology are just as bad. In learning good grammar, you should also learn the meaning of words.

Bad grammar marks a person at once. Errors in agreement, double negatives, show careless thinking and careless learning. Any salesperson, experienced or not, should listen to himself speak (use a tape recorder) and root out faulty grammar by getting a good manual and reviewing the basics. Everyone can learn to correct his own errors.

A good salesperson should also learn to use the dictionary. Even though you as the seller should take a customer's errors in stride, you should not allow yourself to lapse into the bad habit of slipshod language. Such abuses as *irregardless* for *irrespective*, *infer* for *imply*, and so on, are common enough in daily life, but the conscientious salesperson will pride himself on his good speech.

Unfortunately, the contemporary vocabulary is being expanded all the time by coined words and "bureaucratese" which violate the principles of clarity and conciseness, and in the business world especially, they are impossible to avoid altogether. Nonetheless, you should try to make your sales presentations clear and effective, even if you find yourself having to use some business jargon. In particular, don't allow yourself to use currently fashionable jargon and inflated expressions that you know yourself are silly.

Here are some pointers:

- *Conciseness.* Effective salespeople get to the point. They know that prospects don't like them to ramble on, and they repeat a point only when it is necessary to do so, or for particular emphasis.

- *Clarity.* If you have your ideas clear in your own mind, you should be able to present them clearly to others. If what you say sounds confusing, the customer will think you don't know your own product, and certainly he will not.

- *Use simple language.* Use brief, simple words instead of pompous-sounding ones. Say "This copier," not "This photographic duplicator."

- *Creativity.* Without being obviously clever, try to use the right word for the situation. This means having a vocabulary that goes beyond trite expressions and jargon—and certainly beyond slang. One way of learning to speak creatively is to be aware of everything that is going on in a particular situation—being alert to place and time and people. Another is to expand one's vocabulary by reading books and consulting the dictionary.

THE SALES PRESENTATION

Another way to learn creativity and variety in speech is to write. Try writing out a sales presentation completely. This will give you practice in choosing the right words and will probably—if you use the dictionary—make you aware of mistakes in usage that you can correct. Using a thesaurus can introduce you to words that you are not familiar with.

After you have written out a presentation, read it aloud several times, then try to remember—not word for word, but in outline and key phrases.

Reciting by rote will sound like a memorization—no more. The important thing is to have the outline clearly in mind. Experienced salespersons like Beth Wilson in our earlier example always make notes of a prospective interview and practice. You can train yourself—alone, or with a friend to act as the customer—and in doing so can also learn how to overcome nervousness.

We have said enough about not using slang or vogue words or too much business jargon. But there is one special category of expressions that salespeople should be especially leery of. These are the inflammatory expressions, some of them old salesman's clichés, that are instant red flags and immediately put the listener on the defensive. The list below is only a sampling. You can add your own.

Phrase	Listener's Reaction
"I'll be honest with you."	"Has he been lying to me all along?"
"You're not going to like what I'm about to say."	"And I'm sure I don't want to hear it."
"You're difficult to sell to."	"So what!"
"You're putting me off, aren't you?"	"I know I am, but that's my business."

Assertiveness

Assertiveness is the quality of stating ideas in a positive and controlled but nonbelligerent way. Agressiveness is self-assertiveness which disregards others' rights in pursuit of one's own ends. Most successful salespeople have some measure of assertiveness. They can speak forcefully when the occasion demands, and yet not sound overbearing or challenging. If a salesperson is afraid to state his ideas emphatically and always bows to the first refusal, he can lose out entirely. The trick is to learn how far to go—how to persuade without being unpleasant. Honesty is always better than hedging, and the assertive salesperson projects trust.

Consider these examples:

Prospect's Statement	Assertive Response	Nonassertive Response
"Is this product really the best for me?"	"I feel it is, definitely."	"Probably."
"Can you promise me delivery in two weeks?"	"I'm afraid I can't."	"Let's see."
"Can you match company B's price for this same product?"	"No, I can't, but I can make up the difference in better service."	"Well, not exactly, but . . ."

We should learn to express our opinions, to ask questions, to face up to things, to be at home with ourselves, to say what is on our minds, in a positive, assertive way. By doing this, we will project an image of being honest. And people will like to be around us because we are so predictable.

People who are effectively assertive are self-sufficient, mature individuals who are able to accept situations gracefully and honestly:

- They radiate enthusiasm.
- They relate warmly to others and usually have a good sense of humor.
- They value the opinions of others and are willing to help, but they are neither timid nor domineering.
- They think beyond the norm and thus become more creative.
- They are sensitive and recognize the realities of life.
- More than anything else, they know how they want to live and what is important to them.

Written Communication

Salespeople regularly have to make proposals and write memos, follow-up letters, interview letters, and so on. The importance of writing clear, concise letters should be obvious, but many a good sales interview has been offset by a sloppy, ungrammatical follow-up letter.

The general pointers laid down for clarity and conciseness in speaking apply even more for the written word. Good diction—proper choice of words—good grammar, clarity, and vigor are necessary. Writing a good letter takes practice, but it will come. At first, following a sample form letter may help; later you can produce your own. Use the dictionary for usage and spelling. Use a thesaurus if you are stuck, though Webster's gives many synonyms. Use a good manual of style (Like Strunk and White's *The Elements of Style*). Know generally what you want to say and in what order. Organize your thoughts in your mind first.

DO'S

- Give each paragraph a topic sentence.
- Be concise, by being brief and to the point, omitting excess verbiage. Do not be wordy or repetitive (but do not be curt).

- Make your style vigorous by using strong words, where appropriate, to get the message across and by using the active voice, not the weaker passive (as in, "A good time was had by all").
- Be creative but keep your language simple.
- Use correct English.
- Edit all letters for syntax, grammar, spelling, and punctuation.

DON'T'S

- Don't use trite expressions such as "we wish to acknowledge the receipt of" or "please be advised that" or "we beg to state that."
- Don't use slang or vogue words like *input, maximize, hopefully, finalize, bottom line.*
- Don't use a lot of redundant phrases, such as "the reason is because" or "it's agreeable and satisfactory" or "anxious and eager" or "the basic fundamentals."

Study Figures 13-3 and 13-4 for the differences between a poorly written thank you letter and a good one.

```
Dear Mr. Thorndyke:

     Permit me to say thank you for the generous time given
my presentation in your spacious quarters yesterday in the
afternoon.

     For your information, your input will go far in maxi-
mizing the scope of my forthcoming proposal.  I am anxious
and eager to do business with you.

     Thanking you in advance, and looking forward to our next
meeting, I remain, very gratefully yours,


Thomas Prolix
```

Figure 13–3. A Poorly Written Thank You Letter

```
Dear Mr. Thorndyke:

     Thank you for the time you gave me yesterday.  From the
information you provided, I shall be able to draft a suitable
proposal.  I want to do business with you, and look forward
to our next meeting.
Regards,


Tom Brief
```

Figure 13–4. A Well-Written Thank You Letter

Conversation

"He is probably one of the most boring people I know. He rarely has anything interesting to say." Everyone has probably made that criticism of someone—but how about yourself? Try to recall your last social encounter in detail. Did you listen well? Did you dominate the conversation? Were you boring? Not many of us can truthfully say that we are never boring. We all tend to say the same thing twice and to ignore what the other person is saying or trying to say.

Conversation as such can be a useful part of selling. Though you may know exactly how you want to go about making a sales presentation, the presentation is only part of the whole conversational framework in an actual sales interview. If your opening conversation shows that you are alert and intelligent, your prospective customer will be inclined to listen attentively when you get down to brass tacks. On the other hand, if your opening remarks are no more than routine—platitudes at best—or banal remarks which make you seem dull-minded, the customer may start thinking wearily of how quickly he can be rid of you.

Here again, you should focus on the customer, not on yourself, and be ready to listen and ask a question or two to keep the conversation going. If you follow this principle in all conversation, social as well as business, you will begin to learn a lot about various occupations, causes, hobbies, and life experiences. This in turn will increase your own awareness and make your life more interesting than it was before. And you will no doubt become more popular to boot, simply because people will feel good when they are with you.

Become better informed. The best conversations consist of an exchange of ideas, and a dull person not only has no ideas to offer but also lacks the wit to ask intelligent questions. You may know your line of products backward and forward, but if you walk into a customer's office on, say, the morning after an important international event that you have not even heard about (even though it is front-page news) you might find yourself embarrassed when the customer wants to talk about it.

That is only one example. No one can be informed on every subject, of course (leaving aside quiz show entrants), but lively, well-informed salespeople will certainly keep abreast of what is happening in their particular field. They will read the newspaper, for both local and national and international affairs. They will know more about the arts and entertainment than just the names of the popular TV situation comedies. They will probably know something about sports, geography, the economy, worldwide inflation, air and water pollution, and so on. And they will never stop being curious and wanting to learn. The world is full of people with surprising breadths of knowledge, and you may find that one of your best customers has a passionate interest in rare stamps, or exotic orchids, or photography. Your interest in what he is interested in will be mutually rewarding and will increase the element of trust.

A few simple hints may help you keep informed of what is going on in current affairs on a daily basis:

- Watch at least one television newscast every day.
- Read your daily newspaper as completely as possible.
- Read a good weekly news and business journal.
- Try to read the special sections in a large Sunday newspaper each week.
- Try to work into your knowledge of current affairs at least one unusual facet about most subjects.
- Try to develop the ability to recall specifics instead of remembering only vague generalities. Here is an example. You are at a social gathering in the Northeast in the month of January. Your community is digging out of two feet of snow. Many of the guests canceled. Everyone is dropping banal remarks about the weather. Suddenly you say, "The FCC claims the new satellite it is launching next July

will predict storms accurately at least 24 hours in advance of when they will hit." Where the conversation goes from there is hard to say, but at least you have let people know that you keep informed, and you have added something to their knowledge.

Voice Quality

Your voice says a lot about you. As soon as you utter a few words, you have projected a very strong image of yourself, and one that will last. Our appearance may change, but our voice alters very little, and your voice probably stays with a customer longer than your face does.

Most people are completely unaware of the powerful influence that their voice has on others. The voice is a valuable tool. Your insensitive use of it can hurt only you, no one else. A quiet, almost apologetic voice defeats you before you start. Conversely, a loud or abrasive voice can turn others off, even faster than a thin, reedy voice. Voices that are too loud, speech that is rushed and booming, the hail-fellow-well-met sort unfortunately associated with a certain salesman type have probably lost their owners more sales than they deserve. But no one likes to be intimidated by a voice, and a good salesperson strikes a happy medium. He does not boom, but neither does he mumble. He speaks clearly, in a well-modulated tone, looking at the customer. Imagine the awkwardness of having a customer say, "Sorry, I didn't hear that—what did you say?"

If you are curious about how you sound to others, or in doubt, try taping your voice on an inexpensive tape recorder. The first time you hear yourself you may be dismayed, but don't let that discourage you. Practice, as all good public speakers do. A loud, harsh voice can be toned down for more effective impact. Some salespeople purposely lower their voices slightly to force better listening by their customer. And certainly an indistinct voice can be improved.

If you really want to, you *can* improve your voice quality. Nationally known speech consultant Dorothy Sarnoff, who wrote *Speech Can Change Your Life* (Dell Publishing), says that apathy is the main enemy of speech improvement. People just do not care. If salespeople want to improve their effectiveness in their chosen profession, they should start with their voices. Here are some hints about the proper use of the voice:

- Try to keep your voice within a reasonable sound range. A good thing to do is to say "yes . . . Yes" in a normal way. Try to keep the voice within that range.

- An apologetic tone of voice can hurt.

- An abrasive voice turns others off quickly.

- Don't rush your speech; it conveys superiority.

- Take a couple of deep breaths before beginning a sales talk. This will help relax tensions which can produce a shaky voice, which, in turn, imperils confidence.

- Interesting voice modulation is an attractive asset.

- Practice your voice with a tape recorder.

- Don't let apathy block improvement.

OTHER AIDS TO COMMUNICATION

Clothing and Accessories

Many people say that "clothes make the person." Fairly or not, clothes do convey an image and are an important aspect of nonverbal communication. This is particularly true in sales. Society has certain criteria for what a salesperson should look like. Or, to put it another way, most customers prefer to buy from those who conform to their notion of capable, responsible salespeople.

All the articles and books on career dressing, and there are many these days, emphasize the importance of good grooming and conservative clothes. Without laying down guidelines, we can say that when you dress for selling you should bear in mind that you are going to mix with certain kinds of people—perhaps a variety of people—and that you are with them for business, not social, purposes. In other words, save party dress for parties, and very casual attire for off hours and weekends. Beyond the general rules of neatness and propriety, we do not have to be strict conformists these days. Department store salespeople no longer have to wear uniform black—but there is something to be said for dressing so that you are not mistaken for a customer. You are the best judge of what is suitable for your weather and customs: in the Middle West in the boiling summer, most men go jacketless, but a Wall Street bond salesman might not risk being so casual. In small towns dress may be less formal than in certain big cities. It all depends upon whom you expect to encounter. But in any case, your clothes should be clean and neatly pressed, and not flamboyant (unless you sell equipment to rock musicians). Men should save their Hawaiian shirts for the barbecue, and women, their low-cut blouses and clanky jewelry for dinners out.

Dressing well does not come naturally to everyone, and those who tend toward dowdiness and cannot seem to choose colors and fabrics that flatter their coloring would do well to consult some of the books on choosing a wardrobe (the local library should have a good selection). Or ask a friend whose appearance you admire to help you pick out a new outfit. We cannot always view ourselves objectively in a fitting-room looking glass. Perhaps you are choosing colors that make your skin look sallow, or styles that are unbecoming. This applies to men as well as women. Many men don't know how to choose a jacket that really fits, or to mix trousers and jackets with shirts and ties. It is better for your pocketbook as well as your appearance to have a wardrobe of well-made clothes which fit well and last several seasons than a closetful of ill-made garments which continually have to go to the cleaners or be pressed, or cannot survive a few washings without looking seedy. And remember too that good posture makes any garment look better on you. A beautifully cut jacket can look terrible if you hunch your shoulders.

Accessories like shoes and briefcases are also important—they can indeed be the final interesting (or fatal) touch, so remember to look down, and try to get a full-length glass to see yourself in. Here are some hints about clothes:

- Suit your clothing to the situation.
- Be neat and clean.
- Stand and sit straight.
- Don't be a carbon copy of every other salesperson—but stay within propriety.
- Study your appearance and select your clothes with care.
- Try to buy clothes that will last (instead of being trendy).
- Choose accessories that enhance the total effect.

Personal Grooming

Dirty fingernails, body odor, or bad breath can ruin any presentation. These will turn off not only the customer but anyone else in the vicinity. Also, keeping hair reasonably groomed in a current hair style is strongly recommended.

BODY LANGUAGE

Body language is a way of communicating without speaking, through signals. In selling, it is a powerful tool for the one who is doing the selling, and, as well, an important way of being able to detect the attitude of a customer. The way people sit, fold their arms, smile, use their eyes, put their hands behind their heads, lean forward or backward in the chair, touch others, and the like can say something quite as clearly as the spoken word.

Kinesics (the study of body language) has investigated the norms of proximity and space, including the way in which particular circumstances determine the space that people insist on maintaining between one another. In recent years, numerous studies have worked out elaborate theories about spatial rights, and the meaning of various postures. Some of this is mere speculation, and attitudes necessarily differ from culture to culture, so that a mannerism taken as friendly in the United States might be insulting in the Middle East, for example.

Morever, attitudes do not always have to mean the same thing. If a customer sits with his hands folded behind his head while leaning back in a chair, he may be showing boredom, but he may just as easily be totally absorbed in what you are saying. One should use common sense.

Still, you as a salesperson can project interest and energy by your attitude. If you sit leaning slightly forward, eyes alert and focus on the prospect, your face smiling, you will show confidence and alertness. The prospect will understand that you are interested in what you are selling, and in him.

It can all begin with the opening handshake—firm and cordial rather than limp or grasping. When you are asked to sit down, do so gracefully (don't flop) and sit straight, preferably not with knees crossed, for that makes it less easy to lean forward. Leave your hands free for handling sales material—don't keep one in your pocket, nor should you scratch your face or pull your hair! Remember:

- Body language does have a place in selling.
- Salespeople should look interested at all times through good eye contact.
- Sit and stand gracefully. In a chair, lean forward slightly.
- Smile frequently. It is infectious!

Reading Body Language

People buy when they are ready to buy, and body language can be a visual indication of readiness to sign an order. Most salespeople understand basic body language. The can usually tell when they have another's attention, even interest. But behaviorial psychologists are now isolating specific signals given by others engaged in two-way communication.

Professional salespeople can learn to recognize these signals to help them make sales.

Again, this is responsible selling. If buyers are ready to buy, they should buy. Most of them will never come out and say, "I'll take it." Prospects don't like to admit to salespeople that they have been sold. They simply do not like to concede victory to salespeople, even to the professionals. Most professional salespeople accept this and help prospects "help themselves," so to speak, in closing sales. Body language signals salespeople that a sale is probable and brings on the order-writing portion of the interview. It does not follow that the first positive body language signal means that you should start writing the order. It is more a matter of feel, gained by experience, that tells salespeople prospects are ready to buy. Here is a partial list of such signals accompanied by pictures to illustrate their normal messages.

Leaning forward, extending arms, smiling broadly with eyes fixed alternately on products or salesperson. This is the strongest buying signal of all. These prospects are sold and it is time to write the order. The eyes can be a telltale signal. Looking away, or out the window, or at the ceiling or distant part of the room usually signifies lack of interest.

Smile. A broad, full smile usually indicates prospect excitement (left photo). A thin tight smile indicates just the opposite (right).

Head cocked. Head to one side indicates prospect interest. It is time to close.

Readiness sitting.
Here the prospect is
leaning slightly
forward with one
forearm on one knee,
the other hand loosely
on the other knee.
The prospect is ready
to proceed.

*Stem of eye glasses
touching lips.* Usually
indicates prospect is in
need of more facts to
make a valid judgment.
Benefits should be
stressed again at
this point.

Church steepling with fingers. This indicates superiority or skepticism. Good salespeople capitalize on this signal by complimenting the prospect on his obvious knowledge of the product or service being presented.

Hands behind head, leaning back. This may mean superiority, or it may mean genuine interest, but it would not indicate that the prospect has made up his mind.

Arms folded. Conveys defensiveness and lack of interest.

Both arms on chair, legs crossed. Boredom or impatience is indicated when a prospect puts both arms on chair arms, crosses legs at the knees, and bobs foot back and forth in a gentle kicking motion.

Locked ankles. This conveys tension. The position is usually brought on by discomfort, feeling threatened, or intimidation by salespeople. It is time for salespeople to slow down and assure prospects they have their best interest at heart, despite how they have appeared.

Chin in hand. Here the chin is supported by the thumb and the forefinger touches the cheek. The prospect is critical of the salesperson and is not ready to buy.

Chin-stroking evaluation. Usually means prospects are actually going through a decision-making process. A reference to benefits at this time might lead to a sale.

Chin resting in one or both hands. This is a usual sign of boredom. Salespeople had better become more enthusiastic, get prospects involved, or ask some pertinent questions about prospect's thoughts on the presentation.

Clenched hands under chin. Usually means prospects feel they have been pressured. It's time for salespeople to be less aggressive, less assertive.

SUMMARY

Effective communication skills are a must for professional salespeople. These include both verbal and nonverbal skills.

Verbal skills include the proper use of voice with particular attention to diction and grammar. Oral presentations should be clear and concise. Becoming a good listener is a strong communication tool. Good listeners have an open mind, use good eye contact, and concentrate on what is being said. Effective assertiveness in verbal communication will help self-confidence. In written communications, strive for clarity, conciseness, and vigor; a poor follow-up letter may undo a good interview. Becoming a more interesting conversationalist by always thinking in terms of others' interests and keeping well informed will enhance communication skills, also.

Along with performance, a good appearance is essential. Body language can help develop effective nonverbal skills for salespeople, and an understanding of a prospect's body signals can be very helpful in guiding a sales interview on the right track.

Good communication skills can be mastered with consistent practice and honest personal criticism. The chapter offered these hints for perfecting communication skills.

- Pay attention to voice, diction, and oral presentations.
- Become effectively assertive.
- Maintain a good appearance.
- Learn to listen
- Learn to write good letters and reports.
- Become a more interesting conversationalist.
- Learn the signals of body language.

KEY TERMS

Body Language   Kinesics
Body Signals   Listening
Diction

REVIEW QUESTIONS

- What is the best way to improve the quality of your voice?
- Why is apathy the main enemy of speech improvement?
- How can diction be improved?
- Name some essentials of good listening.
- What is wrong with using jargon, clichés, or vogue words?

DISCUSSION SUBJECTS

- Do you believe that in selling clothes make the person? Explain.
- In what way is body language important in selling?
- How can you communicate most effectively in writing?
- How can a person become more effectively assertive in a sales situation?

EXERCISES

1. Break up into groups of two to practice listening skills: one listens while the other gives a brief life history, and then the listener repeats the details.

2. Demonstrate before the class the various body postures and what they mean in a sales situation.

3. Write a thank you letter to a customer just sold, including comments about service in the future.

Case Study One

Nelson Carpenter is a successful industrial salesman for a large manufacturer of plastic molding machines. He is a knowledgeable professional, always near the top of the list of the best salespeople of his company.

He has one fault. His diction and grammar are poor. He consistently makes several basic grammatical errors such as "He don't," and he uses words incorrectly. He also slurs his endings and mispronounces words. A new sales manager who recently joined the staff notices these faults at their first meeting.

- Should the sales manager suggest to Nelson that he work on better diction and grammar? Why?

- Why is it important to develop good speaking habits?

- How do you correct bad grammatical habits?

- Why should salespeople rid their speech of jargon and vogue words?

Case Study Two

Lunch at Cissie Jones's restaurant in downtown Cincinnati is always interesting. It is a favorite gathering place of media people. Roy Rivlen, a successful television time salesperson with Channel 16, is trying to convince Lester Blake, head of a local advertising agency, to use his station for some of his clients' advertising.

After finishing a cup of soup, Roy makes his usual presentation. He concludes, citing audience ratings for his station during prime time, and then says to Lester, "Do you have any questions?" Lester has several and begins putting them to Roy, but he soon notices that Roy seems more interested in who is at Cissie's than in the questions. He keeps looking away. He looks at Lester when he answers a question, but when Lester talks, Roy's eyes are always scanning the other tables. After Lester has finished his questions, Roy attempts to close the sale, but his inattention has probably lost him a customer. The luncheon ends with Lester's promise that he will think about it.

Back at the advertising agency, Lester's partner asks about the lunch with Roy Rivlen. Lester responds: "The lunch was OK, but Roy's presentation wasn't much. He didn't even listen to my questions . . . ."

- Explain what is meant by genuine listening.

- Listening is one of the most important communication skills. Explain.

- How do salespeople "open their minds" to prospects to become better salespeople?

- What does listening have to do with becoming a professional salesperson?

Audio-Visual Aids

14

OBJECTIVES

In this chapter you will learn:

- What audio-visual aids are available to the salesperson.
- How to use them effectively.
- What their limitations are.

Ann Kearney and Mary Farrell are attending their company's annual convention at the Broadmoor Hotel in Colorado Springs. Of the company's 210 salespeople, only 30 belong to the exclusive President's Club, which requires exceptional sales. This is the fourth consecutive year Ann and Mary have exchanged first- and second-place ranking in sales (each has won first place twice), and the trip to the convention is part of the award.

They have just left a workshop on the use of audio-visual materials such as video tapes as selling aids. During the coffee break, Ann tells Mary that she seldom uses visual aids because she thinks she does better with her own words. Mary says that she thinks visual aids are an important part of her success. She likes the overhead projector particularly, for its simplicity and convenience. She can carry it to a meeting, set it up quickly, and use it either on a one-to-one or in a group presentation basis.

"I find it very useful for getting my point across, because I can switch from visual to oral at will. I like it especially when I want to make a strong visual impact, like comparing graphs. I just flip on the overhead projector and draw their attention immediately to that. Then when I turn it off and begin myself, the contrast makes it more interesting and creative. It really helps my sales!"

"Not for me," Ann says. "It may be all right for you—and obviously you know how to use it effectively—but I still prefer a chalkboard or a pad and pencil. I find that it's a lot more effective when I draw my own graph in front of the prospect. He thinks I know more. Also, it seems to me that it is more creative and more personalized—as if I were creating it just for him. I like doing my own selling, I guess."

"The visuals don't do my selling," Mary protests. "All I'm saying is that they are superb tools, and they really help me get the point across. My sales results, I think, prove it."

"Well, mine aren't bad, either."

As the two women turn back to the meeting room, they both seem confident, almost smug. They have made their point and are satisfied.

Obviously, the question of using or not using audio-visual aids in selling is a personal one. Some salespeople love them; others shun them. But audio-visuals are certainly here to stay, and as new and more interesting models are developed and put into use, more and more salespeople will begin experimenting with them. Even though professional salespeople recognize that audio-visuals can never substitute for salespeople themselves, they can be powerful catalysts in selling.

This chapter discusses the full range of audio and visual aids, all the way from the product itself, through brochures, catalogues, scratch pads, displays, flip charts, chalkboards, charts and graphs, to more complicated aids like tape recorders, screen projectors, and video equipment, as well as miscellaneous items such as advertisement offprints and newspaper or magazine articles.

THE PRODUCT ITSELF

Nothing sells a product better than the product itself. If the customer can actually see the product and examine it, he doesn't really need pictures or descriptions. For example, you need a lamp for your room and have budgeted for it. You want a nice one. You go to a fancy decorator shop and look around. Suddenly you see a particular lamp that is perfect. You examine it. You touch it. You pick it up. You are sold. No salesperson has to point out the good features or persuade you.

Have you ever bought a new car? All car salespeople agree that the first thing they want to do is to get the customer to slip behind the wheel. One sniff of that new-car smell and the customer is half-sold already, even before he has inquired about all the features of the car or its availability. Salespeople who go out to customers also know how effective the actual product can be, but some products are simply too big to carry around. In this case, visual aids are obviously useful. Visual material such as graphs, charts, and so on can have value in the selling of intangibles such as insurance, or bonds, or services of one sort and another.

DISPLAYS

A display is any visual arrangement of products or services in a store, trade show, convention, meeting, merchandise mart, or similar area. Goods are arranged in as attractive a way as possible to draw attention. Displays are a prominent part of all retail selling, a way of stimulating interest or educating the customer about the benefits of a product or service. In any situation in which the customer is the mover and can choose to enter a shop or pause in a certain department, display is the chief way of attracting interest. Probably most buyers do not set out in search of one specific item, and even if they do, their attention can be drawn to many items that they might have had no intention of buying. No one knows this better than department stores, and display artists are a necessary part of the staff. Skillful decorators can make store windows that convey a store's image better than a sheaf of newspaper ads.

The same sort of temptations to impulse buying that make customers pause in a department store work equally well in grocery stores and specialty shops of all sorts, and in trade shows, fairs, conventions, and so on—wherever people are moving about and probably in a buying mood. The aim of all display, then, is to catch and hold the eye—to make the public stop and look, and then begin to examine, inquire, and, it is hoped, buy. A good salesperson will watch carefully and know the right moment to approach for the questions. Obvious haste can throw a customer off and make him murmur, "Just looking, thank you."

BROCHURES AND LEAFLETS

Strictly speaking, brochures and leaflets that illustrate a product fall under advertising rather than selling, and salespersons are to a great extent dependent upon the company to provide them with such material. But a good salesperson will know their value and use them if possible.

Leaflets and brochures with photographs and accompanying detailed information can be a tremendously powerful aid in selling. Their use in selling anything of a size too large to be shown firsthand is obvious, but they are also extremely useful in selling smaller items because they are a reminder. If you can give a customer a leaflet or brochure which illustrates the product and lists its features and specifications, the customer can study it at leisure and begin to fancy how it would be to have the product. If size is important, he can measure spaces and do some figuring. The brochure will act in your behalf and help prepare for a follow-up call.

FLIP CHARTS

Flip charts—easels, loose-leaf binders, some catalogues—are designed so that the salesperson can easily flip from one page to the next. The easel form, using blank sheets of paper or cards that can be flipped over and replaced by other sheets or cards, is most suited to group presentations. It is portable, though cumbersome. Sellers can flip printed pages back and forth to reemphasize points or benefits, or they can use blank pages in the same way they might use a chalkboard, to sketch out a point or graph or simply to write a word or phrase, tearing off the sheet afterward. This sort of showmanship has to be carried off smoothly. Practice is necessary.

For one-to-one situations, the loose-leaf binder flip chart does a similar job. Using an ordinary three-ring notebook, you could make your own graphic sales presentation, with photographs, lists, and so on.

Most beginning salespeople find a loose-leaf binder a great confidence builder. A regular sales track can be worked out to accompany the page order. The first page would be an opening eye-catching statement, such as, "Have you ever wanted to be financially independent? Page two could then be a sketch showing stacks of money with the question, "How much money do you want?" lettered beneath. This would be followed on successive pages by whatever detailed proposals or plans were appropriate.

CATALOGUES

Catalogues, supplied by the parent company, are a broad category which includes detailed listings of items and prices, perhaps issued monthly, but usually less frequently, with order numbers, sizes, or whatever, often with photographs or drawings, and swatches, depending upon the nature of the product or service. The range is enormous, and here, as with brochures, the salesperson takes what the company supplies. Creativity enters in knowing how to use the material—being thoroughly familiar with the material, first of all, and then knowing at what point in a presentation to introduce it. It should be evident, too, that a good salesperson will grasp from experience whether the catalogues he is supplied with are a help or a hindrance. If a catalogue doesn't work, you as a salesperson ought to feel free to offer a few suggestions for improvement. In some types of selling, the catalogue is the most important tool of all, because it lists the full range of the product and what can be supplied. Even when a computer must be relied upon for checking availability, the catalogue, infinitely portable, is indispensable.

SCRATCH PADS AND PERSONAL VISUALS

Many old-time professional salespeople, lacking the sort of printed visual aids so common today, got along very nicely with scratch pads. They knew how to use a pencil to make a visual impact. It is a simple device that the modern salesperson could well adopt, even if he is accustomed to printed aids, and it can be highly effective simply because it is so personal and immediate. The trick is to use it skillfully, with whatever paper is at hand if necessary, though to be sure a sturdy scratch pad is best.

For example, Francine Duval works for a computer company as a seller of software programs, which are designed to perform a particular service to a customer who already has a computer (The computer is the hardware; the software, like a payroll program, dictates what the computer should print out in the payroll.)

Francine does not like to show her prospects a lot of printouts, so she uses her own scratch pad to point out company benefits. Her presentation goes like this:

"Here is my program," she says, drawing on her pad a circle with an X inside it. "And here is your payroll." She draws a circle with a Y inside it.

"Let's combine these two into one," she says as she draws a single circle with XY in it. "By our joint efforts, we guarantee you four desirable benefits," and as she itemizes them, she jots down the key words on her pad:

"(1) An error-free payroll system [Error-free system]. (2) At a cost of one-half your full-time person now handling it [1/2 full-time person]. (3) At tax time, an efficient way to prepare income tax forms for the Internal Revenue Service [Efficient IRS forms]. (4) And finally, your peace of mind [Peace of mind]."

If Francine wants to use something a little more elaborate than scratch pads, she can easily make her own. Many salespeople actually prefer making their own, even when the company can supply brochures and the like, because they enjoy working out their own way of selling. (And of course some small companies have only a limited amount of visual material.) This calls for creativity and ingenuity, and some salespeople delight in the opportunity to vary a strictly selling routine. Here is a chance to use other skills and training (photography, graphic arts, and advertising copywriting).

CHALK OR MARKER BOARDS

Every Monday morning the commercial loan committee of a large metropolitan bank convenes in the boardroom to review the loans made in the preceding week. The executive vice-president in charge of the commercial division is usually in charge of the meeting, and this morning there is fire in his eyes.

As members pull up their chairs to the long table, their eyes turn expectantly to the wall at the end of the room where Harry Edwards, the executive vice-president, stands waiting. The panel doors are opened up, revealing a blank green chalkboard. The group is hardly seated when Edwards says in a firm voice, "Commercial loan defaults this past month are up 75 percent!"

He wheels around and in big bold letters, writes the figure "75," adds a percentage sign, and then circles it. He then says, "I repeat—75 percent! What in the world has happened to our loan committee? Why are we making such bad loans? Even with the temporary downturn in the economy, we should not be having this high increase in defaults."

Throughout the entire meeting, not another thing is put on the chalkboard, but all present glance again and again at the figure "75%." The effect is compelling.

Not all occasions will permit such a dramatic use of the chalkboard, but chalkboards (usually green or black) with colored and/or white chalk, or white marker boards with broad-tipped markers, can help in any group presentation. As in the above example, their effect is always greatest if they are used sparingly—to illustrate a particular point. They should not be relied on to make a point that the speaker can make more effectively with the spoken word, but they can supplement the voice. All teachers know this, and like the software seller and her scratch pad, you can use the board to jot down key words or figures.

Here are some tips on the proper use of chalk or marker boards:

- Don't write too much on the board.
- Use concise statements or key words or figures.

- Make sure the blackboard is clean before you start. A messily erased board is worse than no board at all.

- Use colored chalk or colored markers for emphasis.

- Beware of chalkboard glare. Here again, a board that is ineffective is worse than no board.

- As a general rule, print rather than write, and make it bold and clear.

- Know in advance exactly what you intend to write and when.

CHARTS AND GRAPHS

Peter Strong is a prosperous salesperson for the largest envelope manufacturing company in the Greater Cleveland area. In selling a potentially large customer, he wants to emphasize that the Carter Envelope Company has improved sales markedly over each of the last three years by keeping up with customers' changing needs. So he says, "Mr. Jones, the Carter Envelope Company has increased its sales each year over the past three years by some 30 percent." Now contrast this with, "Mr. Jones, let me show you a chart from our Annual Report which shows how our sales have increased over the past three years." The chart (Figure 14–1) is clear and immediately understandable.

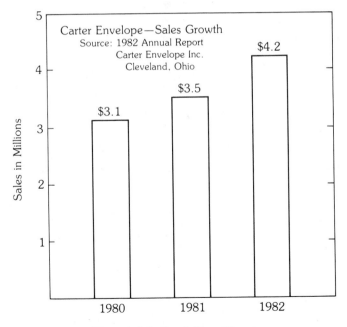

Figure 14–1. A Bar Chart

Charts and graphs can be used in many ways to make a particular selling point in the interview. They can illustrate comparisons, condense statistical information, highlight growth patterns—all aids in the selling process.

It is important to suit the type of chart (or graph) to the subject. Charts are of three main types: bar charts, line graphs, and pie charts. The bar chart, using either horizontal or vertical bars, as in Figure 14–1, is ideal for showing the comparative quantities, extents, sizes, or ranges of things—population growth, sales of a certain product, and so on.

In line graphs, one or more lines trace a trend—unemployment figures, inflation, the value of the dollar, housing starts—over a given period of time. Figure 14–2 shows how two different sets of statistics can be compared in a single graph. More can be shown, but more than three are usually confusing.

The pie chart or circle graph is most familiar as a device for showing how the national budget is being apportioned. The whole circle, or whole pie, is 100 percent and the thick and thin wedges tell the story better than figures. A circle graph (see Figure 14–3) could effectively show a

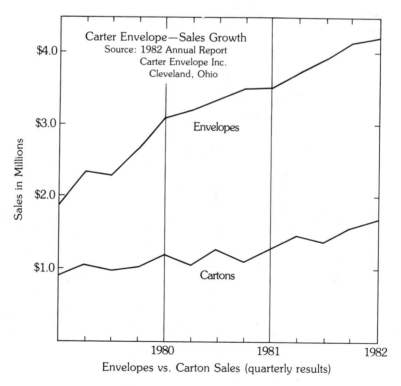

Figure 14–2. A Line Graph

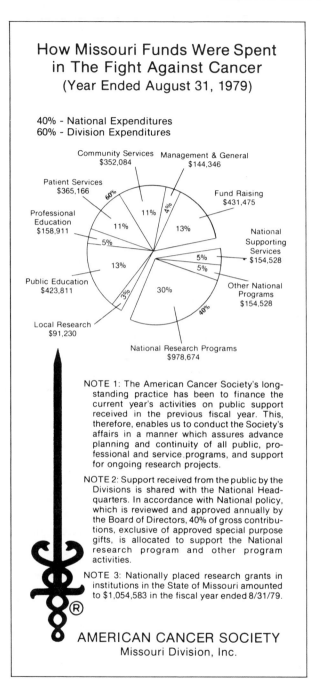

NOTE 1: The American Cancer Society's long-standing practice has been to finance the current year's activities on public support received in the previous fiscal year. This, therefore, enables us to conduct the Society's affairs in a manner which assures advance planning and continuity of all public, professional and service programs, and support for ongoing research projects.

NOTE 2: Support received from the public by the Divisions is shared with the National Headquarters. In accordance with National policy, which is reviewed and approved annually by the Board of Directors, 40% of gross contributions, exclusive of approved special purpose gifts, is allocated to support the National research program and other program activities.

NOTE 3: Nationally placed research grants in institutions in the State of Missouri amounted to $1,054,583 in the fiscal year ended 8/31/79.

Figure 14–3. A Pie Chart

prospective buyer of radio time that in prime time, the largest wedge of listeners are tuned in to Station X, for example, and smaller wedges to all the other stations in the area.

As in all illustrative material, size is important for charts and graphs. If size is misleading, clarity is lost.

Here are some things to keep in mind:

- Make sure the charts and graphs are accurate and up-to-date.
- Where possible, cite the source.
- Do not try to achieve too many things on one chart.
- Make sure the chart is large enough. Too small an exhibit makes it hard for the customer to grasp the meaning quickly.
- Use a chart only if it is really pertinent to what you are saying.

OVERHEAD PROJECTORS

Overhead projectors, because of their enormous flexibility, are a favorite visual aid of many salespeople in a variety of fields. Some of the latest projectors are small enough to be carried in a briefcase. They simply project on a screen, over the heads of the audience, a desired image from a transparency placed on the projector. They can be turned off at will as attention is transferred back to the speakers.

These projectors can dramatize figures, statistics, graphs, cartoons, in a way the speaker cannot, and they offer an interesting and effective change of pace. Who can visualize a series of years with percentage sales increases opposite them when rattled off by a speaker? Very few. Furthermore, the transparencies can be designed for any situation, and even on-the-spot drawings can be made and projected while a presentation is in progress. (Beth Wilson demonstrates this dramatically in the Case Study.)

Other advantages of overheads are:

- They dramatize statistics and other data difficult to describe with the spoken word.
- They offer variety with impact.
- They command audience attention.
- They are portable.
- They are quickly set up and ready to use.

TAPE RECORDERS

Tape recorders, like overhead projectors, can be useful in selling when a special impact is desirable or when the product particularly lends itself to an audio presentation. Cassette recorders, increasingly sophisticated in both design and fidelity, are so common nowadays that no creative salesperson can afford not to speculate on their possibilities as an audio aid. Their use is only limited by one's imagination. Consider, for example, approaching a prospective customer in a distant city with a cassette tape along with a letter introducing a product or service. Prospective customers can listen to the message at their convenience. Or say that your business is the selling of music, seminars, inspirational messages, or psychological aids. You might mail a tape as a sample of your product or play the tape in the prospect's presence.

SCREEN AND SLIDE PROJECTORS
AND FILMSTRIPS

Great advances have been made in recent years in the use of screen projectors with movies, filmstrips, or slides. Closed-loop eight-millimeter film projectors are small, with self-contained screens, and can be carried with ease. They are effective if the films are fresh and up-to-date. Although movies are usually expensive to make and develop, the less expensive and far more flexible hand-held slide projector is a reasonable substitute. Salespeople can show slides as they see fit, and slides are relatively cheap to make, requiring only a few props and adequate lighting.

If portability is no problem, these projectors can be dramatically used to sell products or services. Filmstrips also have a useful place as an audio-visual. Strips are not nearly so expensive to make as films, and the machine is easily portable.

Salespeople use these video aids in specific situations. However, one caution is apparent: no slide presentation or filmstrip can substitute for salespeople themselves. They are all aids. They cannot do the selling alone, but only in conjunction with personal selling techniques.

VIDEO EQUIPMENT

Here again, size and weight can be a drawback. If the nature of your product or service is such that customers will come to your offices, video can be a powerful stimulant, but no one can carry video equipment around easily from place to place.

At regional meetings or other group gatherings, television can be put to good use. Far more flexible than the movie projector, television can be stopped or started at will, with great ease. Its great advantages are its faster and less expensive production costs and its realism, since staff salespeople and real-life satisfied purchasers can appear on screen.

A moderately priced portable camera and recording set are all that are needed to record informal sessions of headquarters' people describing the latest products or services available. Here, too, advances are a matter of time, and, cost permitting, television will no doubt increasingly enter into sales and promotion work.

MISCELLANEOUS AUDIO-VISUALS

Some miscellaneous aids that can be properly categorized under audio-visuals, are reprints from advertisements or stories in newspapers, magazines, newsletters, periodicals, and the like.

A Polaroid camera, or any camera, can be an effective tool in certain sales situations. A representative of a landscaping firm could use a camera to take a "before" picture and then, after working out a plan, return and show the prospective customer what he proposes. Actual photos in this way can be the basis for drawings which can show better than words what the landscaping service can do.

In this instance, the salesperson necessarily works with designers and landscape architects. The possibility of enlisting the aid of freelance commercial artists is also suggested here. Indeed, fruitful collaboration between salespersons and artists may solve many problems. Even on a tight budget, ideas can materialize if imagination is used. If your ideas are fresh and you know what you have in mind, you can usually find someone who will be happy to help you carry them out. Investigate the possibilities of printers, small ad agencies, commercial artists if you have an idea that you think will work and need a professional to execute it.

Reprints of newspaper or magazine articles can also add a certain authority to sales presentations. These should be chosen with care, but they can be useful. Used creatively, material of this sort can add just the right touch to a presentation.

Finally, in this category are statistical tables. At times the salesperson may want to present certain numerical information, and tables are a standard form of organizing such information. Tax tables are but one example.

SUMMARY

Psychologists tell us that 87 percent of all lasting sensations are visual. We retain strong visual memories of a magnificent sunset, a snow-covered mountain pass, ocean waves pounding a beach. In selling, visual impressions can be powerful, and audio-visual aids are indispensable.

The variety of audio-visual aids is vast, ranging from the product itself, through simple aids like scratch pads, to the most advanced equipment. Not all aids can be useful at all times, and every salesperson must choose what he thinks works best for him, and at what times. There is a happy medium between trying out every latest sales gimmick and never ever varying the old routine. Old customers may welcome a new approach; new customers may be intrigued.

As with all other sales aids, audio-visual aids must be used smoothly, never clumsily, in the right place and for the right length of time—as aids to, not substitutes for, your own words. Sometimes a picture is worth a thousand words, but pictures alone are not usually enough. In other words, audio-visual sales aids should be looked upon as tools—tools that will add interest, stimulation, and entertainment to most sales situations.

KEY TERMS

Audio-Visuals	Flip Charts
Brochures	Loose-Leaf Binders
Cassettes	Marker Boards
Catalogues	Overhead Projectors
Chalkboards	Personal Visuals
Charts and Graphs	Reprints
Easels	Screen Projectors
Filmstrips	Slide Projectors

REVIEW QUESTIONS

- Is a picture always worth a thousand words?
- What does back-of-the-envelope selling mean?
- How can cassette tapes help in sales?
- Why are overhead projectors becoming so popular in sales situations?

DISCUSSION TOPICS

- What are some of the problems that may arise in the use of a chalk or marker board?

- Discuss the possible pitfalls of using charts and/or graphs.

- Could the use of audio-visual materials ever violate the professional concept of selling? Explain.

- Discuss the use of video tape in a sales situation.

- What would be a sales situation involving the use of catalogues as a visual?

EXERCISES

1. Using materials from the bookstore, prepare a transparency for a projector promoting or presenting a concept or a product. Comment on the various techniques.

2. From the newspaper collect three different types of graphic visuals for class discussion.

3. Draw up a pie chart showing how your monthly living expenses are apportioned by percentage among food, clothing, housing, transportation, and miscellaneous categories.

Case Study One

Ron Draper is based in Chicago and has the surrounding states of Illinois, Wisconsin, Minnesota, and Indiana as his territory. He sells steel couplings and conveyor belts to many manufacturers in the area.

One particular manufacturer in eastern Indiana is unavailable to Ron. The vice-president has told him that he does not have time to discuss Ron's products over the telephone. He refuses to give him an appointment. Operating on a tight time schedule, Ron feels it is unwise to make a trip over to eastern Indiana to attempt a cold-call visit with the vice-president.

Ron's sales manager agrees that because of other commitments, it is simply not worth the trip for him to go over and try to see this manufacturer. However, since this manufacturer is potentially a large customer, what can Ron do to contact him?

- Discuss what audio-visuals could be used to approach this customer by mail.

- What kind of third-party influence could be used here?

- In view of the possibility, wouldn't a cold call be justified? Explain.

Tony Frank has sold industrial molding machines for years in and around Pittsburgh, Pennsylvania. When he first started out, he used to use his catalogue, but he abandoned it several years ago. He now carries all the information around "in his head," so he claims, and the only thing he actually has with him is a current price list. And he only has that because it changes so often.

He thinks audio-visual sales materials are a crutch. Though it may be all right for beginning salespeople to use them, he feels that, being an old pro, he might look silly to some of his customers if he used visuals. He does, however, appreciate the importance of diagrams or drawings to make his points graphically. So he carries with him a supply of white envelopes as well as a pad of yellow legal size paper that he can pull out of his briefcase at a moment's notice.

Although Tony's sales results are superior, the new sales manager feels that Tony could sell a lot more if he would simply use some of the company's latest visual sales aids, produced at considerable cost by a local advertising agency. Tony disagrees.

- Who is right here?
- Is there a place for back-of-the-envelope selling in today's climate? Explain.
- What dangers are there in relying on memory instead of visuals?
- How could Tony and the sales manager strike a compromise on this matter?
- Is there ever a time when visuals might be out of order for use in sales situations? Explain.

15

Group Sales Presentations

OBJECTIVES

In this chapter you will learn:

- The potential of group presentations.
- The possible scope of group sales situations.
- How group and individual presentations differ.
- How to prepare and deliver a group presentation.
- How to hold the attention of an audience.

San Diego, California, whose balmy climate has for many years attracted a well-to-do upper middle class, is a good city for dentists. Although the cost of living there is high, most of its residents seem to have plenty of money and plenty of insurance to assure prompt payment of dental bills. One result of this happy situation is that the dentists in San Diego are usually interested in good and more efficient equipment.

Teresa Marcos sells for the Dundee Dental Supply Company, a large distributor of various lines of drilling equipment and other dental supplies. Marcos has done well. She majored in communications at San Diego State and was recruited right off the campus by Dundee. After one year as a trainee, she was given a small territory in La Jolla. That was five years ago. Two years ago, when a long-established salesperson in the San Diego area retired, she was awarded that lucrative territory.

Dundee currently is selling an expensive and somewhat revolutionary new drilling machine for use in root canal work. This machine features a high-speed drill graded at the tip in such a way as to cause less vibration, and less distress to the patient, than older models.

Teresa has sold several of these new machines from catalogues featuring photographs showing the machine at work. Obviously, the machine itself is too large to carry around from office to office, and Teresa recently got the idea that a group demonstration would be a good way of selling the machine. Now, with her sales manager's backing, she is going ahead with her idea.

Theresa of course knows many of the leading dentists in the area—several, indeed, bought the drilling machine as soon as it came on the market and are pleased—and she also knows the head of the dental society. With these connections she has been able to arrange a demonstration of the machine at the fall meeting of the society. Ordinarily the society does not permit sales presentations at meetings, but Dundee's new machine has had such a stunning imapct on the whole profession that an exception has been made to the rule. Teresa is excited.

She plans her presentation. The machine will be delivered to the meeting and placed in a dental office setting. A factory representative will be there to answer technical questions. In addition, Teresa will have visuals displayed by an overhead projector and alternately with a slide projector. She also assembles handout material that explains the machine in great detail, several testimonials, and cards to pass out to indicate further interest.

Group sales presentations—large like the one Teresa is preparing or as small as three people—are a useful method of professional selling. Appearing before groups is not as difficult as one might imagine. Societies, student organizations, and professional groups in general are accustomed to special programs—including what amounts to sales presentations—and their program chairmen welcome suggestions along that line.

To be effective, sales presentations to professional groups must be carefully prepared. This chapter presents the various kinds of group selling situations, points out some differences between group selling and selling on a one-to-one basis, and discusses techniques for effective group selling.

GROUP SELLING

Group selling can be effective and is appropriate in certain specific, though dissimilar, situations.

Trade Shows

At trade shows, the sales situation is not unlike that of a retail store. The participants have exhibits manned by a sales staff who must be ready to greet people as they wander by on the trade show route and answer their questions, discuss problems, and give demonstrations. In the middle of a demonstration for one customer, other customers may stop to listen, compelling the salesperson to shift at once to group presentation. Although this sort of selling can be exhausting, it may be lucrative. But usually the actual sales come later, as a result of follow-up cards filled out by interested prospects (see Figure 15-1). Only at some shows, such as furniture or clothing, do buyers go for the sole purpose of placing on-the-spot orders.

Dundee Dental Supply Company
1689 South 21st Street
San Diego, California
Phone: (714) 931-9724

Thank you for your attention during my presentation today. I hope you found it worthwhile.

Teresa Marcos

Please check one of the boxes below:

☐ Yes, I am interested.

☐ At no obligation, I am willing to see you.

☐ Not interested at this time.

☐ Yes, I would like to buy one or more.

☐ I would like more information.

☐ I would like to see the equipment in operation.

☐ I am not interested because:

_____

Figure 15–1. A Follow-up Card

Conventions

Salespeople are often asked to be featured speakers at conventions or other large business meetings. Since many leads may result from an effective talk, great care in preparation and delivery is especially important here.

For example, imagine talking to a group of 300 rural bankers about a new customer newsletter which has been highly effective in stimulating consumer loans. Calling on those 300 bankers individually would take days and weeks, whereas one talk to the entire group takes only half an hour or so. In this case, an effective presentation is well worth the time and effort.

Professional Meetings

Professional associations (dentists, among others) use regular meetings as a way of keeping informed about legislative matters, new product developments, and new services offered by various vendors. These are ideal prospecting platforms for salespeople (like Teresa Marcos) with proper sponsorship.

Company Groups

Salespeople in some lines are frequently asked to make presentations before a board of directors, a group of executives, middle-management people, or employees. This often occurs when they are selling a new fringe-benefit plan or something that will affect an entire company and its employees. In this case, the salesperson usually arranges a series of group meetings with selected employees at convenient times.

Student Groups

Sales presentations to student groups are not at all new and have proved to be a good sales technique, especially for clothing manufacturers. These often take the form of fashion shows, perhaps at fraternity or sorority houses or other campus facilities, or they may be trunk shows, when the presenter rents a hotel room and has small groups of students drop in during a two- or three-day period. In any event, orders are taken on the spot.

Home Group Selling

Some of the most successful group sales on record have been made in homes, and some companies sell exclusively this way, rather than through retail outlets. Cosmetics, cooking utensils, brushes, vacuum cleaners, books, wearing apparel—these and numerous other products have all been sold successfully by this method, usually at mid-morning, afternoon, or evening coffees with residents in designated market areas. Some salespeople combine a natural liking for people with this familiar atmosphere—the home—to fashion an attractive sales career for themselves. Homemakers have found this easy-paced sales career ideal for them because while their children are at school, they can have a gathering at a different home in their territory every day. These sales events also provide social outlets for potential customers. A great deal of merchandise is sold in a congenial atmosphere by this method.

Groups in Retail Stores

Department stores and even specialty shops, usually in cooperation with a manufacturer, use group sales demonstrations as a way of drawing crowds into a department—if not to buy the product being demonstrated, then at least to buy something else. The technique is widely used in cosmetics, housewares, and clothing. As at trade shows, it is an exhausting kind of selling, but it can be highly remunerative for salespeople who do it well.

THE TECHNIQUES OF GROUP SELLING

Group selling is very different from talking to one individual over coffee. In group presentations, varied reactions are natural and expected. Some listeners will respond to what is said, others will not, and the salesperson must be alert to the nuances of the assembled group.

Reading an audience's reaction is not always easy. Some group signals are obvious enough, such as noticeable restlessness and the departure of more than one or two persons. At other times, there may be no apparent reaction at all. Listeners may seem attentive, but are they merely being polite? One cannot take in all possible signals from a large gathering as easily as one can from a single person sitting directly opposite. And if you are talking to a group of 250 engineers about the merits of a mini-computer for personal use and you lose them all, you have lost a lot.

Bland facial expressions, nodding, whispering—these are fairly definite signs of boredom, and if these are accompanied by restlessness and departures, you are quite clearly losing your audience. If one person nods off, but nearly everyone else seems to be with you (at least enough to smile when you want them to), then you are doing well. And if you get a response in a question period, you can be sure you have aroused interest.

Selling to a group is a little like giving a good performance, and you must size up the audience. As a salesperson, you often have an advantage over the actor: you know pretty well what your audience consists of, so you can direct your presentation specifically to it. For example, in selling calculators to bankers, you talk about how easy it is to figure interest rates with a calculator. With engineers, you talk about how the machine is made. To the manager of a small specialty shop, a calculator has special advantages that are different from those it has for a large company which has access to a computer bank. And so on. The more you know about your audience, the better you can direct your presentation.

Speaking the Audience's Language

How close should one try to come to speaking the audience's language? In general, the more knowledge one has of the special terms familiar to the audience, the more specific one can be in speaking. This implies a certain amount of research and study, but since salespeople who make arrangements to speak before special groups usually have advance notice and special contacts within the group—the program secretary if no one else—questions can be asked and plans made. What is the audience particularly going to want to know about the product? Will it be totally new to them, or will they be comparing it with a similar one? Are they laymen or highly trained in your special field? Is *your* knowledge of the product as sophisticated as *theirs* is? Perhaps your demonstration will seem boringly simple: what seems intriguing to one group may be old hat to another.

If you ask questions in advance, inquire about previous programs, look at the annual report or other literature available about the organization, you may be able to direct your presentation more specifically. Homework will pay off in interest.

WRITING SPEECHES: THE PREP APPROACH

Speeches to groups require careful preparation. Start by writing down the main purpose of the talk. Teresa Marcos's talk to the San Diego Dental Society, for example, would have the following objective:

- To stimulate interest in purchasing her company's new drilling machine.

That decided, the next step is to carry out the purpose. This is done by assembling material, organizing it, writing out the main part of the talk, and reviewing the subject to anticipate possible questions at the end.

- *Assembling the materials.* Teresa made arrangements for the drilling machine itself to be on hand. Then she obtained testimonial letters from several of her dental customers. An overhead projector used alternately with a slide projector provided helpful visuals. She also has materials and follow-up interest cards to distribute.

- *Organizing the materials.* At what point should Teresa demonstrate the machine? Where should the slide and overhead projector be used? Should the handouts be distributed before, during, or after the formal presentation? The experience of sales managers can be of great help in deciding these matters.

- *Writing the talk.* Here is where salespeople can flounder. How is a talk supposed to proceed? The surest and safest way is to make the point clear at the outset. Be direct, and after introducing the subject, go right on—following the simple but sound order, beginning, middle, and end. This may be bewildering to a beginner even so, and a little formula called the PREP speech formula can be of great help. PREP—meaning *Point*, *Reason*, *Example*, *Point*—is a simple, usable technique to outline any written presentation.

  First comes the point of the talk. Next comes the reason (or reasons) for making the point. Then follows an example—a description or perhaps slides, or an actual demonstration—to amplify the reason. Finally, you repeat the point. In a more complicated talk, the middle portion—reason, example—may be repeated as often as seems desirable, but it is always sensible to state the reasons together before going on to expand on each one.

  Applying the formula to Teresa's presentation, we might have this, for example:

  Point. Dundee's new drilling machine will increase the profit from your practice.

  Reason. It is more efficient and cuts down on overhead.

  Example. Because it uses less electrical power, this new, high-powered drill can reduce energy costs by as much as 25 percent. And by working more efficiently, it saves time for you and your staff.

  Point. Thus, Dundee's new drilling machine will improve your profit from your practice.

From this simple beginning, a full-length presentation can easily be outlined. In Teresa's case, she can now begin to expand the talk by citing more reasons, supported by examples, to buy her product. She can work in her visuals appropriately, to vary the talk and hold audience attention. Each part of the whole should be planned carefully.

After the order is clear, it should all be written down on 3 × 5 or 4 × 6 index cards (numbered clearly in the upper left-hand corner). The parts to be spoken should be clearly written, either in full form, for important statements perhaps, or in some shortened form. Reminders to show slides or demonstrate certain features should be inserted at appropriate places. Remember that these cards are reminders or cues. You should write them out in your own familiar hand and become adept at using them by practicing several times before the actual talk. Total familiarity will make the final presentation that much easier.

A few other pointers are:

- Intersperse visual aids appropriately throughout the talk. It is not wise to rely on visuals alone, no matter how graphically they make the point.

- A creative beginning and end to the presentation are helpful. Experience will help develop your creativity.

- The card outline form is preferable to a speech totally memorized or read word for word.

- In practicing the talk with cue cards, be sure to show the slides, if you are planning to use slides, or demonstrate the features you have in mind, so that you will know how much time it takes. For the spoken parts, practice by using a tape recorder to hear how you sound.

- Find out whether a lectern or table will be available. A lectern is useful for holding notes and other material and can be a comforting support.

- Find out also—if you plan to use slides—what lighting the room has and whether curtains are provided. Nothing is more exasperating to an audience than slides that cannot be seen because the room is not dark enough.

- Practice standing erect, with your feet about eighteen inches apart. Have a critic watch you to see if you sway or slouch. Don't worry about gestures. The more natural and easy your manner is, the better.

- Speak clearly and distinctly, as you would do in any simple sales presentation, pitching your tone to the size of your room and audience. If the microphone you are supplied with performs badly, don't be embarrassed. Feeling nervous is natural, but if you are confident that you know your subject, you should do well.

AUDIENCE REACTIONS

Although audiences can be frustratingly unpredictable, they can also be delightful. Everyone who has spoken to groups of people knows this, and experienced speakers have usually acquired an intuitive sense of how far to prolong a point and when it is best to move on. A beginning speaker may lack the skill to shift from a carefully worked out preparation, but if you bear certain suggestions in mind, you may seldom have to do so.

- *Never talk down to an audience.* Talking down means that you are treating your audience as inferior. This is worse than talking over the heads of an audience, because it is insulting. Talking above is actually flattering. Think of yourself as one who is there to educate, not entertain.

- *Remember where you are.* Suit the situation to the word and the word to the situation. Make a comment or two about the place: the audience likes this. But be sincere. Refer, perhaps, to a specific person or persons in the audience, if there is an appropriate opportunity to do so. Show that you are glad to be with them.

- *Use eye contact.* Look at the audience, glancing only as necessary at your cards. Look to the right, the left, and so on—catching one person's eye briefly now and again. Don't stare at a point in space.

- *Learn to cope with distractions.* If you have never made a group sales presentation before, especially to an audience of more than ten people, distractions of one sort or another can be upsetting. In any large audience, there are bound to be a few coughs, some whispers, rustling of papers, an occasional sharp sound of a dropped briefcase. When these distractions occur consistently, and people start getting up and leaving the room, even the most experienced speaker knows that he is in trouble. No one always has a perfect audience. Moments of absolute stillness in an opera house, when everyone is listening enthralled by an aria, are rare and special moments to be remembered. Even the greatest singers have had an aria spoiled by a cough. The point is to ignore it. Be assured that anyone who has a real coughing spell leaves the room. The person who left so abruptly may be feeling ill or may have another engagement that he must keep. And people who seem to be looking out the window may be listening very carefully to what you are saying. Don't be alarmed. Alarm will show, and your nervousness will transmit itself to the audience. They will start watching you instead of listening to you.

HOW TO HOLD AN AUDIENCE

All that has been said earlier about preparation is the best advice. If you are well prepared—if you know what you are going to say, in what order, and at what length—you should be able to get through in the time you have set for yourself. But say you find yourself confronted with unexpected difficulties: perhaps the room is stifling, or because of bad weather the audience is much smaller than you had expected, or, alas, you simply have a dull group who obviously expected something different. What can you do?

If you are well prepared, you can condense or expand parts of your presentation. Always wear a watch that you can glance at casually. Without cutting short the main portion of your presentation, you may be able to show a few more slides, brought along just in case, or add a few minutes of additional demonstration if that seems to be interesting the audience. Don't resort to repeating things or dragging out every point. Don't try to make a lot of jokes on the spur of the moment. Omit technical details if they seem to be making the audience glassy eyed, but follow through to the end according to plan, and maintain your enthusiasm as if you were an actor on stage. Actors can have the most boring audiences in the world, but they always try to give a good performance. And they know how to improvise if something disastrous happens. If the leg falls off the table, it will at least wake up a sleeping audience!

HANDLING QUESTIONS

Most salespersons speaking to an organized group don't have to worry about hecklers (though someone demonstrating in a department store may), but they do sometimes get the odd interruption from someone who is too ill-bred or too impatient to wait for the question period. Out of courtesy to the rest of the audience, you had best cut such questions short—politely but firmly—unless, as could happen, the question is very pertinent and you quickly see how answering it can amplify a point. But don't dwell on the question. Go on as quickly as possible, or say, "I'll answer that later on, if you don't mind."

In open question periods, usually after the conclusion of the presentation:

- Be fair with the audience. Don't allow yourself to be drawn into a dialogue with one or two avid questioners.

- Choose questioners from different parts of the room, not just at random, for you can find yourself caught in one circle of one part of the room.

- If a question is asked so inaudibly that most of the audience misses it, repeat it for their benefit.

- Don't bluff. If you honestly do not know the answer to a question, say so, and promise the questioner that you will find out.

- Clarify the next step for future action. If you have handout cards for follow-up, make sure that everyone gets one. If these and other literature such as brochures have been left on the seats, remind the audience of the cards at the close. Passing out material can be time-consuming, occasionally confusing, but try to do it smoothly. And be sure that the cards are carefully worded. As in Figure 15-1, the choices should be specific.

At Presidential press conferences, a leading reporter always knows the right time to conclude the session by saying, "Thank you, Mr. President." You may not have such a helper, but a quick glance at the program chairman or someone else you know sitting near you may be a good signal to end the session gracefully. It is more satisfying to hear applause and know that the talk is over than to find that while the avid questioners still go on and on, the rest of the audience has slipped away. The avid questioners will always have a chance later on if they are not satisfied.

SUMMARY

Group sales presentations (to three or more persons) can stimulate many profitable sales, but they require a special approach. The range is wide: exhibits and talks at trade shows and conventions, talks to professional meetings, company groups, student groups, home gatherings, service clubs, demonstrations in retail stores, and more. In all these situations, the aim is to hold the attention of a group, and the more one knows about the group, the more carefully one can direct the presentation.

Writing the actual talk through the PREP method of Point, Reason, Example, Point is a good way of organizing material. The talk should not be written out completely but put down in abbreviated form on cards, along with cues for using video material. Careful preparation is all important. This means practicing the talk, rehearsing the video parts, and putting it all together within the given time.

Audience reactions are what you are interested in, but they are not always easy to judge. The best advice for a beginning salesperson is to ignore the minor distractions and concentrate on the audience as a whole without letting your enthusiasm waver. Total familiarity with your subject and with the organization of your talk gives you the confidence necessary for a skillful presentation. It allows you to be flexible if the unexpected happens and still get your message across as you planned it.

KEY TERMS

Follow-up Card

PREP Approach

REVIEW QUESTIONS

- What are the sales advantages of group presentations?
- How do group presentations differ from individual presentations?
- What are the dangers of "talking down" to a group?
- Why is it important to finish a presentation on time?
- Should questions come during or after the formal presentation? Explain.

DISCUSSION TOPICS

- What is the value of handouts or follow-up cards?
- How do you learn to talk the audience's language?
- Explain the PREP approach in speech writing.
- How can you continue to hold the attention of the audience when there are occasional minor distractions?

EXERCISES

1. Select a topic and prepare and give a five-minute talk using the PREP approach.
2. Choose a subject and give an impromptu sales talk in which you demonstrate good eye contact.
3. In a group, using volunteers, show how you can handle audience distractions, including unasked-for questions.

Case Study One

Sally Meadows is in charge of convention sales for a large golf and tennis resort in North Carolina. The owner of the resort has made arrangements through a friend for Sally to appear before the national meeting of travel agency owners to be held at a famous eastern resort, with several travel editors of outstanding newspapers in the United States also in attendance.

Sally has been allotted 30 minutes for her presentation and has rehearsed her talk many times. She has polished it to perfection, and has timed it carefully to allow five minutes for questions. Though slides—professionally done—are part of her presentation, she is thinking about reading her talk so she won't forget anything.

For handouts, Sally has reprints from an airline in-flight magazine of a flattering article on her resort. She also has an ample supply of brochures and rate cards. She has done her homework on the audience, but has never talked to an actual travel editor of a newspaper, though she has talked to plenty of heads of travel agencies over the years.

- Do you think Sally should read the talk? Explain what other methods might be more suitable.
- How could meeting and interviewing a travel editor in advance of her presentation help here?
- If Sally had not met heads of travel agencies through her work, how might she learn the jargon of the travel business?
- What else could she use for a handout?
- What methods of follow-up are available to her?
- How can Sally train herself to be enthusiastic during her entire presentation?

Oklahoma City, the capital of Oklahoma, is one of the largest cities in the the United States in land area. It is a major oil center—there are several producing wells even on the capitol grounds—and nearby is the city of Norman, home of the University of Oklahoma, known throughout the Big Eight Conference for its high academic standing as well as its legendary football teams.

Sid Johnston works for a major drilling supply company. He has just made a group sales presentation of a new oil-recovery process for residual oil in old wells that are pumping slowly or have been abandoned as dry. By forcing salt water through the porous sandstone containing residual oil, this new drilling process moves residual oil out and up to the drilling pipe. The realities of the international oil situation make such recovery extremely profitable.

The audience consists mainly of the last of an American breed, known as wildcatters—independent drillers who lease land on speculation and put down wells hoping to strike it rich. Most of them are extremely shrewd individuals who love what they are doing and seem to love life. They are tough and resilient, and enjoy a happy—occasionally lusty—camaraderie.

Sid has just completed his talk—not very successfully. Most of it was written out in full, and he was so afraid of losing his place that he hardly looked up, and when he did look up, he merely stared straight ahead blankly.

To start, he told an off-color joke. Then he mentioned that he was a Cornhusker fan—a gauche remark at best, since the University of Nebraska is Oklahoma's chief rival in football. He said, "you guys" at least five times during his talk, and almost every other sentence had an "uh" in it. He did have some colorful handouts, which were available at the end of the talk, and he closed his talk with a promise that he would "stick around" to answer questions if there were any.

- Do you think Sid held his audience?
- Should he have told the off-color joke?
- Did he underestimate his audience, or was he simply trying to talk their language? What is the difference?
- What suggestions could you offer about his eye contact?
- What are the alternatives to reading his speech?
- Was his follow-up after the talk adequate? What else could he have done?
- How could he have "talked the audience's language" here?

16

Managing Territory and Time

OBJECTIVES

In this chapter you will learn:

- Why personal organization helps in the sales career.
- The value of managing territory efficiently.
- The value of managing time efficiently.
- How to use a pocket diary, prospect cards, and prospect files.
- How to plan your weekly organizational tasks.
- How to avoid the most common career traps.

Imagine the Ajax Manufacturing Company's main office on a typical Monday morning in mid-autumn. The air is clear and crisp, the sun is warm. Everyone is feeling good, and "blue Monday" seems to be a tolerable day. Employees arrive promptly at 9:00 A.M. and go directly to their desks. The district manager starts his day by dictating some memos to his associates and sending his reports to the home office. The new order department is busy typing and transmitting orders to the plant. The personnel manager is reviewing résumés and his appointment schedule for the coming week. In bookkeeping, everyone is bent over the books making appropriate entries. The whole office is humming with activity as manager, assistant manager, secretaries, and clerks busy themselves with their work.

But wait a minute. What's going on in the sales department? In the four offices right outside the sales manager's door, all four salespersons are just sitting there fooling around with prospect cards. While the rest of the office is working away, the salespeople are literally doing nothing. As each salesperson is asked what's going on, the answer is the same: "I'm waiting for my customers to call me to place an order." This may sound peculiar, but it really happens in some sales offices.

The point is that, in selling, one has to start one's own momentum each week. The sales job is unlike any other because a consistent and regular work flow does not already exist. Salespeople must organize their work week themselves. No one is going to do it for them. That is why the management of time and territory comes under the heading of personal organization and is absolutely vital in the sales career.

No salesperson can possibly succeed without a clear, well-organized plan of action, which is followed faithfully every day. Under the heading of personal organization come many of the everyday tasks such as record keeping, telephoning, filing, writing letters, drawing up proposals, scheduling appointments, and filling out forms, usually in great numbers.

Personal organization is the sustaining skill in sales. Without careful and continuous organization of both territory and time, not even the most superior salesperson can succeed. This chapter discusses the managing of territory and time. It describes the tools that can help in organization, such as diaries and pocket calendars, prospect cards, file folders, and prospect card boxes, and it explains the use of different kinds of record-keeping symbols.

The chapter closes with a discussion of career traps that all good salespeople try to avoid because they either waste time or have a negative effect on one's attitude.

MANAGING TERRITORY

If there is one thing that drives sales managers crazy at meetings with their sales personnel, it is vagueness—as when a bright salesperson reports on calls by saying, "From nine to ten, I was in the south part of town; then I had to drive all the way to the north end for an eleven o'clock appointment; then I had to go all the way out to the west side at one-thirty for an afternoon appointment, and finally came back downtown for my fourth appointment. I'll tell you, Joe, I felt like I spent the whole day driving."

Any competent sales manager would be upset by this poor territory management. Although territory management may seem to be largely a matter of geography, scheduling and routing are also a part. Salespeople have to understand how to get the best use out of a territory, within a certain time.

However large the territory, the first step in organizing is geographical division. This may sound simple and obvious, but without organization, a schedule can—as in the above example—quickly get out of hand. Whether one's territory is a single city, or a metropolitan area with many suburbs, or several cities and towns over a wide area, even several states, one has to begin with a map. Only by studying a map can one determine the size and nature of the territory and how to get about in it with the least amount of wasted time and effort. By studying a map one can divide one's territory sensibly.

Salespeople who cover a large metropolitan area might divide the area into quadrants, north, south, east, and west. Other divisions such as downtown, industrial sections, suburbs, and shopping areas might also be considered. Each of the areas thus defined should then be assigned a regular time for coverage, and appointments made accordingly.

Many salespeople identify the geographical area on each prospect card by making a notation in the upper left-hand corner ("N" for north, "S" for south, "JCO" for Johnson County, and so on). A system of this sort makes it easy to group cards by area.

Scheduling of calls in a particular section according to priority is the next consideration. Professional salespeople carefully organize their accounts in each area, placing the more profitable ones at the head of the list. Then they plot a route which puts their most important account first, lesser accounts second, and so on, with possibilities for cold calls last.

The next step is to assign a particular time of the week to each territory. This is only sensible time management. Obviously, the amount of time scheduled for each territory depends greatly on the size of the territory and the number of clients or prospective clients, and also on how one travels. Ideally, one salesperson's month in the Middle West might allot a week to Iowa, a week to Nebraska, a week to Kansas, and a week to Oklahoma, but weather and unforeseen delays may cause problems. Traveling by car may be more fraught with difficulties than one imagines, and traveling by plane may also be uncertain. These are matters that every salesperson has to deal with as they arise, and some changes may be necessary even in schedules that involve a small geographical territory.

With a little thought, however, even complicated territories may turn out to be workable. Suppose a salesperson has his office in downtown Chicago in a big office building but has several steady customers in the vicinity of O'Hare airport, some twenty miles west of the city center. It may make sense on certain days not to go to the office at all but to go directly to the O'Hare area and work out from there. All this sort of planning takes is a little imagination and thought.

Carrying several extra prospect cards for cold calls on known or potential customers is another good way of using one's time to advantage. It will not do much good to get back to the office and discover cards of several possible clients in an area one has just visited. Thinking and planning ahead are thus very important. Emergency calls may sometimes take one across town, after a desperate message from an old and reliable customer, but as a rule try to avoid wasting time driving back and forth in a zigzag fashion. Plan your calls.

MANAGING TIME

"Time is our most valuable asset" and "Time is money" may be old saws, but for salespeople they are axioms: in selling *the most important time is the time spent with the prospect.* This is not the bulk of the time. Research studies have shown that successful salespeople spend only about one-third of their working time in front of customers or prospects. But the time for planning and preparation make that one-third profitable—or not so profitable, depending upon how one uses it. In both the field and the office, the salesperson should consider how to use his time to the best advantage.

IN THE FIELD

- Decide how many hours are to be spent in the field on a daily basis.
- Determine the maximum number of hours per week to spend in front of prospects, then do it *every* week.
- Realize that good sales interviews can vary in length, usually from approximately 20 minutes to an hour and a half. Allow one and a half hours for each interview.
- Plan minimum travel time based on good geographical planning.
- Establish a time when you will leave your house every morning and a time before which you will not arrive home in the evening.

- Do any personal business before or after working time.
- Always carry additional prospect cards for cold calls on people in the area in case of canceled appointments, shortened interviews, or other time gaps.
- Avoid long coffee breaks.

IN THE OFFICE

- Give priority to items directly related to selling, such as telephoning for appointments, preparing sales presentations, and personal organization.
- Handle all paper items such as correspondence and filing on a daily basis if possible.
- Place in an "Action" file all matters requiring prompt action.
- Place in a "Later" file all other matters.
- Do required reading at home after hours.
- Avoid idle chats with other salespeople or staff.
- Avoid long coffee breaks.

Salespeople have unusual demands on their time. It takes discipline to organize time effectively. Professional salespeople handle this continuing time problem by specific actions as part of their daily routine to avoid too many demands on their time.

- They regularly set aside a few minutes of each day to analyze how they have spent their time.
- They ask themselves what they accomplished and what they did not accomplish.
- If something did not get done, what was the reason?
- What were the unexpected demands that interfered?
- Were they directly connected with the selling time or were they only personal?
- They reassert their resolve to make better use of their time, tomorrow.

PERSONAL ORGANIZATIONAL TOOLS

A salesperson's personal tools of the trade are neither numerous nor expensive: a pocket diary or calendar, prospect cards (usually 3×5 cards) and a file in which to keep them, file folders, prospect sheets. How many of these and their exact nature are a matter of individual choice, and every salesperson has to work out his own system of abbreviations for identifying customers, calls, and so on.

Pocket Diary or Calendar

Call it a diary or calendar, or make it a weekly-monthly sheet or a yearly what-to-do notebook, but whatever its exact size and shape, a pocket calendar of some sort is the single necessary item for salespeople.

Most people carry a pocket diary, and they use it for recording social as well as business engagements. In it they record appointments, with places and times, expenses, and memoranda of all sorts (usually in a separate column), including notes and referrals (see Figure 16–1). So much goes into the diary that a salesperson should guard it with his life! Besides its primary value as an engagement calendar, consider these points of usefulness:

- It keeps track of cash expenditures and entertainment expenses, valuable not only for the expense account but for tax purposes. (The IRS accepts a valid diary as proof of expenses deducted.)
- It usually provides space for entering the names of referred leads picked up in sales interviews.
- It is a memory jogger, making it possible to check back on previous engagements or to keep track of future ones.

Although diaries are of various sorts, the monthly type is most useful and most popular among salespeople. Most annual calendars are too bulky to be easily carried about, and weekly calendars cover too short a period of time. (It may be added that losing a monthly calendar would not be nearly so great a loss as losing an annual one.)

A monthly calendar should contain the following:

- Pages showing the day of the week, and a space to enter in the date.
- An hourly breakdown by line for filling in appointments, engagements, and expenses incurred.
- Some pages captioned for monthly sales to note the business submitted as well as the business that has been delivered.
- Space for writing names of new prospects.
- Space to make informal notes as needed.

MONDAY JUNE 3

	APPOINTMENTS	NOTES
8	John Johnson at Hilton Coffee Shop	Send Johnson picture of 500B desk computer
9	See S. Taylor at IPEX re slow delivery	Mary Alter referrals:
10	10:30 Mary Alter	Norman Petlovic-SL Metals Pres.-int in desk computers
11	Suite 500 1st Nat'l Bank Parking ($1.75)	Helen Spinavich-Custom Software Co-O-P Mktng
12	Carl Costillo	
1	Lunch Catherine's Coffee Sh. ($9.65)	Dr. Costillo-call Tues. for Bd. meeting or proposal
2	Dr. Sutter for teeth cleaning	
3	Office	
4		
5		
	5:30 Home evening 8:00 Bridge Club	

TUESDAY JUNE 4

	APPOINTMENTS	NOTES
8	8:30 Office	Do pay office bills
9	9:30 Peter O'Malley- my office	Write B-day cards for March. thanks for leads (M. Alter)
10		
11	Austin Jefferson 3914 Broadway	
12		
1	12:30 Lunch w/ Sls. Mgr.	
2	Chamber of Commerce Membership Comm.	Call Sacramento office re Spesin Software
3		
4	3:30 Cameriro's for demonstrat	Proposal- when can I get it?
5	Nancy Chin for Beer re Co's software needs at Fellicio's evening	

Figure 16–1. A Page from a Center-fold Pocket Calendar

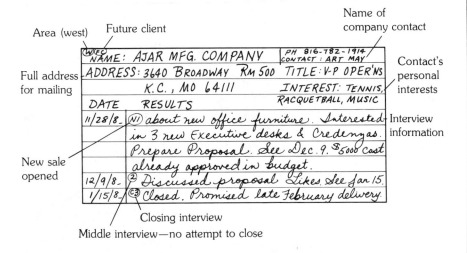

Area (west) Future client Name of company contact

Full address for mailing

New sale opened

Contact's personal interests

Interview information

Middle interview—no attempt to close Closing interview

Figure 16–2. A Prospect Card

Prospect Cards

Just as the pocket calendar is a history of daily life, so the prospect card or customer card is the history of a salesperson's relationship with a customer. It is the working record of each individual customer call. Besides the customer's name, address, and telephone number, the card should list the nature of the business, the name and job title of the contact at the company, the particular items of interest to the customer, and any other details for purposes of small talk (see Figure 16–2). It should also include a column for entering the date and results of each interview.

There is nothing wrong in using the customer card for reference or as a memorandum card during an actual interview, but to avoid possible embarrassment, it is wise never to put anything negative about a customer or a company on the card. Good salespeople never write anything in the presence of the prospect that cannot be seen by the prospect at any time. Put negative comments, if you have them, in your diary later on in private.

The Prospect Card Box

At the end of each week, the prospect cards used during the week should be properly filed in the prospect card box, to be kept in the office for

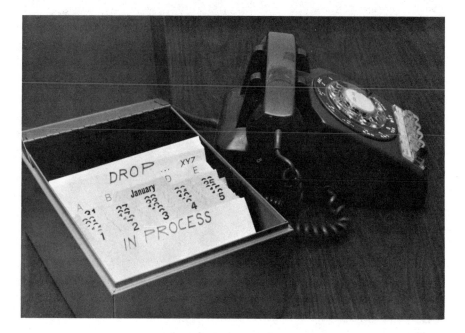

Figure 16–3. A Prospect Card File

future reference. (See Figure 16-3.) The prospect card box contains the prospect cards of current customers and prospects. It should have an alphabetical index, for filing inactive or dormant customers, and a separate section organized according to month and day, so that separate weekly or monthly rounds of customers are automatically placed. Calls or appointments tentatively scheduled for some future date should also be filed in the monthly section.

A certain amount of cross filing may be necessary. Say that a customer asks you to call him some months hence—in June, let us say. Besides filing the card under June, you might also insert a note in the alphabetical file indicating that the customer is filed under June. Too elaborate a system defeats the purpose, however—which is to be able to locate information quickly and in whatever detail the file contains.

Besides the two sections described, the prospect card box should also have an In Process section, with its own main tab marked "In Process." This section, usually at the front of the file box for quick reference, contains the cards of customers whose orders are still undelivered. This section makes it easy for the salesperson to keep track of pending orders on a weekly basis. If a customer buys a typewriter for delivery in two weeks, his card should be placed in the In Process file with a note of the promised delivery date.

The proper ordering of the prospect box begins with the In Process section just described. Then follows a daily file for the current month, in which cards of regular customers or immediate prospects are filed. Customers who say "See you Tuesday the 13th," or "See me next Tuesday, the 9th," or just "See me Tuesday" can be properly filed for weekly or monthly reference. Some salespeople regularly shift these cards so that the current week is always in the front of the section. If next Monday is, say, the 14th of the month, that week's cards will be filed in sequence at the front of the section.

Following the daily file of 1–31 comes the annual file, that is, the months of the year, for the filing of calls tentatively scheduled some months in advance, as when a customer says "See me in October." At the end of the box comes the alphabetical index of customers containing names for whom no calling is in the offing.

One additional section could follow, for prospects you doubt will ever buy from you, marked simply "Drop." It is a good idea to save these cards for an end-of-the-year review. Perhaps one or two can be salvaged.

The prospect card box is an important part of a salesperson's life. If properly used, it can cut down tremendously on the amount of time spent in personal organization. It should be self-evolving, automatically helping the salesperson to stay abreast of sales in process and of future calls.

The Office File Folder

Obviously, not everything can go on a card. More detailed information on each of your customers should be organized in a file folder. This master file will hold all the correspondence and proposals on each prospect who becomes a client. It will contain the details of the client's relationship with the salesperson; products or services sold and other relevant data, miscellaneous notes or telephone messages, and pertinent notices of product changes which might affect the customer or action on the customer's products or services. If the letters on file do not indicate what you have sold to that customer, a copy of the signed order or a dated listing of purchases should be kept. Cross reference to the prospect card in the file card box will provide complete information on every account.

Sometimes these files can get to be enormous, as customers buy more products or services. In these days of duplicate and triplicate copies, it is not unusual for the file of a steady customer to become packed with all kinds of material over a year's time. It is not a bad idea to sort out extraneous material once a year. On the other hand, if the needs of a customer demand a continuing accurate and minute record (such as in computer software where changes may require frequent reference to the file), then perhaps a master file of that customer could be set up in a file drawer called "Master File Customers." Each year a new yearly customer's file might be put in the drawer, appropriately identified with the customer's name for the current year. Each office file folder should contain the customer's name on the outside (to be filed in alphabetical order) and should be placed appropriately in a file drawer marked "Customers" or "Clients." As the files begin to increase in number, more file drawers will be needed. Each drawer may be marked to contain customer files in limited alphabetical groupings. One drawer, for example, might contain A–B. The next might be marked C–F, and so on.

Every salesperson adapts this general method of filing to suit his own needs. It is sometimes useful to have a simple history of customer contacts included in the file folder, in which supplementary data are noted, that being a good way also to keep up an inventory and a ready reference file of the goods and services purchased by particular customers.

FUTURE CLIENTS

Consider this situation. Christine Lee is a successful salesperson in San Francisco. She grew up in San Francisco's Chinatown where her family has had a successful restaurant for several generations. Christine was not interested in going into the restaurant business and thought she might have a career in something connected with drama. But while taking courses in drama and speech at the University of San Francisco she fell in love with a marketing course that she took as an elective. Selling seemed a good idea: it would be a way of using her training in speech, and as a career it promised more security than acting.

Christine at 36 is an enormously successful sales representative of a leading national manufacturer of office furniture. For the past eight years she has been one of the company's top five salespersons, and this year she has been chosen to be on a discussion panel at the company's annual convention in Fort Lauderdale, Florida.

Christine is especially well known for her almost uncanny ability to seek out and eventually develop top-flight customers who become permanent clients. One of the questions asked of her in the panel discussion relates to this ability. Christine's answer describes how she works:

If I'm calling on someone who has no need or interest in buying from me at that time, I make a quick mental judgment of whether that person is a potential customer or not. If I think he is, I immediately pull out a prospect card and start writing the name and address on the card and some pertinent information.

In the upper left-hand corner I write "FC" for future client. When I get back to my office I start a file folder, labeled in the upper left-hand corner "FC," with the client's name and the date. Even though I may not have a piece of correspondence or order blank or proposal or anything, I have the folder, and it serves as a reminder to call the prospect at some future time—usually about a year later. I don't visit the prospect but call him on the telephone and refresh his memory of our earlier meeting.

I note this conversation in the file, and I also file away anything I happen to learn about the prospect—newspaper clippings, for example. If I send any literature to the prospect, I note that too. I might, for example, have a file entry that would simply say, "6/18/80—sent *Wall Street Journal* article on new office displays." In any event, anything I accumulate, I put in that special "Future Clients" file.

By having a separate file, I do not clutter up my prospect card box by keeping cards on people who are not yet customers, but at the same time I am building good future client relationships. I have found that many customers like to be approached slowly like this, and when I call them I never use pressure.

Some salespeople keep future client prospect cards also in the monthly section, filed according to the date of the original contact. This provides an automatic follow-up system for calling future clients at least once a year. The cards are annotated as necessary and are always there for easy reference.

Many salespeople, as Christine Lee also mentioned in her comments, pass up potentially fruitful customers by failing to develop them properly. Developing clients in the way Christine does is challenging, and the satisfaction comes when one is able to erase the "FC" and retransfer the prospect card to the active customer file.

WEEKLY ORGANIZATIONAL TASKS

A mark of successful salespeople is their careful attention to organizational tasks on a regular weekly basis. Personal organization cannot be done intermittently or casually. The procedure must be adhered to week in and week out if the whole personal organization scheme is to work. That is why successful salespeople continually refer to personal organization as the sustaining skill. It literally keeps the salesperson going. Outlined below is a typical weekly organizational procedure:

- Set aside a particular period of two to four hours every week, preferably at the beginning or end of the week, for deskwork.
- Complete all order blanks of sales made the preceding week and submit them to the order department.
- Fill out a weekly activity report of calls made, orders written, and prospects secured.
- Follow up on calls of the preceding week, completing the information on the prospect cards, and, in the files, noting what proposals have to be made up for the coming week's calls.
- Prepare the next week's schedule:
   Assemble proposals for the week's sales.
   Pull out client cards that are listed for appointments (these may already be somewhere in the monthly calendar file).
   Review prospect lists, arranging the sheets in order of priority for phoning for appointments.
   Use the telephone to make appointments for the week ahead.

After all the appointments are fixed, pull out the proper cards and arrange them in order by day (add a few blank cards and other customer cards also). These constitute the week's working file. Salespeople who regularly call at the office each day may prefer to carry with them only those prospect cards for a particular day's appointments instead of a full week's; others may find this inconvenient. In any case, the week's working file should be kept separate from the main file.

Naturally, every salesperson has his own preferences in the matter of when to tackle the organizational tasks: some like Friday afternoons, because not many clients want to talk with salespeople after three o'clock on Fridays; others like Monday mornings when they are fresh; some like the weekend. The essential thing is to make this period of time a priority commitment, a habit, and that takes discipline.

Use of Abbreviations

Abbreviations are also a matter of individual choice, though certain ones are more or less standard. Circling them makes them stand out on a card. A few are:

- FC *Future client*
- SC *Seen calls.* This could also be CS—calls seen.

- NI *New sales interview*, meaning that a potential sales situation has been opened. This is a meaningful interview.

- MI *Middle interview*, meaning that further information is sought or an attempt to close has failed. Too many cards labeled "MI" would suggest that you are visiting rather than selling.

- CI *Closing interview*, where one has asked for the order and tried to close the sale.

- DI *Delivery interview*, the interview where actual delivery of the product or service occurs.

- IC *Influence call*, made on a center-of-influence for new prospect names (see Chapter 7).

- SI *Service interview*, when the customer is contacted to service an existing account. No sale is involved.

A consistent use of abbreviations in both diary and prospect cards is a useful shorthand—a quick, convenient way of describing the stages in a continuing sales relationship.

CAREER TRAPS

There are several traps that can sabotage any sales career. Professional salespeople work hard to avoid them.

The Negative Image Trap

It is easy for a salesperson to become negative. Sales slumps, broken appointments, product delivery delays, and the like take their toll on even the most successful salesperson. This negativism must be defused before it becomes obvious to prospects and customers. A negative attitude throws up a communication barrier in any sales interview. Sensing the salesperson's poor mood, the customer withdraws—the sales potential is dead. The negative image trap can be beaten by:

- Accepting setbacks as a normal part of the sales career.

- Not projecting negative feelings to the customer. Carrying them into a sales interview is courting disaster.

- Recognizing that negative feelings (and the situation that created them) will pass.

Naturally, this is easier said than done. But take a tip from successful salespeople. They work hard at "compartmentalizing" their customer contacts and sales interviews. They learn to table, for the moment, all negative feelings that may detract from their present actions. They reason correctly that sales are not usually made when salespeople are preoccupied with other matters.

The Entertainment Trap

The entertainment trap is particularly attractive to young salespeople, who often feel they can buy themselves success with their expense accounts. Experienced salespeople know better. They know that their own tongues may be loosened if they drink with prospective customers. They recognize that the big night-on-the-town is not only expensive but could even intimidate prospective customers. And the giving of gifts to prospective customers is tantamount to bribery.

Limited entertainment, of course, is all right. Many good salespeople like to buy breakfast or lunch, or perhaps coffee, for customers, particularly when they are dealing with Expressive personality types. They do not view this as entertainment but as a comfortable way to do business. Such an event is viewed as a professional courtesy, not as a bribe. In this manner, they avoid the entertainment trap.

Company policy is often a controlling force here. Some companies may feel appropriate entertainment is an acceptable, even required activity for their salespeople. Hospitality rooms with free food and beverages is quite common at trade shows and conventions where customers' orders are solicited. Professional salespeople follow these rules of thumb:

- If the entertainment is incidental to the sale, it's all right.
- If the entertainment is such that the prospective customer might feel manipulated or compromised in any way, it should be avoided.

Of course, there are exceptions for substantial or long-term customers. And sometimes salespeople and their customers develop valid friendships. If that is the case, there is no longer a question of using entertainment to buy business.

The Spending Time with Other Salespeople Trap

Another trap prudent salespeople avoid is spending too much time with other salespeople. Studies indicate this occurs most frequently when a salesperson is new in the business and looks to his colleagues for help and reassurance.

Frequently, a new salesperson makes sales calls with an experienced member of the sales force. This can be productive. Neophytes learn from proven successes how to:

- Approach people.
- Assess their dominant personality tendencies.
- Make sales presentations.
- Answer objections.
- Close sales.

They learn to use the tools of their trade—how to make cold calls and how to fill in empty time in the field. They learn how to prospect and to cope with loneliness. Ambitious salespeople should take care, however, not to spend too much time with colleagues, just socializing. Salespeople do not sell to other salespeople; they sell to prospects.

The Vanity Trap

Successful salespeople never take success for granted. They know they are good, and they also know why they are good—because they put the buyer's needs ahead of their own.

Professional salespeople do not spend time massaging their own egos. They cannot be self-centered and still earn the trust of their customers. If they do become self-centered, it is immediately telegraphed to the customer, and they lose that customer's confidence, which was responsible for their success in the first place. Here's how successful salespeople remain humble:

- They remind themselves that their customers make them successful, and their customers don't like salespeople who brag about themselves.
- They keep their egos in balance. They know they are good, but never take their customers for granted.
- Instead of trying to overwhelm their customers with their expertise, they give talks at sales meetings, pass on tips to new salespeople, and write helpful articles for others.
- They continually work on their shortcomings.

The Criticism Trap

Finally, professional salespeople do not talk down their competitors' products, services, or salespeople to their customers. They may be aware of, and feel strongly about, the negative aspects of a particular company, salesperson, service, or product, but they will not voice this to a customer. There are good reasons for this.

People who hear negative things about others are generally suspicious of the motives of those they hear them from. Furthermore, downgrading competitors is unprofessional because it implies the role of judge and jury. That is the customer's role. Salespeople are advocates, not judges. Therefore, professional salespeople simply do not criticize. They may answer objectively when asked a question, but they will not pursue the point.

Suppose Jolen Whitecomb, an industrial equipment salesperson, is asked a direct question by a prospective buyer: "Jolen, I know International is one of your keenest competitors. But, I hear their service is really poor lately. Have you heard that?"

Let's assume that Jolen has heard that International's service is poor. But listen how professionally he answers this question: "Yes, Mr. Ambrose, I have heard that, too. But you know, on balance, it's a great company, and I'm sure whatever service problems they do have will be worked out in the very near future. Now, as I was saying..."

Successful salespeople do not capitalize on a competitor's product shortcomings or on the ineptness of its sales staff. They do not want to sell by default. Such sales tactics rarely pay off and may come back to haunt them someday.

Emotionally mature people find something unpleasant about discussing others' faults. Competent salespeople know this and live by a code that says "Don't knock the competition." They don't have to tear down others to build themselves up.

SUMMARY

The proper management of territory and time, and careful and regular attention to all paperwork, are essential parts of the sales process. Salespeople cannot possibly succeed unless they outline a plan of personal organization and follow it. Disciplined management of both territory and time will result in more time spent with prospective buyers.

Managing territory and managing time go together. The good salesperson knows his territory and works out a sensible way of covering it to best advantage with the least amount of wasted time. This means maintaining an accurate customer-prospect file, studying the map, and making appointments wisely to ensure the maximum number of hours in the presence of prospective customers. Most salespeople try to keep a regular daily starting and stopping time, and they avoid time wasters such as personal business and long coffee breaks.

The schedule also has to provide for a set time each week for record keeping, telephoning, filing, writing letters, drawing up proposals, scheduling appointments, and filling out order blanks and weekly activity reports. Conscientious adherence to one's personal schedule and orderly habits of work are essential.

The chapter also described the aids to organization: the pocket diary or calendar for recording daily business as well as personal engagements; prospect cards for recording information on prospective buyers and future clients and prospect card boxes for proper filing and weekly and monthly follow up of them; and office file folders for organizing information on customers.

A discussion of career traps ended the chapter. Managing one's attitude is as important as managing time and territory. The salesperson who wants to succeed must be constantly on guard against behavior, attitudes, and practices that might jeopardize his or her career.

KEY TERMS

Career Traps

Pocket Calendar

Prospect Cards

Prospect Files

Territory Management

Time Management

Weekly Organizational Procedures

Weekly Activity Report

REVIEW QUESTIONS

- Why is territory management important in selling?
- What does the phrase "time is money" mean to the salesperson?
- Why should the salesperson carry a pocket calendar instead of using an office or desk calendar?
- What is kept in the "In Process" section of the prospect card box?
- What is meant by the term "future client"?
- Why do some customers respond negatively to entertainment?

DISCUSSION TOPICS

- Why is personal organization so important in selling?
- Discuss the reasons why salespeople should strive to be in the presence of prospective buyers a minimum number of hours each week.
- Discuss the various other personal organizational tools available to salespeople.
- What is wrong with long coffee breaks?
- Discuss the importance of a fixed time every week to do personal organization.

EXERCISES

1. Find a map of your local metropolitan area. (If you live in a rural district, get a map of the entire state.) Then divide up areas by initials on the map for north, south, east, west, central, and so on. Using a fictitious sales field, number the areas according to priority 1, 2, or 3, depending on your understanding of customer values.

2. Interview a working salesperson on the contents of this chapter and draw up a report. Some questions that could be asked are:

    How much time do you spend in front of customers or prospects each week?

    How do you arrive at a priority list of your customers or prospects? Do you set aside a time each week for personal organization? When?

    What kind of pocket calendar do you use: weekly, monthly, annual?

3. Write out a daily schedule on a sheet similar to Figure 16–1, showing calls and using abbreviations to describe each call. Make some hypothetical notes on the right side of the page.

Carlos Garcia is a real estate salesman in Laredo, Texas. After ten years of effort with the leading commercial agency in town, he is one of the top three salespeople among the staff of twenty-four.

One of Carlos's strong points has always been his personal organizational ability, and a three-hour period for deskwork on Saturday mornings has long been a fixed part of his schedule. Lately, however, he has been spending Saturday mornings at home with his two little girls, now seven and eight years old.

Carlos used to get a lot done on Saturdays—not only filing and correspondence but also thinking, about his own future, about possible future clients. He also made occasional telephone calls to clients to arrange appointments for the following week. On Monday mornings he did the bulk of his telephoning.

At first, Carlos thought he would be able to rearrange his schedule and take care of his personal organizational work on Friday afternoons after three, but he finds that he is constantly interrupted by telephone calls and by two younger salespeople who greatly admire him and want to talk over sales ideas with him.

Carlos genuinely likes to help other salespeople, but he wishes he could be left alone so that he could get his work done. He has told the switchboard operator to hold his outside calls, but he can't do much about the in-office calls from staff personnel, including his sales manager, who has a habit of calling to talk on Friday afternoons.

He doesn't know whether he should go back to his old schedule, thereby depriving himself of much wanted time with his children, or try to find some other time during the week for desk work.

- What should Carlos do? Should he go to his sales manager for help?
- Is there any way Carlos can secure his privacy during office hours?
- Would there be any problems if Carlos brought his personal organizational work home? Explain.
- What are Carlos's other alternatives, if any?

Case Study Two

Janet Tipton is a moderately successful salesperson for a business journal in Nashville, Tennessee. She started out as a journalist—she majored in journalism at college, worked for a local newspaper for two or three years, and then got a job with this same business journal, a monthly publication geared toward business executives in the Nashville area.

After writing articles and doing interviews for a time, Janet became interested in the advertising side and switched over to sales.

She still likes selling, but her sales manager thinks she is spending far too much time on personal organization, particularly on the long-hand letters she loves to write to prospects she has called on during the week.

Janet insists that this letter writing is a necessary part of her image-building. She feels strongly that her creative letters do much to condition prospects to buy from her. Her sales manager agrees, but thinks she simply cannot afford the office time required to write these letters. He wants her to spend more time in the field.

- What can Janet do to increase her time in the field?
- Can her sales manager help her? How?
- Discuss ways Janet could write all these letters and still increase her field activity.
- Can Janet have the best of both worlds here? Explain.

Following Up and Building a Clientele

17

OBJECTIVES

In this chapter you will learn:

- The value of client building.
- The use of follow-up as the key to client building.
- The reasons customers become repeat buyers.
- What makes a good delivery interview.
- The techniques of successful follow-ups.
- How to handle customer complaints.

Houston, Texas, in the heart of the Sun Belt, the largest city in the entire south-southwest, is a city of great diversity. It is an industrial giant, financial hub, and one of the nation's major oil centers. Besides having one of the world's largest concentrations of petrochemical works, it has space and science research firms, electronics plants, steel mills, shipyards, grain elevators, packing houses, and a variety of factories manufacturing and assembling a vast array of products.

Ted Miller came here 15 years ago with a national packaging products company which has been one of the leaders in expanding and developing the tape industry. Its reinforced tapes are widely used and imitated; reinforced tapes have indeed made binding twine almost obsolete on most kinds of packaged goods.

Ted has acquired a near monopoly on sales of tape to medium-sized manufacturing companies in the area, but he is beginning to run into some stiff competition. He is a good salesman and has made large sales, but he has never made any special effort to go after repeat purchases and the purchases of other products. His method of operation has been primarily to ascertain the basic needs of a particular manufacturing concern, make the sale, and then assume that the company will reorder on its own as the need arises. This requires a minimum of customer contact after the sale.

Linda McDermott, a recent graduate of Baylor University, where she majored in marketing, turned down Dallas in favor of Houston because the company she works for (a direct competitor of Ted's company) convinced her that Houston has a solid market for their packaging products. Her sales manager has told her that Ted Miller's company dominates the market in Houston and that she will have to prove her worth—and that of her product—to the various purchasing directors who have been accustomed to dealing with Ted. Linda realizes this: after considerable market research, she has concluded that the best customers for her products would be the same companies Ted has pretty much had to himself for the past 15 years.

During Linda's first week in Houston, on three separate occasions when she talked to purchasing directors, she heard criticisms of Ted's lack of follow-up. One comment was, "Ted's a great salesperson, but once he makes a sale you never hear from him again." Another customer said, "His products are fine and his company services the account when necessary, but Ted's never around to answer any complaints and I don't like having to call the home office all the time." The third said, "Ted could do a lot more good with us if he would give us better service and call on us from time to time just to see how we are doing."

Later comments and hints have borne out Linda's sense that she has a golden opportunity in Houston. Ted's clients like his company's products and like him too, but they say that he never follows up, never calls on them. The only time they hear from him is when he wants to write another order.

Linda explains all this to her regional sales manager who comes down from Dallas twice a month for a day to talk over Linda's sales. The sales manager is excited about this opening and tells her, "Linda, this is a great opportunity. I know Ted's products are first rate, but obviously his follow-up is poor. All you have to do is to make a reasonably competitive presentation and then follow through with good service, and we will secure a great market down here." Now, one by one, Linda is picking off

Ted's customers in the Greater Houston area. Ted has tried to recover, but it is too late.

The moral is obvious: building a successful clientele of repeat buyers demands follow-up and service. Professional salespeople recognize that building customer loyalty will ensure repeat sales—continuing reorders and new orders of different products. It means "growing vertically" with customers.

This chapter discusses the importance of follow-up and client building, the reasons why customers like to buy from the same salesperson, and the ways of building a clientele. It also discusses the delivery interview and the necessity for thanking the customer for the business and the value of asking for referred leads at that time. Planned call-back is discussed along with the various methods of keeping in touch with the customers. The chapter closes with a discussion of ways of handling customer complaints.

WHY FOLLOW UP AND BUILD A CLIENTELE?

Successful salespeople know the value of repeat sales to satisfied customers. Developing steady customers with potential for growth is much easier than continually trying to sell new customers. Ted Miller, being from the old school, never appreciated this point. As long as the market was there and he could find enough new customers, he did not have to bother about building up his current customers.

With competition on the rise, new customers are not so easy to find as they may once have been. It is only sensible to try to build a clientele of repeat buyers, and most professional salespeople today prefer the vertical growth concept over selling a large number of customers. Repeat sales build customer loyalty and are in the long run far more profitable than an equivalent number of new sales spread among several customers.

CUSTOMER LOYALTY

There is no special mystery behind customer loyalty. People simply like to deal with a person whom they know and trust—in the way that they like to frequent a favorite restaurant, or go back to the same vacation spot, or buy their clothes at the same shop, often from the same salesperson, year after year.

A busy customer likes knowing that someone who understands his needs or problems will be available to help. Salespeople who give their customers reliable service are always welcome back. Their dependability allows customers to concentrate on other details of their business.

Customers give repeat business to salespeople for the following reasons:

- They are satisfied with the products purchased.
- They know they can count on the continuing service.
- They like the sales representative who sold them and feel a sense of loyalty to him.
- They like the easiness of dealing with familiar salespeople.

DELIVERY INTERVIEW

Not all types of selling involve a delivery interview as such: no salesperson actually delivers a truckload of parts or an oil-drilling rig. But when delivery of a product or papers necessary to the commencing of a service is a natural part of the sales cycle, this last interview can be of great importance.

Inexperienced salespeople, eager to get on to the next sale, often fail to appreciate the value of a well-executed delivery interview in yielding future sales to the same customer, and frequently solid referred leads as well. The delivery interview is in many ways a courtesy call. It starts with the practical, that is, the presenting of the product itself or the papers that begin the service. Then the salesperson reaffirms the client's reasons for buying the product or service as well as his good judgment in doing so. The next step is to discuss any particulars concerning the product—other appropriate personnel who may be called upon for service, and so on. At this time, too, the salesperson explains the operation of the product or service to the appropriate employees.

Properly handled, this interview is not the conclusion but the beginning of a solid relationship between the client and the company that the salesperson represents. Even if the salesperson should be shifted to new territory, the relationship should continue. So he takes care to explain and answer questions fully. When he leaves, he can feel satisfied that his clients are satisfied.

One successful salesman for a computer software company attributes his success in holding clients to his ability to get along with customers' employees at all levels. He talks to everyone on an equal basis, from the highest officer in a company to the factory line worker.

He explains: "Over the years, I have found that good customer relationships are helped by the customers' feeling they are equal or even above me in intelligence, not only with relation to the goods and services

I am selling, but in other matters as well. This doesn't bother me at all. I just want those people to feel the sincerity I honestly want to project. I never talk down to them. And the fact they feel they are sharper than I am is OK with me. Frankly, I have learned that some customers like to feel just a bit superior to those who are selling them goods or services. I don't know why, they just do."

The final portion of the delivery call should be with the decision-maker—purchasing agent, or whomever—to thank him again for the business and reaffirm the continuing service to follow. After such comments, the ideal time for asking for referred leads is at hand. This is covered in Chapter 7.

Depending on the goods or services sold, the delivery interview may take up the better part of a working day, and competent salespeople never try to squeeze in this call. They plan carefully and allow plenty of time, knowing that this interview can be the foundation for building future vertical growth with a customer.

PLANNED CALL-BACK

Successful salespeople usually plan a call-back on the customer after a suitable interval. Setting a time is a matter of choice. Often it is done by telephone later, but some salespeople like to set a time at the delivery interview as their final comment after procuring referred leads. If the product sold is new to the employees, or complicated, the customer may be glad to know that the salesperson will be calling in at a given date to answer questions. Planned call-back is particularly important if the product itself has been delivered by truck or some such way rather than by the salesperson himself. If the product sold has had to be installed, call-back would properly come as soon as the work is done (perhaps while it is being done). In this case it would be the equivalent of a delivery interview, to be followed by another call later on. The most important point here is not *when* the call is made, but that it *is* made.

KEEPING IN TOUCH

Coca-Cola built an empire from creative and persistent advertising over the years so that the word "Coke" became synonymous with "soft drink." Professional salespeople want to get their customers conditioned in much the same way, so that they will think of them automatically whenever they require additional service. They do this by not letting the customers forget them. Keeping in touch is possible through a variety of creative ways. Here are some proven methods:

- A predelivery letter (see Figure 17-1).
- A note reminding the customer of the first interview (see Figure 17-2).
- A short written note after delivery asking if everything is all right.
- Restating availability by a simple phone call.

MODERN OFFICE SYSTEMS ASSOCIATES

12 APPLETREE COURT
ST. PAUL, MINNESOTA 55420
(612) 853-2398

Dear Mr. Smith:

    Thank you again for your order of the word processor. My company and I are both grateful. You have made a sound purchase, and we look forward to a long and satisfying relationship with you and your fine company.

    I shall deliver the processor on March 9 as agreed. At that time I shall be happy to explain its operation to your staff and answer any questions they may have. Until then,

               Yours sincerely,

Figure 17–1. A Predelivery Letter

- Impromptu goodwill calls.
- Cards at special times of the year, such as Christmas and Thanksgiving, particularly to good clients.
- Brief telephone calls on items of mutual interest, such as customer's mention in local newspapers.

5237 Verona Road • Vallejo, California 94590 • (415) 939-6866

Dear Mr. Burstein:

    It was a year ago today that we met in your office. I have not forgotten you and appreciate your continuing confidence in me and my company.

    I hope we shall be able to serve your fine organization for many more years. Please call me if I can be of service.

                Regards,

Figure 17–2. A Customer Anniversary Note

- Fliers about product changes or other information, accompanied by a handwritten note.
- Miscellaneous but related information such as company announcements or sales progress reports.
- Letters containing newspaper items of interest to the customer.
- Notices of achievement awards and honors earned by the salesperson. These are best sent by the sales manager not the salesperson (see Figure 17-3).

Such methods of keeping in touch build strong customer-salesperson relationships. The letter from the national sales manager makes Mr. Gray pleased for Linda McDermott and pleased on his own behalf too, since he can say to himself, "After all, I contributed an awful lot to her good sales record." He may of course turn around and decide that he should try to help Ted Miller out by giving him a sale, but chances are he will stick with the successful Linda McDermott.

Every customer is different, of course, and it is only natural, too, that large customers get rather more attention than small, occasional customers. Some types of sales—a new bookeeping system, for example, or word processors for an entire department—may require several postsale sessions and numerous call-backs, whereas other sales are comparatively routine. But even the most modest sales require some keeping in touch. One should never make assumptions about a customer. Quite apart from maintaining your own reputation as a courteous and dependable salesperson, your call-backs to small customers could lead, through referral, to other customers in the same area. And just as easily, slighting a customer because he seems unimportant might lose you a large order some day.

Professionals never ignore any customer account. They do what is required to nurture and expand all their accounts, and they look upon the time it takes for call-backs as an investment in their own future and a valued opportunity to build customer goodwill.

ADDITIONAL WAYS TO BUILD GOOD CUSTOMER RELATIONSHIPS

- Keep them abreast of changes affecting products or services they have purchased.
- Become a resource person for customers requiring or requesting allied product or service information.

R.A. DALTON COMPANY

114 MAYO DRIVE
NEW SMYRNA BEACH, FL. 32069
813/663-8143

Dear Mr. Gray:

I thought you might like to know that Linda McDermott has just received our company's Outstanding Salesperson's Award for high sales last year in the state of Texas. Her sales of 152 percent of quota were substantially helped by your company's orders.

Thank you again for your continuing support. We are proud to have Linda on our sales staff.

Regards,

Randy New
National Sales Manager
R.A. Dalton, Company

Figure 17–3. A Letter from a Sales Manager

- Do favors for customers, even when sales are not involved. Helping a customer's terminated employee find a new job would be an example.

- Write notes to the customers' employees who use the products or services involved.

- Help customers get business whenever possible.

- Talk favorably about customers to others in the community. This frequently gets back to the customer. People like to hear they have been mentioned favorably.

These miscellaneous activities may take a little time and effort, but they are all useful ways of building more favorable customer relationships and goodwill.

HANDLING CUSTOMER COMPLAINTS

In our industrialized society, with technology outpacing almost any other aspect of manufacturing, it is little wonder that things sometimes go awry. Machines are not as flexible or inventive as human beings are, and one small breakdown can sometimes stop a whole manufacturing or business operation. When this happens, the one who sold the product that failed has to bear the brunt of the complaints.

Suppose, for example, that just one week after receiving that nice letter from Linda McDermott's sales manager, Mr. Gray finds that his packaging system, sold to him by Linda, has broken down because of a defective part. No one can blame Linda; she only sold the system. But it is up to her to see that the part is replaced—or the whole system if necessary. The way she handles the matter may have a great influence on any possible future sales to Mr. Gray's company (or perhaps to anyone he happens to talk to).

Most customer complaints are valid. Occasionally misunderstandings arise about how to operate a product or use a service; in these cases a visit by the salesperson to the customer's premises can solve the problem. For more serious complaints, a good salesperson should be especially solicitous.

- Listen to the complaint attentively.

- Paraphrase the complaint in the customer's terms, repeating it to the customer orally, or in writing if appropriate.

- Apologize for any misimpression or unanticipated malfunction.

- Be truthful about how much time or expense will be necessary to correct the problem, but do not promise more than you can give.

- Be courteous and patient, even when the customer seems to be unreasonable. Professional salespeople never lose their tempers.

- Follow up quickly and decisively in getting the complaint handled.

Remember, the customer is always right. If the complaint is valid, the customer is not to blame. Courtesy, integrity, and dependability must always be the basis of good salesperson-customer relationships, even when it is the salesperson who has to prove the worth of himself and his company.

SUMMARY

Sales follow-up and client building are essential in the professional sales career. They build customer loyalty and guarantee repeat sales, and they help salespeople to grow vertically with their clients—that is, to sell clients more products and services.

Customers like to deal with the same salesperson over and over, but only if they are satisfied with the products and services. The customer likes dealing with a dependable salesperson, and knowing that he, the customer, is helping the salesperson adds to the solid mutual relationship.

Building a clientele is a steady process of maintaining relationships after sales have been completed. It begins with the delivery interview, where the features of the product or service are reviewed and discussed with appropriate employees and referred leads are solicited. The salesperson expresses gratitude again for the sale.

The planned call-back nurtures the relationship. So does keeping in touch with customers by occasional notes, goodwill calls, birthday cards, reminders of product changes, telephone calls, and letters from the sales manager about any honors and awards the salesperson has received.

The chapter also emphasized the importance of handling customer complaints quickly and courteously. Even when the customer is very annoyed or angry about a breakdown or failure, the salesperson must respect the customer's position and try his best to solve the problem to his satisfaction.

KEY TERMS

Delivery Interview

Follow-up

Goodwill Calls

Planned Call-back

Vertical Growth

REVIEW QUESTIONS

- Why is the follow-up so important?
- What is meant by vertical growth?
- Salespeople should not make false promises. Why?
- Why should salespeople ask for referred leads in the delivery interview?
- List three ways a salesperson could keep in touch with customers between calls.

DISCUSSION TOPICS

- Explain why customers want to develop permanent relationships with salespeople.
- The delivery interview is the key to client building. Why?
- Explain the significance of the planned call-back.
- Should salespeople or their managers inform customers of sales achievements and awards? Why?
- Explain how the frequency of the call-back may vary.

EXERCISES

1. Break up into groups of three. Role play the delivery of a product, with one student playing the salesperson, another the customer, and the third, a critic. Exchange roles.

2. Interview two salespersons to find out how they keep in touch with customers. Write up a short summary for class discussion.

3. In class, name a valid customer complaint and call on your fellow students at random to answer the complaint as an experienced salesperson would.

Bob Pulaski represents the largest conveyor system manufacturing company in the country, located in Elkhart, Indiana. After 15 months soliciting, proposing, and discussing, he has sold a good-size conveyor belt system to a large agricultural equipment manufacturer in DeKalb, Illinois. His original contact was the vice-president of operations, but most of his association has been with the plant manager, Jason Marquis, and it was through Jason that Bob made the sale. They met several times and redesigned the plant setup to accommodate the conveyor system. After the system was installed, Bob spent three days in the plant going over details with production-line supervisors and other employees who will be responsible for operating and maintaining the system.

As he is having a cup of coffee in the late afternoon of his third day at the plant, Bob asks Jason to name a date when he can call back to see how things are going. Jason seems to think no such call is required: "I feel as if I had manufactured this thing myself, and so do many of our line people out there. Anyway, at the rate we work, I'll be too busy to see you in the near future, so why don't I just call you if I need you? I appreciate your concern, but I can't promise to take the time away from my duties here for a goodwill visit with anyone—even you."

Somewhat dejected, Bob stops at the office of the vice-president, his original contact, but the vice-president, busy with other matters, wants Bob to deal with Jason from now on—and says he is not in any position to question Jason's opinion in the matter of calling back.

Bob had hoped that frequent contact with Jason would eventually lead to referrals to other plants owned by the same company elsewhere in the country. But when he brought the subject up with Jason over coffee, he was rebuffed. Jason said he simply did not have the time.

- Under these circumstances how can Bob have any planned call-back?
- Will written communication help?
- Would it be wise for Bob to try to arrange to see Jason Marquis after working hours? Explain.
- Is there any way Bob could get some referrals to other plants around the country? Explain.
- Could Bob's sales manager be of any help here? If so, how?

Case Study Two

It is three o'clock on an afternoon in early April. In the district sales office in Madison, Wisconsin, of a nationally known office equipment manufacturing company, Mary Swenson is feeling especially happy and pleased. She has just found out that she will be getting an income tax refund. The weather is delightfully warm after a brutal winter. After a bit more work on personal organization and filling out her weekly report sheet, she has one minor service call to make, and at 5:30 she will be meeting two friends for cocktails and dinner. Just then the telephone rings.

It is Marv Rothman, the assistant dean of the law school. Mary knows him because she sold him one of her company's copying machines for the law library. The students and faculty of the law school do a great deal of copying on this machine, using both legal and letter-size paper, and for some months the machine has had steady, continuous usage.

"Mary, the blasted paper tray broke, and we can't seem to get the metal clips to snap in so that we can use the legal-sized paper. The tray holding the regular-sized paper is OK, but not this one. How soon can we get a replacement?"

A sick feeling begins to creep into Mary's stomach, because she knows exactly what Marv Rothman is talking about. The company has had a chronic problem with this clip-on section, and it is not the first complaint she has had about this same defect. Apart from this one detail, the machine has always been efficient and trouble-free.

The research and development people say there is nothing wrong with the design, only with how the machine is used. They say jamming the tray is what causes it to break. For the last six months they have been trying to produce a good substitute part, but so far have not come up with the answer. Mary was aware of this and told Marv of the possible defect at the time of the sale, but she hoped he wouldn't have trouble. To make matters worse, she knows that there aren't any replacement parts on hand in Madison at the moment, although normally there are. Repair is not going to be a quick and simple matter.

The phone call continues: "So I'm wondering, Mary, if you could get some of these parts over here Monday—Tuesday at the latest. The students are working on their moot court case before some of the judges from the Circuit Court, and we'll be needing that machine desperately."

Mary, sighing inwardly, repeats the problem; "Now let me see if I understand what you're talking about, Professor Rothman: the little clip-on fasteners for the legal-size paper tray have broken, and there is no way that you can lock the tray into the machine so it will work. Is that correct?"

"Yes, that's it."

"Well, I understand what the problem is and, first of all, I want to apologize for any kind of machine breakdown. If you recall, I mentioned this possible problem when I delivered the machine. I'm sure when you got the machine, you didn't figure this would happen and neither did I. I will, of course, get on this right away and see whether I can come up with something on Monday."

- What are Mary's alternatives in this situation?

- Would it be a good idea for Mary to postpone her routine service call and go over to the law school at once to look at the machine? Explain.

- Should professional salespeople always mention machine weaknesses as Mary did? Explain.

- Is Mary wrong in not frankly telling Marv Rothman that she probably cannot get the parts by Monday?

18 Selling Creatively

OBJECTIVES

In this chapter you will learn:

- What creativity means.
- How to use it as a technique in the sales process.
- How to use drama and entertainment in sales presentations.
- How to appeal to the senses.

Jack Smart, 42 years old, is an experienced and highly successful life insurance salesman with one of the leading companies. For the past 15 years he has been a Chartered Life Underwriter, a high honor bestowed by the American College of Life Underwriters on life insurance salespeople who complete college courses in finance, insurance fundamentals, and allied fields. He is also a life member of the Million Dollar Round Table, an organization of the most highly skilled salespeople in the world, founded by life insurance salespeople for the purpose of exchanging ideas, improving techniques in understanding buying motives, and helping the life insurance industry keep pace with changing trends.

Jack started in the life insurance field at the age of 26 as a general salesman. For many years he sold standard policies to young families; then he went on to sophisticated pension plans, business insurance, investment plans, and so on. For the past eight or nine years he has dealt exclusively in estate planning for business and professional people. He keeps up with changes in finance and insurance, and his continuing study of creative approaches to the sales process has helped him maintain a high closing ratio.

Jack has been asked to speak to the Estate Planners Association in Pittsburgh, Pennsylvania. This is an association of attorneys, accountants, trust officers of banks, and life insurance agents which strives to bring a team approach to estate planning.

Jack's talk focuses on creativity in the selling of life insurance, particularly to people whose estates are of some size and therefore liable to heavy inheritance taxes. In talking with prospects, he says he tries to explain the potential benefits in terms that the buyer can grasp imaginatively:

"When I am asking a customer to buy a mortgage life insurance policy, I try to make him see that he has a need for it by saying something such as: 'Why don't we guarantee your lovely home for Marge and little Susan and Peter as long as they need it, in case of your death?'

"In selling a trust instrument to a prospect, I might say: 'Let's let someone else deal with all those investment and financial details. What you need is a reliable supply of good food, warm clothing, and a decent vacation for you and your family once a year.'

"In other words, creativity in selling is for me simply using an imaginative and personal approach instead of a routine one. Using creativity has increased the closing ratio of my sales by:

- Getting customers' attention and interest more rapidly.
- Stimulating the customer's thinking through unusual approaches.
- Emphasizing needs in a more vivid way, and
- Reinforcing conviction to purchase the product or service offered." (See Figure 18-1.)

Figure 18–1. A Diagram of Creative Selling

This chapter discusses the various aspects of creativity and the ways in which creativity can be developed and used to enliven sales presentations and increase sales. Some of the ideas in this chapter have been touched on before, especially in some of the earlier chapters in Part Four on communication skills, audio-visual aids, and group sales presentations. Here we are interested in creativity in a more general sense, and we shall look at ways in which a salesperson can, by using creative imagination, make selling more interesting to both himself and his customer.

Creativity is essentially an expression of the imagination, in which observation and memory also play a role. Two simple little tests demonstrate the way in which the creative imagination sees beyond the expected or obvious.

In the diagram below, which line is the longer?

Now read the following statement at least three times: "Failing grades of students result in forfeiture of grade-point standings of previous efforts."

In the first test, the vertical line appears at a glance to be longer than the horizontal line, but in fact the two lines are equal in length. Now try to remember how many f's are in the statement (test 2.) The correct answer is eight, but the tendency is to recall the outstanding words and leave out the prepositions, which account for three of the eight f's.

Creativity in selling is the application of this same kind of imagination and recollection. It means using awareness and personal attention as a way of appealing to a prospect's needs and desires, even when the prospect may not have expressed those needs and desires. In the case study, "Selling in Action," Beth Wilson appealed to Carl Brown's dreams of the future by reminding him of his staff in the field and his plans to expand. She sensed that by subtly recalling his long-range plans, she would make him realize that the important thing was to buy 30 overhead projectors, and that he was instead wasting time on a lot of rather unimportant details such as the appearance of the case for the projector.

CHARACTERISTICS OF CREATIVE SALESPEOPLE

Creative salespeople like Beth Wilson seem to share certain characteristics which they are able to use to great advantage. Besides the fact that they all really enjoy selling, they have a very special kind of enthusiasm:

- They love a sales challenge and relieve occasional boredom by experimenting with creative ideas in sales situations.
- They are interested in people and show it by being good listeners as well as good conversationalists.
- They look ahead and are resilient. If a certain approach falls flat, they do not dwell on mistakes or nurse guilt complexes but go on to some better approach.
- They are observant.
- Most of all, they have imagination.

WHY CREATIVITY WORKS IN SELLING

Creativity works in selling probably for the same reasons that certain salespeople like to be creative: people are stimulated by new approaches, which lift them out of the boredom of daily life and, perhaps, of stereotyped sales appeals, and they welcome something that challenges their imagination in a new and different way.

In the chapter on Group Presentations we saw how one can hold the attention of an audience by projecting enthusiasm and by using visual aids and demonstrations that are carefully chosen for the particular audience. The emphasis was on educating rather than merely entertaining. There is, however, a place for entertaining in selling. Quite apart from the usual, perhaps overemphasized, meaning of the word—wining and dining—which is another matter altogether, entertaining can be a creative way of leading an individual customer into thinking and seeing from your point of view.

Offensive antics will not entertain, but creative showmanship may. Many great teachers not only inspire their students but at the same time entertain them. Entertainment can stimulate students to learn simply because they enjoy the learning process they are going through. By the same token, salespeople can entertain if they sense that a customer will respond positively to the experience.

Not all customers will like amusing or clever showmanship, and a professional salesperson will know what is appropriate and on what occasions.

CREATIVITY IN ACTION

Showmanship and Drama

Think of a skillful trial lawyer summing up a case before a jury, using each phrase, each gesture to impress the jurors with his cause. Or think of the flourish with which a wine steward presents the wine list, disappears for the proper length of time, and reappears to give suggestions. In answer to a question, he never says, "This wine is good," or "That one is bad." No: he talks about aroma, bouquet, color, and the appropriateness of the wine to the dish. And a good wine steward always treats the novice wine drinker in such a way as to make him feel enriched by the experience.

That is showmanship—a kind of entertainment.

Think of an interior decorator who brings a very special lamp to a client's house, places it in just exactly the right spot, and says enthusiastically, "There! That *makes* the room! It brings all the colors together, picks up *that* orange and *that* blue—and the light there is beautiful." In this kind of showmanship, the timing is perfect, the gestures are perfect, and the language is carefully phrased for the right effect.

It must be realized that some products would seem to have a natural affinity with showmanship. Beth Wilson was able to use the overhead projector effectively; copy machines, typewriters, and similar audio-visual products fall in the same category. One does not need visual aids to dramatize them, because they are visual in themselves. But there is hardly a product that cannot be dramatized by words or photographs.

Creative Language

Using words in an unusual yet attractive way can often mean the difference between a yes and a no from a prospect. Sometimes, word pictures which stimulate the imagination are far more powerful than any photograph or other visual aid. Consider the following examples:

- "Vacationing in Portugal is not an experience—it is an emotion."
- "Your golf ball will fly out of the rough with this club."
- "Jogging could become an addiction with these shoes."

- "Shedding this weight will liberate you."
- "Your life will never be the same after tasting this wine."
- "What you are buying from me is peace of mind."
- "The aroma intoxicates, the taste inspires."

These are much like advertising appeals, but there is no reason why a salesperson, too, cannot try to persuade by using vivid language. So long as the statements are not intended to falsify, they are perfectly sound aids to selling.

Visual Aids

As pointed out in Chapter 14, visual aids such as displays, brochures, scratch pads, flip charts, chalkboard, and so on can all be used to enliven a sales presentation. In recent years some very distinguished photographers have been turning out beautiful work for annual reports. Their photographs prove how exciting all kinds of seemingly unexciting objects can become if photographed by someone with sensitivity and imagination. Close-up pictures of finely tooled machinery, superbly made nails, tires coming off an assembly line—all these and more are common today. The creative salesperson will recognize possibilities in the product he is selling. A hardware salesperson has a treasure trove of items at hand to sell in an imaginative visual way.

Appeals to the Senses

Although appeals to sight and hearing are most usual in selling, smell, taste, and touch should not be overlooked. Nearly everything on earth appeals to (or repels) more than just one sense: fabrics to sight and touch (and sometimes smell and hearing); food and beverages to taste and sight and smell and touch—sometimes to hearing (snap, crackle, pop!); Music alone appeals to just one sense—but silence is part of music too, and in selling certain things like copiers or ceiling tiles, for example, it is silence that can be appealed to. And perfume, though primarily a matter of smell, has been successfully advertised through the medium of television—visual—making a secondary appeal to what one might call a sixth sense, the imagination, in which the very name of the perfume becomes the key.

By using imagination, the salesperson can experiment with using more than just the obvious appeals.

Creativity—Some Examples

Here are other ways creative ideas can be applied in sales situations:

- Salespeople get customers involved by having them fill in blanks in a proposal form.
- Salespeople selling pocket calculators drop them on the floor three or four times to show how sound the solid-state components are.
- Copy machine salespeople ask customers to put several different types of paper through the copier to see how good the performance is.
- A winery invites its prospective customers to sample several varieties of wine.
- Salespeople for residential landscaping firms bring a pot of flowers to place in a key corner of the garden to suggest a certain flowering shrub.

CAN CREATIVITY BE LEARNED?

New salespeople may feel that creativity is something that can never be mastered—that one either has it or does not have it. As with all skills, mastery will take time, but creativity definitely can be learned.

Try, for a start, writing your name a different way—just to see whether you can do it. Try parting your hair differently, just to see how it looks. Go on from there: think of a different way to drive to work, or take the bus instead. Try your hand at a hobby completely new to you, or try cooking a totally new cuisine. If you are a sports fan, go to a concert; if you always watch TV, read a book some evening instead—or play checkers, or look at the stars.

Go beyond yourself. All the suggestions given in Chapter 13 on learning to be an effective conversationalist can be applied here as well. Become interested in others by asking questions. Read the newspaper to see whether it will provoke your imagination.

Reading is knowledge, and one thing can lead to another. If you see a film made from a book, read the book too—and then read some more works by the same author. If you travel, follow a list of required reading first, and then lock at things yourself with a knowledgeable eye.

Try some opposites. If you work in the city, go to the country. If you work in the suburbs, go to the city. Go to a museum. Set yourself a challenge: if you sell sewing machines, try really learning to sew by making something you can wear yourself. All good outdoor gear salespeople are experienced backpackers, and the same kind of practical knowledge can help any salesperson be more creative. Creativity in this sense is imaginative intelligence.

Knowledge of one's product comes first and has no substitute. Creativity is the art of being able to demonstrate the product so that others appreciate its value or merit and see that it will for them fill a need or satisfy a desire.

SUMMARY

This chapter began with Jack Smart's definition of creativity as an acquired ability to look beyond the routine in sales approaches.

Creativity helps in the sales process by arousing customer interest, stimulating thinking, emphasizing needs in a memorable fashion, and reinforcing customers' convictions. More than anything else, creativity in selling requires imagination. The creative salesperson has that imagination, along with enthusiasm, a love of experimentation, resiliency, and an interest in people.

Entertaining customers by using showmanship and drama, expressing ideas in unusual ways, using visual aids, and appealing to the senses (sight, hearing, smell, taste, and touch) are all perfectly good ways of stimulating a customer's interest and making him use his own imagination about your product. A professional salesperson will use discretion and never offend.

Creativity in selling is a skill that can be learned, starting in small ways in everyday life. Simply changing habits and patterns can set off one's creative imagination, and in time ideas will come naturally as a part of making selling a daily challenge.

KEY TERMS

Buyer Stimulation   Creativity

Creative Language

REVIEW QUESTIONS

- What is creativity?
- What is its importance in the sales process?
- How can language usage be more creative?
- Is showmanship unprofessional?

DISCUSSION TOPICS

- What are the barriers to becoming more creative?
- How can a salesperson develop creativity?
- Discuss creativity as it relates to the five senses of sight, hearing, smell, taste, and touch.
- Discuss the general things salespeople can do in their private lives to help them become more creative and thus more effective in selling.

EXERCISES

1. Think of a product larger than a breadbox and smaller than a wheelbarrow which could be put to use in a small, independently owned retail store. Plan a creative sales presentation, preferably using some appeal to the senses. Be specific about the product and the store.

2. Using photographs or pictures cut from magazines, prepare a striking visual presentation of a specific line of products. Make notes of what you intend to say while showing the visuals.

3. Do the creativity exercise on the facing page. Compare notes with your classmates.

CREATIVITY EXERCISE

Many professional salespeople work at being creative. They develop the ability to look beyond the routine. Here is an exercise that will stimulate your creativity. Find the word that is common to each series. It may be linked to either the beginning or the end of the listed words. Enter two words that continue the series in the blanks provided. For example:

Basket   Base   Foot   _____   _____

The common completion word is ball. Your entries could be *golf* for *golfball* or *game* for *ballgame*. As selection progresses, the linking words become less familiar, stretching the creative process.

1. Score   Time   Credit   _____   _____

2. Cran   Blue   Black   _____   _____

3. Day   House   Bulb   _____   _____

4. Shoe   Window   Wooden   _____   _____

5. Law   Dining   Jump   _____   _____

6. Pickle   Wine   Water   _____   _____

7. Bed   Torture   Maid   _____   _____

8. Goal   Season   Fence   _____   _____

9. Morse   Ethical   Dress   _____   _____

10. Air   Ship   Country   _____   _____

11. Snake   Cherry   Orchestra   _____   _____

12. House   Grade   Marm   _____   _____

Carol Musgrave first got into the computer world while studying mathematics at the Massachusetts Institute of Technology. She worked part-time as a software designer for a computer company near Boston.

Carol went on to get an M.B.A. degree at Stanford, and then from among several offers chose to go with the second largest computer manufacturing company in the world, located in the Northeast. She was a service representative for a brief time, then shifted, at her own request, to being a marketing rep. She likes the excitement of selling, especially talking to decision-makers of large organizations about buying expensive computer hardware.

Carol has now been with the company 10 years. She is very good at selling, but the senior vice-president in marketing has often urged her to put more creativity, more drama, into her sales presentations. Carol's argument against "creativity" is that she always deals with the decision-maker in the presence of the in-house computer expert and is therefore able to sell her product in a straightforward fashion. Besides knowing the computer hardware field backward and forward, she also has the mathematical skill to formulate and solve most computer software problems. She has never been worried about not being able to sell, nor can management cite a single sale she has lost because of lack of dramatic selling technique.

A large banking conglomerate with headquarters in New York City has invited a bid from Carol's company for what will be the largest computer sale on record in the United States (to exceed $20 million). Two other companies have also been asked to submit bids. One of the two is probably too small to handle the order, but the other one is the largest computer manufacturer in the world, and competition will be intense.

After an exhaustive study of the specifications submitted by the conglomerate bank, and after months of investigation and rewriting of software programs, Carol's company is satisfied that it is in a position to make a very competitive presentation to the esecutive board of the bank and its in-house computer experts, who will sit in on the meeting.

Carol and the marketing vice-president again discuss the wisdom of her preparing a few dramatic byplays just in case she needs them for this important sale.

- Should Carol follow her marketing vice-president's suggestion?
- Discuss three possible dramatic touches she could have ready for this presentation.
- What appeals to the senses would be appropriate?

The agricultural college at Kansas State University in Manhattan, Kansas, is one of the best in the nation. A few years ago Gene Poutek received a degree in ag economics there (with a minor in chemistry), and he now works as a salesman for a large conglomerate which deals in agricultural chemicals and irrigation equipment. Gene is currently assigned to the irrigation division of the company and is being groomed to be one of the company's senior account executives.

In this particular case, Gene is interested in selling one of his company's mobile irrigation systems to a large produce grower in the Rio Grande Valley near Brownsville, Texas. This system is a huge affair which has to be transported in parts by at least two trucks and then assembled in the field. Gene has pictures and catalogues of the equipment and has used them successfully in the past, but in this instance he feels the need for something more.

Not only is it a potentially big sale, but Gene knows that his prospect is interested in a competitor's system (which in some respects is superior to his). Heretofore Gene has always been able to offset points against his system by emphasizing the superior maintenance service for which his company is noted. He is searching for some creative way of demonstrating the dependability and superiority of his company's service.

- How should he go about it?
- Could he use testimonials? How?
- Are there other visuals Gene could use in this situation?
- Whom should he go to for help?
- Could he creatively entertain the customer here? How?

Getting and Keeping a Job

PART FIVE

Carol Pfander

Background Carol Pfander is an eminently successful actress (and therefore salesperson) in television commercials. Her career has followed the plodding, planned progress of the tortoise, rather than the mercurial pace of the hare, which, contrary to general belief, is similar to the paths of most performing artists.

She received her B.A. in Speech Education from the University of Missouri–Kansas City and, through a graduate assistantship, earned her M.A. degree in theater in 1967. During that period she was active as a performer in what is now the highly respected and successful Missouri Repertory Theater.

After completing her master's, she worked with the University of Missouri and the Missouri State Council on the Arts as tour coordinator and company actress to help form the first statewide tour of the Missouri Vanguard Theatre Company, sponsored by the Missouri Repertory Theater.

Carol's career in commercials began in these early stages as a necessary means of support. Her first commercial work was in Kansas City. Later she traveled to California to enter the commercial field on a national scale. Her first product was for a laundry product. She refers to this as a "clean beginning."

Carol moved to New York City in 1969, pursuing work in television commercials and other acting opportunities. She played a major role for several years on NBC's soap opera *The Doctors* and has since worked in other areas of television, but has always concentrated on television commercials.

Sales Achievements   Over the years, she has sold both on camera and on radio a variety of products—practically everything that can be bottled, boxed, tubed, canned, or otherwise presented to the consumer. This includes Campbell's Soup, Ajax Cleanser, Hour After Hour Deodorant, National Airlines, Prell Shampoo, Dristan, tires, insurance, banks, and sweaters.

Her Comments on Her Career   "I am most grateful to have somehow succeeded in a profession that is highly competitive to an awesome degree. For every one commercial that is filmed or recorded, there are hundreds of highly qualified performers capable of doing the job. I believe success lies in obtaining an adequate background in the field, being tenacious, and then getting the hang of it, which only comes with experience.

"Part of getting the hang of it comes, I am beginning to realize, from selling yourself. In the commercial acting field, the actors sell themselves on several levels. They first must sell the advertising agency on their ability to perform as professionals in a high-pressure situation. Television commercials (which cost thousands of dollars to produce) are usually filmed within a day or a few days, with little time for serious rehearsal. In radio, the recording session is usually one hour.

"Actors usually have about 15 minutes at most to convince the agency of their ability in an audition. In that 15-minute audition, actors must also attempt to convince the ad agency's client that they have all the qualities that will interest and appeal to the client's potential customers across the country. It's the task of being all things to all people within the scope of a given product.

"Finally, and most important, commercial actors are involved in a seemingly public, but really very personal, sales situation—selling a product to whomever may be watching or listening. This involves a one-on-one relationship with the potential buyer. The final responsibility rests on the performers' ability to convince that one person of their personal integrity and the integrity of the product. Most performers occasionally will, as I have, decline a job when it is personally impossible to believe in the product or when one cannot morally justify selling it. If you really don't believe in it, no one else will.

"There you have it, then—salesmanship at many levels and often performed in a short period of time. But what profession doesn't require similar salesmanship relative to the specific needs of that profession?"

19 | Getting the Job

OBJECTIVES

In this chapter you will learn:

- Why it's wise to research a company.
- How to prepare an effective résumé.
- How to write interesting application letters.
- What interview techniques will help you land a job.
- How to develop negotiating skills in the job interview.
- What qualities employers want in salespeople.

Richard Nelson Bolles's manual for job hunters and career changers, *What Color Is Your Parachute?*, has become a classic since its publication in 1972, because the techniques it describes are timeless.[1] Bolles has simplified the techniques of his approach into three basic keys to success: (1) isolate exactly what you want to do and where you want to do it; (2) learn all you can about the organization you are interested in; and (3) approach the one individual in that organization who has the authority to hire you for the work you have settled upon as your life career. The underlying theme of the book is that getting a desirable job is

360

[1] Richard Nelson Bolles, *What Color Is Your Parachute?*, rev. ed. (Berkeley: Ten Speed Press, 1979).

a difficult procedure requiring relentless pursuit.

This chapter discusses methods of getting a sales job and the decisions that the job hunter must make during the process, beginning with choosing the desired geographical area, reading up on the companies in that area which have sales jobs and learning what person is best to write to, and preparing a résumé. Next, beginning with letters of inquiry and application, the chapter emphasizes ways of preparing for the interview and some aspects of the interview itself. Negotiating benefits, when the applicant gets to that stage during the interview process, is also described in detail, as are the various ways of following up the interview and keeping in touch with the prospective employer.

CHOOSING A GEOGRAPHICAL AREA

It seems unlikely that a would-be salesperson could have no feeling one way or another about a geographical location, and one's choice of a location starting out would seem to be more wide open than it might be later on. It can be a very important decision, because once ties are made, breaking away can be difficult.

Sometimes, *what* one sells is far more important than *where*. Quite obviously, someone who wants to sell winter sports equipment has to stay reasonably close to the snow—but there is a great deal of choice still possible.

For a vast number of other products and services, location is purely secondary, and therefore, ideally, a matter of individual choice. Insurance, real estate to some extent, investments, computers—these can be sold anywhere. The trick is to make the decision and find the job. Many people prefer to stay where they grew up and are not faced with making a geographical choice. Others are eager for new horizons.

Frank Rose has just received his Associate of Business degree in marketing from Spring Valley Junior College in Evanston, Illinois. Frank grew up in Cicero, Illinois, and has been living in Chicago. He would like to leave the cold and crowded city behind and move to the Southwest.

Frank has never been in the Southwest, but it appeals to him for a number of reasons. He thinks he might like the Dallas–Fort Worth area or perhaps Arizona, either Phoenix or Tucson—but he has a lot of questions. What is the climate really like? How high is the cost of living? Are there many jobs available in selling—and for what kinds of companies? Frank is black; will that make things harder for him? He doesn't want to spend all his money going around looking for a job and be disappointed.

Many young graduates are faced with this same problem. Very sensibly, they know they must do some research—perhaps get a few leads or even arrange some interviews. How can they go about this?

The campus library is a logical starting place. Most university and college libraries have a large assortment of periodicals as well as reference books (and helpful librarians). Anyone interested in selling, as Frank is, can study the trade magazines, area surveys, business periodicals, and the like. Certainly the library will have the answers to questions about climate, cost of living, the rate of unemployment, cultural advantages, and so on.

Having decided that the area sounds worth trying, Frank's next step could be the college placement office. Because of the great mobility of Americans, college placement offices usually have a good relationship with large firms that have a continuous need for new personnel. They rely on each other to satisfy their needs. Frank, through his college placement office, could get in touch with similar campus offices in Texas and Arizona.

The placement office might also have the names and addresses of alumni living in the Southwest who have offered to help students and recent graduates get started (this is particularly true of large universities with far-flung alumni). At least Frank might be able to find out from them what opportunities there are for selling office equipment and supplies (his choice) in the areas he has in mind.

If Frank asked around among friends or family, he might discover a few more helpful leads and learn more about the cities from a personal point of view. The chambers of commerce would happily send information, too, and travel agencies could give him brochures, perhaps maps.

It is well to remember that getting the first job may require starting out in a place one does not particularly like and spending two or three years there. Opportunites are not always available in what one regards as the ideal location. These thoughts should be kept in mind in the discussion that follows.

FINDING OUT ABOUT THE COMPANY

Finding out about a company means finding out what a company deals in, how large it is, where it is headed, what its policies are, and so on. Finding out about several companies is usually no more difficult than finding out about one, if they are all in the same field, and especially if, as is true in some industries, a great many companies are located in the same general area.

This sort of research is not as difficult as it sounds. Here again, students can start with the college placement office and the school library. Other sources to consult are:

- Annual reports. These are always available for publicly owned companies. Reports of privately owned companies may be less easy to obtain but could be consulted upon inquiry.

- Chambers of commerce. Encouraging business in their communities is part of their job, and they usually have information on selected companies.

- Periodicals and newspapers. The *Wall Street Journal, Forbes, Business Week*, and other business magazines are all good sources of information, not only for the major companies but from time to time small ones as well. Most good libraries carry several daily newspapers whose financial sections would be helpful. If one is really serious about a special city or town, subscribing to the local newspaper for a month or two would be an excellent idea, not only for checking on the job market but also for learning something about the town itself.

- Personal contacts. These may not always be possible, but they are of obvious value if firsthand. Hearsay information—from the friend of a friend—may not be worth listening to.

GETTING THE RIGHT CONTACT

Finding out whom to apply to—and who actually will do the hiring—can be much more difficult than finding out what the company's financial standing is.

A telephone call to the company, with a request to speak to the sales manager, may produce favorable results. One has to begin somewhere. If you explain that you are interested in working there and would like to learn more about the organization, the sales manager may be pleasantly surprised. It could be refreshing to hear that you are not looking for a job yet but want to inquire about the company's job programs.

Here again, talking to employees is always helpful if it can be arranged. Someone on the clerical staff or at the middle management level who has nothing to do either with the personnel department or the hiring and firing processes would be ideal, since there could be no question of bias or pressure involved.

WRITING THE RESUME

The most important career document for people seeking employment is the résumé or data sheet. (The term *vita*, from the Latin word for life, is not generally used in business, though a vita is essentially the same as a résumé.) Though the two are much alike, the data sheet usually has selected information in abbreviated form and often requires an explanatory letter to enlarge on information outlined. The résumé gives more explanation.

The résumé is the best form to use in applying for a sales job. It should contain a heading, including name, address, and telephone number. Next should come work experience, in reverse chronological order so that the most recent job appears first. This is followed by education and training, then activities and interests, and any other personal data that you think important. References may be included.

All the above information should be arranged to impress the prospective employer. If a student is preparing a résumé, educational qualifications naturally precede work experience, which is presumably minor.

Federal, state, and local laws forbid employers from asking about any applicant's race, color, religion, national origin, maiden name of women or parents' names, sex, age, marital status, address, or using any other means to elicit such information from applicants. However, it is not unlawful for applicants to furnish such information. Circumstances should dictate the revealing of such information. Omitting this sort of information will not hurt you, since the employers want to comply with the law. If additional information is needed, the applicant might check with the closest office of the Equal Employment Opportunity Commission (a federal agency.) Also, older applicants do not have to reveal their age.

References are usual. Although many employers feel that names given in a résumé are of little value because they will rarely give a candid opinion (having been selected for a favorable opinion), it is far better to include two or three names than to say "References on request." If you have good references, it is only natural that you should want a prospective employer to know about them.

You should ask permission from anyone whose name you want to give as a reference. Regardless of how employers may feel about the value of references in sizing up applicants, references are checked, by letter or telephone, and it is only fair to give your references the opportunity to decline in case they feel reluctant to recommend you. In any event, the prospective employer is free to contact any of your former employers or educational institutions to verify your record or ask for additional information.

Other things to remember:

- The purpose of a résumé is to get an interview, not a job.
- Be concise and to the point.
- Do not put anything in a résumé that might invite controversy. Examples would be religious persuasion, political party, negative opinions about anything.
- Emphasize leadership skills and activities as well as any other activities that might show selling ability.
- Leave out high school achievements unless exceptional. They are not usually helpful.
- Account for all elapsed time periods, even if nothing seems pertinent. Time gaps in résumés arouse suspicion.

Many people make the mistake of putting too much information in their résumés with the hope of acquiring a job. At best, a résumé will get a quick glance from the person who is responsible for hiring. The best résumés are carefully selective so that the person who will hire you—in many cases the same person who interviews you—can see quickly what your main interests are and what there is about your background and training that might make you the right person for the job. Omit things that you yourself feel are unimportant because they no longer interest you. Be specific about anything that you want to emphasize and that seems relevant. Here are two more points to remember:

- Job objective. This should be "Sales-Marketing." This tells the employer you have interests in the sales career and other areas of marketing such as sales management.
- Emphasize points that relate to selling. Chapter 3 discusses qualities that the employer looks for: personal responsibility, self-motivation, and evidence of leadership abilities. Leadership abilities and a competitive spirit would be indicated by participation in athletics, extracurricular activities, or grades. The ability to communicate with people, another desirable quality in salespeople, could be indicated by speech and drama courses and debating experience.

Figure 19-1 is a good example of a résumé for a recent college graduate. Note how degrees, extracurricular achievements, and honors and

```
                        FREDERICK RAY JOSKI
                       2320 West 91st Street
                    Overland Park, Kansas  66022
                          (913) 718-4942


OBJECTIVE:  Position in Sales-Marketing.

EDUCATION
    September 1981-May 1983    Bachelor of Science in Marketing.
                              University of Kansas, Lawrence, Kansas
                              Grade Point Average, 3.6
                              Courses included:
                                  Fundamentals of Marketing (3 hours)
                                  Sales and Sales Management (9 hours)
                                  Business Communications (3 hours)
                                  Speech (3 hours)
                                  Communication Skills (3 hours)
                                  Psychology (6 hours)
                                  Business Law (3 hours)


    September 1979-May 1981    Associate of Arts Degree.
                              Johnson County Community College, Olathe, Kansas
                              Grade Point Average, 3.8

EXTRACURRICULAR ACTIVITIES    Vice-president, Student Government.  Served three
                              years on Student Government Council at
                              University of Kansas.  Duties included arbi-
                              trating disputes between student groups and
                              faculty and speaking before student assemblies.

                              Actor, student drama society.  Speaking roles
                              in four plays. Assistant producer, senior
                              year, of Hamlet.

                              Student Marketing Club, active member.

JOB EXPERIENCE
(part-time in college)        Assistant manager, Dumpby's Drive-in.  Duties
                              included hiring and training part-time staff.
                              Paid approximately 50 percent of school ex-
                              penses through this position.

HONORS AND AWARDS             Best actor.  Junior year in Our Town.  Awarded
                              by Student Theatre Guild.

OTHER INTERESTS               Jogging, tennis, music, reading.

                              Willing to relocate.
```

Figure 19–1. A Student Résumé

awards are underlined. This focuses the prospective employer's attention immediately. Also, leadership skills are highlighted. Frederick doesn't just say he worked at Dumpby's Drive-in; he makes it clear that he hired and trained others, which indicates self-responsibility, a sought-after sales skill. Note also that courses relating to the selling career are specifically mentioned.

LUCILLE ANN GREENFIELD
1469 West Palm Street
Jacksonville, Florida 32209
(904) 943-7621

OBJECTIVE: Position in Sales-Marketing

WORK EXPERIENCE
1977-present
Personnel manager and training director. Sweeny's Fashion Stores, Jacksonville, Florida. Responsible for screening, testing, and interviewing job applicants. Have designed and implemented six-month on-job-training for all staff and sales personnel. Currently conducting communications, assertiveness, and motivational workshops. Also design annual performance audits for executive staff, write job descriptions for all personnel, and supervise employee benefit programs.

1974-77
Administrative assistant to president. Sunshine Food Products, Orlando, Florida. Supervised secretarial pool; conducted in-house training; arbitrated employee complaints; interviewed and tested clerical candidates for possible employment.

1968-74
Private secretary to John Kornfeld, vice-president. Grove Realtors, Inc., Orlando, Florida. Composed business correspondence. Kept personal and business accounts. Arranged meetings with clients and prospective clients. Handled travel arrangements.

EDUCATION
September 1964-May 1968
Bachelor of Science Degree (History Major). University of Miami, Miami, Florida. Active in student drama and debating society. Worked as waitress in evenings to help with college expenses.

COMMUNITY ACTIVITIES
1975-76
Volunteer, American Cancer Society. Orlando, Florida. Duties included organization of Fund Crusade and speaking to variety of volunteer groups.

1979-80
President. Personnel Managers' Association of Jacksonville, Florida.

HONORS AND AWARDS
Special Citation. American Cancer Society, Florida Division, for leading Orlando unit to highest percentage increase in state in 1976.

Shakespeare Award. For outstanding student actor at University of Miami, 1968.

OTHER INTERESTS
Surfing, tennis, traveling, classical music.

Willing to relocate.

Figure 19–2. A Nonstudent Résumé

In a nonstudent résumé (Figure 19-2), work experience, in this case extensive, is listed first because it is more recent and of much more importance than college experience to the prospective employer. The job the applicant presently holds precedes the others. Community activities are listed, and special honors, but only one college award which seems especially relevant.

At higher levels, particularly in highly skilled professions where research and publications are taken for granted and may be numerous, the résumé (in this case often referred to as a vita) is necessarily longer and more detailed, but here, too, conciseness is important.

Other hints about résumés are:

- Do it well. Allow yourself plenty of time to outline and then write it.

- The résumé should be typed, preferably on good-quality white paper, and if possible on a good typewriter with a new ribbon. If corrections are necessary, they should be made neatly.

- The résumé should be free of grammatical errors, misspelled words (including typos), and punctuation errors; be sure to proofread carefully.

- Plan the layout in the most attractive form possible (see Figures 19-1 and 19-2). Underlining job descriptions and other key phrases draws interest quickly.

- Photocopies of résumés are perfectly acceptable (and preferable to carbons), but they should be clear and readable; the quality of the original is in this case particularly important.

- Résumés should always be sent with a formal application letter, the two folded together and mailed in a business envelope.

THE APPLICATION LETTER

Whether the application letter is an unsolicited letter or is sent in response to a known sales-marketing opening at a company, it should be well done, It should be neat, always an original, and typed on 8½″ × 11″ paper on good white bond with no heading. Use the personal business letter style. Again, it must be free of errors. It should not exceed one page in length. Always address it to a specific person whenever possible rather than "Manager, Personnel Department." A little research will reveal this name.

The application letter has three main parts:

1. *Opening.* This should refer specifically to the job you are applying for.

2. *Body.* These middle paragraphs should indicate the source of your information (in other words, how you found out about the opening) or tell why you are interested in the sales position. A brief statement of your qualifications, and how they would fit company needs, comes next. The résumé enclosed should be mentioned specifically.

3. *Conclusion.* The closing paragraph should encourage the prospective employer to act or indicate that you plan to follow up the letter with some action.

Application letters, like résumés, take time and thought. A great deal may depend upon your wording (as well as on the general appearance of the letter), and several revisions may be necessary before you get it right.

Figure 19-3 is a typical application letter from a college senior, written in this case to apply for a specific sales job on file with the college

```
        Mr. F. R. Green
        Marketing Vice-President
        Thomas R. Simon Company
        3240 West Dearborn
        Chicago, Illinois


        Dear Mr. Green:

            A sales position with your company excites me.

            When I read your job description in the placement office
        here at Loyola and did some research on your company, I
        knew you had the ideal career opportunity for me.  I can
        contribute much to your organization.

            Enclosed is my resume highlighting my qualifications.
        I like people, am self-motivated, and have engaged in many
        leadership activities on campus.

            My qualifications seem to be exactly what you need.  I
        shall be calling you for an appointment within the next
        few days.

                    Sincerely,



                    John Eager
```

Figure 19–3.   An Application Letter for a Specific Job

placement office. The letter is creative and concise, and its confident but not arrogant tone implies that the applicant may have good selling ability. The ending, particularly, is meant to show the prospective employer that the applicant has initiative and is really interested in going to work.

Figure 19-4 is an unsolicited letter from a person already employed who wants to shift to a selling career. This provocative letter should get an

```
Mr. Allen Marks, Sales Manager
Overfelt Company
1355 Peach Street
Atlanta, Georgia


Dear Mr. Marks:

     I would like a sales career with your progressive
company.

     When I decided to make a career change into sales, ex-
tensive research pointed to your company as one of the most
marketing-minded companies in the entire Southeast.  I want
to be a member of your sales force and grow with you.

     The enclosed resume emphasizes my special communication
and leadership skills.  My experience in banking and real
estate sales should be readily transferable to your line of
office equipment.

     I am eager to discuss this with you and shall be calling
you within the week for an appointment.

                         Sincerely,


                         Evelyn Crabtree
```

Figure 19–4.   An Unsolicited Application Letter

appointment. The fact that research has been done on their company is sure to interest many employers, and it might be the best way to get an interview. The purpose of a résumé and an application letter is, as said before, to get an interview. Getting the job comes later.

CONTACTING THE COMPANY

Remember that the person you want to reach is the decision-maker, usually the sales manager, not the personnel director. Research will tell you who the decision-maker is. Your letter should be sent to that person. If the letter and résumé have been properly done, chances of getting an interview are excellent.

Usually the decision-makers in organizations are impressed by an assertive approach. Taking the time to find out who these decision-makers are, and sending them a résumé with a creative letter, will impress them favorably.

Sometimes your letter and résumé will bring a written response very quickly. If none is forthcoming, call for an appointment, usually seven days after mailing the letter. Generally, an appointment will be granted.

If for any reason an appointment is not granted after several attempts, try to find another decision-maker in the company who might have some influence on the person you first wrote to. This, too, may fail—there will be refusals, especially in certain locales and probably at certain times of the year. Try not to be discouraged. Applying for a job, and getting the interview, can be quite as challenging as the job itself.

Persistency is the motto. One can learn a great deal from interviews, and the last interview may turn out to get you the best job of all.

PREPARING FOR THE INTERVIEW

Whoever said that first impressions are lasting ones was accurate when it comes to job interviews. One should prepare very carefully for an interview. Besides keeping in mind all the qualities that employers look for in salespeople, as outlined in Chapter 3, and the use of communication skills, body language, and dress (Chapter 13), you should follow certain procedural steps.

When you call for an appointment, write down the exact time and place of the interview. This may sound elementary, but it is an unfortunate applicant who *assumes* that an interview is to be held in a certain place and then discovers two minutes before the interview time that the appointment is elsewhere. Do not rely on memory but write the time and place down and keep the paper in a safe place. (Writing down *any* important time or fact is always better than trying to remember it.) Also write down the full name of the company, the name and title of the person you are to see, and the address. Take this information along on the interview. If you are uncertain about the correct pronunciation of the name of the person you are to see, call the company switchboard operator and ask. Be sure the interviewer's title is clear.

Your research on the company will have given you some helpful facts—the age and history of the company, the location of its plants or offices, the variety of its products or services, its growth rate, its prospects for future growth, and so on. This background information gives you something besides yourself to talk about during the interview, and material for questions.

Some of your questions may be spontaneous, but you should prepare for the interview by making a list of questions having to do with the company, not yourself. (Take a pen and notebook containing this information, allowing some extra pages for making notes during and immediately following the interview.) Keep in mind that the most important thing is the job *opportunity*. Salary and benefits are a matter that is broached later.

In the interview, you want to impress upon the interviewer your interest in the opportunity with his company. You want to project confidence but not cockiness, willingness but not servility. You want to show that you are serious about your future and want to learn how to be a good salesperson. Some good questions to ask are:

- What kind of training program do you have? How long does it last? Where is it held?

- Does your training program outline all your various product and service lines, including those of your competitors?

- What is the sales territory involved? How large is it? How many accounts does it have? What size are the accounts?

- What back-up service does the company provide to help its sales force in the field?

- What about training in answering objections, closing the sale, personal organization, and prospecting?

- Do you have company schools, meetings, conventions, seminars, and the like? How does one qualify for them? Where and how often are they held? Does the company pay the expenses?

- What activity goals are expected in the field each week—that is, number of calls, interviews, referred leads, and so on?

These questions should be written down, and answers should be written down during the interview. Tell the prospective employer you are "making some notes, if that is all right." The answers you receive will tell you a great deal about the sales opportunities of the company—and your interest will impress the person conducting the interview.

All the notes you make should, of course, be factual. Never include any personal remarks—write only what you have been told, as if you were reporting a speech. Interviewers have been known to ask, "Do you mind if I see what you have been writing?"

Leave questions about salary and fringe benefits to the last. They will come up in due course, and it is not tactful to rush them.

Listed below are further interview hints:

- Each interview will be different, so do not expect anything but wait to see what happens.

- Be attentive, listen well. Don't talk too much. Answer questions and inquiries with minimum comments.

- Sometimes you may not get all your questions answered. Don't press the matter.

- Don't smoke even if the interviewer asks you if you would like to have a cigarette.

- Maintain good eye contact.

- Sit straight, leaning slightly forward.

- Maintain a pleasant expression.

- Remember that it is normal to be nervous.

- Remember the companies want to hire good salespeople. They never find enough.

- Be prepared to discuss your résumé in detail.

Finally, there are some opinions likely to be sought from you. Prospective employers usually ask several probing questions of those they interview. Think out answers to such questions in advance and rehearse, to yourself if necessary, your answers to these typical questions you may be asked:

- Why do you want a sales career? (Opportunity for personal growth, unlimited income, and freedom.)

- Where do you want to be 5, 10, or 15 years from now?

- What can you tell me about yourself?

- Why do you like our company?

- What have you done in the community?
- Do you enjoy working alone?
- What have your previous jobs taught you?
- What does the word "commitment" mean to you?
- What is your personal financial situation?
- What are your other interests?

Questions of this sort help the interviewer decide whether the applicant has an acceptable sales profile. Your answers should be truthful, but they should also be slanted toward the sales opportunity being discussed.

THE INTERVIEW

A sample interview shows how preparation helps. Pamela Rogers, a recent graduate of Auburn University, is applying for a sales job with a large book distributing company in Birmingham, Alabama. She majored in English and marketing and feels this background qualifies her for the field of book selling. She has done everything properly for the interview as outlined above.

Pam has an appointment with Jason Quill, the marketing vice-president. He makes the final decision on all salespeople hired at Southern Distribution Company. He is impressed with Pam's résumé and application letter and looks forward to meeting her.

As Pam is shown into Jason's office, she feels a momentary alarm. How on earth did she get herself into this terrifying situation, she wonders. She has a sense that all the cards are stacked against her, but she is wrong. The organization needs talented salespeople, and Pam should tuck this away in her mind. It is certainly normal to be frightened, but if you have prepared adequately, there is no reason to panic. No interview is exactly like talking to an old friend, of course; on the other hand, a little nervousness can make the applicant that much more alert during an interview.

Pam hopes to bring out in the interview some of the things she did in college that show leadership, self-motivation, and creativity. She did a lot of jogging in school, but she realizes that jogging does not prove anything particularly except self-discipline, certainly not much in the way of communication skills. But she hopes she can say something about having been on the women's basketball team at Auburn, because that shows a spirit of competition and ability to work as part of a group.

She also wants to emphasize that she has a broad interest in reading. Ordinarily that might not particularly apply to the sales field, but in this case, because she would be selling books, she very wisely will try to capitalize on her background and interest in books and reading to indicate her knowledge and interest in the product.

Not all interviewers oblige by asking the right questions—that is, the questions the applicants want them to ask. After dozens, perhaps hundreds, of interviews, some sales managers have developed their own skillful techniques, often designed to throw the applicant off guard so as to see how he reacts to pressure. An interviewer might suddenly ask:

- What is your weakness?
- What is your worst personal fault?
- Do you see anything wrong with our organization?
- Is there anything you might not like about the job?
- What drawbacks would you find in working for us?

Quick thinking obviously helps an applicant in such a situation. If you listen carefully and pause slightly while you consider your answer, you may be able to frame the response in such a way that it turns in your favor.

Thus, if someone asks about personal weakness, a good reply would be, "I have, I believe, been criticized for being too loyal." Or if someone says, "What drawbacks would you find in this job?" a positive answer would be, "Well, I could say that the job would be very hard—it would involve an extraordinary amount of work. But that's what I want. I want to learn and I want to do a good job." If someone persists about a personal fault, the response might be, "Some say that I have a tendency to work too hard," or "I spend too much time learning about things," or "I ask too many questions."

Any of these answers would impress the interviewer with the adroitness with which you handle a seemingly stressful situation under pressure. Rehearsing some of these negative trick questions with a friend would be wise in preparing for the interview.

Assuming, then, that the interview has gone well, it is time to move on to that part of the interview—or the follow-up interview—in which terms are discussed.

NEGOTIATING SALARY AND BENEFITS

Normally an interviewer will not move to a discussion of salary and benefits unless he is really interested in the applicant. It is the interviewer's prerogative to close an interview without discussing anything that suggests hiring—though this does not necessarily indicate uninterest.

Nierenberg in his best seller *The Art of Negotiating*[2] says that in successful negotiation, everyone wins. Furthermore, not only does everyone win in a negotiation, but needs and their satisfaction are a common denominator in negotiation. The same can be said of the sales placement interview.

The employer is looking for a salesperson; the applicant is looking for a platform for his own fulfillment which he hopes to find in a particular sales job. Both need to win: that is, the company needs to get the applicant, and the applicant needs to get a job on satisfactory terms.

The opening phases of the process of negotiating benefits in the sales interview normally involve the discussion of salary. After the employer is satisfied that the applicant is right for the job, and the applicant is satisfied that he wants the job, the process of negotiating benefits properly begins. It usually starts with the interviewer's saying something like, "So you think you would like to come to work for us," or "I think we have some mutual interests here. Let's talk about salary and the other benefits." If all has been going well and the applicant is fairly sure of his ground, and there is a clear lull in the interview, the applicant could say, "I really think I would enjoy working here, and I should like to discuss the range of your salary structure." Any kind of innocent phraseology like this is adequate to move into the area of negotiating benefits. Here are some things to remember about negotiating benefits:

- The interviewer knows exactly what the salary range is for similar sales jobs.

- The interviewer knows roughly what the minimum required living income is in that area.

- The interviewer is in the driver's seat.

- Normally, there is not one fixed salary amount for any sales job. A fairly broad salary range is usually available.

Thus, if the employer says, "Our starting salary for this job is $12,000," the applicant's immediate answer might be, "I see." If intuition tells the prospective applicant it may be more, he could say, "I see. Is this a fixed figure or is it negotiable?" A discussion may ensue.

Employers sometimes ask the applicant what sort of salary he would need to work for the company. At that time, it is effective to pull out a written or typed budget and go over the figures with the interviewer (see Figure 19-5). This section of the interview is not to be taken lightly. One

---

[2] Gerard I. Nierenberg, *The Art of Negotiating* (New York: Simon and Schuster, 1968).

must settle salary and other fringe benefits before employment can begin.

Since fringe benefits usually make up 20 to 25 percent of the salary, it is proper to discuss them along with salary. This means asking about car, expense accounts, group life insurance, accident and health insurance, sick pay, pension, days off, paid holidays, and vacations.

Fringe benefits are continually expanding, and often they are decisive in one's choice of a company. This stage of the interview is the proper time to find out all you want to know about fringe benefits as well as such matters as annual performance reviews and salary increases. For a beginning salesperson, field performance is usually reviewed every

---

BUDGET

Your figures should reflect the minimum amount required in each item for an acceptable standard of living. Figure all expenses on a monthly basis.

Fixed Expenses		General Expenses		Other Expenses	
Rent or mortgage*	$_____	Food	$_____	Recreation	$_____
Utilities	$_____	Clothing	$_____	Other:	$_____
Income taxes	$_____	Car expenses	$_____	_____	$_____
General insurance	$_____	Lunches, incidentals	$_____	_____	$_____
Life insurance	$_____	Laundry, tailoring	$_____	_____	$_____
Health insurance	$_____	Medical and dental	$_____	_____	$_____
Debt repayment (if any)†	$_____				
Total	$_____	Total	$_____	Total	$_____

Least amount needed for total monthly living expenses $_____

*Rent, food, clothing, car expenses, and recreation can be inflated somewhat.
†Watch debt repayment. If for a car, stereo, or boat, it may convey financial immaturity. If for student loans, needed furniture, it may portray responsibility.

Figure 19–5.   A Budget Worksheet for Use in an Interview

week. Salary increases usually depend a great deal on sales results—in other words, they depend on the salesperson, since most salespeople go to work on some kind of salary guarantee plus performance commission.

Even though salary and benefits have been discussed, an interview can often end without the interviewer's having made a real offer. It is usual for a company to interview several people for a particular sales job, sometimes over a period of several weeks, each interview being conducted along the same lines, even down to discussing salary and benefits. This makes the after-interview follow-up an equally important part of getting the job.

FOLLOW-UP AFTER THE INTERVIEW

The most important thing in the interview follow-up is to write a personal letter immediately after the interview so that the interviewer gets it the very next day, if at all possible. Even a handwritten note is sufficient, provided the writing is legible.

This letter should be brief, cordial, and specific. It should express gratitude for the meeting, touch on some specific favorable aspect of the interview, and close with an appropriate "next action" comment.

Prompt follow-up letters indicate to the prospective employer that the applicant has some of the essential qualities of a good salesperson: an interest in the job, the ability to follow through, creativity and observation, self-motivation, sincerity, and courtesy.

Figures 19-6 and 19-7 show two follow-up letters. The second is more imaginative and has more impact, and it is only slightly longer than the first. It shows thought.

After the letter has been sent, and a week, but no longer, has gone by, it is in order to telephone and ask for another appointment. Do not ask over the telephone whether or not the job has been filled. People do not usually like to discuss these matters on the phone, and one cannot very well ask bluntly, "Have you made up your mind yet?" or, "Do I have the job?" By asking for another appointment, you are showing that you are still very interested in getting the job. It is also tactful in that it solicits a response. If no second appointment is granted, then at least you know where you stand. It is not always the case that companies, especially when there are many applicants, notify the rejected ones that the job has been filled.

Assuming, then, that a second interview has been granted, but the job is still up in the air, the applicant should enter, sit down, and seize the initiative in a nice, but firm way. He might say something startlingly frank like, "I have been thinking about the job opportunity here, and I am eager to go to work for you. I could start next week." This remark would get the question out in the open early, and in most cases would elicit an honest answer. The applicant would then have to react accordingly.

```
        Ms. Marion Herschberg, Sales Manager
        Viking Products, Inc.
        2821 South University Drive
        Fort Worth, Texas

        Dear Ms. Herschberg:

            Thank you for the time you gave me in your office
        yesterday afternoon.

            Your comments about Viking's growth and its need for
        dedicated salespeople were impressive.  I'm interested!

            I shall call you in one week, as agreed.

                            Sincerely,
```

Figure 19–6.   A Follow-up Letter

```
Mr. Morten Schmidt, Sales Manager
Gordon Container Corporation
1325 Bay Street
Seattle, Washington

Dear Mr. Schmidt:

     That was an interesting interview in your office
yesterday.  Thank you.  No wonder you are successful!

     Your observation that the career offers unlimited
opportunity for growth and income impresses me.  That
is why I want to be a salesperson with your organization.

     I look forward to our next meeting Thursday after-
noon.

                    Sincerely,
```

Figure 19–7.   A Follow-up Letter

Don't be hesitant about asking for the job. Applicants have a perfect right to, and many employers like to hear them say they want the job. The worst that can happen here is that the answer is no.

A strong way to reinforce this is by immediately stating assets that could be beneficial to the company. Summarize the reasons by saying:

- "This job—selling—is what I like to do."
- "I think I will be good at it."
- "I like the future opportunities being offered by your company."
- "You have a fine reputation in the community."
- "I believe my performance and personality will be an asset to your company."

LETTER OF ACCEPTANCE

A letter of acceptance is not always required, but it is always worthwhile. It may add that extra note of responsiveness which will start the relationship off in a pleasant and polite way. It is particularly appropriate where the job being accepted is in another part of the country.

Letters of acceptance have a fixed format which should be followed. They should open with a confirmation statement, followed with an appropriate comment about the new relationship, and close with a reiteration of the starting date. (See Figure 19-8). Salary or other fringe benefits agreed upon are usually not mentioned, even though they have been agreed upon.

SUMMARY

Substantial sales jobs are available almost anywhere in the country. If one wishes to find a job in a new area, some preliminary research through the library, college placement offices or alumni, the local chamber of commerce in the city one is interested in, travel agencies, friends, will provide answers to questions about climate, cost of living, job opportunities, and so forth, and help you decide whether the choice is right.

Additional research on the company or companies that interest you is also a good preliminary. Published annual reports, business journals, chambers of commerce, personal inquiry, local newspapers can all provide information. In your research you are also apt to find out whom you should actually apply to—that is, who will actually be doing the hiring.

Preparing the all-important résumé is the next step. Here, adequate time and care are always worthwhile. The résumé should be concise and clear, listing name, address, and telephone number, work experience and education (or the reverse), followed by activities, interests, and any other pertinent data. The résumé must be typed neatly and contain no errors.

The application letter which accompanies the résumé should also be concise, but an interesting opening can suggest your personality and

```
Ms. Grace Miller, Marketing Vice-President
Wilson Travel Service
1355 Commonwealth Avenue
Boston, Massachusetts

Dear Ms. Miller:

      This will verify my acceptance of your offer of employ-
ment with the Wilson Travel Service.

      Selling group travel packages for your company is going
to be an exciting challenge.  I am eager to start!

      I shall be on your doorstep Monday, June 1, at 8:30 a.m.
as agreed.

                        Thank you again,
```

Figure 19–8.   A Letter of Acceptance

draw interest. It should be specific and clearly suggest a call from the applicant for an appointment. The interview itself requires special preparation. Though you may be asked some unexpected questions, you should be ready to talk about the company and yourself in such a way as to show the interviewer that you are the right person for the job.

During the interview, you should keep in mind what employers are looking for in salespeople (as outlined in earlier chapters). Even if you feel nervous, you should use good communication skills, so as to impress the interviewer with your ability to perform well in tight situations. In the last part of the interview (or a follow-up interview) in which salary and fringe benefits are negotiated, straightforward questions are quite in order.

The interview follow-up consists of a personally written note to the interviewer and a call by telephone for another appointment. One should not be modest about asking for the job—that is what you are there for. And if you get it, a warm letter of acceptance starts the relationship well. If you do not get the job, try again. The fifth or sixth interview may bring you the best job of all.

KEY TERMS

Budget Worksheet

Data Sheet

Résumé

Vita

REVIEW QUESTIONS

- How does research on the company help in the job process?
- What is the primary purpose of a résumé?
- Why should great care be taken in preparing the résumé?
- In the job interview what should be emphasized in the area of extracurricular activities?
- What is the underlying principle of all successful negotiation?

DISCUSSION TOPICS

- Why would travel agencies be a good source for learning about an area where you wish to work?
- If there are no annual reports available, name three local sources where you could get information on a company.
- Why is it important to include job objectives in the résumé?
- Why should a résumé be concise?

- Is it ethical to inflate a budget? Explain.
- Why is it important to try to arrange the interview with the decision-maker?

EXERCISES

1. Prepare your own résumé for a possible job in sales. Include the names and addresses of three references whom you have called for permission.

2. With a partner, act out a job interview, taking the role of Frederick Joski (in Figure 19-1) as the interviewee.

3. Apply for a sales job at a company and report in class on the experience.

It is a rainy day in January. Edwina Young is being interviewed for a selling job with a paper products company in Portland, Oregon. Edwina is from a small town in northern California and knows something about lumbering and paper, but she has never sold paper before. Back in California, after graduating from Humboldt State University, she sold advertising for the local newspaper and also worked for a time as a typist in a lumber mill.

Edwina moved to Oregon partly because she wanted a change and partly because she thought Portland sounded exciting and less formidable than San Francisco. Since coming to Portland six months ago, she has taken a couple of postgraduate courses in marketing and has had a part-time job selling in a retail store, but this is her first application for a job that she seriously hopes will be the start of a career.

Bill Wood, the sales manager, liked Edwina's résumé and was struck by her personality in the first interview. Now they are ready to talk about salary and benefits.

Edwina has brought a budget worksheet with her. After living half a year in Portland, she knows how expensive things are—rents are much higher than back home, and although she shares an apartment with a friend, she expects to be spending more on clothes, especially, for the job she hopes to get, and probably, inevitably, more for food and other things as well.

Edwina estimates that she will need $1200 a month just to get by. Bill Wood's offer of $1000 is disappointing, but Edwina realizes that she is not experienced and perhaps cannot expect more. It does not seem likely that Bill will go higher.

- What should Edwina say about the salary?
- If Bill refuses to go higher, what should she do?
- How could Edwina use her budget worksheet effectively here?
- What is the basic principle of negotiation that Edwina should keep in mind in this situation?

Louis Leveque is a recent graduate of the University of Maine where he majored in business. He grew up in Maine. His father, originally from Canada, has worked up from a modest start to the point where he now has a small farm of his own on which he raises potatoes.

Louis likes Maine, but he has a sense of adventure and a desire to see a little more of the country. He thinks he would like to get into selling, preferably with a company dealing in farm implements or perhaps canning equipment—one that covers the whole of New England.

He has heard about a company down in the Boston area that appeals to him. He has checked up on its territory, and he has also asked a few questions around Orono and knows that the company has not really expanded its coverage of Maine, so he is hoping his knowledge of the state will interest them—besides his affability and a fine college record.

Louis is on his way to Boston—partly for the trip, but mainly to apply to the company in person. He doesn't know anyone at the company, but he hopes he can get an interview anyway.

- How should Louis go about finding the decision-maker to talk to at the Boston company?

- What could he learn from the company's annual report that would be helpful?

- What about the chamber of commerce? How should he approach it?

- In preparing his résumé for an eventual interview, should he mention the fact that his father is a potato grower in Maine? Why or why not?

- In preparing for the negotiating aspect of the interview, is there any way Louis can find out what the going rate is for starting salaries for the job he wants?

Commitment and Activity

OBJECTIVES

In this chapter you will learn:

- The need for full commitment to the sales field.
- The value of quality and time commitment.
- The importance of learning the skills of selling.
- What personal growth in selling means.
- Why field activity is so important.
- Why personal auditing and commitment to the company are essential.
- How to understand self-motivation.
- The value of a positive mental attitude in selling.

No one seems very active on this hot, humid August afternoon in Washington, D.C. Congress is out of session, and though the city is full of tourists, they are mostly sitting in the shade. Pat O'Riordan has just completed another sales call on the manager of a kitchen appliance store.

Pat is a printing representative. Mr. Finch, the store manager, uses a large amount of direct mail advertising to his large block of customers.

Although he buys printing from Pat occasionally, Mr. Finch feels that Pat has never seemed particularly interested in his orders, nor has he made any suggestions that might stimulate additional ones.

Pat heads for the Homestead, his favorite bar in the area, for a beer. He does this almost every day, completing his calls around four-thirty. He likes a few beers with his other single friends, many of whom do not arrive until after five-thirty when they finish work.

Pat feels he does his share of calling although he gripes to his friends about his poor potential. He never works on Saturdays, never gets his activity reports in on time, and is always complaining about his lack of new prospects and leads. He feels strongly that his sales manager should find leads for him.

Pat O'Riordan is failing and will soon be looking for another job. Although he is an experienced salesman, he lacks commitment.

Compare him with Nancy Borelli, a seasoned restaurant equipment saleswoman who simply cannot find enough hours in the day to see everyone she wants to.

She always carries old customer cards for drop-in calls when her appointments are finished in early afternoon. She is convinced that keeping at the job is the key to sales results, and she hates to waste time when she runs out of appointments.

If these back-up customers are not available, she makes drop-in cold calls; and if these don't suffice, she finds a place where she can fill out her day's results on prospect cards. And she always has something worthwhile to read in her briefcase. Most of her working days last until five-thirty. Though she enjoys being home, she hates wasting time on the job. She is succeeding. She is committed.

Successful salespeople, particularly those who have been selling for several years, agree that commitment is the key to success in selling, especially in the early years. You cannot simply be a salesperson: you must be sincerely committed, and part of being committed is knowing that selling is the career for you. You must be willing to risk failure to succeed. This requires a healthy self-image and disciplined activity in the field.

In *The Influence of Fear on Salesmen*, Frank Budd says: "The person with self-esteem is not so quick to interpret temporary setbacks as failures, nor does he enter his commitments half-heartedly, always keeping his escape route in sight, like a visitor who stands with one foot inside the house and the other on the front porch." People who are skeptical of their power to achieve are not totally committed: "Self-doubt manifests itself in a variety of ways, but one of the most common ways is semi-commitment."[1]

The sales field requires exceptional commitment to succeed. The rewards are certainly worth it. Many would suffer temporarily for long-term economic and social freedom.

This chapter is primarily concerned with commitment as it relates to activity in the field, the main area of a salesperson's interest. Before salespeople can commit themselves to field activity, however, they must commit themselves to several related aspects: first of all to the career itself, then to the time it takes to learn the fundamentals of selling, to learning communication skills, to product knowledge, to professional and personal growth, and to personal auditing of progress. The benefits of loyalty to the company as well as the pledge to being competitive and forming success habits are also reviewed. Basic to all these is an over-riding commitment to a positive mental attitude, assuring the much needed healthy self-image.

COMMITMENT TO THE CAREER

Necessity is the mother of invention, but desire certainly is the mother of success. It all starts with desire. It is not easy.

In other fields of endeavor, in all the professions—medicine, law, accounting, teaching, architecture, engineering—long years of study and training are necessary before one can begin at the lowest rung of the professional ladder. The same kind of commitment that inspires the beginning medical student is essential to the person starting out in selling—a commitment not just of time but of time spent learning fundamentals.

A beginning salesperson must be willing to put aside certain other, no doubt attractive, interests in life until he, like the young intern, learns facts and skills. Without that learning time, success rarely will come. Selling can be an attractive and highly remunerative permanent career—indeed, its freedom and high income potential have drawn many people to switch to selling careers at all stages of life. This is what the good salesperson has to remember, rather than thinking of selling as a stepping-stone to something else.

It is unfortunate but true that many companies doom sales trainees to failure when they recruit them as future marketing executives. They

---

[1] The *Influence of Fear on Salesmen* (Cincinnati: National Underwriter Co., 1975), p. 35.

slight the role of the salesperson in marketing by saying, "Of course, you'll have to spend one or two years at most out in the field as a salesperson to learn the ropes before you come into the home office."

In other words, the sales career is, they seem to say, an unpleasant experience which must be endured to get into management. Such an approach has two negative effects:

1. It implies that good marketing executives do not have to have successful sales experience. Though their experience may not have to be extraordinary, it should be sufficient to give them an understanding of salespeople's problems in the field.

2. It suggests that salespeople are somehow second-class company citizens. In truth, the situation is quite the reverse.

Salespeople who start under these misguided directions feel they can get by with a part-time commitment. The companies have seriously misled them, and many companies, the wiser for having learned the hard way, are now recruiting people for permanent sales careers and giving them solid training. If management possibilities are mentioned, it is with the caution, "If you prove your worth as a salesperson—"

TIME COMMITMENT

The learning period for a good beginning in selling is a minimum of three years. Only in that long a period can any salesperson—no matter what the product—learn the fundamentals of his field and begin to be really comfortable with the range of techniques of selling. Mastery, as in any field, takes a good deal longer; it can really only come with experience, as in any human pursuit. In one year, or two, or three, the salesperson only encounters so many sales situations, has to meet and overcome only so many objections, deal with only so many different sorts of customers. Experience comes gradually—and it is after the basic techniques are second nature that the salesperson can really begin to appreciate the excitement and challenge of new sales situations, in which experience can be counted on to give insight.

COMMITMENT TO LEARNING COMMUNICATION SKILLS

Certain communication skills are an important part of selling. Earlier chapters have discussed these at length: Chapter 13 analyzed the basic communication skills, including speaking and writing as well as body language, especially important to the salesperson in understanding customers' reactions; Chapter 12 discussed the important techniques of closing a sale; and the case study, "Selling in Action," showed how one saleswoman used closing techniques and communication skills to get an order from a prospect whose personality she had given considerable thought to.

Besides learning how to say things effectively and how to listen attentively, the would-be successful salesperson has to learn how to cope with rejection and its allied ills, fear and stress. These were covered extensively in Chapter 6. Learning how to get along in slow times as well as busy ones is part of the training period, too, and it is in this area that commitment becomes crucial. Setbacks are much harder on the half-committed than they are on the committed, and they tend to be cumulative if they are not handled forcefully.

In all aspects of these communication skills, role playing can accomplish a great deal. Some companies conduct clinics in which particular sales skills, such as closing the sale or asking for referral leads, are demonstrated. These and other techniques of formal sales training programs will be dealt with at length in the following chapter. Here, it is enough to emphasize that the committed sales person welcomes every opportunity to learn from skilled professionals, either in formal sessions or in joint calls and conversations.

COMMITMENT TO PRODUCT AND SERVICE KNOWLEDGE

Knowing the product or service does not mean knowing just your own products or services; it means knowing your competitor's as well, and, indeed, the range of the product field. How can a pharmaceutical salesperson, for example, be competent without having some understanding of drugs in general, as well as of his own company's line and those of competing manufacturers? In this field, as in many others changes may come frequently, over a wide range of products, and keeping up may be extremely difficult.

Salespeople are supposed to sell, and no one suggests that they have to be experts in the field they are selling. The designers and inventors and scientists are the experts. But the salesperson should be thoroughly familiar with whatever material is provided him by the company in the way of product information. Before anything else, he should know the facts and have the figures on whatever his company has to offer. It should also be realized that in these days of keen competition for jobs, many very well-trained people are entering the selling field—rather than devoting more years and time to additional study and training in order to work at the research level. (This is reflected in a number of the case studies.) This means that it is no longer enough merely to have selling skill.

Professional salespeople flock to industry conventions and trade fairs, not just to display their own lines but to take stock of their competitors' lines. Among salespeople in a particular field, there is often a great sense of friendly rivalry—not cutthroat competition—and trade shows give an opportunity to discuss product or service differences openly. The feeling here is that no company has a monopoly on quality, and a friendly comparison of product differences is mutually beneficial in keeping everyone informed and in that way serving their customers better.

One single-lens reflex camera may have a wider range of lenses than another, or a simpler focusing mechanism, or it may be lighter in weight; a good camera manufacturer's representative knows the differences and can admit excellence where he recognizes it. This is part of keeping abreast of product developments. And since no one knows better than customers what the public wants, sales representatives are frequently in the best position to pass on news about a competitor's new product.

Product knowledge is a continuing challenge and a permanent part of the sales career. Professional salespeople must keep growing.

COMMITMENT TO PROFESSIONAL AND PERSONAL GROWTH

The ancient Greeks described happiness as the pursuit of excellence. In the carrer of selling, people must nurse a continuing commitment to professional as well as personal growth, trying always to broaden their perspective. Making high commission dollars with a topnotch company is wonderful, but growing in other areas should accompany the ascent up the ladder. Professional salespeople want to talk intelligently with their customers about many things other than what they sell. They do this by becoming a whole person with broad, not narrow, career and life perspectives.

There must be civic involvement. There must be industry involvement. These will not only aid the sale of products and services but also help salespersons contribute more of themselves to their communities. People are impressed with community doers, and customers will respect and admire salespersons who are obviously committed to professional growth in the broad sense.

Over the years, many salespeople demonstrate their sense of professional responsibility to their careers by becoming leaders in their own industry organization or trade association. It is a way of keeping up with the profession and with one's professional colleagues.

COMMITMENT TO PERSONAL AUDITING

Personal growth requires personal auditing. Polonius's advice to his son in *Hamlet*, "This above all: to thine own self be true," could well be heeded by every salesperson.

Honestly assessing individual sales progress, by such things as weekly, monthly, or yearly analysis, is invaluable. Professional salespeople periodically sit down with their superiors—sales managers or whomever—for an objective discussion of how well they are progressing. Some salespeople have their own self-analysis forms which they make part of their regular personal review. Often the company undertakes an annual progress review, in which growth objectives are mutually agreed upon and individual performance is evaluated (see Figure 20–1).

If the salesperson understands what the objectives are and agrees to them (often in writing), they become part of a joint effort toward a common objective. In other words, in management by objectives (MBO), as it is called, a genuine, horizontal relationship between salesperson and sales manager is established. When managers have a feel for the abilities of their salespeople, objectives can be realistic—neither too high nor too low—and between managers and sales staff there is a healthy give and take. Reasonable objectives are agreed to by both parties and periodic review meetings, weekly or monthly, are set.

For the process to work effectively, salespeople, not management, must take the initiative for:

- Writing down results versus goals for the period discussed.
- Explaining the reasons for exceeding or falling short of the goals.
- Writing down corrective actions to be taken.
- Arranging for the interview with the manager.
- Eliciting the concluding comments by the manager.

If management by objectives works in this fashion, it can be a wonderful way to stimulate salespeople to assume responsibility for their own career development.

Monthly review:_____ For month of:_____ 19_____
                              (name)

As a member of our sales force, we are eager to share with you your yearly progress to date. The annual objectives selected by you, after mutual discussion with your manager, have been endorsed fully by us. We want these objectives to be meaningful and attainable.

	Annual Quota	Cumulative Goal to Date	Received to Date	Results (+ or −) to Date
COMMISSIONS	$	$	$	

	Average per Week	Actual Average per Week		Results (+ or −) to Date
WEEKLY ACTIVITY				
Seen calls	_____	_____		_____
Opened cases	_____	_____		_____
Closing interviews	_____	_____		_____
New facts	_____	_____		_____
Qualified referrals	_____	_____		_____
SALES	_____	_____		_____

Your comments for objectives exceeded: _____

_____

Objectives not reached:_____

_____

What have you learned during this period? _____

_____

Sales Manager comments: _____

_____

Date_____ Signed: _____
                                    (salesperson)

Date_____ Signed: _____
                                    (sales manager)

Other Comments: _____

Figure 20–1.   Sales Objectives Review

COMMITMENT TO COMPETE

Professional growth and competition are overlapping commitments. The commitment to reach stated goals, to compete, is an essential part of setting objectives and analyzing one's progress. Being competitive is a natural part of the sales career, and a disinclination to compete is a deterrent to good salesmanship. Competition is the catalyst that makes good salespeople better.

Not all salespeople have a competitive sense to the same degree. Probably every would-be salesperson has some measure of it or he would not be interested in selling in the first place, but too much competition in others may have a negative effect on some beginning salespersons. To maintain a healthy competitive spirit, one has to accept that, in sales, competition is a way of life.

- Learn your product well. Compare it with your competitors' products, learning the benefits and weaknesses of each. Knowledge is a powerful tool in competition.

- Keep the competitive sense in proper perspective. It is not meant to hurt people but to be a stimulus to performance.

- Winning is part of the career.

- Engage in outside competitive activities to help develop the competitive spirit. Take part in sports or charity or civic membership drives that have specific goals. Attaining those goals will build confidence.

- Try to test your sales abilities against those of well-known successful salespersons by calling on one of their best customers. This is not only a challenge but also a way of finding out why those customers prefer the competitor's products to your own.

There is excitement in stepping into the ring with a respected competitor and matching selling skills. As long as personalities are left out, trying to win is a strong motivator.

Finally, if there is no competition in sight, simply be competitive with yourself. Set your own goals and beat them.

COMMITMENT TO THE COMPANY

Commitment to the company is a natural accompaniment to knowledge of the product. Most good salespeople have an honest, practical commitment to their companies. Although they realize that the competitive system under which they sell will always produce some better products and that competitors sometimes have the advantage, they believe in their company's essential worth. They have a practical commitment which says, in effect, "All right, so my company isn't everything. But for me, it's 95 percent of what I need, and therefore I am going to back it and sell its products for all I am worth, making up for any deficiencies by giving better service." Behind most long-tenured, successful salespersons are long years with a particular company. Those who float around from company to company not only get confused trying to learn various products but also lose all sense of loyalty and dedication to their career. Loyalty works both ways: good companies make a special effort to help their loyal field forces, and the pros help the company.

COMMITMENT TO FORMING SUCCESS HABITS

Many years ago, Albert N. Gray, a marketing officer with the Prudential Insurance Company, made a significant speech at the annual meeting, in Philadelphia, of the National Association of Life Underwriters, an organization of sales agents from the top life insurance companies in the United States. In his talk, entitled "The Common Denominator of Success," he described what he had learned as the result of an extensive field trip designed to explore the secrets of successful insurance agents. The answer was a timeless credo, as applicable today as it was back in 1941. Essentially, he discovered that the people who are successful are those who discipline themselves to do, who form the habit of doing, things that people, by nature, do not like to do. In the sales field, he explained, this principle applies in four categories:

1. Successful *calling* habits: call on those who can afford to buy, need your service, and will buy from you.
2. Successful *selling* habits: learn sales skills and use them consistently.
3. Successful *work* habits: be organized and follow a strict level of field activity on a daily basis.
4. Successful *prospecting* habits: continually search out new leads, build markets, and enlarge your calling list.

All this amounts to a commitment to succeed.

COMMITMENT TO FIELD ACTIVITY

All the commitments we have discussed so far find their ultimate expression in field activity. Here is where the action is. Here is where success lies.

For the architect, it is the drafting board; the surgeon, the operating room; the lawyer, the courtroom; for the salesperson, it is the territory. Making calls, knocking on doors, seeing people, presenting products, isolating needs, getting commitments—this is what selling is all about.

Out-of-office diligence is absolutely vital to the survival of any salesperson in any field. Though adequate preparation is essential, the level of success is determined by the amount of time spent profitably in front of prospects or customers. Salespeople simply have to make profitable calls to succeed. This means following up referrals or other sound leads, not making round after round of cold calls.

Not all salespeople can be as successful as Ernie Nelson. Ernie sells office supplies in Saint Louis. He goes from office to office carrying two briefcases full of such ordinary items as typewriter ribbons, paper clips, pens, pencils, scratch pads. He does not even introduce himself. He simply says, "Is there anything you want today?" It's a little like the old London muffin man, and the secret is lots of hard work and regularity.

By making 30 calls a day, Monday through Friday, Ernie makes a nice living. Most of his calls are cold calls, though he has regular customers and could probably get more if he had the time. He may not spend as much time analyzing his growth potential as some salespeople do, and his route requires little travel time, but he is a true salesman.

The Numbers Game

All kinds of formulas are around describing the proper amount and type of activity that a salesperson should aspire to, or should actually perform in a given period, usually a week. What should be the number of weekly calls made? How many sales should result? Ernie's formula, if he has one, is simple: 150 calls a week. Obviously, there can be no single answer when there are so many variables.

Most company marketing departments adopt minimum weekly (or daily) levels of calling activity as benchmarks for their field forces. From experience, they know approximately how many calls are necessary before the new salesperson learns the ropes. And it does not take long for the sales manager to find out who is more effective than others.

Most sales managers try to work closely with new salespeople for six months or so, trying different activity levels to strike the proper quota. Ideally, a salesperson sets his own quota after that time, based on a knowledge of his territory and his customers. He sets his own daily pace with a goal in mind. As one successful farm implement salesperson put it, "If I see five new people a week, talk to five old customers, and pick up 15 new prospects from whatever source, I know I've done it. My past record indicates that."

Although activity may vary by industry or company, all salespeople and sales managers recognize that planned activity "by the numbers" is essential, particularly in the early years of a sales career.

Salespeople who do not accept this principle often fail. Many beginners, equipped with the strong ego that makes a good salesperson, honestly feel that they can succeed without seeing a lot of people. They think that by using their intelligence they can prove the old system wrong and make just as many sales as their cohorts but without working nearly so hard.

The old system is not wrong. Though plums may occasionally fall into the laps of the lazy, the experience of thousands has proved beyond any doubt that success comes to those who follow a minimum activity level week in and week out throughout their careers.

In almost any other calling, activity is generated by outside forces. Executives, accountants, bankers, lawyers, dentists, all have their activity determined by others. The kind of salespeople that this book is concerned with must seek out their customers. They must have a commitment to selling.

COMMITMENT TO A POSITIVE MENTAL ATTITUDE

A lasting foundation for all of the commitments we have been discussing is the one intangible ingredient that is probably the most important commitment of all: having a positive mental attitude. This is a gift salespeople give themselves. It starts with a good self-image. Successful salespeople usually understand their parent-child-personality relationships with their customers (along the lines discussed in Chapter 5). They are aware of themselves and of others and of the subtle interplays that can affect all human relationships.

All human beings, not just salespeople, can improve their feelings about themselves and heighten their self-image. Here are a few suggestions, listed at random, many of them familiar from earlier chapters:

- Recognize strengths and weaknesses and set goals accordingly. Unrealistically high goals are foolish.

- Put past failures aside. Dwelling on failure does not lead one toward positive goals.

- Refrain from excessive self-criticism. Belittling oneself in comparison with others is self-pity and copping out.

- Meditate occasionally; reflect on goals and desires.

- Appreciate one's own good qualities.

- Be optimistic. Look at the bright side of life, especially with prospects.

- Be pleased at having achieved short-range goals.
- Be glad to do not great things but little things in a great way, every day.

This kind of self-awareness is the best form of mental therapy. In the competitive field of selling, it is a measure of growth. Reflecting on goals and the quality of life helps the salesperson maintain equilibrium and balance in the two parts of his life—personal and working. Being committed to one's career in this sense means being committed to a life full of field activity, but at the same time enjoying that life and taking pride in one's part in it.

SUMMARY

In discussing the necessity of full commitment and full field activity in the sales career, this chapter emphasized the importance of learning and growth over a beginning period of not less than three years, much as in other professional fields. Experience has to be based on a good foundation, in which techniques, products, and skills are learned and tried out toward the end of personal achievement.

Thus there have to be commitments to learning communication skills, to acquiring product knowledge, to professional growth, including competitiveness. Good salespeople like to know where they stand and how they are progressing. Although self-imposed goals are best, meaningful management by objectives helps in that it gives the salesperson fixed but realistic objectives of activity, sales, and commissions. This kind of mutual setting of objectives, along with a commitment to product knowledge, is part of the commitment to the company that makes selling a rewarding and lifetime career.

Commitment to success habits—calling, selling, personal organization, and prospecting—goes along with the commitment to field activity, the place where success lies. The experienced salesperson realizes that there are no shorts cuts, no easy ways: though adequate preparation and planning are essential, the time that pays off is the time that is spent in front of serious customers. This means following a schedule week in and week out.

Behind all this must lie a commitment to a positive mental attitude. Maintaining a good self-image, a gift salespeople can give themselves, is the measure of growth in the competitive field of selling and the key to successful field activity.

KEY TERMS

Field Activity

Management by Objectives (MBO)

Success Habits

REVIEW QUESTIONS

- Why is full commitment to the sales career important?
- How many years are usually required to learn the fundamentals?
- Why should you be loyal to a company?
- Why is field activity essential to success in selling?
- Name the four success habits.

DISCUSSION TOPICS

- How does a salesperson get involved in community or industry activities?
- Why is management by meaningful objectives so valuable to sales-people?
- Why must good salespeople nurture a positive self-image?
- Do you feel that activity is always the key to success in selling? Explain.

EXERCISES

1. Describe what commitment to the sales career means to you.
2. Discuss the importance of a balance between personal life and working life.
3. Write a one-page essay on how to build a good self-image. Discuss in class.

Molly Curtis has recently become a sales trainee with a rather new computer software firm outside Pittsburgh. The company is enterprising and hopes to make strides against some of the more established software companies, and it wants its salespeople to carry out fairly aggressive field prospecting.

Molly was formerly a secretary in a sales organization and switched voluntarily to sales, partly because she thought it was a field in which she could do well. She has a great interest in psychology and studied it in college (though she does not have a degree). She still reads and keeps a lively interest in the subject.

Now that she is a sales trainee, she has the notion that, although she is inexperienced in selling, she has a better understanding of people than most beginning salespeople and is a keener observer of body language and so on, all of which is going to be a definite advantage in selling. She really thinks she will do much better in a minimum number of calls per week and rather resents the emphasis on certain quotas.

Her sales manager, Alice Hamilton, disagrees. She says that no matter how smart you are, a high activity level is important in the early months of any sales career. As a sales manager for 20 years, Alice thinks she knows best.

- Do you think Molly is right?
- Is the sales manager's experienced judgment sound?
- Is Molly's commitment to the sales career lessened by her stubborn belief in her own untried sales abilities?
- Should the sales manager make an exception in Molly's case?

**Case
Study
Two**

Jim Shelton is from Gary, Indiana, and now lives in the south suburbs of Chicago. He is a steel salesman. He grew up in the steel business, his father having been employed in one of the large plants in Gary. Jim knows the business inside out and loves his work.

He now works for one of the largest steel companies in the United States, selling to some of the top fabricators and manufacturers in the Chicago area. They respect Jim highly, and he has always been successful. In fact, he has been one of the leading regional salespersons for the last eight years.

However, with the recent influx of foreign steel at much lower prices, selling his product has become increasingly difficult. This, of course, concerns him deeply, but he has tremendous loyalty to his company.

One of the things that has always bothered Jim is that his regional sales manager has insisted that he be involved in the community in various activities, have a high profile, and maintain a reputation as a "doer." Now, with competition making sales more difficult, he is finding that, in order to keep up, he has to make more calls to develop more customers, and that means less time for community work.

Jim's company is very conscious of the poor public image it has long had in many communities because of its former practice of polluting area streams with waste materials. It no longer engages in this practice, after a government investigation nine years ago which resulted in a consent decree in court, but it still has the old image to live down. The regional sales manager's insistence on Jim's community work is part of this general company policy.

Jim is aware of all this, but in a special meeting with his sales manager, he has asked that, in view of the foreign steel competition, he be permitted to drop some of his community activities.

- As his sales manager, what would you answer?

- What alternative methods of selling, if any, could Jim take to save time?

- How could Jim adapt his community commitments to give himself more time for selling?

- Would changing his employment to one of the foreign steel companies be a good solution for Jim's problem?

- Do companies have an obligation to be involved in their communities? Explain.

The Importance of 21
Good Sales Training

OBJECTIVES

In this chapter you will learn:

- Why good sales training programs are important.
- Why such programs must be written.
- Why sales training must be continuous.
- What makes an effective sales trainer.
- How psychology helps in sales training.
- Why sales-skills training is important.

Professional salespeople are made, not born. On-going training is essential for growth and success. Simply having knowledge of the aspects of selling is not enough.

In the early days of commercial selling, there was no such thing as sales training. It used to be said that a good salesman was born, not made. "Here's the catalogue; now get out and sell" was all the advice a salesman got, and of course the turnover was great. There was a brief exposure to the products in the line, and then the sales manager gave each salesman several order blanks and told them to get out on the street and call back only when they had made some sales.

Barney Stockwell, a bright and extremely competent commercial loan officer at the Shawmut National Bank in Atlanta, Georgia, shakes his head when anyone brings up this old lackadaisical way of turning out salespeople. As an aggressive commercial loan officer, Barney spends almost every afternoon in the field, soliciting new clients and selling them on the value of transferring business to Shawmut National.

When Barney began as a loan officer at Shawmut ten years ago, he wasn't told much about his duties. He was given a two-page job description which ended with the statement: "Your main concern must be to avoid making risky loans." The bank's training in the essentials was rudimentary; the phrase "sales training" wasn't even mentioned. Barney had to learn his job gradually by observing the established loan officers and asking questions. It was an apprenticeship of the old-fashioned sort.

Barney never dreamed that he would have to go out and sell banking services. But when Shawmut National set up its new, aggressive marketing program, requiring commercial loan officers to spend at least half of each day in the field soliciting new customers, it very wisely set up a comprehensive, in-house sales training program. This program has helped Barney's progress and increased his income, and he would not trade it for any old apprenticeship: "Our training program," he says, "has no place for the pressure tactics most of us thought the sales career would involve. To me, the most important thing about any sales career is the training, and we have an excellent program here at Shawmut."

Industry studies have shown that there are two basic reasons for high turnover in sales personnel: poor recruiting and poor training. This chapter discusses the importance of having good, long-range training programs, with clearly written and specific sales manuals. Training should always be conducted by someone who is thoroughly familiar with the program. It should include all aspects of selling, from sales skills and product knowledge to responsible sales techniques. It should also include some kind of self-audit system and joint work with successful salespeople.

THE IMPORTANCE OF CONTINUITY

From the company's point of view, a long-range training program is a sound investment. With the high cost of recruiting, hiring, and training salespeople these days, turnover is a costly business, and a program that can reduce that cost and result in a well-trained sales staff makes good sense indeed.

Long-range training usually means a minimum period of three years. Depending on the products or services involved, the initial program may require intensive training for at least three or four months.

Some companies take this first training period very seriously. Some of the sophisticated computer corporations, for example, take their prospective salespeople off to a retreatlike atmosphere for three to four months of intensive training before putting them in the field. Life insurance companies often train their agents in the home offices for one or two months, or encourage local offices to have training periods of fixed lengths before allowing salespeople to start regular calling.

However long, or wherever conducted, this first period of intensive training should familiarize salespeople with all products or services and should include fundamentals of sales skills. (Figure 21-1 is the schedule of a two-week initial training program.) After this intensive period, a second stage should continue training for several months with close supervision. The supervisory period should become gradually looser as salespeople begin to move toward being on their own.

Finally, salespeople assume independent status except for required reporting of activity and sales and periodic progress reviews with their sales manager.

There is no magic moment when salespeople arrive at this independent stage. Some, eager to get to the field, break away from formal training early; others go slowly.

THE WRITTEN SALES MANUAL

In today's complicated sales world, particularly where product knowledge itself can be almost overwhelming, a written program for salespeople is absolutely essential. Although direct sales training, either individual or group, is necessary and desirable, it is usually not enough. Salespeople today have a great deal to master, and not all of it can be learned in classes, even in several sessions. There must be some sort of written manual that can be studied and referred to when questions arise.

Some companies call such a manual their sales bible. Although these manuals are continually revised to reflect product or service changes, the fundamental sales skills remain little changed. Any written sales program or manual should contain the basics:

- Product or service fundamentals
- Prospecting methods

- Market development techniques
- Overall sales skill training, including role playing
- Personal organizational procedures and tools, including time and territory management
- All sales presentations in current use
- Closing techniques, including appropriate answers to objections
- Client-building methods
- Communication skills in selling
- Creative sales ideas
- Competition product knowledge

Week: (first)   New Trainee:_____

TIME	MONDAY	TUESDAY	WEDNESDAY	THURSDAY	FRIDAY	SATURDAY
8:30 A.M.	Orientation— Introductions Review Sales Manual, S.M.	Demonstrate overall approach to S.M.	Record opening interview on video tape.	Demonstrate opening interview on television to S.M.	Read "Personal Organization" in Sales Manual.	8:30-12:00 noon in office.
9:30 A.M.	Company and office history Awards/Benefits/ Compensation	Demonstrate presenting products to S.M.	Read "Prospecting and Selective Marketing."	View video tape on prospecting, Part 1.	Read "Getting the Most Out of Your Daytime Activity."	Review of week, prepare questions for Monday meeting with S.M.
10:30 A.M.	Discuss sales process —an overview of the sales cycle. S.M.	Read "Isolating Needs."	Read Section A of Price Manual (underline at will).	Study Section C of Rate Book on delivery and installation.	View video tape on servicing accounts.	
LUNCH						
1:00 P.M.	View video tape on sales tracks.	Read "Getting the Dollar Commitment."	Review taped opening interview. Record it again on video.	Read "Specimen Order Blank".	Learn referred lead talk, practice on audio cassette.	
2:00 P.M.	Read "Sales Process." View overall approach on video tape.	Discuss "The Savings Commitment." S.M.	Overview of product and service fundamentals (to be studied in evenings) S.M.	View video tape on prospecting, part 2.	View video tape on personal organization.	
3:00 P.M.	Read "Presenting Your Products."	View video tape on presentation of products and services.	Read: "Our Company and Yours" (underline at will).	Review Salary and Compensation Plan.	Read "Art of Closing" in Sales Manual.	
4:00 P.M.	Practice overall approach.	View video tape on professional selling.	Read Section B of Price Manual (orders).	Study Section G of Servicing Accounts.	Read "The Written Proposal" in Sales Manual.	
5:00 to 5:30 P.M.	Practice presenting your products on audio cassette.	Practice opening interview on audio cassette tape.	Practice opening interview on television.	Read "Getting Referrals" in Sales Manual.	Informal meeting with sales manager.	
Evening	REVIEW OF DAY AND READ AND REVIEW SECTIONS IN SALES MANUAL ON PRODUCTS.					

Figure 21–1. First Week of a Two-Week Initial Training Program (S.M. = Sales Manager)

- Procedures on writing and submitting orders
- The delivery interview
- Postsales service
- Customer contact and client building
- Audio cassettes and video playback material, if possible

A complete written program is a ready reference on selling techniques, information, and skills, and it also gives the salesperson a convenient notebook for marking refinements and things that seem to work particularly well. Experience teaches, and the sales training manual will eventually become the salesperson's reference, as well as training, manual.

Week: (second) _____   New Trainee: _____

TIME	MONDAY	TUESDAY	WEDNESDAY	THURSDAY	FRIDAY	SATURDAY
8:30 A.M.	Meeting with S.M.	Review "Customer List."	Demonstrate opening interview on television.	Demonstrate closing on television.	Review entire two weeks. S.M.	8:30 to 12:00 noon in office.
9:30 A.M.	View video tapes, Part 1, Psychology of Close.	View video tape on psychology of closing sale.	Handling Objections workshop. S.M.	Discuss delivery interview. S.M.	Write out questions S.M.	Review of week Prepare for Monday phoning.
10:30 A.M.	View video tape on customer file box.	Review "Sales Talk."	View video tape on transanalysis.	View video tape on customer service.	Question period. S.M.	
LUNCH						
1:00 P.M.	Prepare pocket diary for current month.	Read Sections E and F of Price Book Manual (underline at will).	Read "Fear, Stress & Rejection" in Sales Manual.	View video tape on four personality types.	Study telephone technique in Sales Manual.	
2:00 P.M.	View video tape on Motivating the Prospect, Part 1.	Writing the Order workshop with staff at order desk.	Read "Ethics and the Customer" in Sales Manual.	Read "New Products and Services" in Sales Manual.	Workshop on telephone techniques. S.M.	
3:00 P.M.	View video tape on Marketing the Prospect, Part 2.	Complete sample order and submit to order desk.	Work through sample problems from price book.	View video P-09 on coordinating corporate dollars.	Accumulate prospects for telephone next week.	
4:00 P.M.	Study target markets in Sales Manual.	View video tape on personal attitudes.	Demonstrate referred lead track. S.M.	Have planning session; set quotas. S.M.		
5:00 to 5:30 P.M.	Learn three motivating anecdotes in Sales Manual.	Practice closing on television with S.M.	Practice closing interview with S.M.	Tape sales ideas.	Final meeting with S.M.	
Evening	ACCUMULATE 200 PROSPECTS ON PROSPECT SHEETS (ANY SOURCE). FILL OUT SHEETS COMPLETELY.					

Figure 21–1 (continued).
Second Week of Training Program

THE EXPERIENCED TRAINER

A good sales training program should be taught by someone who has been through the same program or a similar one and has had experience in the field. If all businesses realized this, training programs would achieve more, no doubt, and achieve it more quickly. This is not the salesperson's problem, of course—or it is his problem only in that he may be the loser.

Not all experienced salespeople make good teachers, and those best suited to the trainer-teacher role must themselves learn some techniques of teaching others. Nonetheless, no one who is inexperienced in the ups and downs of selling is really competent to train others to sell. Trainers who have made some great sales, who have felt the thrill of writing orders, can project to their trainees an enthusiasm that cannot be matched by those with no field experience.

The skilled trainer is a skillful salesperson also, which means that he has a thorough knowledge of the product and an appreciation for the necessity of having that knowledge. He also knows, or has learned, how to analyze performance, how to conduct skill sessions and sales clinics, and how to motivate others.

Industry wastes thousands of dollars every year by placing unqualified salespeople in sales management positions. Headquarters marketing departments seem to make these errors all the time. Sometimes, outstanding salespeople, lured by the attractions of, they think, more prestige, security, or income than in straight selling, insist on giving sales management a try. Frequently they are disappointments to all concerned.

The fortunate and serious sales managers build healthy relationships with their salespeople. They share a general concern for the business of selling and can appreciate the plusses and minuses of the sales and management careers. A sales manager's life is not easy, though many salespeople may think so. Frequently, the pressures to meet quotas, recruit, train, and improve the standing of their districts more than offset the apparent increase in prestige and income that sales managers enjoy. It takes a good sales manager to understand that training others is quite different from making it on one's own, so to speak. In sum:

- To survive, salespeople have to be concerned primarily with themselves and not others. Managers' concerns must always be directed toward their salespeople.

- Managers must have patience, knowing that it is their place to inspire rather than order.

- They must be flexible and open to suggestions from trainees.
- They must not mind being chained to a desk.

Good sales trainers seem to have these characteristics in common:

- They get satisfaction out of seeing others succeed.
- They like to reach sales goals through the combined efforts of others.
- They remain cool under changing conditions such as swings in the economy or sales slumps.
- They are particularly adept at teaching transferrable sales skills.
- They are inspiring teachers.
- They are leaders.

TRAINING IN PRODUCT KNOWLEDGE AND SERVICES

Gaining product knowledge is a continuous process. In our busy industrial-technological society, sales products and services change so rapidly that the salesperson needs all the information he can get on not only current and past but also future product developments. Product information is usually brought together for salespeople in sales manuals, catalogues, binders, or other sorts of printed materials that can be carried in the field. Continuing study, industry-wide conventions, and information bulletins help salespeople stay reasonably abreast of even the most advanced product changes. Schools, seminars, and meetings are a standard part of the training provided by many companies.

It goes without saying that price, technical, and service changes must be made known to those who sell the product. Misquoting a price, being unaware of changes in technical equipment, or failing to inform customers of service changes is not only embarrassing but potentially damaging to the company itself. Companies therefore, on the whole, do all they can to impart product and service knowledge to their field forces on a continuing basis.

Besides the regular issuing of printed material and scheduled training sessions, many large sales offices maintain libraries for the use of their salespeople. And, of course, one of the sales manager's continuing responsibilities is to see that salespeople are kept informed about their own product and, very often, of those of the main competitor as well.

TRAINING IN RESPONSIBLE SALES TECHNIQUES

A skill is somewhere between a science and an art, involving both the learning of facts and the practice of creativity. In a good training program such as the one set forth in Figure 21-1, selling skills are taught along with product knowledge, for it does little good to teach one without the other. The business world has many people exceptionally well informed in product knowledge and services who are quite unable to sell because they have never learned selling techniques.

In a good training program, the emphasis is on practice and role playing. From simple memorized presentations, trainees move on to more challenging role-playing situations, in which the trainer plays the salesperson and the trainee the customer, and then the reverse.

The trainer criticizes every performance, and, like an actor, the trainee repeats his presentation again and again until it becomes part of his personality.

This can be exhausting work. Every part of the sales presentation, from the opening remarks to the closing, must be thoroughly rehearsed and criticized. Only then does the trainer step aside and let pairs of trainees move on to practice additional skills on each other or on video or cassette tapes.

Companies usually maintain training clinics on a continuing basis. Perhaps a trainer finds her charges are not closing enough sales. So she might call for a Friday afternoon closing clinic. Here, factual sales situations are agreed upon and trainees volunteer to role play the scene.

"What should Fred have said there?" might be the comment, or "What did Mary do that was so effective in writing the order here?" Training sessions on specific details are valuable and necessary parts of any training program, and group learning in this case is far more effective than individual learning. By putting trainees on the spot, group sales-skill training forces control and builds confidence. And for many, candid criticism from a friendly group of fellow trainees may be far more effective than well-intended criticism from a highly skilled trainer. As one presentation is criticized, by the trainer or the group, all can learn.

Occasionally, experienced salespeople join the trainees in such sessions. They participate by playing the salesperson and asking the "customer" to be tough and difficult. Then the trainees perform, using the experienced person's techniques. By the time the session is over, the trainee's confidence has zoomed.

Another tool more and more used in training sessions is the video camera playback system. Much as a coach uses playbacks of a game, the sales trainer can video-tape a session and play it back immediately for analysis. This is particularly useful in analyzing details such as handling and demonstrating products; body language, posture, and gestures; skill in making presentations and handling objections; and of course the overall effectiveness of specific parts of a presentation, such as closing.

THE SELF-AUDIT SYSTEM

Through daily, weekly, monthly, quarterly or annual reports, a good sales training program should provide salespeople with a method of assessing their progress toward realistic goals.

Salespeople like to know where they are going and what is expected of them. They like having a continuing measure of their progress and growth. So they like to set production goals. But these goals must be realistic to be meaningful.

Goals set so low as to be unchallenging are self-defeating. In a way, salespeople have to be challenged to be responsive. Professional salespeople can't be part-timers with time on their hands.

Goals that are unrealistically high can also be devastating. Beginning salespeople often set unreasonable goals and when they fail to reach them become discouraged and depressed. It is here that trainers must assume responsibility for setting reachable goals.

The management tool called management by objectives (MBO), which was referred to in the preceding chapter, is a way of working out a genuine joint effort by both salespeople and managers. Properly designed, it should:

- Set mutually agreeable annual sales and income goals.
- Set mutually agreeable activity goals.
- Provide for periodic review.
- Require analysis preparation by the salesperson for the periodic review.
- Make the salesperson responsible for arranging the review interview.

Figure 21-2 shows a completed monthly accomplishment form, in which the salesperson has answered specific questions about his goals, work habits, and plans, together with an analysis by the sales manager. By obliging salespeople to explain in writing what they are doing well or

Monthly accomplishment analysis *Greg Tandy*
(name)

For month of *March*   19 *83*

Goals for 19 *83*

GOALS:	Volume		Cumulative Goal to Date	Made to Date	Results (+ or −) to Date
	Month	Year			
COMMISSIONS	$2,000	$24,000	$ 6000	$ 4564	−1436
NUMBER OF SALES	10	120	30	31	+ 1

ACTIVITY:	(Weekly) Number			(Weekly) Number	
Seen calls per week	25		25	21	−4
Opened cases per week*	5		5	5.5	+.5
Closing interviews per week†	5		5	4	−1
New facts per week**	5		6	2	−3
Qualified referrals per week	30		30	36	+6

*Need and dollar commitment have been firmly established.
†You ask for the order at least five times.
**New facts procured on potentials who are not prospects now.

Greg Tandy
(Signed)

Figure 21–2.   Monthly Accomplishment Form (page 1)

PLEASE COMMENT ON FOLLOWING:

GOALS

Which goals most satisfactorily achieved and why? *Number of sales.*
I have been using better closing skills - also
qualifying prospects much better.

Which goals least satisfactorily achieved and why? *I'm behind in commis-*
sions. I'm relying too much on large sales. I need
to increase my activity for more sales, even though
smaller.

WORK HABIT GOALS

Which goals most satisfactorily achieved and why? *Opening up cases*
better because of more quality prospects and
finding more needs by patient counseling.

Which goals least satisfactorily achieved and why? *New facts per week -*
not up to my requirements. I tend to overlook
this in favor of immediate sales.

What do you feel the problems are (if any)?
I need to be more active in developing future
clients.

What are your plans to overcome the problem(s)? *Allocate more interview*
time per call so I can develop future clients.
It takes time to explore the potential
with such prospects.

(After completion, please arrange definite appointment for analysis interview.)

Figure 21–2 (continued).   Monthly Accomplishment Form (page 2)

ANALYSIS INTERVIEW

<u>GOALS</u>   Date of Interview *April 2, 1983*

Most Satisfactory

1. Number of sales – this is fine. I'm proud of you.

2. Referred leads. This is the key to future sales and client building. Referrals, as you know, are the best leads available, particularly if they're qualified well.

Least Satisfactory

1. Commissions. I agree that increased activity is the answer here. Big cases are nice, but you have to go after numbers – even if it means smaller sales.

2. New facts. You are getting lots of referrals, but apparently when you see them you are giving up too easily. By spending more time with them, you will be able to develop them profitably in the future.

Other Comments

Overall, I like your attitude. You are assuming self–responsibility for your field results. I like that.
Keep up the good work. Let me know if I can help.

Signed *Mel Grossman*
Sales Manager

Figure 21–2 (continued). Monthly Accomplishment Form (page 3)

poorly, this kind of performance analysis stimulates thought and considered action to correct problems. To work, MBO must be realistic in its goals and nonauthoritarian in its implementation (see Figure 21-3). The salesperson is, after all, working in great part for his own success and satisfaction.

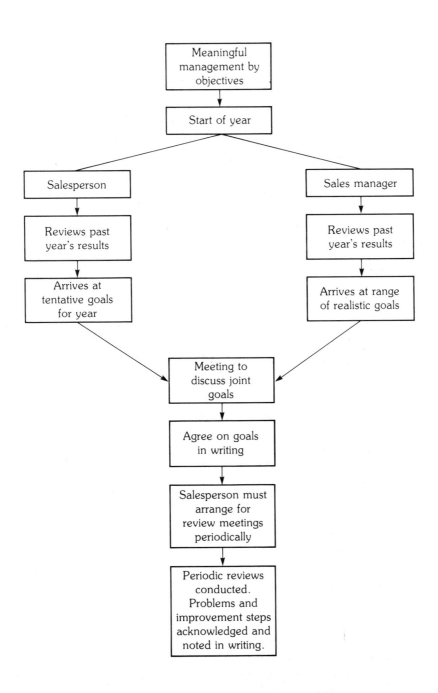

Figure 21–3. Management by Objectives: How It Works

COOPERATING WITH SUCCESSFUL SALESPEOPLE

Some companies have lengthy in-house training programs, whereas others have only brief ones, feeling that early field experience is top priority. In either case, training should not end abruptly once the session is concluded.

Besides helping in the formal training program, skilled professionals should be ready to help neophytes on a planned but informal basis, and the company should encourage this sort of cooperation. Informal discussions, joint field work, buddy systems—any arrangement that gives the new salesperson the chance to ask questions and learn from the skilled professional should continue for as long as the new salesperson feels the need for advice.

Though many skilled salespersons are unsuited to conduct group training programs, they are usually very willing to help beginning salespeople succeed by sharing knowledge learned from experience—as the newcomers will someday share theirs. Though the formal training ends, the learning continues.

SUMMARY

This chapter emphasized the importance of effective sales training. Intensive at first, it must be continued over an extended period of time. It should be written and presented to sales trainees for study in a sales manual, and training sessions should be conducted by experienced salespeople who are at the same time good teachers. Not all successfull salespeople have the patience necessary to teach others—salespeople are by nature usually independent. A good trainer or sales manager wants to see others succeed.

Good training programs should include extensive training in product and service knowledge and sales techniques. Product knowledge, from sales manuals, bulletins, video and cassette presentations, company schools, and so on, is of utmost importance, especially in highly technical fields, and most companies take that aspect of training very seriously. Training in selling skills is most effective in group sessions or training clinics, in which trainees practice every aspect of sales presentations, with trainers and with each other, to learn skill and confidence.

The chapter closed with a description (and an example) of a self-audit system based on meaningful management by objectives (MBO). When realistic goals are agreed upon by salespeople and their managers, and salespeople evaluate their progress first, before discussing it with the manager, performance takes on a new meaning.

KEY TERMS

Joint Field Work

Sales Manual

Self-Audit System

Trainer

REVIEW QUESTIONS

- What are the two main reasons for turnover in sales personnel?
- Why should a sales training program be long-range?
- Why should such a program be written and presented to the salesperson?
- Why don't successful salespeople necessarily make good sales trainers?
- What is role playing in sales training?

DISCUSSION TOPICS

- Is it possible to have a good sales trainer who has not been through the program himself? Why?
- What is the main reasons for having role-playing clinics before the closing interview of a big sale?
- What is meant by "responsible sales techniques in training"?
- Discuss why a good sales training program should involve proven successes with new salespeople.

EXERCISES

1. Divide into groups of five or six. Appoint one of the group to explain a new product or service to the rest of the group of salespeople. Each group should evaluate the effectiveness of its own presentation.

2. Write up a set of goals in activity and sales for the coming year, based on sound management by objectives. Assume that your trainer at the annual planning session thinks the goals are too low. Pair off with a fellow student and act out the planning session.

3. Call on a local business and ask for a copy of its sales training program. Discuss it in class.

Case Study One

The Ace Printing Company has recently hired Bill Hicks as a new salesman. The new lower cost printing offered by Ace is the result of a major breakthrough in the lithography process. Because the new process is fairly simple, salespeople can explain it to customers without any long training session. Ace is now going after some accounts who have been doing business with standard, old-line companies which have not adopted this new process.

Jim Hunt, the sales manager, has told Bill that since selling printing is a matter simply of showing the catalogue and quoting prices, a written sales training program is not necessary. He prefers to train his staff (now six) in individual sessions, including joint calls for the first two weeks. After that the person is on his own. Furthermore, Jim thinks most salespeople wouldn't read a training manual anyway, since people like to learn on the job.

- Do you agree with Jim's position? Explain.
- Does the newer, simpler lithographic process really make a sales training manual unnecessary?
- How can Bill develop a self-audit system with no sales training program?
- What benefits can Bill expect from making joint calls with successful salespeople instead of with Jim himself?

Jane Leary is a recent graduate in chemistry from Rutgers University and is now a sales trainee at a large chemical firm in her home state of New Jersy. She had thought of going on for graduate work and becoming a research chemist, but a recruiting program caught her attention and she switched goals. Now she finds herself the only woman in a training clinic of 15 men.

The company has been conducting formal training clinics for about a decade now and runs them well. The manual is excellent, and product information has been thoroughly brought together in catalogues and brochures. The video tapes showing chemical processes and industrial use of the products manufactured by the company are excellent.

Jane has absorbed all this material and feels competent in product knowledge, but she is having trouble with sales techniques. To put it bluntly, she feels embarrassed in some of the role-playing interviews, and mortified by some of the well-intentioned but frank criticism. She wonders whether she has made a mistake in going into selling.

- What can Jane do to overcome her embarrassment?
- What can the other trainees, and the trainer, do to help her?
- Will product knowledge be enough?
- Would joint sales calls be more helpful to her as a way of gaining confidence?

22

Law, Ethics, and the Consumer

OBJECTIVES

In this chapter you will learn:

- How laws can affect the selling career.
- The types of laws covering the sales career.
- What ethics means.
- The relationship between ethics and sales.
- The need for ethical conduct in selling.
- The meaning of the consumer movement.

Paul Quincy sells industrial paint in Ohio. On this particular day he is in Dayton, where he is calling on a small manufacturer of automobile trunk lids for compact automobiles. Paul's paint is used as a sealant for the trunk lids to prevent corrosion and other wear and tear due to exhaust fumes, water, and oil. He has done business with this company only sporadically in the past. He is a highly competent salesperson and has been at his job some twenty years, ever since his graduation from Ohio State University.

Over coffee with the local purchasing agent, Paul learns that there is another company bidding for the same job at about the same price. Paul is used to this. He knows he is in a highly competitive field and offers to the purchasing agent his usual arguments about better service and prompt delivery. These have placed his company in good standing in the past and have resulted in his procuring many repeat orders for his industrial paint products.

However, the purchasing agent hints that times are pretty rough right now and that he has not even been able to buy any clothes, much less the new suit he usually buys at this time of year. Paul is disturbed by this conversation, particularly when the purchasing agent pursues it, indicating subtly that if somehow Paul would give him a suit, he would most certainly get the order.

Paul has experienced similar approaches before and has always ignored them. He knows that giving preferential price reductions to anyone is illegal. He also feels such an act is against his personal ethics. His reputation for integrity has been established firmly with his customers and his company for years.

As the talking proceeds, however, it becomes very clear that the purchasing agent is prepared to double the order, which would raise Paul's commission on this sale by some $1700. The purchasing agent has the authority to double the orders and would be willing to do it if, he suggests, he knew somebody who could "buy suits cheaply" for him.

Paul is certain that the company needs the paint, and he would be happy to have a reasonable order in the usual way. He wishes the purchasing agent would shut up. If he reports the purchasing agent to the management, he knows the agent can deny everything and say that he was only talking in a general way about the economic situation and inflation and having to postpone clothing purchases. And if he ignores the implied bribe, he is sure the competitor will get the business.

Paul quickly decides against any kickback. He is angry at the purchasing agent for implying he would do anything unethical. But he will not compromise his conscience. He says, "There's no way I can help you here. I'm sorry but I just can't." So he loses the sale. Paul is upset, but feels his integrity is too important to him personally to enter into such an arrangement.

Paul's experience is typical of the ethical choices that can face salespeople in normally routine selling. This chapter will discuss this matter as well as larger legal and consumer problems from the standpoint of both law and ethics and will pay particular attention to laws as they affect business and salespeople.

The ancient Greek philosopher Plato considered these questions centuries ago. Most philosophers agree that there are immutable truths (willful murder is always wrong) and situational truths (it is all right for a man to steal food for his starving family) in personal ethics.

In selling, these lines frequently cross, and they vary from one industry to the next. Within certain limits, what is ethical in one situation may be less than ethical in another. The most we can do is to discuss some ethical situations that frequently arise and offer some ways of handling them.

Ethical conduct in business is not unchanging. Some things that were once considered highly unethical—such as lawyers advertising—are now considered not only perfectly legal but quite ethical. A few years ago, many states had statutes prohibiting the replacement of existing life insurance policies with other similar plans. Now, a number of laws have been liberalized to permit such changes where the policyholder benefits from the change.

In the field of selling, public awareness of price fixing and international thefts of trade secrets has made it obligatory for salespeople in the field to steer clear of even the mildest forms of gift giving, which used to be common.

THE LAW AND EARLY CONSUMERISM

Caveat emptor—let the buyer beware—was the Roman expression for the kind of business ethics that more or less prevailed until fairly recent times. This is not to say that there have not been many honest tradesmen and sellers. Especially when they had an established clientele, tradespeople were quick to make amends for shoddy goods.

It was only, in fact, as the relationship between manufacturer and consumer loosened and then disappeared almost altogether with the rise of the Industrial Revolution that the consumer began to lose his rights. With no one to complain to except the storekeeper, consumers had to beware. All too frequently, the storekeeper himself was being exploited, too, by the manufacturer. The result, emerging only gradually, of these abuses was protective laws, the early beginnings of the consumer movement. These laws have been of two broad categories: those that affect the consumer indirectly, and, more recently, those that affect the consumer directly. Over the years, a body of federal law has been constructed which indirectly affects the consumer.

- The Sherman Antitrust Act of 1890 made it possible for the federal government to intervene in the regulation of competition. The Sherman Act had two main provisions: (1) contracts, combinations, and conspiracies in restraint of interstate and foreign trade were illegal;

and (2) monopolies and attempts to control entire industries through mergers were illegal. Further defined in the act as illegal were conspiracies to fix prices, to limit controlled production, and to divide markets or territories for customers. The act also prohibited any other activities that might unreasonably restrain healthy business competition.

- The Clayton Antitrust Act, passed by Congress in 1914, attempted to clarify the confusion caused for business persons and others subject to the Sherman Act. It was much broader in scope than the Sherman Act and tried to prevent harm to competition before it occurred. This act has three major sections; Section 1 makes price control illegal if its effect is to create a monopoly or lessen competition; Section 2 prohibits a seller or lessor of a highly desirable product from requiring purchases of other or less desirable products to obtain the former; Section 3 limits mergers of large companies that would tend to discourage competition, disallowing a larger corporation from buying out its competitor except under stringent rules and regulations. The act also legalized peaceful strikes, picketing, and boycotts.

- The Federal Trade Commission Act of 1914 created a Federal Trade Commission charged with preventing "unfair methods of competition and commerce and unfair or deceptive acts or practices in commerce." This commission became the investigative body of the violators of antitrust laws and unfair competition or trade practices. It can issue cease-and-desist orders and levy fines for any business engaged in interstate commerce.

- Among laws administered by the FTC is the Consumer Credit Protection Act originally passed in 1968. It has been amended several times to include consumer protection in such areas as credit cards, electronic funds transfers, equal credit opportunity, fair credit reporting, fair debt collection, and truth in lending.

- The Robinson-Patman Act passed under Franklin D. Roosevelt in 1936 was a supplement to the Clayton Act. Its purpose was to guarantee equal treatment to all buyers of a commodity from a company and to prohibit price discrimination in goods of a like grade in quality shipped in interstate commerce where the effect would be to lessen competition or create a monopoly. Thus, a large corporation such as General Motors, with its vast assets, would be prohibited from cutting its prices substantially to drive other auto manufacturers out of the business. The buyer who knowingly pays a discriminatory price is also in violation of this act.

Many states have adopted similar laws. Most states now follow the principles enunciated by the above laws.

Typical of other laws indirectly affecting the consumer are laws administered by the Securities and Exchange Commission. Here Congress attempted to protect the public from fraudulent stock arrangements and purchases. The Foreign Corrupt Practices Act outlaws bribery or other unethical practices to procure business from countries outside the United States. Although these may only remotely affect the consumer; they are nevertheless indicative of a recent trend to protect the consumer from large corporate abuses. This is currently referred to as the consumer movement.

CURRENT CONSUMER LAWS

Within the last 20 years a whole series of new laws have come onto the scene which directly affect the consumer. Currently, many such laws are the subject of heated controversies and lawsuits.

- The Equal Employment Opportunity Commission, which is an outgrowth of the civil rights laws, prohibits business from discriminating against hiring or retaining anyone on the basis of age, race, religion, creed, or sex.

- ERISA (Employment Retirement Income Security Act) requires protection of the pension benefits of consumers who work as employees for organizations. The law requires adequate funding and fair vesting of certain employee pension rights. Thus, employees can reasonably anticipate their pensions when they retire.

- The Environmental Protection Act sets maximum levels of earth, air, and water pollution and sets penalties for companies that do not comply. This act has had the general support of citizens' groups all over the country.

Many of the cases brought to the courts at all levels, under the above laws and numerous state, county, and local laws of a similar nature, have been settled in favor of the plaintiffs—that is, the consumers. Many are still under litigation, and more are filed every day.

PRODUCT LIABILITY SUITS

Product liability suits are a more recent trend, and here again the consumer frequently has the court on his side. The long abused public, feeling cheated, defrauded, or misinformed about the nature of a product or service purchased, wants its money back with interest. Fines have been levied against the defendants; in some cases imprisonment has resulted. Courts are awarding not only actual damages for defective products, but in some cases punitive damages also.

It is not surprising that companies are trying to guard themselves by calling in products that are found to be defective. Though the cost of such recalls may be enormous, the cost of potential damages awarded for death or injury due to a faulty brake system or transmission malfunction may be far higher. Even when the defects appear to be minor and perhaps not even widespread, recall is the safe thing to do.

Although automobiles seem to be especially defective, to judge from the number of recalls, they are not the only products recalled by any means. Recalls of canned goods are common. At Christmas time, toys are scrutinized especially by consumer groups and recalls occur. Flammable baby clothes and nightwear, paints, industrial masks—the list is long.

In essence, the laws have stimulated the consumer movement, and the consumer is at last gaining strength as an effective monitor of defective products and services made available to the public.

THE ROLE OF SALESPEOPLE

Under these circumstances, if for no other reason, salespeople who sell any product or service must be aware of their company's and their individual liability. Most companies keep a close watch on their public image, part of which is, of course, projected through the sales staff. More and more, salespeople are being cautioned against any misrepresentation, however slight, of a product or service and warned of the legal consequences that could ensue. Here are a few basic cautions:

- Lying about products or services to the detriment of the customer exposes the salesperson to a lawsuit.

- Rebating any commission when it is illegal to do so could also cause the loss of the salesperson's right to do business. It would probably cause immediate employment termination.

- Not following through on promised service can expose a salesperson to liability.

- Making false promises about a product can be the subject of a lawsuit. In most cases, it is the company that will be sued, since salespeople are usually considered as acting as agents of the company, and attempts by companies to escape liability by saying the salespeople are independent contractors usually are to no avail. Nonetheless, the salesperson owes it to the company not to promise what it cannot give.

Salespeople must bring a high degree of personal integrity to their careers. It is important that they know their liabilities. Many companies have laws and regulations in manual form for distribution to their salespeople. If not, it is up to the salesperson to acquire this important information.

CONSUMER'S RIGHTS

The four-point consumer protection program passed by Congress at President John F. Kennedy's urging in 1963 was the first substantial bill of rights for the benefit of the consumer. This program included the following consumer rights:

- The right to safety
- The right to be informed
- The right to choose
- The right to be heard

Nine years later, Congress began to build a faster momentum by passing additional consumer-oriented laws. These, coupled with the vast array of laws discussed earlier, gave consumers a whole new set of rights.

Under this pressure, and spurred also by high-quality Japanese competition, the sloppy workmanship, mediocre service, and the "we couldn't care less" attitude at some levels of our manufacturing and distribution process are changing.

In particular, Ralph Nader's documented criticisms of government and industry over the past 15 years have made the public aware of its rights and of the abuses it has suffered. Nader has been responsible for at least eight major federal consumer protection laws and numerous other advances in the areas of health, pollution control, and access to government information. His unflagging efforts have built an effective national network of citizens' groups whose ultimate goal is to give all citizens means of resolving their grievances and for achieving a better society.

ETHICAL AND MORAL RESPONSIBILITIES
OF SALESPEOPLE

So far in this discussion, emphasis has been on the legal aspects of fraud and misrepresentation. But salespeople should do more than merely be aware of their liabilities and those of the company they represent. The legal areas are fairly clear. Ethics is a less precise territory.

Ethics, in the popularly understood sense, concerns itself with value judgments as to what are right or wrong acts. It may involve the study of rules that people live by or ought to live by. It could, therefore, be said to deal with what people ought to do.

Yet, barring specific religious points of reference, it is difficult to state what people ought to do in specific situations, especially in the highly complex industrialized society in which we live.

One may, of course, ask the basic question, "Why be ethical? Why not do what one impulsively wants to do and let it go at that?" There are perhaps many ways to respond to such questions, but an appropriate answer is that *not* to be ethical is to be less of a whole person. It makes no more sense to ask one, "Why be ethical?" than it does to ask a mathematician, "Why be precise?" If you want to be a mathematician, you have to be precise. If you want to be fully human, you have to be ethical. Admittedly, everyone is stuck with being human, but being ethical is part of being a whole person.

Being ethical need not be incompatible with self-interest. Indeed, it might even be successfully argued that being ethical entails the pursuit of one's self-interest so long as others are not hurt in the process. There is the proviso, however, that conflicting interests are to be resolved by generally agreed upon rules, such as moral laws—thou shalt not kill or steal—or civil laws. Such rules enable the more effective pursuit of individual self-interest in society. For example, when there is a need for gasoline rationing during an oil shortage, the majority of people will voluntarily set aside their own self-interest for the common good. In selling, salespeople should likewise set aside their own self-interest in sales situations and think in terms of the customers' best interest. This is one of the tenets of professional selling. To do this may require a rather thorough self-analysis of what is about to be done. Paul Quincy probably asked himself these questions when he refused a kickback and lost the paint sale:

- Is it reasonable? Is the action I am about to take reasonable? Would a responsible person do this?

- Will it hurt anyone? Will this act hurt the customer, my company, the public, the community?

- Will it hurt my self-image? Will I feel bad about this? Will it detract from me as a person?

- Will it pass public scrutiny? Would the public endorse what I am about to do? Would my company say, "Go ahead"?

- Overall, what does my conscience tell me about this deed?

Most of us, through constant interaction with others in society, form reasonable consciences that we call into play throughout life.

Thus, salespeople should be ethical and develop their own sense of integrity simply because there is no better or workable alternative. Studies and surveys over the years have proved beyond any measure of reasonable doubt that customers like doing business with salespeople and firms that have reputations for being honest and ethical. Since trust and confidence stand at the heart of the art of successful selling, it behooves all salespeople to adopt and practice a strong code of ethics and personal integrity as they go about their daily tasks. This means telling the truth at all times and using responsible sales techniques. Thus, no harm befalls their customers. Figure 22-1 shows the responsibility in graphic form.

The moral or ethical responsibilities of salespeople fall into three main areas and several lesser ones. The three main ones are: to themselves, to the company, and to their customers.

To Themselves

Salespeople must assume responsibility for their own personal growth and integrity in what they do in their daily selling activities. They must use their time wisely, so that they grow and learn. In a way, their responsibility to their family, industry, and community is part of their responsibility to themselves, for only by being a whole and complete person can one be truly responsible. By being a whole person and recognizing the overlapping of responsibilities, the salesperson assumes the personal integrity that he must have to be truly successful. That kind of integrity cannot be acquired by pursuing selfish ends and ignoring wider responsibilities. One owes it to oneself to be honest. If one has personal integrity, personal honesty, one cannot easily be dishonest with company, customers or anyone else.

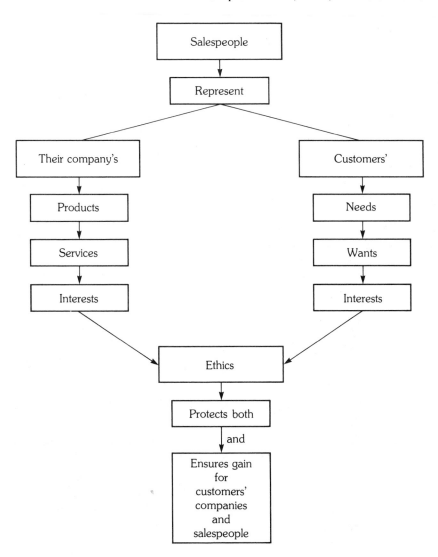

Figure 22-1.   A Salesperson's Responsibilities

To the Company

The kind of commitment and loyalty toward one's company that was emphasized in Chapter 20 is essentially the ethical responsibility that we
are talking about here. It is a mutual responsibility, and neither party can
violate it at will. A salesperson owes it to his company to represent it fairly

and honestly, to use his time to mutual profit, to give the kind of service that the company stands for—and in which, indeed, it has the greater stake. No salesperson should ever misrepresent his company just to make a sale and get a commission. By the same token, no company should ever ask its sales staff to sell products it knows to be defective. This has been mentioned before and needs emphasizing. If the company expects loyalty from its sales staff, it must be loyal to them.

For the salesperson, responsibility ro a company can mean a great many things, some easier to follow than others.

- Adherence to company policies. Generally, salespeople should follow company policies at all times. Even though personally disagreeable, such policies have been worked out over a period of time as the most workable programs for an organization. Thus, if a company asks its salespeople to work from 8:30 A.M. to 5:00 P.M., Monday through Friday, it is unfair to sleep in occasionally and not start calling until, say, 9:30 A.M.

- Accuracy on order forms. All these policies were made for specific reasons and salespeople have an obligation to adhere to them. If a particular policy is so distasteful that salespeople feel it is unfair, like promising quicker delivery than is probable, it should be discussed with sales managers.

- Personal use of company property. We are not talking about fraud, but of seemingly trivial things like having a pool secretary type a personal letter, or using the company copy machine for some purpose unconnected with company business, or taking home supplies of pencils, paper clips, note pads, and the like. These may seem like minor offenses, but they are offenses. Telephone calls fall in the same category. Many companies have special lines which reduce the cost of individual phone calls. Does that mean that salespeople have the moral right to make unnecessary personal calls on the grounds that the company can afford it? Is it really all right to use a company typewriter for personal reasons after hours? There are many gray areas here. The best rule would always be, if there is any doubt at all, don't—or check with the trainer or sales manager.

- Misuse of company time. Taking extra-long lunch hours or taking off early from work is a misuse of company time. Being out of the office and working on one's own gives salespeople a freedom and flexibility rare in the business world, and it is tempting to fudge. The salesperson has to remember that his freedom must not be abused. The salesperson loses, as well as the company.

- Expense accounts. Companies know salespeople have to spend money to make money, and on the whole expense accounts are reasonably generous. There is no need to inflate expenses, and professional salespeople rarely do. They keep careful and exact records and are armed with proof in case questions arise (see Figure 22-2). Limits necessarily vary, depending on territory and other

THE METZGER COMPANY

NAME: *Patrick O'Meara*
TITLE: *Salesman*

ADVANCE AMOUNT: — 0 —
DATE:
FOR:

DATE	CHARGE*	EXPLANATION	AMOUNT
3-21	Meals	Lunch with J. Carston at Green's Cafe	9.36
3-23	Travel	To and from Monroe city to see Garvey Co. (90 miles @ 20¢)	18.00
4-1 to 4-4	Travel	To Chicago for District Sales Meeting (air ticket & Hotel Room Receipt attached) including Meals & Tips	387.50
4-15	Phone	Long Distance to Ardmore on Nogales Case	7.19

TOTAL EXPENSES	422.05
LESS ADVANCE	—
NET DUE	422.05

Patrick O'Meara
Signature

Apr. 30
Date

Jen
Approved

*Phone, travel, lodging, meetings, meals, and the like. Receipts required for air fares, lodging, and entertainment.

Figure 22–2. An Expense Reimbursement Form

things, but so long as salespeople adhere to the spirit of expense accounts, problems generally do not occur.

- Incentives and contests. Beating one's fellow salespeople honestly in a contest or other incentive program builds self-esteem and ego and makes up for some of the rejection that occurs daily in the field. Everyone knows that cheating to win is wrong. But what if the cheating consists of urging customers to buy an item they don't really need "to help me win a trip"? This kind of cheating, as well as sandbagging, the practice of holding back previously written orders until a certain contest date, is just as wrong—and not at all rare. Even if the aim is to heighten incentive, management must be careful not to force sales-people to use high-pressure selling tactics simply to win a contest. District managers must not compel salespeople in the field to resort to tricks so that the district can win an award.

- Moonlighting. Working at another paying job after hours is questionable from an ethical standpoint. Successful selling requires a great deal of energy, and diluting it by working somewhere else, even on your own time, is in a way cheating. This is another gray area, however. No company can have total claim on an employee's time.

- Competitive selling. Competition with fellow salespeople in one's own company can be fierce, but most salespeople manage to keep it on a decent level. If one resorts to trickery, one is liable to be tricked oneself, and no one wins. Fellow salespeople within a company have to maintain a respect for one another's clientele, and for one an-other's referrals and even casual leads. That is part of company ethics. Trying to weasel in on someone else's territory is not honest.

To Their Customers

Chapter 17 discussed in detail the necessity of honesty, trust, and confidence between salesperson and customer and their importance in building a clientele. Ethical conduct is implicit in this relationship, but owing to the very nature of selling, personal judgment can sometimes falter.

- Misrepresentation. One of the most difficult areas to define is that of misrepresentation of products or services. Salespeople swept up with enthusiasm for and belief in their products or services can get carried away. In the heat of the moment, they may make unreasonable claims for the product they are selling. It ought to be sufficient to say that salespeople should remember that customers' interests always come first. Beyond that consideration, and from a purely practical standpoint, overstating quality does not help you get repeat orders and build clientele. Fly-by-night salesmen make outrageous claims; professional salespeople do not.

Leaving pure misrepresentation or unreal assurances of service aside as obviously unethical, there are shadings of claims that occur every day—they abound in commercial advertising, as any television watcher knows. Sometimes claims to superiority are a matter of opinion and cannot be proved one way or another: two companies may turn out commercial bake ovens that are well made and nearly identical in features. The customer must ultimately make the choice. Or if one has a feature more advanced than another, the salesperson can say, "Yes, Ajax does have a more sensitive timer, but ours is thoroughly tested and we guarantee full replacement if anything goes wrong."

- Confidential information. Often, a salesperson's clientele may include several customers who are themselves strong competitors with one another. This sometimes puts the salesperson in the awkward position of being pumped for information which, indeed, the salesperson may have received quite innocently in the course of a sales interview. Professional salespeople treat all conversations with customers as strictly confidential and will under no circumstances pass on anything—business or personal—that they know to be private. If a customer asks about another customer's business, the professional salesperson says, simply but firmly, something such as, "I understand your interest in finding these things out, but unfortunately I do not feel I can breach a confidence here." Such remarks will increase respect for you, too, by the person asking.

- Entertainment. Of all the issues facing salespeople in the area of personal ethics, none prompts more controversy than business entertainment.

Exactly what is business entertainment? From building goodwill to an outright attempt to buy sales, business entertainment presents an infinite variety of situations for salespeople. Industry cuts a wide swath on what is acceptable here. Liquor and beverage salespeople, for example, buy drinks all the time for their prospective customers.

Insurance salespeople like to sell over breakfast or lunches with their clients. As one successful insurance salesperson says, "I find that breakfast and lunch are ideal settings for sales presentations. And I so inform my prospect. My prospect is away from office interruptions, and having a meal with anyone is usually relaxing."

In certain businesses, lavish entertainment is taken for granted. It has long been standard practice to introduce new food products with large parties for the media food editors. Madison Avenue is good at arranging unusual and very expensive outings. Travel agents and columnists are routinely flown to new resorts or hotels so that they can in turn get the ordinary tourist to go there too. Sportswear salespeople frequently hand out tickets to athletic events to their valued customers. The list is endless.

Many salespeople never see a part of this world, but most of them entertain customers occasionally on a modest scale. Sales managers usually expect this and allow for it in the budget. A few rules seem to apply here:

Be conservative in entertainment.

Never try to buy business by entertaining. It can never substitute for the regular sales process.

Save more lavish entertainment for after the first order or so.

Tasteless entertainment is worse than none at all.

Entertainment is never a substitute for dependable service.

Gear the entertainment to the customer's preference when possible. A drink after work, a golf game, a baseball ticket, may do more than a meal in a posh restaurant.

Modest gifts may be perfectly legal and ethical. Desk calendars, pocket diaries, ballpoint pens, and other items of the sales promotion sort, usually of slight monetary value, do no harm and can build goodwill.

One office equipment salesperson who has been dispensing an attractive company desk calendar for years says she has over three hundred customers and community leaders who like these calendars. Many times when she speaks with one of these leaders, even if she hasn't seen him for years, she gets remarks such as, "Where is my calendar this year?" Nominal gifts, then, are acceptable. But larger gifts like turkeys, cases of wine, blocks of cheese—these must be made with discretion. Some companies, aware of abuses, expressly forbid both giving and accepting gifts of this sort.

To Their Competitors

Salespeople have a responsibility of understanding the necessity of competition in the business world. They know that their competitors have a rightful place in the market just as they do, and they keep any criticism on a product level.

Trying to win a customer away from another company is a legitimate challenge, but the fight should be fair and square, a match of selling techniques and value of product and service. No salesperson should try to win by any sort of trickery or personal backbiting. If a customer seems justifiably dissatisfied with the service he is getting from another company's representative (as in one of the cases in Chapter 17), a salesperson should of course promise better service, and if the customer gives you the order, see that he gets it. But deliberately talking down another company's salesperson as a way of soliciting an order is unethical in the extreme.

On the whole, salespeople maintain a friendly rivalry and welcome the opportunity to exchange ideas at sales conventions or meetings. They respect one another's product and competitive spirit.

To Their Professional Organization

To become better trained and sustain high ethical standards, salespeople have an obligation to join their own industry sales organizations. Thus, they can help educate and inform themselves. They can also discipline their cohorts for unethical conduct.

To Their Community

Salespeople have an obligation to the community in which they live and work. They must be aware that unethical sales practices will hurt not only the salesperson's image, but the community as well.

Salespeople have wonderful talents that charities, churches, school districts, as well as many others, need in their communities. Their communication skills, enterprise, and enthusiasm have done wonders for a variety of groups throughout the country over the years.

Besides, community involvement offers an ideal opportunity for salespeople to become favorably known in their areas. Customers seem to like to do business with salespeople who are active in their communities.

INDIVIDUAL ETHICAL CODES

Salespeople must establish for themselves an individual code of ethics. To do this requires proper blending of company policy with their personal consciences.

Following the Golden Rule, or religious tenets, or learning from experience that life has a way of punishing evil, will help form this code of individual ethics for salespeople. The Golden Rule, "Do unto others as you would have others do unto you," makes a lot of sense as an ethical base for salespeople.

Everyone likes to be treated with dignity and respect, which also means fairly and honestly. Salespeople need only think of *themselves* as their customers, and treat them as they would like to be treated in the same situation.

The American College of Life Underwriters, in Bryn Mawr, Pennsylvania, administers the international Chartered Life Underwriters program (CLU). These college courses are primarily designed to broaden the general economic knowledge of life insurance sales agents. Twenty hours of college credit courses must be successfully completed, and a certain amount of sales experience accumulated, before the CLU degree is confirmed.

At the graduation ceremony, each graduate publicly pledges himself to uphold the CLU code of ethics: "I shall in the light of all the circumstances surrounding my client, which I shall make *every* conscientious effort to ascertain and understand, give him that service which, had I been in the same circumstances, I would have applied to myself." This version of the Golden Rule has been the hallmark of professional life insurance sales agents for years.

Integrity is the foundation of the trust so vital to the customer-salesperson relationship. Integrity could be the foundation of livable, personal, ethical standards. Honesty is always the best policy.

SUMMARY

This chapter began with a discussion of the evolution of consumer protection laws in our industrialized society. As we became industrialized in the middle of the last century, abuses fostered by some large companies prompted the federal government to pass several laws which affected the consumer indirectly.

In addition to these federal laws, state and local laws have been passed to supplement and put teeth into the national laws. Salespeople must become aware of these laws. Violation of them might risk individual or company liability. Most companies inform their salespeople of these laws and regulations as they affect the marketing of their products or services.

Beyond merely recognizing legal constraints, salespeople also have to develop some code of personal ethics in selling. This means recognizing responsibility to oneself, one's company, and one's customers, first of all, understanding that the whole foundation of the sales process is built on trust and confidence. These, in turn, are primarily built on mutual respect for the truth between customer and salesperson, resulting in an ethical balance of purpose.

KEY TERMS

Antitrust

Fair Trade Contracts

Monopolies

Price discrimination

Price Fixing

Product Liability

Restraint of Trade

REVIEW QUESTIONS

- Why have so many laws protecting the consumer been enacted?
- What laws have an impact on the sales career?
- What is meant by ethical conduct?
- What is the salesperson's ethical obligation to the competitor?
- Why is the sales career so open to ethical misconduct?

DISCUSSION TOPICS

- Can an action be legal and still be unethical? Explain.
- What is the basic difficulty in defining a code of ethics?
- Explain what is meant by an ethical obligation to oneself.
- When is entertaining a customer proper and when is it improper?

EXERCISES

1. Draw up an expense account for money ethically spent on customers. (Use information in this chapter as criteria.)

2. Recite your version of the Golden Rule as it might apply to individual sales situations.

3. With a partner, act out a situation in which a salesperson turns down the offer of a bribe from a potential customer. Try to answer the offer in such a way as not to offend the customer, for purposes of future business.

**Case
Study
One**

Ron Davis is an agent with the Millennium Life Insurance Company in Louisiana. He sees a client of his who wants him to replace a policy that the client has bought from another company. The policy is two years old. A close analysis indicated that, so far as cost was concerned, the policy-holder would be better off by dropping the two-year-old policy with the other company and taking out a new one with Ron's company. Ron explains to the policyholder that the two-year contestable period will apply here—that is, under his old policy the company has two years in which to contest its insurance, and after that time they would be forever banned from questioning it.

By taking out this new policy, a new two-year contestable period would start running. Ron has urged the policyholder to keep the old policy in force until the new one is issued in case there should be any problem passing the physical examination.

The law says that any policy replacement must be reported if a policy is over one year old. Ron feels very strongly that he is doing his client a favor because, all things considered, his company's policy is cheaper than that of the first company, even though the first policy was taken out two years ago.

In filling out the application, Ron answers yes to the question, "Is this a replacement of an existing policy?" He feels the law requires this, even though he feels justified in the replacement.

- Should Ron have done this? Why or why not?
- In view of all the facts, does the moral question overrule the legal question here?
- What ethical questions are involved in this sales situation?
- Since the policyholder cannot be hurt here, isn't Ron's "yes" going a bit too far? Explain.

Tony Toshido works as a salesman for the Aloha Realty Company in Honolulu, Hawaii. He specializes in sales of real estate to well-to-do Hawaiians who own large amounts of property on the island.

His latest venture is the selling of a new group of condominiums recently constructed in the picturesque fishing village of Lahina on the leeward side of Maui Island. While selling the first one, Tony notices a crack in the foundation in the basement. He checks with the contractor, who says the crack could get worse, but only if a severe tropical storm should occur. Such storms usually bring street and basement flooding. They do not occur often. The last one was ten years ago.

From the builder, Tony learns that the engineers took something of a calculated risk in their specifications: chances of a severe storm were too small to justify heavier, more expensive foundations. The builder thinks it would be all right to ignore these cracks unless someone asks about them, and if that happens, explain the situation truthfully. When queried on the matter, the building inspector made light of the crack and said he thought the foundations were up to standard.

- Is there an ethical problem here? Explain.
- Since the building inspector said it was all right to sell the condominiums with the present foundation, doesn't this make it all right for Tony not to say anything to his prospects? Discuss.
- Tony prides himself on being a professional. What would be the professional thing to do here?
- Could he tell the truth and still urge customers to buy? Explain.
- Is any aspect of the consumer movement involved here? Explain.

Glossary of Key Terms

Action The final stage of the Formula-Need theory, in which the prospect takes the necessary steps to purchase the product or service offered.

Alternative-Question Closing Asking the client to make a decision on a minor point ("Do you want the red or the blue?") in an effort to close. Many prospects dislike saying "Yes, I'll buy," so the opportunity to express a preference about some usually unimportant detail of the sale permits the customer to save face.

Amiables One of Merrill and Reid's four social profiles, Amiables are primarily relationship-oriented. Like Expressives, they tend to display feelings openly, but are less assertive and more interested in being agreeable and cooperative, even conforming. Amiables like salespeople who are warm and open.

Analyticals One of Merrill and Reid's four social profiles, Analyticals are thinkers. Although not usually decisive or forceful, they have control over their emotions. In making buying decisions, Analyticals want both a great deal of information and the time to assimilate it.

Answering Objections An essential part of selling. If the salesperson cannot answer a prospect's objections satisfactorily, the prospect is not likely to buy. Professional salespeople should welcome objections (they are usually buying signals) and answer them sincerely and knowledgeably.

Antitrust laws Federal laws that aim to prevent harmful competition in business. They prohibit conspiracies to fix prices in order to create monopolies or lessen competition, and prohibit

larger corporations from buying out their competitors, except under stringent rules and regulations.

Asking for the Order A crucial moment in the selling process. Most salespeople first attempt to ask for the order (close) with the alternative-question method. The salesperson may also save his most convincing selling points for this moment, in case the client brings up further objections.

Assertiveness One of Merrill and Reid's three dimensions of human behavior. Assertive people state their opinions with assurance, confidence, or force.

Assumptive Close The salesperson assumes from the beginning that the prospect will buy, and this positive attitude may in itself effect a successful outcome. When closing, the salesperson asks a question that assumes a sale will be made, such as "Whom do I see to get a check?"

Attention The first stage of the Formula-Need theory, in which the salesperson procures the undivided attention of the prospect with appropriate small talk. A minute or two of conversation breaks the prospect's previous chain of concentration and prepares him for the next phase of the selling process.

Audio-Visuals Sales aids that appeal to the prospect's eye or ear—pictures, drawings, overhead transparencies, film strips, catalogues, tape recorders, slides, and the like.

Behavior Skills The art of responding productively to the behavior of others. In sales, effective listening and good verbal and nonver-

441

bal communication are important behavior skills.

Body Language   A way of communicating without speaking through body signals. The way people sit and fold their arms, for example, are as revealing as the words they speak. An understanding of body language and the ability to employ it effectively are powerful tools for the salesperson.

Body Signals   The unspoken "words," or "vocabulary," of body language. Because body signals can have a range of meanings, the salesperson must be cautious in interpreting them.

Boomerang Method   The salesperson, by presenting the reason for the prospect's objection in a new context, turns the reason for the objection into a reason for buying the product.

Brochures   Supplied by the parent company, these pieces of promotional material are very helpful to the salesperson. Photographs and accompanying detailed information help sell items that are too large to fit into a sample case. Brochures are useful in selling smaller items as well, because they act as a reminder once the salesperson leaves the prospect's office.

Budget Worksheet   A personal budget prepared by a job applicant for use in negotiating salary in an employment interview for a sales position.

Buyer Interest   Any indication from prospects that they are interested in buying. Such an indication may be a statement such as "We really could use a new typewriter" or an inquiry about specific product features.

Buyer Reluctance   Some prospects find it difficult to say yes, even to the purchase of a product they like and need. The experienced salesperson can usually overcome buyer reluctance by uncovering the reasons for the prospect's unwillingness to say yes (it may be a personality trait or an objection to some product feature) and responding appropriately.

Buyer Stimulation   Intensifying the customer's interest in products and services through unusual, dramatic, or otherwise creative approaches.

Buying Signals   Any verbal or physical signal indicating readiness to buy. The prospect may ask about delivery or payment terms, for example, or may signal by smiling, nodding, and leaning forward.

Can't-Be-Perfect Method   The salesperson answers the prospect's objection that other products have features superior to his with the comment that, of course, his product is not perfect—no product is. He then points out that he can offer the prospect some feature his competitors' products do not have—for example, good servicing.

Career Traps   Behavior that can sabotage any sales career, including the negative self-image and attitude trap, the entertainment trap, the spending time with other salespeople (rather than prospects) trap, the vanity (over personal success) trap, and the criticism (of competitors) trap.

Cassettes   The use of cassettes and cassette recorders as sales aids is limited only by the salesperson's imagination. Cassettes can be sent to prospects in distant cities, along with a letter introducing a product or service.

Casualty Insurance   Insurance on automobiles, property, and businesses against theft, fire, or other damage. Casualty insurance covers all the various liability risks of a large company—workers' compensation, fire, personal property, business interruption, and so on.

Catalogues   In some types of selling, catalogues are the most important tool of all, because they list the full range of products. For other salespeople, catalogues are optional selling tools. The creative salesperson is thoroughly familiar with the catalogue and knows at what point in a presentation to introduce it.

Centers of Influence   Any person who has considerable prestige, power, or connections in a particular city, area, industry, or profession is a potential center of influence. Centers of influence, if properly developed, become mentors, anxious and willing to help the salesperson they believe in, mainly by suggesting prospects. Centers of influence must be carefully developed and thanked for their help.

Chalkboards   Properly used, an effective supplement to an oral presentation. Salespeople should use them only to highlight important points and always print clearly and boldly.

Charts and Graphs   Charts and graphs that are accurate, up-to-date, clear, and immediately understandable can be used in many ways to make a particular selling point in the interview. They can illustrate comparisons, condense statistical information, highlight growth patterns, and the like.

Closing Props   Documents that need to be initialed, signed, and/or dated in order to close a sale. These props are kept in broad view throughout the entire closing interview, and the salesperson uses them to record the responses to the alternative questions he or she asks the prospect in attempting to close.

Cognitive Dissonance   In selling, an after-purchase state of anxiety experienced by many customers; it occurs when an individual's beliefs, opinions, or feelings are in conflict with each other ("I should have bought Ms. X's product; it was cheaper"). Responsible salespeople always make the effort to anticipate this problem during the sales process in order to reduce its effect or eliminate its entirely.

Cold Calling   Calling on an unfamiliar person or firm without an appointment. It is a wonderful way to fill the time gap created by cancelled appointments or shortened interviews. It can also be used to test new sales ideas, to discover new territory worth developing, or to counteract a slump.

Commitment   A firm indication by a prospect that he or she is willing to do business with the salesperson making the presentation.

Commodity Brokers   Inside salespeople who use the telephone to buy and sell such goods as coal, steel, grain, corn, and soybeans for their customers. They must have exceptional training and the kind of temperament that can survive in a risky, volatile business environment.

Communication Skills   Skills that facilitate effective communication with others: good vocabulary, voice quality, and diction, as well as assertiveness, authentic listening, the proper use of body language, and writing skills.

Conviction   The fourth stage of the Formula-Need theory, which usually occurs in the closing interview. In this stage, the prospects are convinced that they need the salesperson's products or services, that they do not need those of the competitors, that they want to do business with the salesperson in question, and that they are ready to buy now.

Counselor Probing   A low-key approach to the sales interview in which salespeople help prospects examine their needs and set priorities by delving into the prospect's thinking about the products or services that the salesperson is offering. (Also called "counselor selling.")

Counterpoint Method   A good way to counter a customer's statement that a competitor's product has more favorable features than the product the salesperson is presenting. The salesperson admits the truth of the statement and then counters the effect by demonstrating that the particular features of the competitor's product are not needed by the customers. The advantages of the product or service in question are then stressed.

Creative Stimulation   A method of conveying thoughts, images, or concepts by using words in an unusual and attractive way, a method that has much in common with advertising appeals. Sometimes vivid word pictures that stimulate the imagination are far more powerful than any photograph or other visual aid.

Creativity   In selling, the ability to use an imaginative and personal approach instead of one that is simply routine. Using creativity increases sales.

Data Sheet   An abbreviated work-history document which often requires an explanatory letter to enlarge on information outlined.

Decision-Maker   The person who is empowered to buy what a salesperson has to sell. Professional salespeople want the decision-maker involved in the selling process early, and frequently achieve this by convincing screeners or delegated subordinates that they can discuss their product adequately only with the decision-maker.

Delivery Interview   Properly handled, this interview is not the conclusion, but the beginning of a solid relationship between the client and the salesperson's company. The interview consists of presentation of the product or papers that begin the service, the salesperson's reaffrmation of the client's reasons and good judgment in buying the product, and a discussion of any particulars concerning the product.

Demonstration Aids   Visual aids that help salespeople demonstrate their products, verifying their claims by proving them on the spot, and adding interest, drama, and impact to their presentation.

Desire   The third and most lengthy stage of the Formula-Need theory, where the salesperson's sales presentation and manner stimulate the prospect's desire for the salesperson's product.

Diction   Choice of words, especially with regard to correctness and effective communication. Proper diction is very important to the salesperson, who should keep in mind these four general points: conciseness, clarity, use of simple (not pompous) language, and creativity.

Direct Mail A form of prospecting in which sales letters and brochures are mailed directly from company headquarters to a list of prospects (generally compiled by the salesperson), with the goal of creating interest in the company's services or product. A 5 or 6 percent response is considered standard for 100 pieces of mail. Many good salespeople try to keep a continual direct-mail program in operation.

Discretionary Income The amount of total income that is not preallocated for the purchase of such necessities as food, rent, debt reduction.

Drivers One of Merrill and Reid's four social profiles. Drivers are assertive and action-oriented. They control their feelings and are geared toward results rather than people. The salesperson should present a Driver with several alternate summarized solutions to the problem at hand, without attempting to tell him or her what to do.

Easels Large flip charts that are more suited to group presentations because of their greater visibility. Sellers can flip printed pages back and forth to reemphasize points or benefits, or can use blank pages in the same way they might use a chalkboard.

Ego Trap A possible snare for the successful salesperson. Carried away with self-importance, the salesperson loses humility and perspective (and eventually customers). To avoid this, the successful salesperson must keep in mind that a period of great success may be followed by a slump.

Emotional Buying Motives Motives that stem from feelings or impulses. Emotional buying motives sometimes play a part in industrial sales (friendship with the salesperson would be one example), but generally they are the dominant and sometimes the only factor in consumer sales. Some emotional buying motives are pleasure, social approval, convenience, and status.

Expressives One of Merrill and Reid's four social profiles. Expressives are warm and outgoing. They are dreamers, highly opinionated, and can be very emotional and impulsive. Opinions of others are important to them, and they don't like to argue. Expressives like social recognition; hence they like being entertained by salespeople.

Extrovert Carl Jung's term for the person who looks outward. Extroverts are generally categorized as outgoing, fun-loving, highly social individuals.

Fair Trade Contracts Agreements between producers and vendors that commodities bearing a trademark or brand name be sold at or above a certain price.

Field Activity A salesperson's out-of-office work—the time spent knocking on doors, seeing people, and presenting products. Though in-home or in-office organizational work is essential, the level of a salesperson's success is determined by the amount of time spent profitably in the field, in front of prospects or customers.

Filmstrips Useful audio-visual aids. Filmstrips are far less expensive to make than films, and the projector is easily portable.

Flip Charts Easels, loose-leaf binders, and some catalogues which are designed so that the salesperson can easily flip printed pages back and forth to emphasize points or benefits. Salespeople can also use blank pages in the flip chart the same way they might use a chalkboard, tearing off the sheet afterward.

Follow-Up A key to client-building and customer loyalty. Follow-up is the post-delivery interview process of regular, salesperson-initiated contact with customers.

Follow-Up Card Presented to prospects at a group presentation or trade show. It includes a brief statement from the salesperson thanking the prospect for his or her attention, as well as space in which the prospect can indicate desire to buy, desire for further information, and the prospect's name, address, and other pertinent information.

Formula-Need Theory (AIDCA) A theory of selling developed in the early 1900s, stating that the sales presentation should be based on the customer's needs and wants. It is a five-stage process which includes attention, interest, desire, conviction, and action. Each stage must be successfully negotiated before the next is introduced.

Goodwill Calls Non-sales calls made to establish and maintain good relationships with customers.

Guaranteed Salary A guaranteed salary (as opposed to straight commission) eases potential financial pressures on beginning salespeople. As salespeople gain experience, they often move away from this method of compensation to either straight commission income or a combination salary/commission income.

Help Sheet A suggestion sheet given to a person who is a potential source of referrals. It has blanks for name, profession, address, phone number, and the like. This sheet is left with the potential source person in the hope that it will serve to jog his or her memory and produce a listing of prospects by the time the salesperson calls again.

Hierarchy of Needs Psychologist Abraham Maslow's conception of five basic levels of needs common to all people. These needs in ascending order are: physiological, safety, social, self-esteem, and self-actualization. Each level of need must be achieved before going on to the next level.

Hot Buttons Prospect needs that may surface during the counselor probing process. It is the salesperson's responsibility to help the prospect establish priorities for these needs.

Impending-Event Close The salesperson informs the customer of a change in, say, price or product line that will be occuring in the future and which makes it advantageous for the customer to sign the order as soon as possible.

Industrial Salespeople Those people who sell to manufacturers, wholesalers, and distributors the raw materials, fabricated parts, and other items used in various stages of manufacturing or assembling all kinds of products. These salespeople must have a good technical knowledge of the product.

Inside Salespeople Those who sell in a store or office. The customer comes to the salesperson, rather than vice versa when he needs a particular product. Inside salespeople sometimes do very little selling, merely serving as order clerks.

Intangibles Salespeople Those who sell products or services that involve a concept, an idea, or a process. Since such products or services cannot be seen or felt, people who sell intangibles must use their imagination to paint effective, persuasive word pictures of their wares.

Integrity The inner quality of ethical strength, demonstrated by honesty and reliability, possessed by professional salespeople.

Interest The second stage of the Formula-Need theory of selling, where the salesperson tries to stimulate interest in his products or services. It involves an opening approach to eliminate any pressure the prospect may feel and to assure the prospect that the salesperson he is dealing with is professional, honest, and well-meaning.

Interview Checklist An ordered list of important information about a particular prospect or company, as well as points to be covered in the sales presentation. Salespeople review these checklists prior to appointments to remind themselves of everything to be covered.

Introvert Carl Jung's term for the person who looks inward. Introverts are usually categorized as retiring individuals who engage in careers like engineering, accounting, and research.

Invalid Objections Reasons for not buying that can be overcome ("I want to think about it" or "I'd like to check with other companies first"). Some invalid objections indicate reluctance to buy, but others are buying signals, telling the salesperson that the prospect is definitely interested, but that a particular objection must be satisfactorily answered.

Isolation of Needs The process whereby the salesperson, in conjunction with the customer, clarifies specific needs for products or services.

Joint Field Work Two salespeople working the same territory as a pair. It is frequently employed as a teaching device.

Kinesics The study of body language that investigates the meaning of various postures and the norms of proximity and space, including the way in which particular circumstances determine the space that people insist on maintaining between one another. Body-language norms differ from culture to culture.

Leadership Leadership is the ability to inspire others to do what the leader wants them to do. Salespeople can profit from developing leadership skills because they must influence prospects to motivate themselves to buy a certain product or service.

Listening Good listening is one of the most effective tools salespeople can employ, for listening can literally make sales. Attentive salespeople listen for the customer's reactions, for their hidden objections, for their reasons for not buying. To listen effectively, a salesperson must keep an open mind, concentrate, ask appropriate questions, show interest by body language and facial expressions, and hear the other person out.

Loose-Leaf Binders Can be used as flip charts. The salesperson can create a personalized graphic sales presentation using an ordinary three-ring notebook.

Management by Objectives (MBO) A form of management in which the salesperson and the sales manager mutually evaluate the salesperson's performance and agree upon growth objectives. Thus, improvement becomes a joint effort toward a common objective.

Manipulation Manipulation in selling involves the use of intimidation or unfair, exploitive, or fraudulent methods to achieve a sale. These sales tactics are harmful to prospects and salespeople alike; no salesperson who uses them will build up a pool of loyal customers.

Manufacturer's Representatives Independent contract salespeople who usually represent several companies or fields. A manufacturer's representative whose agreement with the manufacturer gives her or him exclusive rights to sell a particular line in a particular territory, or has products that complement each other, can find this type of work very profitable.

Marker Boards Like chalkboards, but brighter because they are used in conjunction with colored marking pens. An effective supplement to an oral sales presentation if used sparingly and if the salesperson prints boldly and clearly.

Market Analysis Doing research to obtain information on the needs, buying habits, and size of a particular market, in order to assess its potential—to discover whether or not there are enough prospects to merit development, and if so, what kind of strategy is likely to prove successful.

Marketing Equation Product or service development, price, distribution, advertisement and promotion, and finally sales are the constants which must be balanced in this equation.

Mirror Response The salesperson captures the substance or the form of the prospect's objection in paraphrase in order to demonstrate understanding of it.

Monopolies The exclusive control by a group of companies of the means of production or the selling of certain products or services.

Nests A nest is a cluster of potential customers. Nests are found everywhere—in a certain pro-

fession, geographic location, or business. When a nest is developed, the imaginative salesperson tries to sell from the top down, to generate a continual flow of good sales.

Offering-of-Premium Close The offer of an additional item, service, or benefit to the customer who signs the order now.

Outside Salespeople Salespeople who work outside of the office, seeking out prospective customers and selling products and services at the customer's convenience.

Overall Approach A generalized approach used by professional salespeople as they begin sales interviews. A good salesperson personalizes this approach by pointing out problems peculiar to the prospect's field or needs.

Overhead Projectors Portable, quickly set up, and easy to use, overhead projectors command audience attention and offer salespeople the chance to dramatize statistics and other data difficult to describe verbally. Projectors offer flexibility because transparencies can be designed for any situation or created as the salesperson speaks.

Parent/Adult/Child A central concept of transactional analysis. According to author Eric Berne, people have these three ego states coexisting in their persons at all times. Salespeople should monitor their ego states carefully. The salesperson who reacts and responds as an Adult will be the most effective in all sales situations.

Personal Responsibility An essential quality for all professional salespeople, personal responsibility is a combination of several qualities, including self-discipline and self-motivation, which are necessary both for the salesperson's own success and for customer satisfaction (ensuring that products and services are properly sold and serviced).

Personal Visuals Visual aids that the salesperson himself creates to give his sales presentations a personal touch.

Physiological Needs According to Maslow, these are the most basic needs—for food, air, water, clothing, sex, sleep, and shelter.

Planned Call-Back Particularly important if the product has not been delivered personally by the salesperson who sold it. A planned call-back is a date fixed by the salesperson and customer for the salesperson to return for an interview after the product is delivered, a necessary part of follow-up.

Pocket Calendar The single most necessary item for salespeople, in which all activity and planned activity is recorded on a daily basis. Many salespeople also enter names of referred leads picked up in sales interviews, cash expenditures, entertainment expenses, and the like.

Pre-Approach Letters An outgrowth of the direct mail method, but considerably more selective than direct mail. The salesperson develops a list of prospects and each week sends a certain number of pre-approach letters to selected people on the list. Sometimes the letters are sent over the signature of the sales manager, or even the president of a firm. These letters, if creative and well-written, often result in appointments and may condition the prospect to view the salesperson and the product or service favorably.

Pre-Approach Process Preparation by salespeople prior to a presentation. All preparation has three specific phases: gathering information on the prospect and the prospect's company, assessing this information to see if the prospect is indeed a potential buyer, and preparing a suitable approach to the sales presentation.

PREP Approach An approach to preparing a speech, consisting of the following sequence: point, reason, example; and point.

Presentation All effective sales presentations have certain characteristics in common: they capture and hold the prospect's attention; maintain his interest; isolate valid needs; establish the prospect's confidence in the salesperson; and involve the prospect through questions and discussion.

Price Discrimination Charging different customers different prices for the same product or service.

Price Fixing A process in which two or more companies conspire to set artificial prices on similar products and services, often in order to drive out competition.

Product Liability The idea that the manufacturer has the legal responsibility not to defraud, misinform, or underinform (with the intent to deceive) consumers about the nature of their products. Courts award not only actual damages for defective products, but in some cases punitive damages as well.

Professional Salespeople Those who put the customer's welfare first, possess superior product knowledge, and use responsible sales techniques.

Proposal Sometimes called a case study, it is a written description of the way a product or service can be designed to satisfy a particular customer's needs. Proposals are written for a specific product or service to be used by a specific client in a specific environment.

Prospect Cards Cards upon which salespeople record all pertinent information about prospects and customers, including name, address, telephone number, nature of business, items of interest to customer, as well as the dates, times, and results of all interviews.

Prospect Files Used to file prospect cards, a good prospect file should include an alphabetical index for filing inactive or dormant customers and a separate section to record weekly or monthly customer visits.

Prospect Sheet A form to record the names of prospects, along with such information as occupations, addresses, and the name of person who referred the prospect. The more information the salesperson has at his disposal before contacting the prospect, the greater the likelihood of a sale.

Qualifying Prospects The process of getting as much information about a prospect as possible, to see if he or she has enough potential to warrant an interview.

Question Method The salesperson counters a prospect's objections with a series of arguments framed as questions ("You are planning to install solar heating, someday, aren't you?"). The questions should never be intimidating or designed to confuse the prospect.

Rational Buying Motives These are based on analysis, logic, and utility. Rational buying motives are usually the basis for sales of products to business and industry. They include low purchase price, increase in profitability, long product life, and the like.

Referred Lead Also known as the endless chain method, a referred lead is a lead (the name of a potential customer) obtained from a satisfied customer.

Restraint of Trade The attempt to eliminate competition, create a monopoly, maintain prices artificially, or otherwise tamper with the free market.

Résumé   Used in applying for a sales job, the résumé includes the applicant's name, address, phone number, job objective, work history, education and training, activities and interests, and references.

Requalifying Prospects   Reassessing the prospect's need to buy, ability to buy, and willingness to buy from the particular salesperson. This should be done early in the closing interview so that the salesperson does not waste time with someone who is not going to buy.

Responsiveness   One of Merrill and Reid's dimensions of behavior. Responsiveness is the degree to which people show their feelings or react overtly to influences, appeals, or stimulation. Less responsive persons tend to be cautious, serious, and rely primarily on logic. More responsive people are people-oriented, informal, fun-seeking, dramatic, open, and impulsive.

Safety Needs   The second level in Maslow's hierarchy of needs, this need is for economic and physical security, including freedom from illness.

Salary/Commission Combination   In the combination pay plan, the company guarantees a certain minimum salary to the salesperson, and anything over that amount must be earned by commissions. Most salespeople prefer this plan because it gives them both a fixed floor on their income (usually geared to the salesperson's basic income requirements) and the incentive to sell over that floor to make more money.

Sales Cycle   Encompasses the entire sales process from the knock on the door to the signing of the order. It breaks down selling into three basic skill areas: prospecting, personal organization, and closing.

Sales Manual   A written program for salespeople that can be studied and referred to when questions arise. It contains product or service fundamentals, prospecting methods, market development techniques, personal organizational tools and procedures, creative sales ideas, competition product knowledge, all sales presentations in current use, and other sales techniques, information, and skills.

Sales Slumps   Three or more weeks without any sales. Slumps are a natural part of selling; nevertheless, they are usually warning signals that something is wrong. To break out of a slump, the salesperson must analyze sales interviews objectively to determine what went wrong.

Samples   Used in the sales interview, a sample of the actual product is a strong motivator to buy. Since it is tangible, a sample may stimulate a prospect's interests by appealing to his senses of sight, hearing, touch, and (sometimes) taste, and smell. Letting the prospect handle the item himself generally has a strong positive impact on sales.

Screen Projectors   Closed-loop 8-millimeter film projectors that are small enough to be easily carried and set up. An effective sales tool if the films are fresh and up-to-date.

Security Salespeople   Those who sell stocks, bonds, mutual funds, money market funds, futures, options, and the like. Most of their business is done over the telephone. These salespeople must have exceptional training, knowledge, and personal integrity.

Self-Actualization   The apex of Maslow's hierarchy of needs, self-actualization is self-fulfillment or self-realization. It comes to a person whose four basic needs have been met and who is now motivated to achieve her or his full potential professionally, or simply as a human being.

Self-Audit System   Used by salespeople to assess their progress toward realistic goals. Management by Objectives is one such method because it helps salespeople set realistic goals and assess their progress toward their attainment.

Self-Esteem Needs   Fourth of Maslow's hierarchy of needs, these needs motivate people to strive for success in their careers or communities. Companies must provide salespeople with some sort of yardstick to measure their own worth and thus fulfill their career-based self-esteem needs.

Self-Motivation to Buy   The process in which a potential buyer motivates himself to fulfill a perceived need. Although salespeople cannot actually motivate anyone to buy, they can create an atmosphere that encourages self-motivation by communicating an understanding of the prospect's needs, giving satisfactory answers to customer questions, and appropriately presenting products or services as fulfillments of customer needs.

Selling   The process of helping prospects motivate themselves to buy wanted or needed products or services.

Slide Projectors More portable and flexible than film projectors, a slide projector is a valuable audio-visual aid. Slides are relatively cheap to make, requiring only a few props and adequate lighting.

Social Needs Third in Maslow's hierarchy of needs, these are the needs for love and friendship. People need acceptance and emotional support from their peers, their families, and their communities.

Social-Style Profile The four social styles described by David Merrill and Roger Reid, which are measured by the basic dimensions of human behavior—assertiveness, responsiveness, and versatility. The four styles are Analytical, Driving, Amiable, and Expressive.

Success Habits In sales, the habit, acquired through self-discipline, of performing tasks that are unpleasant yet lead to success. These habits are broken down into four areas: calling, selling, organizational work, and prospecting.

Summary-of-Benefits Close After completing the presentation, the salesperson summarizes the benefits of the product or service, and then asks for the order.

Tangibles Salespeople Such salespeople sell products and services that can be seen or held. Sensory perception can sometimes do more to sell these products than the salesperson's efforts.

Target Marketing The development of one particular market. The concept behind target marketing is that the commonalities of the targeted occupation or business makes the approach worth the effort. By becoming specialized, salespeople are better able to answer questions and serve customer needs, and thereby gain and keep more customers.

Territory Management A well thought-out plan that allows the salesperson to cover a territory in the most efficient way possible. It is a matter of geography, scheduling, and routing.

Testimonials Statements, usually letters, from satisfied customers commending a product, service, or salesperson. It is to the salesperson's advantage to obtain testimonials that will be appropriate to the situations and related to the needs of prospects.

Third-Party Method Neutralizing a particularly strong prospect objection by mentioning satisfied customers who think favorably of the product or service.

Time Management Scheduling activity in such a way as to make the most efficient use of time.

Trainer A sales trainer trains salespeople in group or individual situations. Ideally, a trainer is a skilled salesperson who also knows how to analyze performance, how to conduct skill sessions and sales clinics, and how to motivate others.

Valid Needs Actual prospect needs ascertained through dialogue between the salesperson and the prospect.

Valid Objections Sound reasons for not buying that can effectively block a sale. There are three valid objections: "I don't need it," "I can't afford it," and "I won't buy from you."

Versatility The extra dimension of human behavior (Merrill and Reid) which permits people to deal with other people's social styles. Salespeople can learn versatility by learning how to listen attentively, to live with confrontation, to resolve conflict, and to use feedback well.

Vertical Growth Selling more to the customers one has, rather than broadening the prospect pool.

Vita Similar to a résumé, a vita is more specifically an in-depth presentation of the work and educational history of a job applicant.

Weekly Activity Report A weekly record of the number of new prospects acquired and of the calls, interviews, and sales made by the salesperson. Generally turned in to a supervisor or sales manager.

Weekly Organizational Procedures A system that must be followed in a disciplined fashion in order to enable salespeople to develop and maintain a productive pattern of activity. Salespeople must set aside a particular period of two to four hours every week (preferably at the end or beginning of the week) for this desk work.

Workaholics People who do not maintain a proper balance between work and personal lives. Workaholics have meager social lives and few intimate relationships with others. In addition; the excessive time invested in work does not generally pay off in terms of additional success—another case of diminishing returns.

"Yes, But" Method The salesperson introduces a point that challenges the prospect's objection—but only after affirming a point of agreement.

Index